Adorno and Theology

**Other titles in the Philosophy and Theology series include:**

# Adorno and Theology

*Christopher Craig Brittain*

t&t clark

**Published by T&T Clark International**
*A Continuum imprint*
The Tower Building
11 York Road
London SE1 7NX

80 Maiden Lane
Suite 704
New York, NY 10038

www.continuumbooks.com

**British Library Cataloguing-in-Publication Data**
A catalogue record for this book is available from the British Library.

ISBN:   978-0-567-56929-5 (Hardback)
           978-0-567-26108-3 (Paperback)

Typeset by Newgen Imaging Systems Pvt Ltd, Chennai, India
Printed and bound in Great Britain by CPI Antony Rowe Ltd, Chippenham, Wiltshire

*While there is a beggar, there is a myth*
*Walter Benjamin*

# Contents

# Contents

# Contents

# Acknowledgements

I would like to thank my family, friends and colleagues who have supported me throughout the completion of this book. The debt owed to my parents Robert Brittain and Pat Craig is incalculable. My brother Jonathan taught me much about the limitations of religious traditions. Ruth Craig helped nurture my initial appreciation for the aesthetic. Marsha Hewitt introduced me to the work of the Frankfurt School, while Ken Mackendrick ensured I was sufficiently caffeinated to carry on reading. Katja Stößel, Philip Ziegler, Andrew MacKinnon, and Brian Brock kindly agreed to read previous drafts of this material. The Wabash Centre provided a summer research grant in support of the project.

Sections of Chapter 5 appear in a different form in: 'Political Theology at a Standstill: Messianism in Adorno and Agamben', *Thesis Eleven* 146 (2010). They are printed here by permission. Chapter 6 includes some material published previously as 'From *A Beautiful Mind* to the Beautiful Soul: Rational Choice, Religion, and Adorno'. In: *Marx, Critical Theory, and Religion*, ed. Warren Goldstein (Leiden, Boston: Brill Publishers, 2006), 151–77. This is included with permission from Brill.

This book would not have been possible without the support and inspiration provided by my wife and partner Katja. She remains the greatest witness to me of the beauty to be found even in the midst of 'damaged life'.

# Introduction
# Adorno *and* Theology?

It is becoming fashionable to hail a 'return to religion' in contemporary philosophy and critical theory. Philosophers as diverse as Richard Rorty, Gianni Vattimo, Slavoj Žižek, and the late Jacques Derrida have turned to the subject of religion in their recent work.[1] Jürgen Habermas made some notable shifts in his position towards religion since 11 September 2001, going so far as to engage in a dialogue with Joseph Ratzinger shortly before he was elected Pope.[2] At the same time, this seeming re-emergence of interest in religion within North Atlantic societies has also produced a counter-reaction. A so-called 'New Atheism' movement, involving outspoken intellectuals like Richard Dawkins, Sam Harris, Daniel Dennett and others, has made impassioned appeals to exclude the supposed 'irrationality' of religion from any serious consideration within secular society.[3] This perspective, far from calling for a renewed study of religion and for greater attention to how it shapes the lives of its practitioners, warns that religion is inherently dangerous and inimical towards democracy.

In such an intellectual climate, the thought of Theodor W. Adorno has much to contribute. For Adorno's philosophy does not fit into either faction of this contemporary engagement with religion, which enables it to offer a fresh perspective on a debate that is increasingly becoming polarized and reduced to rhetoric and stereotype. Theology, as this book will demonstrate, plays a significant role in his articulation of Marxian philosophy, despite his being a materialist and an atheist. Although Adorno developed a scathing criticism of rationality and the traditions of the Enlightenment, his references to theology do not serve to replace the ideals of modernity, or to uncover some postmodern trace of the 'other-of-reason'. Instead, Adorno is interested in theology because he thinks it reveals important insights into existing social conditions. His use of theological concepts is intended to help realize the ideals of Enlightenment reason, not overcome them. In the context of contemporary debates over 'post-secular' reason, the relationship between traditional moral values and scientific knowledge, and the complex nature of increasingly pluralistic and multi-faith societies, Adorno's thought represents a significant resource.

## Adorno and Theology

In November of 1934, having quickly relocated to Oxford from Hitler's Germany, Adorno wrote to his friend Walter Benjamin (who had himself fled to Paris): 'If I can contribute any aspirations of my own to [your] work, without you taking this as an immodest suggestion, it would be this: that the work should proceed without qualms to realize every part of the theological content and all the literalness of its most extreme claims.'[4] A month later, Adorno writes even more passionately in this regard: 'it seems to me doubly important that the image of theology, into which I would gladly see our thoughts dissolve, is none other than the very one which sustains your thought here – it could indeed be called an "inverse" theology. This position [is to be] directed against natural and supernatural interpretation alike.'[5]

'Theology' is a word found throughout Adorno's writing, but its role within his critical philosophy remains surprisingly neglected and misunderstood. When his references to theology do receive attention from his readers, it is generally only to lament it as an unfortunate lapse in his work. Why would an atheist materialist make positive references to theology, unless it is evidence of 'pessimistic resignation' or 'privileged ivory-tower quietism'?[6] His most famous student, Jürgen Habermas, suggests that Adorno's interest in theology was merely a product of despair brought on by the dark years of the Second World War, in which he lost confidence in human rationality and modernity, and history for him 'faded into the Golgotha of a hope become unrecognizable'.[7] Demonstrating a more nuanced and appreciative understanding of Adorno's references to theology is the principal task of this book.

## Theodor W. Adorno

For those unfamiliar with Adorno's thought, a brief introduction to his life and work will serve to put this discussion into context.[8] He was born Theodor Ludwig Wiesengrund-Adorno in Frankfurt am Main on 11 September 1903. His Jewish father was a successful wine merchant, and his Catholic mother an Italian opera soprano. After completing his doctorate in philosophy at the University of Frankfurt in 1924, Adorno moved to Vienna to study music composition with Alban Berg. He began a career as a musicologist and composer, while starting his *Habilitation* (or post-doctoral dissertation) in 1926. After a dispute with his supervisor in Frankfurt, Hans Cornelius, Adorno completed a study of Kierkegaard under Paul Tillich. It was published in March 1933, on the very day that Hitler came to power.

Adorno collaborated with a close circle of left-wing academics who were associated with the Institute of Social Research, an interdisciplinary collective of Marxist intellectuals in Frankfurt. The Institute brought together the disciplines of philosophy, sociology, psychology, economics and the study of culture, in order to determine how progressive politics might be nurtured within the Weimar Republic. After the war, as it grew in reputation, the Institute came to be known as the 'Frankfurt School'.[9] Adorno and his friend and colleague Max Horkheimer were the Institute's most prominent figures, along with other notable intellectuals including Herbert Marcuse, Friedrich Pollock and Erich Fromm.

Hitler's rise to power had immediate impact on Adorno and the Institute, as all of its members at the University immediately lost their jobs on political grounds. Adorno was able to secure a position at Oxford University as an advanced student until he and he wife Gretel were able to immigrate to New York in 1938, with the help of Max Horkheimer. There they sought to continue their work, eventually moving to Los Angeles during the war. In 1953, after considerable wavering, Adorno and Horkheimer agreed to return to Germany and take up professorships at the University of

Frankfurt. The Institute of Social Research was reconstituted, and became a prominent voice within West Germany during the period of reconstruction. After a lively career that would make him a household name within Germany, Adorno died of a heart attack on 6 August 1969.

## A Brief Introduction to Adorno's Philosophy

Adorno is perhaps best known for three elements of his thought: the concept of the 'dialectic of Enlightenment', his project of a 'negative dialectics', and his frequently quoted remark that 'to write poetry after Auschwitz is barbaric'. For the purpose of this introduction, it is useful to briefly summarize these aspects of his work, and attend to how misunderstandings of each have contributed to the view that Adorno's philosophy results in a pessimistic despair that seeks refuge in an otherworldly theological escape.

The manuscript *Dialectic of Enlightenment* was written collaboratively by Adorno and Horkheimer in 1944.[10] This complex text is famous for one of its primary arguments: the assertion that, in its attempt to grasp and understand nature in its entirety, Enlightenment reason forces its object into a rigid schema, and so ultimately fails to comprehend what it seeks to know. Because it is driven by fear of nature and myth, rationality continues to be shaped by nature and thus continuously dominates its object of inquiry rather than successfully understanding it. The 'dialectic' contained within the Enlightenment, then, is that it continuously transforms into its opposite. Reason turns itself into a self-generated myth: believing that it possesses perfect knowledge and pure objectivity.

Adorno's conception of the dialectic of Enlightenment is related to his commitment to what he calls 'negative dialectics'. If reason does indeed impose a false structure upon objects in the world, so that it is unable to grasp what does not comply with its artificial ordering, Adorno argues that a more adequate form of thought must become aware of its own dominating nature, and ruthlessly criticize itself. He calls the manner of reasoning that is blind to its own dominating impulse a form of 'identity thinking'.

Negative dialectics strives to achieve a form of non-identity thinking. Although all thought, to even conceptualize something, must identify it in some way, non-identical thought remains conscious of this dilemma, and refuses to imagine that its present representation of an object is adequate to its reality. Adorno contrasts his approach with that of Hegel and Marx, for whom dialectical thought involved the weighing of opposing positions and contradictions with the goal of achieving an increasingly progressive conceptualization of truth. Distrustful of the notion of inevitable progress, Adorno insists that thought is never adequate to its object, and so truth can only be approached negatively – through the act of an ongoing immanent self-criticism.

A common accusation against Adorno and Horkheimer's description of the dialectic of Enlightenment is that their criticism of reason is so thorough that it effectively undermines the very idea of rationality itself. In the influential view of Habermas, *Dialectic of Enlightenment* embodies a 'performative contradiction' through its paradoxical criticism of reason on the basis of reason.[11] A similar interpretation leads Albrecht Wellmer to conclude that such an 'aporia' reduces Adorno's philosophy to a 'negative theology', with the result that his work conceives of human experience 'in ecstatic terms rather than as a real utopia; the happiness that it promises is not of this world'.[12]

Similar charges are made against Adorno's articulation of negative dialectics. Susan Buck-Morss asks, 'Did the perpetual motion of Adorno's argument go anywhere?'[13] Critics frequently accuse Adorno's work as collapsing into mere negativity, trapping his philosophy in a hopeless nihilism. Such a view suggests that Adorno's anti-foundationalism leaves him without any firm grounding upon which to confront existing social injustice, so that his work has no recourse but to invoke a longing for some otherworldly deliverance that might arrive from outside of history.

Those who read Adorno's philosophy in such a fashion frequently cite a third element of his thought as evidence to support this interpretation. Not long after returning to West Germany from his wartime exile, Adorno made the provocative statement that 'to write poetry after Auschwitz is barbaric'.[14] In his writing, Auschwitz is not only a symbol of catastrophe for the Jewish people; it also represents a damning condemnation of modernity.

Having himself narrowly escaped Hitler's Germany, he writes, 'Auschwitz confirmed the philosophy of pure identity as death'.[15] The Nazi 'Final Solution', Adorno insists, imposed a new categorical imperative on human beings: 'to arrange their thoughts and actions so that Auschwitz will not repeat itself, so that nothing similar will happen'.[16] His work, therefore, views existence as 'damaged life', for he is convinced that 'our perspective on life has passed into an ideology which conceals the fact that there is life no longer'.[17]

It is from such a perspective that Adorno once suggested that poetry ought not to be written after Auschwitz. His intention was to alert his audience against the tendency to paper over the horrors of the Holocaust with simplistic and sentimental recourse to some hidden meaning or purpose behind the event. His slogan is meant to prevent any refuge in theodicy. Furthermore, after living in the United States, Adorno became highly sensitive to the power of advertising and marketing in shaping public opinion and political attitudes. He was concerned that practically any concept or image could be manipulated to serve the purposes of capitalistic ideology or to support egotistical self-satisfaction. In the dynamics of what he calls the 'culture industry', even a symbol as desolate as Auschwitz could be domesticated and used to pacify and console human beings or to assist in forgetting the horrific realities of human history.

Some critics, however, argue that Adorno's slogan against poetry is the clearest sign that his philosophy has thrown the baby out with the bathwater. Traumatized by the horrors of the Hitler era, it is suggested, Adorno refused to allow any possibility for hope or new life. For if there can be no poetry, does this not mean there is nothing left to celebrate or nurture? Such an attitude would be nihilism at its bleakest. Is it not, as some ask, a gloomy version of Gnosticism, which associates all of human history with the forces of evil, and locates the Good, if it exists at all, in some pure heavenly realm?[18] What this impression of Adorno neglects is the often unmentioned fact that he would later withdraw his provocative statement:

> I would readily concede that, just as I said that after
> Auschwitz one *could not* write poems . . . it could equally

well be said, on the other hand, that one *must* write poems . . . [A]s long as there is an awareness of suffering among human beings there must also be art as the objective form of that awareness.[19]

What might the reader of Adorno's work make of this retraction, and how does wrestling with this reversal relate to his interest in theology?

## Adorno's 'Inverse Theology'

This volume demonstrates that, far from representing a resigned pessimism, some dark version of Gnosticism, or a desperate longing for other-worldly salvation, Adorno's philosophy is motivated by a deep and sustained commitment to confront the realities of human suffering. His criticism of the traditions of the Enlightenment is not motivated by a rejection of the Enlightenment, but intends to rejuvenate it and defend its ideals. Behind Adorno's relentless criticism and negative dialectics is an enduring and determined search for a better world. What remains to be recognized is the role that his concept of theology has in nurturing this quest.

Robert Hullot-Kentor suggests that 'theology is always moving right under the surface of all Adorno's writings' and 'penetrates every word'.[20] This should not be misunderstood as support for the view that, in the end, Adorno's critical theory represents a despairing flight from reason into the comforting arms of some mystical theological consolation. Adorno develops an 'inverse theology', which probes 'the wounds which this order has and which . . . it inflicts on us'. For Adorno, these 'wounds' are located in the tensions and unresolved contradictions found in the present social order. He argues that 'suffering is objectivity that weighs upon the subject', and that the task of critical social theory is to uncover and analyse this weight of objectivity.[21] Theological discourse is an important object of study for Adorno because he understands it to be an expression of these wounds and sufferings. Furthermore, he argues that theology illuminates how thought and experience constantly reach beyond the limits of the given moment. This is to say that, in theological discourse, Adorno observes experiences and expressions that challenge the dominance of the current social *actuality*, as religion both testifies to, and gives expression to, a concern for alternative social *possibilities*.

Adorno's concept of an 'inverse theology' does not engage in correlating present problems with theological themes, in a manner similar to the methodology proposed by the Christian theologian Paul Tillich. Tillich suggested that contemporary society presents the *questions* to theology and the Christian theological tradition is subsequently examined for *answers* to these questions.[22] Responses to such questions are shaped by Christianity, which might sometimes require some revision based on contemporary experience. Adorno's approach inverts the ordering of Tillich's theory of correlation. For him, theological concepts – such as the prohibition of images of the divine ('*Bilderverbot*'), redemption, justice, and the messianic – challenge and question society. It is then human beings, within their social situation, who are charged with constructing the answers to such questions. An 'inverse theology' is thus not a top-down imposition of idealist concepts; rather, the theological element in Adorno's work is employed to crack open existing life; to make room for new insights.

## Perils and Clarifications

In addition to the considerable complexity of Adorno's thought, there are numerous perils that a book like this must guard against. The first is that of appropriating Adorno's fragmentary remarks on theology in order to turn him into a closet theologian. Over the course of this volume, illustrations of this tendency will be explored in some detail, but such analyses serve to make plain that Adorno is not a theologian. Any transcendence of existing social conditions is, for him, contained solely within material human history, and resourced solely by human agency. Adorno rejects positive theology, and he also criticizes negative theology. Instead, his deployment of theological concepts defends what he calls an 'inverse theology', which directs our attention, not into the heavens, but deep into the wounds and sufferings among human beings and within present social conditions.

A second peril of a book like this is to fail to illustrate effectively the relevance Adorno's philosophy has for contemporary theology. Although Adorno is not a theologian, neither does he advocate an anti-theology. This volume demonstrates that his work resonates with numerous concerns and issues found in modern Christian theology, including the crisis theology of Karl Barth and Latin American Liberation Theology. Furthermore, it shows how Adorno's writing offers an invaluable critical resource for analysing trends in contemporary theology, including the contemporary interest in 'spirituality' and the use of rational choice theory to support strategies focused on church growth. Moreover, Adorno's debates with sociology and the philosophy of science offer provocative avenues for theology to explore as it wrestles with the other disciplines in the academy. While Adorno does not offer theology a positive foundation upon which to secure a systematic theology, his work offers a rich and fruitful critical lens through which theology can examine and scrutinize present trends within its own discipline.

A third danger to avoid when discussing Adorno's work is the temptation to present his philosophy as a 'system' or 'method'. Adorno insisted on the unsystematic nature of his project, and rejected constructing philosophical edifices upon foundational first principles. His preferred mode of writing was in the form of focused essays, not sustained organic tomes. Summarizing the complexity of his thought into thematic divisions necessarily overly simplifies and misrepresents his work; at the same time, presenting it in an intelligible and digested form is necessary to encourage others to read him. This book will, therefore, seek to establish a careful balance between clear exposition and faithful presentation of Adorno's work.

## From Systems to Constellations

Adorno's preferred model for philosophical reflection was not the construction of systems, but immanent criticism of existing structures, as well as assembling together what he called 'changing constellations'. For Adorno, systematic philosophy (and, by extension, systematic theology) represents a form of identity thinking.

A system's first loyalty is to the rules of logic and non-contradiction, rather than to the objects it intends to describe. It thus inevitably neglects or ignores that which does not conform to its requirements. As Adorno argues in his lecture 'The Actuality of Philosophy', philosophical reason is not sufficient to grasp the totality of the real. Rather, 'the text which philosophy has to read is incomplete, contradictory and fragmentary'.[23] Given this perspective, Adorno suggests that critical thought is left with two alternative strategies from that of system building. First, by criticizing existing systems on the basis of its own premises, an immanent critique helps to uncover hidden contradictions, assumptions, and 'unintentional reality' within present social existence. This serves to bring false assumptions into consciousness, and to foster awareness of the ways in which existing society influences thought. Adorno's second alternative to system building is drawn from the work of Walter Benjamin, who proposed that 'constellations' served as a useful model for dialectical reason, because, 'ideas are to objects as constellations are to stars'.[24] Concepts only proximate the reality they seek to articulate and describe, a fact that the rigid and precise structure of a system has a tendency to mask and forget. Adorno proposes, therefore, that philosophy gather objects and experiences 'into changing constellations' – or 'changing trial combinations' – in order to explore how they illuminate and contrast with each other.[25] This enables it to momentarily break reality open, if only to achieve momentary or partial insights.

## Religion and Theology

Some clarification at this point is required to distinguish between the terms 'religion' and 'theology'. Within the academic study of religion, an intense debate rages over whether it is possible to define what is distinctly 'religious' about certain forms of subjective human experience, structures of discourse, or communal practices.[26] Across the vast differences among human beings and cultures, it is indeed astonishingly difficult (if not impossible) to identify a trans-cultural 'essence' within a universal genus of 'religion'. Adorno's use of the term 'religion' is generally in reference to what he took to be the two most prominent expressions within Western Europe during his lifetime: Judaism and Christianity. This is, thus, how the term will be used in this book. Rather than suggesting a specific theoretical definition for religion, references to 'religion', 'religious experience', or 'religious practices' simply refer to the institutional existence of Jewish communities or Christian churches, or to the experiences and activities of individuals who are practising members of those communities.

The term 'theology' is less clearly delineated in Adorno's writing. More specific than the term 'religion,' the word generally refers to the theoretical discourse of a religious community. But it also has roots in the Western philosophical tradition, where it is more precisely defined as reasoning about God, or at least the ontological structures which give shape to existence. Adorno's usage of the term shifts between both of these elements of common meaning. Although he is often quite critical of the merits of theology as a theoretical discipline, Adorno does treat it as having a rational component. There is no question for Adorno that theology involves processes of reasoning, and, as such, is related to the general philosophical search for truth. Thus, in some instances, Adorno discusses theology in reference to the rational discussion about topics related to the concerns traditionally considered to be 'religious': the existence of God, the purpose and meaning of suffering, the nature of death and the possibility of immortality, etc. However, on other occasions, Adorno's deployment of the term draws on tradition-specific concepts that carry with them some particular content. In particular, he frequently employs specific concepts from the Jewish tradition, such as redemption, the messianic, and the *Bilderverbot* (prohibition on images of the divine).[27]

## The Structure of the Book

The presentation of this volume develops according to the spirit of Adorno's approach to philosophy. It will not, therefore, seek to construct a precise and systematic analysis of Adorno's thought for the purposes of a philosophy of religion or a systematic theology. Nor will it seek to locate his work in the history of philosophy and thus identify all of his sources and influences. Instead, the book brings Adorno's thought and some elements of Christian and Jewish theology into different constellations, in order to explore how they illuminate each other. Furthermore, some contemporary trends in Christian thought will be subjected to an immanent critique, in order to demonstrate how Adorno's writing offers a fruitful challenge to a number of problematic emphases. The primary intention is to offer an example of how Adorno's thought offers a distinct and engaging dialogue partner for theology, while demonstrating that his concept of an 'inverse theology' is at the core of the moral impulse that motivates his work.

The first chapter serves as a further introduction to Adorno's thought, highlighting in particular his understanding of the 'dialectic of Enlightenment'. The chief focus of the discussion is to provide some initial orientation to Adorno's philosophy, as well as to explore his nuanced understanding of 'materialism' by contrasting it with two prominent theological perspectives of the same.

Chapter 2 offers an analysis of the important influence of Immanuel Kant's philosophy on Adorno's work. The examination demonstrates how Adorno interprets Kant's 'block' against knowledge of things-in-themselves. To help clarify Adorno's approach, his treatment of this question is contrasted with that of the Christian theologian John Milbank. The key distinction that emerges is the distinct way in which Adorno conceives of possibility in relation to actuality.

Chapter 3 confronts a frequent charge against Adorno, which is that his work implies a subjectivist access to secret inner knowledge, which renders it an anti-scientific form of abstract Platonism. This accusation is discussed through an analysis of a debate that emerged between Adorno and the philosopher of science Karl Popper. What is particularly striking about this discussion is how both parties in the 'Positivist Dispute' label their opponent's work as being a 'crypto-theology.'

The fourth chapter serves as the heart of this volume, exploring directly Adorno's understanding of theology. This is developed in dialogue with other interpretations of Adorno's work, and particularly with attention to how Adorno's view emerges out of his conversations with Walter Benjamin, and his engagement with the literature of Franz Kafka. What is highlighted by the discussion is the central importance of the concept of the *Bilderverbot* for understanding the description Adorno himself gives of his work: an 'inverse theology'.

Chapter 5 offers a consideration of the political implications of Adorno's thought. The challenges confronting Adorno's critical theory in this regard are illustrated with reference to his dispute with the German student movement in the 1960s. This is complemented by an analysis of his view of the relationship between theory and practice, as well as a discussion of Adorno's relationship to Liberation Theology. The chapter closes by highlighting the role that the concept of the 'messianic' has in his thought, which is illustrated by placing his approach in a constellation with that of Giorgio Agamben.

A prominent aspect of Adorno's social theory is his critique of the 'Culture Industry'. This is analysed in Chapter 6 and is contrasted with the concept of 'spirituality,' as well as with the prominence of rational choice theory in the contemporary study of religion. This engagement with Rodney Stark's work, along with an illustrative discussion of the film *A Beautiful Mind*, demonstrates how Adorno's critique of ideology relates to the study of religion and society, and opens up new possibilities to explore about the relationship between theology and social science.

Chapter 7 brings this study to a close with some attention to Adorno's aesthetic theory, particularly through an analysis of his philosophy of music and his concern with the question of whether poetry can be written after Auschwitz. Adorno's efforts to 'think with the ears' is linked to his view of prayer as 'attention', and some of his fragmentary aphorisms on the nature of love are explored to help connect his aesthetic insights with a more inter-relational approach to theology. These elements of his thought are explored in relation to different theological interpretations of his work, and particularly through his appreciation of the poetry of Paul Celan.

Throughout the book, Adorno's inverse theology is shown to be rooted in reason and critical thought. It refers to a utopian vision that is attentive to the possibilities for society which remain unrealized, and is deployed to criticize existing life on that basis. In the quest to transcend the bonds that dominate the subject, and in the search to uncover the causes of suffering, Adorno argues that one achieves a glimpse of freedom, along with a trace of

objective truth. By analysing this perspective, this book demonstrates that theology is far from a marginal concern in his work.
Adorno was convinced that, without the critical distance opened
up on the brokenness of life by assuming the perspective of an
inverse theology, one surrenders life to the sufferings of the *status
quo*. While Adorno insists that one must remain silent about God,
he also argues that one must at the same time continue to search
for the possibility that the world could be otherwise. In his
philosophy, it is an inverse theology which helps prevent the
conventions of the *status quo* from silencing those who cry out
against oppression and who work for a more human and rational
society.

# Chapter 1
# Materialism, Theology and the Dialectic of Enlightenment

At the close of 1843, Karl Marx completed the introduction to his 'Contribution to the Critique of Hegel's *Philosophy of Right*'. He wrote, 'For Germany, the *criticism of religion* has been largely completed; and the criticism of religion is the premise of all criticism'. Marx argued that, after Ludwig Feuerbach had demonstrated that '*man makes religion*', human beings were free to criticize the very foundations of society, since the 'general theory of this world' provided by religion had been undermined and revealed to be an illusion.[1] Such a premise assumed that religion was the source of irrationality, passivity, and narrow dogmatism, so that, once its shackles were removed, human beings would be free to live rationally and peacefully. In subsequent years, however, the socialist movements of Europe experienced political defeat, which was followed by the emergence of fierce disputes between rival factions. By the turn of the century, it was apparent that, despite the Marxist critique of religion, socialists were far from immune from the dogmas of nation and ideology. This was made all too clear when, in 1914, millions of working class soldiers clashed with each other on behalf of their nation states in the trenches of the Great War.

Some intellectuals began to suspect that a 'spectre was haunting Europe', but they were now concerned that it was not the imminent arrival of the Communist ideal. Determining what this 'spectre' was that lurked beneath the surface of European society became the focus of a number of 'Western Marxists' in the aftermath of the First World War. Having observed the enthusiastic participation of trade unions in the war efforts of many nations, and disillusioned by the dogmatism of the Second and Third

Communist Internationals, such intellectuals sought to articulate a humanistic and un-dogmatic interpretation of Marx's philosophy in opposition to the official Soviet position.

The thought of Theodor W. Adorno emerged out of this developing perspective, and he became one of its most prominent and influential voices. Adorno's attempt to understand the collusion of progressive thought with dogmatism led him to return to an analysis of religion or – more precisely – to a concern with interpreting the influence and role of Christianity and Judaism within Western culture and society. He agreed with Marx that the criticism of religion is the premise of all criticism, but as he observed the preponderance of dogmatism within the social movements of his age, and as he witnessed the decline of emancipatory utopianism in the face of the growing dominance of pragmatic science, he concluded that Marx had been incorrect to conclude that the criticism of religion was largely *complete*. In his view, a 'bourgeois' criticism of religion can be as problematic as the escapist theology and ideological spirituality that Marx challenged. Furthermore, the role of religion as a symbol through which human beings express their suffering and hope had also not been exhaustively analysed by Marx. Such a conviction led Adorno to make reflection on religion a key aspect of his critical social theory; for 'the revolution has suffered the same fate as the Second Coming'.[2]

The relevance of Adorno's concerns for the present context could not be more striking. In both academic and general cultural discourse, the place of religion and theology within social and political life has recently received considerable attention and renewed interest. Since the terrorist attacks in the USA on 11 September 2001, and subsequently in London on 7 July 2005, an increasing number of intellectuals have called into question the assumption that, in modern societies, religion will become increasingly marginalized. This has coincided with the intriguing development of a so-called 'return to religion' in some circles of philosophical and cultural theory. Philippa Berry, for example, observes that 'one of the most unexpected results' of the postmodern critique of science and reason 'has been to revive interest in those once-tabooed aspects of "otherness"; which can broadly be termed spiritual or religious'.[3] This development has been met with an equal-and-opposite reaction. Prominent natural scientists and journalists like Richard Dawkins and Christopher Hitchens, repelled in particular by extreme expressions of American Christian evangelicalism, as well as by some militant versions of Islam, have insisted that affirmation or respect for religious traditions amounts to irrational delusion. According to these 'New Atheists', religion is an enemy of rationality, science, democracy, and morality.

Adorno's own approach to theology is more nuanced than either of these two firm polarities. Adorno neither embraces traditional religion, nor dismisses it as inherently alien to modern rationality. With regard to both religious enthusiasts and militant anti-religious advocates, Adorno's thought will initially appear paradoxical. He is an atheist and a Marxian materialist who thinks that progressive thought cannot do without theological elements. Similarly, in his determined attempt to defend the traditions of the Enlightenment against irrationality and oppressive political forces, he urges his audience to recognize the Enlightenment's deep connection to mythology. Finally, to defend the legitimacy of science, he accuses scientists of harbouring their own mythological devotion to a mistaken belief in objective facts.

This chapter illustrates the broad concerns and context within which Adorno develops his approach to theology. It locates the roots of his interest in theology in the emergence of the Institute of Social Research at the University of Frankfurt. This preoccupation is primarily the result of Adorno's perception of the limitations of Marxian theory, as well as his sense of the deep weaknesses in the Enlightenment's concept of reason. The discussion then turns to an explication of how Adorno understands Enlightenment rationality to be intertwined with myth, in a dynamic he calls the 'dialectic of enlightenment'. The impact this position has for how he conceives of materialism demonstrates that Adorno's critical theory offers a rich resource for analysing contemporary debates over the place of theology in contemporary thought. This will be explored with some reference to how the thought of Christian theologians like Paul Tillich and John Milbank both resonates and contrasts with Adorno's perspective. This comparison demonstrates that, for Adorno, if theology is to have any role in assisting materialism to overcome its limitations, it must first pass through the wounds in historical existence opened up by human suffering.

## Adorno, the 'Frankfurt School' and Religion

Adorno himself had an ambiguous relationship with Christianity and Judaism. The product of an assimilated German Jewish father and an Italian Roman Catholic mother, he was baptized in the Catholic Church as an infant, although he was not himself a practitioner of a religious tradition, and he associated himself with Marxian atheism early in his life. Nevertheless, Adorno's writing makes frequent references to Christian and Jewish theological concepts, a preoccupation that has often puzzled his interpreters. Why would a committed Marxist and a sophisticated atheist bother himself with theology and metaphysics? For many of his contemporaries, theological discourse was considered an antiquated relic of the pre-modern past. When Adorno makes them objects of serious study, his critics often dismiss it as irrational romanticism or the result of a pessimistic longing for consolation in a suffering world. It is important to recognize, therefore, that Adorno's interest in theology follows directly from his understanding of rationality and the social context in which he lived. In a society increasingly dominated by technical thinking and the authority of natural science, as well as consumerism, he understood theological discourse to be among the few places in which concern for truth and a just society were retained.

Adorno's approach to theology was certainly an uncommon one in the academic circles he moved in. Philosophy and sociology generally assumed the legitimacy of the so-called 'secularization thesis': the presumption that, in modern Western societies, religious communities and discourse will become increasingly marginalized in the face of science and the differentiation of spheres of expert knowledge. This process of 'rationalization' is assumed to ensure the gradual relocation of sources of authority (including political, epistemological, and moral) away from the realm of traditional religious communities and to an external 'worldly' secular sphere. The broadening distinction between the separate realms of the 'religious' and the 'secular' is one that comes at the expense of the former. Theology and religious belief are to be relegated to the private sphere, having no relevance or role in the day-to-day business of public life. They represent mere remnants of pre-modern tradition, which enlightened minds and societies ought to be mature enough to leave behind. The secularization thesis presumes that, as societies become increasingly industrialized, this marginalization of religion is both unavoidable and irreversible.[4]

Adorno began to develop an alternative analysis of this narrative of modernity with his colleagues at the Institute of Social Research at the University of Frankfurt. The Institute had emerged out of a 'First Marxist Work Week' organized by the German businessman Felix Weil in 1922. Its founding purpose centred on the 'hope that the different trends in Marxism, if afforded an opportunity of talking it out together, could arrive at a 'true' or 'pure' Marxism'.[5] This aim proved to be an elusive goal, but given that this problem impacted directly upon Adorno's subsequent thought, it is instructive to attend to the early work of what would become known as 'the Frankfurt School'.

Under Max Horkheimer's leadership, the Institute sought to develop an interdisciplinary study of society, incorporating the disciplines of philosophy, sociology, psychology, economics, political theory and, subsequently, cultural analysis. Horkheimer invited Adorno to join the work of the Institute initially as an expert in musicology. The first research project organized by Horkheimer focused on an analysis of the political views of the German working class. It sought to uncover the social and psychological structures of Weimar society, and the extent to which the working class might be relied upon to maintain their left-wing sympathies in crisis situations. The study's conclusions suggested that the Institute's founding optimism about Marxism as a social movement was likely to be disappointed. As one of Horkheimer's early reflections illustrates, he had little confidence in the revolutionary potential of the workers: 'Unlike the pre-war proletariat, *these* unemployed . . . do not possess the capacity for education and organization . . . [Their] impatience . . . is found, on an intellectual level, only in the mere repetition of Communist party slogans'.[6] In his estimation, the working classes were too internally divided to form a politically unified 'proletariat'. The interests of employed workers were often in conflict with those of the unemployed, and this was complicated further by issues of class, region, and gender. As he became increasingly disturbed by events in Russia in the early 1930s, Horkheimer argued that a thorough re-examination of historical materialism was required.

Although Horkheimer was highly critical of socialist politics in Germany, at the same time he resisted abandoning what he understood to be the key insights of Marx's philosophy. He thought it vital to challenge the emerging popularity of Karl Mannheim's 'sociology of knowledge', which argued that cognitive structures are directly related to social structures. Mannheim understood this 'situational determinism' to permit sociology to achieve a new understanding of 'ideology'. By suggesting that particular notions of ideology often serve only to dismiss the views of one's opponent, Mannheim intended to develop a broader 'total concept' of ideology, one that acknowledged that all worldviews represent 'ideological' perspectives on society.[7]

Horkheimer considered this shift towards a more neutral perspective on ideology deeply problematic. In his opinion, Mannheim's claim that forms of knowledge simply 'correspond' to the situation of a certain social group effectively undermined the Marxist understanding of 'false consciousness'. It suggested that there could be no 'non-ideological' perspective from which to criticize ideology, so that one must adopt a relativistic view of truth. Horkheimer intended to defend a more Marxist understanding of ideology, so that social injustices and contradictions could be criticized from a perspective that was not regarded as merely one ideology among others.[8]

This perspective left Horkheimer in a difficult theoretical position. After rejecting the relativism he saw in Mannheim's work, how was he to avoid adopting a rigid dogmatic position of the kind he witnessed among many socialist political leaders? Immediately following his comments on 'the Impotence of the German Working Class', Horkheimer's reflection turns to a discussion of 'Atheism and Religion'. His remarks suggest why religion was becoming a primary concern of his as he sought to articulate a Marxist theory of society in response to the social conditions he was witnessing:

> The complete emancipation from any and every belief in
> the existence of a power which is independent of history,
> yet governs it, is a lack that is part of the most primitive

intellectual clear-sightedness and truthfulness of modern man. And yet it is enormously difficult to avoid making a new religion of this very absence. As long as the horrors of life and death . . . have not been reduced by the efforts of a just society, even the spirit free of superstition will seek refuge from its distress in a mood which has something of the reassuring quiet of the temple, though that temple be built in defiance of the gods.[9]

This reflection raises a concern that will be shared by Adorno throughout his life: why are the emancipatory impulses of Marxism so vulnerable to being reduced to a new form of rigid dogmatism? Why is one false notion of the absolute so quickly replaced by another false notion of the absolute? Such questions led him to revisit the traditional Marxist dismissal of theology, as he wrestled with the dilemma that confronted emancipatory politics following the decline of the German workers' movement.

This reconsideration of the function of religion within society did not imply uncritical appropriation. Adorno remained a harsh critic of historical religious traditions like Christianity, particularly for its ideological support of the nation state, and for encouraging people to passively bear injustice while hoping to attain reward in some blissful afterlife. Nevertheless, he also grew to appreciate how Christianity and Judaism often maintained a vision for a better life. In such utopianism, Adorno identified a goal similar to that of Marxian social theory. Friedrich Engels himself had identified numerous connections between his thought and the utopian impulse of Christianity, particularly in the form it took among radical reformers in the sixteenth century like Thomas Münzer.[10] Adorno's nuanced attitude towards theology is influenced by this appreciation, as well as by the observation that the failures he criticizes in historical religions can be found in a similar form within numerous socialist movements, including a dogmatic over-simplification of social ills, and the idealization of the 'revolution-ary' potential of certain groups (i.e. the 'proletariat'). From his perspective, these supposed socialist and atheistic theories resem-ble the abstract and otherworldly elements that Marx identified as belonging to religion. Adorno criticizes, therefore, the assumption among some Marxists that once human beings recognize that consciousness is dependent upon material conditions, they will as a consequence master these conditions and become free. Furthermore, Adorno laments the fact that once socialist politics began to uphold revolutionary political goals in a rigid and uncompromising manner, it became counterproductive and even anti-humanist. Even more disturbingly, he recalls that, according to Marx and Engels, 'all misery and horror along the way toward that goal must be put up with for that reason'. Adorno argues that this mistake results from their belief that truth is what is most stable, most solid, most dependable, so that any immediate suffering or potential victims of the pursuit of truth become inconsequential. In effect, these two great revolutionary critics of abstract knowledge had fallen victim to the same basic philosophical error they had criticized: they turned their own theory into an absolute claim of knowledge that neglects its own roots in a particular social context. For Adorno, thought can never become so secure of its possession of the fullness of the truth.

Adorno's approach to theology agrees, therefore, with Marx that, 'the criticism of religion is the premise of all criticism'; yet, for him, in contrast to Marx, this criticism is not yet complete. Despite the fact that historical materialism has unmasked metaphysical ideas as human constructions rooted in history, and despite the shift in authority from religious truth claims to scientific theory, dogmatism and mystification remain. It is simplistic to declare, as Horkheimer wrote, that 'God is dead. It would be truer to say that thought has died'.[11]

Adorno's perspective on theology was shaped by this early social research by the Institute. But these more sociological concerns, along with the research projects associated with them, were abruptly interrupted by the rise of the National Socialist Party in Germany, and the appointment of Adolf Hitler as Chancellor in 1933. The following year the Institute was searched by the police and closed, accused of 'activities hostile to the state'. More than one third of the University of Frankfurt's faculty lost their teaching positions, including Adorno and Horkheimer. By this time, however, Adorno and many of his colleagues had already fled the country, and the Institute's resources and library transferred to France and subsequently Switzerland. Adorno initially hesitated to leave Germany, but eventually arranged to become an 'advanced student' at Oxford University. He remained there until 1937, when, with Horkheimer's assistance, he was able to emigrate to New York, where Horkheimer had already settled and set up the New School for Social Research with the support of Columbia University.

The shock of this forced emigration was intensified as Adorno watched the horrors of the war unfold from a distance. As the nightmarish rumours concerning the destructive campaign against the Jews in Europe began to circulate, Adorno's analysis probed deeper into the culture of the West for an explanation for the violence and brutality that had erupted in his native country, which he considered to be the most cultured and philosophically advanced in the world.

## Dialectic of Enlightenment: Reason, Myth and Mimesis

Adorno's concern to uncover the sources of domination contained within the Western philosophical tradition led him to reflect deeply on the nature of human rationality. In this discussion, he largely equates religion with the concept of 'myth'. Here Adorno is informed by an intense discussion of mythology in the late nineteenth and early twentieth centuries, during which myths were understood to be primitive examples of an attempt to rationalize and understand events in nature. Johann Jakob Bachofen, for example, argued that mythological stories evolved from more primitive societies, which were more closely tied to the cycles of nature than modern communities.[12] He suggested that, as societies evolve, they shift from myth to the rationality of logos. A view of this kind is often found within German idealism, and was a source for Friedrich Nietzsche's conception of the difference between the Dionysian and Apollonian aspects of Greek thought.

Adorno's view of myth is also similar to that of the anthropologists E. B. Tylor and J. G. Frazer, insofar as he conceives of mythological stories as attempts to understand and control the natural environment.[13] For Adorno, myths are primitive explanations for physical events. Whereas some conceptions of myth tend to view them as possessing some non-literal or symbolic meaning (as is the case for the theologian Rudolph Bultmann or philosopher Ernst Cassirer), Adorno understands them more as an early form of imitative reasoning. They are not, therefore, simply irrational, but are (inaccurate) forms of rational thought. Myths, in his view, are rooted in prelinguistic experiences, and so seek to express what other forms of discourse cannot capture. He draws particular emphasis from the French anthropologist Roger Caillois, who links mythology to 'mimesis'. Caillois suggests that myths are attempts to copy, and thus relate to, the forces of nature.[14]

Adorno revisited this territory with Max Horkheimer in the 1940s, as they collaborated to write *Dialectic of Enlightenment*. In this text, they locate the roots of instrumental rationality in mimetic practice of the kind observed in anthropological studies of human cultures. For them, the early roots of mimesis can be observed in the manner in which animals adapt to their surroundings for purposes of survival (the chameleons changing colour; the feigning of death in the face of danger, etc.). This practice finds similar expression in prehistorical shamanic rites that intend to pacify the violent forces of nature by imitating them, or in acts of the magician, who draws magic circles, steps into them and 'imitates demons; to frighten or placate them he makes intimidating or appeasing gestures'. While this action is manipulative, it still acknowledges nature as an independent object beyond human control. Furthermore, nature is not made into an object of knowledge, but is identified *with*; the magician does not believe he has the power to control nature, but instead attempts to become part of the same order from which the threat emanates.[15] Adorno suggests that both mythology and modern rationality are rooted in this dynamic, except that in his view, rationality goes still further than this by seeking not only to imitate nature, but also to control it.

Adorno's suggestion that mimesis and reason are profoundly interconnected anticipates some more recent trends within the study of religion and feminist theory. Some scholars of religion emphasize the central role of ritual and religious practices for shaping human subjectivity and worldviews. Within certain articulations of feminist theory, a stress on the significance of embodied practice for the construction of identity is developed in similar fashion. Catherine Bell, for example, suggests that 'ritual activity concerns knowledge (ritual mastery) that is "reproduced through practices made possible by the framing assumptions of that knowledge"'.[16] Adorno's theory of mimesis resonates to some extent with this view, and he is certainly prepared to agree that human reasoning itself is shaped by the activities through which it is put to work, and that it is influenced by the context out of which it emerges. Human beings often learn through imitation, including their very manner of reasoning. What Adorno does not accept, however, is that reason is nothing more than a symptom of cultural imitation and practice. In his view, reason can point beyond the boundaries of existing experience and context, and expand the horizon of human thought beyond the conventions of the *status quo*.

This point will be taken up further below. For the present discussion, it is instructive to remain with the argument in *Dialectic of Enlightenment*. In the first excursus, which interprets Homer's epic poem *The Odyssey*, Adorno suggests that Odysseus' battle against 'irrational nature' and myth be understood as a prototype for the development of the rational bourgeois subject. Odysseus defeats the mythic figures he encounters by combining the imitation of nature with rational cunning and deceit. This accomplishment comes at a price: the repression of his connection to nature. As Adorno states it, 'the human being's mastery of itself, on which the self is founded, practically always involves the annihilation of the subject in whose service that mastery is maintained'.[17] To outwit the Cyclops, Odysseus changes his name to 'Nobody', but his mimicry of a nameless person is the enactment of the truth of his own identity. He cannot enjoy nature, because knowledge has become something based on control: the human being knows things 'to the extent that he can manipulate them'.[18]

As the dialectic of enlightenment progresses from the mimicry of nature in prehistorical times to the myths of the ancient world, and into the metaphysics of the modern age, various conceptual models are left behind. Adorno argues, however, that a mimetic moment remains secretly contained within them all, and that it continually resurfaces in various ways. 'False mimesis' results in a loss of its fluid approach to its object. One's fear of nature becomes a violent rage that expresses itself in such destructive historical forces as anti-Semitism and misogyny. 'False' mimesis tries to make 'the surroundings resemble itself'; it 'displaces the volatile inward into the outer world, branding the intimate friend as foe'.[19] As Karla Schultz states, 'Odysseus, longing for a home, establishes himself as master'.[20]

This dynamic is summed up in *Dialectic of Enlightenment* in the following manner: 'Myth becomes Enlightenment and nature mere objectivity. Human beings purchase the increase in their power with estrangement from that over which it is exerted. Enlightenment stands in the same relationship to things as the dictator to human beings'.[21] Adorno argues that when thought forgets its relationship to the natural environment, and to the object it seeks to understand, its 'false clarity is only another name for myth'.[22]

Adorno concludes that the supposedly demystifying practices of thinking often themselves become a new form of mystification. For example, one might accurately determine that a specific religious claim about the world is erroneous, but such an achievement by no means represents an escape from bias, ideology, or wish-fulfilment. Adorno argues that, in their drive to establish totality through concepts, philosophy and science are guilty of developing theories abstracted from society. In effect, materialism can often turn into is opposite: an ideological assumption about objects in the world. In this dynamic, thought forces objects into the mould of theory, and annihilates what does not conform. Such 'identity thinking', Adorno asserts, is an act of violence against the 'other'. It represents a drive to make unlikes alike; a drive that leads him to reconsider the nature of the knowing subject. The central thrust of Adorno's theoretical work becomes, then, an attempt to recognize the non-identity of the 'other' which remains outside the boundaries of identity thinking.

It should be stressed again that Adorno does not conclude that reason itself ought to be abandoned; nor that it is hopelessly corrupt. His analysis does not lead him to anticipate a version of the postmodern 'death of reason'. Such a position would, for him, amount to a resigned nihilism. Rather, Adorno argues that rationality, despite its tragic flaws, remains the source of that critical reflection which is capable of uncovering hidden forms of domination. It is also the source of ideal concepts like freedom and justice. Drawing from a distinction found in the work of the sociologist Max Weber, Adorno distinguishes between purposive-driven reason and rationality concerned with more substantive concerns, like morality and aesthetics. His view is influenced by his colleague Horkheimer, who presented the outlines of this perspective in an agenda-setting essay, 'Traditional and Critical Theory'. Horkheimer argues that 'traditional theory' fails to acknowledge the social location of its assumptions. He locates this understanding of science in the context of a bourgeois society dominated by techniques of industrial production. Traditional theory, or what both Adorno and Horkheimer will increasingly refer to as 'instrumental reason', fails to acknowledge that facts and theories can 'be understood only in the context of real social processes'. Such a programme, to be undertaken by a 'critical theory of society', Horkheimer argues, 'is a theory dominated at every turn by a concern for reasonable conditions of life'.[23]

The contradictions between the rational concept of society (its ideals and intentions) and the human experience of suffering, and between the attempt to control one's natural environment and the experience of powerlessness are, for Adorno, evidence of the irrationality of society and the incompleteness of scientific knowledge. This tension necessitates an appreciation for the ways in which human thought and action influence the world, but also a recognition of the fallibility of these same powers, and the fact that the world often acts upon human beings against their will. How this perspective shapes Adorno's approach to studying society and to theology will now be the focus of our concern.

## Materialism and Demystification

For Adorno, one of the principal implications of this formulation of the dialectic of Enlightenment is how it challenges assumptions about scientific and intellectual knowledge. Chapter 3 will explore in detail how this influences his view of scientific method. But it is important to initially focus more generally on how this under-standing of the entwinement of myth and rationality shapes his understanding of materialism and human society. In Adorno's view, much of what passes as objective sociological method amounts to what he labels 'positivism', by which he means an emphasis on identifying value-neutral facts. He laments that a great deal of the sociology of his age was limited to the reporting of statistical observations about behaviour, or the results of qualitative subject interviews, the results of which are taken to be 'facts' about social existence. For Adorno, however, such an approach not only remains blind to its own assumptions and biases; more significantly, it neglects how social life is made up of 'congealed relationships'. He criticizes the sociological traditions of both Max Weber and Emil Durkheim for failing to adequately address this reality about social existence. Weber's reduction of social existence to means-ends rationality, and his attempt to achieve a value-neutral perspective free from philosophical concepts, ignores not just the reality that all thought is dependent on concepts, but also the problematic nature of rationality. Durkheim's position on 'social facts' as impenetrable and opaque leads, in Adorno's view, to either the reduction of the object to a mere instrumental 'thing', or to the simple acceptance of the *status quo* as the only possible world.[24]

Adorno's critical theory of society is concerned to analyse how life and thought are conditioned by social interests, but in a way that does not jettison the concept of truth or a better society. In opposition to the sociology of knowledge tradition (e.g. Mannheim), Adorno insists that sociology should not abandon the aim of uncovering and criticizing false consciousness. His approach, therefore, develops a dialectical concept of society, which intends to bring together society's unintelligible opacity (Durkheim) as well as its reducibility to the human, and thus its intelligible character (Weber). The objects of sociology, Adorno argues, exist in a field of relations, which are shaped by these relations. Sociology does not study 'things' with certain properties; rather the proper focus of analysis is on how the relationships between different social agents and environments influence one another. When, for example, sociologists preoccupy themselves with attention to opinions or individual subjective reactions, it is 'completely forgotten that these reactions, being something mediated, derivative, secondary, do not have anything like the certainty ascribed to them'.[25]

This perspective shapes how Adorno conceives of materialism, which bears directly on his resistance to a simplistically reductionistic attitude towards religion. Against the common notion that a materialistic study of human behaviour rids human beings of delusions, beliefs, and ideology by undermining them with attention to 'real' and concrete 'facts', Adorno argues that what passes as materialism is often itself based on metaphysical assumptions. Naturalistic explanations for social behaviour are frequently dependent on presuppositions about human beings, or present society, or even about matter itself and how one studies it. Adorno criticizes the manner in which materialism can be reduced to establishing a method that treats all of its objects as the same. He argues that, 'once the object becomes an object of cognition, its physical side is spiritualized from the outset by translation into epistemology'. When this occurs, the particularity of an object is ignored. It is forced to fit into the mould of a generalized method, and thus its concreteness – its materiality – is ultimately ignored. For Adorno, a different kind of attention must be given to the objects that materialism studies: 'It is by passing to the object's preponderance that dialectics is rendered materialistic'.[26] The assumption that an object, as it presents itself directly to the theorist, represents the truth of its material reality remains, in Adorno's view, blind to the compulsion of material conditions that shape it. The materialism of a dialectical theory of society must, therefore, remain focused on discerning such influential dynamics.

Such a view shapes Adorno's attitude towards distinctions like reason and myth, secular and sacred, materialism and idealism. In *Dialectic of Enlightenment*, he argues that efforts to de-mystify thought can unwittingly turn into a form of mystification. Reason can become its opposite if it treats its object as a simple thing to be isolated and controlled. As in the example of Odysseus, a drive to control and manipulate one's environment through cunning can subtly become a situation in which one's own freedom is undermined. Thought aimed at overcoming a certain belief system might succeed, only to impose a new set of assumptions on the world that is similarly incomplete and mythological in nature.

It is useful to turn briefly to the example of the concept of 'class' in order to illustrate more fully the concerns Adorno brings to the concepts of materialism. True to his Marxian roots, Adorno grants significant importance to the category of social class. But in his use of the concept he emphasizes that, for Marx, class is not fundamentally a quantitative concept based on a certain level of wealth or poverty. Class is a relational category – highlighting the relationship of an individual to the means of production.[27] Adorno continues to stress the category of class, even in the face of considerable criticism from sociologists who observe that it is sometimes difficult to describe differing workers as members of the same class given numerous distinctions between them (salaries, education, etc.).[28] He does not deny this problem, but argues instead that these complications and contradictions reveal that the concept of class is aporetic. Although the category is problematic, it points to a significant reality. It is not a natural or essential notion, but a socially constructed one. It is indeed misleading to describe a variety of very different workers as sharing the same status in society but, at the same time, this is not just any simple misidentification; it is a situation that is performed regularly every day. Rather than dismiss a social concept when he runs into a contradiction like this, Adorno concludes that this concept is socially produced – part of the result of the relationship workers have with the means of production and society in general. He insists, then, that it would be a mistake to jettison the concept of class because of its apparent contradictions. The task of social theory, he argues, is to exhibit and interpret such contradictions.

With this perspective, Adorno articulates what will become a common argument against 'vulgar materialism' in contemporary theory. Drawing particularly from Hegel's philosophy, Adorno argues that material objects are not present at hand in an immediate and uncomplicated manner. In his view, it is thus a fantasy to imagine that one can escape one's illusions simply by attending to 'material reality'. At the same time, Adorno also resists positions which take this challenge to materialism as an opportunity to jettison the original intentions of materialism completely. Adorno is not a 'post–Marxist', nor does the critical edge of his thought resemble what often passes for 'post-secular' or 'postmodern' thought. His criticisms of Marxian materialism are intended to focus more precisely and adequately on concrete social reality and the emancipatory goals of Marxism, not to abandon them. The force of his argument is rather to highlight how difficult it is to get to the bottom of this social 'concreteness'.

## Adorno and Theological Materialism

Adorno's criticism of a rigid and positivistic understanding of materialism resonates with the preoccupations of some notable Christian theologians. Christian theology has considerable interest in challenging an understanding of human life that limits experience and possibility to what can be observed in present concrete material existence. If what counts as reality is limited to what can be physically observed within the current economic and social structures, then there is little warrant or imaginative space to consider alternative possibilities which transcend the self-evident realities of the *status quo*. This clearly challenges any reference to an unseen divine reality, and any valuing of non-quantifiable experiences or values. To clarify how Adorno's position is distinct from prominent critiques of materialism within Christian theology, it is instructive to compare his view with similar discussions by John Milbank and Paul Tillich.

John Milbank's work echoes some of the general criticisms of Marxian materialism articulated by Adorno. Milbank argues that 'the forces of so-called progress — science, rationalism, and materialism — are far more precisely allied to capitalism than Marx realized'.[29] He thus seeks to develop a 'nonreductive materialism' which, if it is to avoid treating objects as if they are inert, must view matter as self-transcending. He argues, however, that how this reality is theorized by philosophy is usually in an 'etherealized' or 'idealized' manner. Here he is referring to the Kantian notion that the 'thing-in-itself' cannot be known to the subject. He also alludes to the Hegelian idea that the separation between subject and object will only be reconciled by absolute knowledge. In either case, Milbank argues, such abstract treatments of matter suggest that 'real material' will be made subject to some logical process or pure will. In other words, he is concerned that the object will be dominated and colonized by the subject who is viewing it.

Clearly this argument resonates with Adorno's criticism of reason in *Dialectic of* Enlightenment; the difference between Milbank and Adorno's treatment of these issues is in how they respond to this problematic. Milbank suggests that in order to prevent the object from being dominated by the reasoning subject, 'materialist socialism needs to invoke theology'.[30] What Milbank means by 'theology' here is a positive and systematic ontology. Only through the embrace of the Christian metanarrative, which describes God's graceful creation and relationship with all things, can philosophy maintain an ontology that is capable of guarding matter's incomplete self-transcendence. Christian theology alone, Milbank maintains, is able to nurture a subjective attitude towards matter that respects its elusive but significant reality. And so he concludes that 'a hope for socialism is possible only if the cosmos is secretly . . . hospitable to human harmony'.[31]

From the perspective of Adorno's thought, such a resolution of the problem does not represent an advance beyond, but a retreat behind, Hegelian philosophy. Hegel sought to overcome Kant's dualism between the thing-in-itself and the knowing subject by introducing a dialectic in which the subjective concept is brought into permanent confrontation with the object. Adorno faults Hegel for resolving this permanent dynamic through his suggestion that subject and object are reconciled in Absolute Spirit. Like Marx, Adorno considers such a move to be abstract, and thus Hegel's achievement is reconciliation in name only. But he does appreciate how at least in Hegel 'mediation is never a middle element between extremes', so that 'mediation takes place in and through the extremes, in the extremes themselves'.[32] Adorno follows Hegel in this conviction, devoting his attention to a close scrutiny of both the particularity of an object as it eludes the grasp of philosophy, as well as to the dynamics within the knowing subject. Adorno consistently refuses to resolve the complexities of these dynamics; no form of mediating institution or theoretical apparatus will serve to bring dialectical reflection to an end.

# Materialism, Theology and the Dialectic of Enlightenment

From the perspective of Adorno's position, Milbank's theological materialism seeks to bring the dialectic between subject and object to an end, by enveloping the object into a secure context defined by the Christian metanarrative. This requires a god's-eye perspective on the part of the philosopher or theologian. In order to suggest that theology serves to secure a true grasp of materiality, one must have access to a divine ontology from a source located outside and beyond the subject. But how does the subject access such knowledge? In Milbank's work it is solely achieved by being shaped by the disciplining technologies of the Christian church. But in Adorno's view, such an ecclesiology effectively swallows the subject as well as the object. His criticism of materialism does not follow a direction towards theology of the sort advocated by Milbank. In Adorno's view, the 'theology' that materialism requires, as will be demonstrated in detail in Chapter 4, cannot be a positive ontology, but only an 'inverse theology'.

It is interesting to contrast Milbank's contemporary attempt to reclaim socialism for Christian theology with an earlier effort to do the same by Paul Tillich. In this case, Adorno addresses Tillich's work directly. Tillich was an important acquaintance of Adorno's. In 1928, Adorno's postdoctoral supervisor rejected his attempt to obtain *Habilitation* status at the University of Frankfurt. The following year, however, Tillich was appointed to a chair in philosophy at the university. A theologian with socialist sympathies, Tillich developed an affinity with Horkheimer, and agreed to supervise Adorno's study of Kierkegaard. Like Adorno, Tillich was expelled from his teaching post in 1933, and both fled the Nazi regime to New York, where they continued to correspond.

Tillich became famous in Christian theological circles in North America for the development of what he called a method of 'correlation'. This approach interprets the questions facing the human condition in terms of existential philosophy, psychology and sociology, and then seeks to provide theological answers to the issues identified. In books like *The Socialist Decision* and *Political Expectation*, Tillich approaches Marxism and politics in such a manner, and it was this aspect of his thought that Adorno objected to most directly.[33] Tillich views politics through an existential philosophy of history, in which human beings are confronted by the reality of their 'finite freedom' in the midst of a specific and perilous situation. In an essay that Adorno gave particular attention, Tillich writes,

> Man is finite freedom. This is his structure. And everything human is included in this structure, all his relations to man, world, and God. Man is not infinite freedom as we say God is. Nor is he finite necessity as we say nature is. Man is freedom, but freedom in unity with finitude. The whole doctrine of man is a description of such an astonishing and unique structure as that of finite freedom.[34]

Tillich argues that 'Religious Socialism' makes finite freedom the ultimate criterion for social organization and justice. This implies subsidiary principles like self-determination, equality, and community, in which individuals are empowered as agents to exercise 'creative freedom' in their socio-historical context. Tillich understands himself to be in solidarity with socialist political movements, while at the same time correcting what in his view are the limitations of Marx's materialist anthropology. Essentially, he accuses Marx's account of human nature to be reductive and mechanistic. This robs socialism of its moral and creative impulse. The source and support of 'creative freedom' cannot, according to Tillich, arise solely from the material social situation, 'but originates from that which is beyond man's being and its brokenness, from beyond being and freedom'. It is being related to 'that which is beyond being' that enables the individual to connect with 'the root of the prophetic-eschatological element in socialism'.[35] Although this argument is developed rather differently from that of Milbank, its basic structure is similar. Dialectical materialism, in Tillich's view, needs to be reunited with a theological vision that appreciates the unity of materialism and idealism, and between spirit and matter. Like Milbank, materialism is urged to embed itself in an ontology provided by Christian theology.

In a letter to Tillich in 1944, Adorno sharply criticizes his former supervisor's account of religious socialism and his interpretation of materialism. He challenges Tillich's attempt to reconcile the conflict between materialism and idealism, proletariat and bourgeois, through the evocation of a future harmonious world 'that can in no way be explained in terms of present reality'.[36] In Adorno's view, the philosophy of history presented by Tillich has essentially been reduced to mythology.[37] Seeking to shun the rigid dogmatism of a Marxist theory he considers reductive and mechanistic, Tillich conceives of the 'true human being', whose horizontal freedom is enabled by a vertical relationship to something beyond history. For Adorno, this is not to mend the social order, but to abandon it by creating an abstract ideal of human existence: 'The definition of the human as "finite freedom" . . . is as methodologically arbitrary and "external" as it would be to define the human being's particular distinction from the animal via the earlobe'.[38] Tillich's anthropology describes humans as being both part of history, while at the same standing outside of it. Adorno argues that this nurtures the illusory notion that it is possible to escape the influence of the social environment, and implies that human agency is 'free-floating' above history.[39]

Whereas Milbank's theological challenge to materialism calls for incorporating it into a Christian ontology, and Tillich's criticism of socialist politics argues for a concept of human essence, Adorno resists shifting attention away from the complexity of material reality through the deployment of concepts that mask society's internal contradictions and elusive nature. In his view, the limitations in materialist theory cannot be so easily resolved by the introduction of some mediating concept to mend the rupture between knowledge and matter, subject and object. Adorno argues that the appropriate response to the complexities of materialism is not to seek after some fixed metaphysical or methodological certainty, but is rather to encourage an attentive sensitivity to social suffering, and a commitment to try to bring it to an end. Dialectical materialism is more a practice of thinking oriented towards the utopian goals of happiness and the end of suffering, than it is an ontology of matter or history.

Adorno's philosophy of history argues that historical existence is filled with catastrophe. He insists that 'the concept of the autonomous human subject is refuted by history'.[40] Thus, against a position like Tillich's, he argues that 'history is not a characteristic quality of the human being, but rather it is the epitome of all suffering'.[41] Suffering is a central focus of reflection for Adorno, and a primary element of his appropriation of Marxian analysis.

In *Negative Dialectics* he writes, 'The need to lend a voice to suffering is the condition of all truth. For suffering is objectivity that weighs upon the subject; its most subjective experience, its expression, is objectively conveyed'.[42] Suffering, in Adorno's view, reveals the presence of injustice or incompleteness. Thus, critical thought must scrutinize 'the stigmata of existence' to uncover such contradictions.[43] Any role that theology has in assisting materialism to overcome its limitations must pass through these wounds in historical existence.

For Adorno, theory has an emancipatory impulse which points it beyond the merely existing reality that stands before it, while at the same time preventing thought from leaving behind a focus on present social conditions:

> [T]he telos, the idea of Marxian materialism, is to do away with materialism, that is to say, to bring about a situation in which the blind compulsion of material conditions over human beings is broken, and in which alone the question as to freedom could first become truly meaningful'.[44]

Clearly this position raises a number of questions. What does it imply for politics? Perhaps even more controversially, what are its epistemological implications? Such issues will be explored in subsequent chapters. The primary relevance of the present discussion of materialism is how it influences Adorno's attitude towards theology. In the next chapter, the philosophical framework out of which Adorno develops an alternative role for theology in support of materialist concerns will be examined, particularly as it emerges out of his interpretation of the thought of Immanuel Kant.

# Chapter 2
# Actuality and Potentiality: On Kant and Metaphysics

Adorno opens his lectures on metaphysics with the observation: 'Today metaphysics is used in almost the entire non-German speaking world as a term of abuse, a synonym for idle speculation, mere nonsense and heaven knows what other intellectual vices'.[1] In a world increasingly dominated by instrumental rationality, pragmatism, and the methodologies of the natural sciences, concerns with metaphysical truths are pushed to the margins of academic discourse. Admittedly, Adorno himself distrusts philosophies that claim to outline the structure of being, or seek to derive first principles to guide subsequent philosophizing. He is also critical of much that is traditionally associated with metaphysics. In his 1965 lecture, however, he urges his students to resist the dismissal of what he understood to be the core of metaphysics: a concern for the 'world behind the world we know and can know'. Throughout Adorno's work, this complex attitude towards the metaphysical is paired with a rather ambivalent appreciation of theology. He directs harsh criticism towards metaphysics and theology, and yet refuses to dismiss them entirely. This results in a paradoxical tension, which complicates his interpretation of both theology and rationality.

This chapter examines Adorno's understanding of metaphysics, specifically as he develops it in relation to the philosophy of Immanuel Kant. The key distinction that emerges is the way in which Adorno conceives of possibility in relation to actuality, and how these relate to what has become known as the 'Kantian block'. The analysis demonstrates that Adorno's work intends to prevent the concepts of experience and freedom from becoming fixed invariants in the face of a contemporary preoccupation with factuality and 'vulgar materialism'. This highlights the importance that Adorno's idea of freedom has for opening a conceptual space to imagine the possibility that the brokenness of contemporary life might be otherwise.

The analysis of Adorno's reading of Kant also brings into view the form he thinks theology can take in post-Kantian philosophy. After Kant argued that the metaphysical ideas of theology were beyond the scope of 'pure reason', theology was left in a difficult position. Ought it to ignore the boundary Kant established between reason and theology, and thereby be dismissed as irrational or pre-modern? Or should theology seek to work within the confines of the Kantian block, and labour to identify some ongoing relevance for itself? Adorno's response to this dilemma is to draw an important distinction between *possibility* and *actuality*, which suggests an understanding of theology that is exclusively negative and largely devoid of content, but which serves to keep open a space for *possibility* through an attentive scrutiny of actual social existence. To highlight how this approach to the problem is distinct from another prominent interpretation of Kant, Adorno's position will again be contrasted with that John Milbank. As this comparison shows, whereas Adorno's critique of Kant leads him to a critical theory of society focused on an analysis of *actuality*, Milbank defends an ecclesiology that participates in future *possibility*, but only at the expense of attention to present social existence.

## The Kantian Block

Adorno's philosophical approach to theology shares much in common with Immanuel Kant. Kant's 'Copernican revolution' in philosophy in the eighteenth century was in response to David Hume's sceptical challenge to the established understanding of a universe bound together by causal laws. Kant was concerned that Hume's empiricism demolished natural theology and rational philosophy, and threatened to undermine confidence in human reason, along with both political and religious authority. As the previous chapter illustrated, Adorno's approach to materialism is concerned to defend a form of philosophy that takes concrete material reality seriously, without reducing all thought to mere acceptance of surface reality, or to a simplistic affirmation of the *status quo*. Similarly, although Adorno's critique of rationality demonstrates that reason remains entwined with myth even when it tries to escape from it, he does not intend this accusation to be an attack against reason, but an important element of its defence. Adorno's work explores the boundary between rationality and myth, culture and ideology, and the manner in which these are shaped by social experience. And in his efforts to formulate such a position, Kant remains a central dialogue partner.

Kant's solution to the challenge of David Hume's empiricism was twofold. First, he agreed with Hume that philosophy cannot have access to the hidden structures of reality. But Kant then constructed a new basis upon which to ground confidence in human knowing: the thinking subject. Agreeing that philosophy had to admit that ultimate truth was inaccessible, so that cognition could no longer claim the capacity to master its object, Kant argued that cognition could study itself. The manner in which a subject comes to make judgements about the world could be identified. Hume's objections to the possibility of *a priori* knowledge could be met by asserting that reliable knowledge depended, not on immediate access the object, but on the thinking subject.

Kant argued that this shift to a focus on the *a priori* foundations of human thinking saved knowledge from scepticism. Furthermore, whereas Hume had opposed reason and faith, Kant was no longer compelled to do so. He contrasted *knowledge* with faith, because he argued that there are reasonable forms of faith, to which human beings can have access. Thus, while faith cannot be said to constitute 'knowledge', the Kantian might still say it can be rational. The significance of this move is not lost on Adorno. He observes, for example, that modern theology's tendency to place the claims of theology in extreme opposition to knowledge (here he has Kierkegaard and Karl Barth in mind) is possible only because of 'the sharp distinction Kant made between knowledge and those metaphysical categories'.[2] Adorno himself, however, finds this clarification between knowledge and reason to be crucial, for it supports his utopian distinction between actuality and possibility.

But Adorno is not content to simply repeat Kant's philosophy of religion, for he raises some primary concerns about a number of central Kantian assumptions:

> Kant's metaphor for the land of truth, the island in the ocean, objectively characterizes the Robinson Crusoe style of the ivory tower . . . Kant boasts of having surveyed the Isle of Cognition, but its own narrow self righteousness moves that isle into the area of untruth, which he projects on the cognition of the infinite. It is impossible to endow the cognition of finite things with a truth derived, in its turn, from the absolute in Kantian terms, from reason – which cognition cannot reach. At every moment, the ocean of Kant's metaphor threatens to engulf the island.[3]

Here Adorno follows Hegel's insistence that one must not only determine the conditions for the possibility of experience, but also the conditions that make such a transcendental inquiry possible.[4] By radicalizing Kant's assertion that all knowledge is mediated by experience, Adorno problematizes the distinction Kant makes between 'thinking' and 'knowing'. A pure form without any content is not merely unknowable, Adorno insists; it is also unthinkable: 'a thought in which we do not think something is not a thought'.[5] He observes that the Kantian categories make experience possible, but argues that they are also made possible by experience, and so may change as experience changes.

Adorno questions, therefore, the Kantian understanding of experience. Kant argues that all experience involves a combination of sensible intuition with a concept (or a form of understanding). Both of these elements are required for experience to be possible, yet Kant also believes that one can separate these two from each other in order to examine them philosophically. Adorno is not convinced that this is possible. Separation in this way implies that experience amounts to 'adding up . . . factuality and concept', as though it was manufactured by pure concepts acting upon the raw material of intuitions.[6] This argument is similar to that presented by Hegel, who argues that the manner in which Kant connects the categories to things-in-themselves fails to adequately explain the origin of sensations: 'On one side there is the Ego, with its ... synthetic unity ... But next to it there is an infinity of sensations and, if you like, of things in themselves. Once it is abandoned by the categories, this realm cannot be anything but a formless lump'.[7] Hegel's additional remarks in his *Lectures on the History of Philosophy* are not unlike Adorno's accusation that Kantian concepts 'manufacture' experience: 'with Kant the thinking understanding and sensuousness are both something particular, and they are only united in an external, superficial way, just as a piece of wood and a leg might be bound together by a cord'.[8]

Developing this viewpoint, Adorno articulates a criticism of the Kantian block. Kant's prohibition of metaphysics, he argues, is dogmatic, for it claims that the conditions of the possibility of experience are unchanging. Kant states that one can *conceive* 'freedom' cognitively, but Adorno argues that this implies that it is impossible to *experience* this freedom. In effect, the Kantian block argues for the impossibility of ever knowing a thing-in-itself. Thus, Adorno claims that 'the Kantian system is a system of stop signals. The subjectively directed constitutional analysis does not alter the world as it is given'. The 'block [it] projects on truth is the self-maiming of reason'.[9]

Adorno does not simply argue that Kant's conclusion is mistaken; he believes it emerges out of the historical conditions of a society in which experience is increasingly modelled on industrial production and exchange-value for its own sake. The block 'is a social product', and so one cannot simply wish it away. Adorno locates the roots of the concept in bourgeois resignation. Just as the modern subject often finds herself alienated from her aspirations and desires, the search for truth is hampered by social reality. Thus, though faith and religion are not completely eliminated in the Kantian system, such longings are 'postponed until Sunday', and are only 'permitted a kind of Sunday-existence'.[10]

Adorno's appreciation of Kant's insights is supplemented by his intention to show that Kant's account of experience need not legislate the limits of all *future* experience. Like Hegel, he worries that when Kant speaks of the *noumenon* as a limiting concept, he cuts himself off from any meaningful discussion of an 'essence' behind 'appearance'. The world of appearances acquires, therefore, an ontological monopoly, so that only what currently exists can be considered 'real'. What is unknown (or forever concealed behind immediate experience) disappears completely from view. Hegel argued that, when Kant claims reason is confined to providing mere postulates or regulative ideals and does not supply its own content,[11] rational thinking becomes dependent upon external sources for content. This limitation threatens to reduce thought to mere sense-certainty: 'In this way thought, at its highest pitch, has to go outside for any determinateness; and although it is continually termed Reason, is out-and-out abstract thinking'.[12] In opposition to Hegel, Adorno does not suggest that reason is capable of grasping the 'infinite', but he intends, like Hegel, to argue that an overly rigid interpretation of the Kantian block risks being reduced to mere acceptance of the already existing within the *status quo*, thereby hindering critical reflection, and legislating the boundaries of all future experience.

Adorno argues that all concepts are entangled with experience, and appeals for the recognition of an 'affinity' between concept and object. This idea is developed in response to Kant's resolution of the problem of how to connect pure concepts of the understanding with sensible appearances. Kant argues that there must be a third element, a 'transcendental schema', that mediates between them.[13] These schemata are necessary and universal attributes of things within time, in order for the expression of temporal relations to be possible, and they are produced by the 'transcendental imagination'. When Kant states that this is 'an art concealed in the depths of the human soul',[14] Adorno argues that here Kant is making a metaphysical claim, and not merely an epistemological one.[15] Adorno considers this to be revealing, for Kant discovers within his own argument that some account must be provided of how concepts and intuitions relate to one another. Adorno states that,

> the immediate antithesis of receptivity and spontaneity,
> of sensibility and understanding is actually already sublated
> in the course of the Kantian analysis itself, and thereby . . .
> Kant granted a certain *placet* to the speculative deliberations
> with which I have been engaged here.[16]

Adorno regards this insight as evidence of Kant's own metaphysical presuppositions. The fact that Kant must speak of an imaginative 'third thing' linking concept and object in his notion of the transcendental schematism is understood by Adorno as signalling that Kant has separated the two latter terms too radically.[17] 'Pure' concepts, 'pure' intuitions, and the imagined schemata remain equally unintelligible to Adorno. Here 'Kant does *the very thing that he forbids reason to do*. He constructs something from pure thought'.[18] As evidence against this possibility, Adorno uses Kant's own argument against itself: because 'all subsumptions of an object under a concept' must be '*homogeneous*', Adorno concludes that 'the concept must *resemble* its object in a certain sense'.[19] 'Pure' concepts and 'pure' intuitions are not thinkable. Adorno's project seeks to answer, therefore, not how pure concepts may be applied to pure appearances, but as Simon Jarvis summarizes it: 'how *impure* concepts can interpret *impure* objects'.[20]

For Kant, objects are formed by the exercise of the conceptual forms upon intuition; therefore, they are treated in a way that is already determined by concepts. An object cannot be known as it is 'in-itself', but merely as a phenomenon. Yet, Kant also argues that one must be able to think of an object 'in-itself' in order to avoid treating appearances as if nothing actually exists behind them. If a concept is to be true and not just something arbitrary, then one must of necessity postulate that it is influenced by an object 'it-self', however unknowable its true nature might be.

Adorno's notion of the 'preponderance of the object' represents an attempt to wrestle with this contradiction, and to question how knowledge of the object as it is in-itself might be possible. Adorno agrees with Hegel that it is more consistent not to separate the thing in-itself from the thing as it appears to consciousness, yet he also believes that Kant's inconsistency here is revealing. For Adorno, the thing in-itself bears witness to what he calls 'the non-identical' (although the two terms are not simply interchangeable). If one absolutely prohibits the possibility that an object can be known in-itself, argues Adorno, the result is a scepticism in which the object will always be pre-formed by the concept, and therefore hidden and controlled.

Adorno's 'groping for the preponderance for the object' is shaped by the view that 'not even as an idea can we conceive a subject that is not an object; but we can conceive an object that is not a subject'.[21] He is not suggesting that one can have immediate access to the object 'in-itself'; nor does he believe one can easily filter out the conceptual layers added to it by the subjective observer. Instead, he insists that 'the object's preponderance is solely attainable for subjective reflection'.[22] Subjectively mediated identifications and truth claims must be pushed to the point of collapse through a negative dialectic. He advocates an attempt 'to use the strength of the subject to break through the fallacy of constitutive subjectivity'. The preponderance of the object, therefore, does not amount to a vulgar materialism. Neither 'society' nor 'history' is installed as immediately given or available; nor even are 'brute facts'. He insists that 'the idea of a concrete object belongs to the critique of subjective-external categorization, and to the critique of its correlate, the fiction of a factuality without definitions'.[23]

Adorno's defence of the possibility that the quality of human experience may change, along with his insistence on the preponderance of the object, also leads to a critique of Kant's understanding of freedom. While a detailed study of Kant's moral theory is beyond the scope of the present discussion, some brief remarks serve to highlight the distinction between Kant and the more Hegelian perspective of Adorno.

In the *Critique of Practical Reason*, Kant argues that 'speculative reason could think of freedom without contradiction, but it could not assure any objectivity to it'.[24] Whereas the third antinomy in the first *Critique* argues that a causality different from the laws of nature ('freedom') cannot be specifically known, but also cannot be disproved, the second *Critique* argues that the concept of freedom is given objective reality by moral law. As Simon Jarvis observes, 'the objective reality of the moral law is not established by freedom; rather the objective reality of freedom is established by moral law'.[25] In a sense, then, Kant essentially demands that freedom exist. The moral law, states Kant, 'is a sufficient substitute for any *a priori* justification'; it 'proves its reality even for the critique of speculative reason'.[26]

Adorno argues that Kant's 'idea of freedom turns into a paradox' at this point. While the third antinomy of the first *Critique* concludes that it can neither prove nor disprove the reality of freedom, in the second *Critique* Kant attempts to demonstrate that even though freedom cannot be theoretically proven, it is given 'objective necessity' by the validity of the moral law that is 'forced upon us'. Adorno concludes that Kant twists himself into a contradiction when his moral theory asserts the practical objectivity of freedom while at the same time presenting experience as being grasped through laws of causal determination. This effectively treats 'empirical human beings as if their will were demonstrably free', while in fact experiencing their actions as determined. For Adorno, this amounts to turning freedom into captivity, and it implies that freedom will never be realized in history.[27]

This criticism of Kant resembles that of Hegel, whose critique of the Kantian conception of practical reason mirrors his criticism of Kant's theoretical reason. Just as Hegel objects to the lack of content Kant grants to reason (leaving it at the mercy of its surrounding environment), he argues that the emptiness of Kant's categorical imperative leaves it dependent upon external contingencies. Practical reason treats its prior motivation as something external to itself, rather than as being related to a deeper rational nature.

Adorno's fascination with this problem results from his conviction that the contradiction in Kant's thought is not simply a failure of logic or philosophical precision. He argues that the root of the problem is both social and historical. The significance that the Kantian project holds for Adorno is in how it both describes the world 'as it ought to be', but also at the same time the actual world of 'unfreedom'.[28] Human beings should have freedom and, in fact, because society is a human construction, humans also have the capacity to freely change this society. And yet, society also shapes and limits the individual subject, frustrating the exercise of true freedom. Adorno cautions that the accusation that Kant's position on freedom is without content can result in a position that 'falls behind' Kant and into an arbitrary support of custom or tradition. Although Adorno agrees with Hegel that Kant's moral theory is problematic, he realizes that it also 'stipulates the universal legal norm, and thus, despite and because of its abstractness, there survives in it something of substance: the egalitarian idea'.[29]

Adorno's understanding of freedom does not simply amount to advocating the ability to act without compulsion. He realizes that the attempt to eliminate all compulsion on the basis of free moral action inevitably turns into legislated behaviour. His account of freedom, therefore, emerges out of a negative perspective. One cannot posit freedom without including some element of compulsion. Adorno insists, however, that this does not mean that the concept is meaningless: 'freedom turns concrete in the changing forms of repression, as resistance to repression'. He continues, 'there is no available model for freedom save one: that consciousness, as it intervenes in the total social constitution, will through that constitution intervene in the complexion of the individual'.[30] The experience of unfreedom can be challenged and altered. Adorno's critical theory is meant to prevent the concepts of experience and freedom from becoming fixed invariants, determined by a social ideology or imposed by a particular local narrative. The concept of absolute freedom helps to leave open the possibility that it might be realized in the future.

Adorno recognizes that the *Critique of Pure Reason* attempts to retrieve certain aspects of 'metaphysical experience', which is 'the inspiration of Kantian philosophy'. The pure concepts of the understanding, which set limits upon knowledge and reason, already demonstrate that reason is transgressive of such limits. Here Adorno makes a crucial point: 'The question whether metaphysics is still possible at all must reflect the negation of the finite which finiteness requires'.[31] This is the moment in Kant's thought that Adorno thinks retains a significant role for theology. For, as will be developed below, Adorno argues that theological concepts like the messianic, the prohibition of images, and the idea of redemption are required to prevent actuality from foreclosing on alternative possibilities.

Adorno's criticism of Kant's problematic distinctions between thought and experience, and the 'block' on metaphysical claims, are motivated by the desire to criticize the separation between *actual* historical experience and *possible* future experience. This is not meant to assist the recovery of formerly held dogmatic claims, but simply to prevent a foreclosure on the possibility for a better world in the future. Adorno believes this may be achieved through a philosophical interpretation of *actuality*; by observing a moment of freedom within thought which reveals the *possibility* that future experience might be otherwise. As Albrecht Wellmer observes, Adorno's interpretation of Kant argues that, instead of 'we cannot know: we do not *yet* know'.[32]

What is important about the Kantian block according to Adorno, therefore, is that it is true to *actuality*: 'the imprisonment in immanence to which he honestly and brutally condemns the mind is the imprisonment in self-preservation, as it is imposed on men by . . . society'. The limitations that Kant identifies in rational thought resemble the restrictions that history and society place upon human activity and freedom. What Adorno resists is eternalizing these limitations by pronouncing them to be 'natural' and by ignoring their roots in social reality. If the 'block' on human knowledge and freedom is interpreted in such a fashion, then future *possibility* is forcibly confined on the basis of the conditions of contemporary society. Adorno observes that, 'as soon as the mind calls its chains by name, the chains it gets into by chaining others, it grows independent here and now. It begins to anticipate, and what it anticipates is freedom'.[33] The Kantian block cannot be thought away or dismissed, but Adorno argues that thinking can show that the social experiences that the block is based on, although real, could possibly be changed.

Adorno's *Negative Dialectics* attempts to resist foreclosing on the possibility of a new form of experience; one not based on mere self-preservation or control of the other. This effort does not amount to the consoling claim that reconciliation between subject and object will inevitably occur in the future, nor that a 'new way of thinking' can be found to lead the way. Rather than emphasizing the 'possibilities of being', his philosophy is directed 'at the existing itself in its concrete historical definition'. One must, he insists, 'criticize the separation of the real and possible from the point of view of reality'.[34]

## Milbank and the Kantian Block

Like Adorno, the theologian John Milbank considers Kant to be a key figure in the dispute over the legitimacy of theological claims to knowledge and truth. But Milbank proposes the precise opposite response to Kant. He argues that the separation between the real and the possible should be criticized from the perspective of the Christian doctrine of God. In Milbank's view, Kant's effort to contain religion within the limits of reason alone, not only strips Christian theology of its content; it also results in the margin-alization of theology by granting to philosophy the permission to determine the limits of knowledge. Milbank's counterproposal is to suggest that 'to reason truly one must be already illumined by God', for only virtuously ordered desire and reason resolve the 'nihilistic contradictions of philosophy'.[35] Distinguishing Adorno's critique of Kant from Milbank's project will help clarify the distinctive nature of Adorno's interest in theology.

Milbank argues that the Kantian block is untenable. Since one can only think in language, 'then it is simply not possible to inves-tigate our thinking instrument — to say what it can or cannot think in advance of its deployment'. He denies the possibility of deriving the Kantian 'categories' through which things are thought, and is especially concerned to show that it is impossible 'to demonstrate that the understanding', or human discursive thought, is clearly limited to judgement of the finite and must not trespass beyond these bounds'.[36]

Like Adorno, Milbank objects to the separation Kant makes between pure concepts and intuitions. He asserts that the claim that 'we possess theoretical "ideas" which we use regulatively with respect to the concepts of the understanding' is a dogmatic and metaphysical position, for 'it is only because one stands meta-physically above phenomena that one is able to determine dogmatically the "range" of concepts like cause, substance, unity, necessity and so forth'. The resulting limit placed on theological knowledge by the Kantian block, Milbank argues, encloses the divine within an aesthetic of the sublime, which produces the following situation: 'the absolutely equal and formally fixed relationship in which we all are, as liberal subjects, stand to the unknown absolute, serves to confirm the world . . . as it is'.[37]

Contrary to the empty formalism he sees in Kant, Milbank argues that any moral theory in which freedom and reconciliation are more than a generalized formal principle is only possible in an unfounded particular *praxis*. Such a specific mode of practice is only found, he claims, in the teaching of Jesus of Nazareth. That Hegel locates the movement towards the realization of this practice in a philosophy of history, Milbank argues, implies an ontology of violence, since it presupposes the necessity of historical conflicts that result in a progressively greater realization of the absolute in history.

From the perspective of Adorno, this position, with its rejection of dialectics, leads Milbank to 'fall behind' Kant, as he embraces an understanding of freedom and morality based on membership in the Christian faith: 'Only in the context of the Christian narrative, not the dialectical metanarrative, should one take seriously the Hegelian view that it is the quest for the Absolute which provides the possibility of social and political critique'.[38] For this to even be possible, however, one must determine the particular characteristics of the Christian form of practice, which Milbank both seems to regard as obvious and fails to describe, despite the fact that throughout the history of Christianity inter-pretations of Jesus' actions have been in dispute. Rather than resolve the problems of Kantian moral theory, then, Milbank withdraws to an abstract and a-historical position. He ends up at the point Adorno says Kant sought to avoid by demonstrating the universality of moral principles: 'he would have had to say that phases and societies in which there is no freedom are not only not rational but not human'.[39] Because Milbank argues that all other narrative traditions, other than Christianity, 'affirm or barely conceal an original primordial violence', he concludes that 'other religions and social groupings, however virtuous seeming, were finally on the path to damnation'.[40]

Milbank responds to the Kantian block by arguing that it remains 'haunted by this question of ontological depth "behind" finite phenomena'. This suggests to him that knowledge is only truly achieved through faith, and that this involves some form of revelation received from outside the finite.[41] In his critique of the Kantian sublime, which resides at the limits of conceptuality and thus cannot be represented, he argues that Kant fails to recognize that the unknown 'is not simply that which cannot be represented, but is *also* that which arrives'.[42] He continues: 'only if reality itself is regarded as "given" from some beyond does it become possible to trust that what is communicated and circulated may assume new meanings'.[43]

One can escape the empty formalism of Kantian liberal political theory, Milbank says, only through 'a kind of collective supra-rational devotion'.[44] The point of human life, he suggests, is to be educated into this kind of devotion. Thus, 'freedom . . . must first of all be the generous imparting of what one has learned'. Such an education 'can never be democratic', for if one is to learn 'one must first submit'. One must 'yield blindly to tradition' before being considered competent enough to claim insight into its logic, or attempt to modify it. Milbank maintains that 'it is only the educated who can determine to what degree . . . a spatial democracy should operate'.[45]

While Adorno's critique of Kant leads him to develop a critical theory of society rooted in an analysis of *actuality*, Milbank develops an ecclesiology that participates in an eschatological vision, looking toward actuality only through the lens of the Christian metanarrative. He argues that 'a claim to know truly, a claim to know at all, as Plato argued, only makes sense within the framework of *meathexis* [sic] (participation)'.[46] This suggests that only the 'insiders' ('the elect'?) can grasp reality 'as it really is', for only they have been taught to see it through the proper lens. Once the object 'is taken apart from God' – viewed in a way that does not presuppose its 'participation' in God – theological assumptions about the world begin to crumble, leading, in Milbank's opinion, to nihilism. Thus he states:

> theology, in the face of secular attack, is only on secure ground if it adopts the most extreme mode of counter-attack: namely that unless other disciplines are (at least implicitly) ordered by theology . . . they are objectively and demonstrably null and void, altogether lacking in truth.[47]

Until one accepts the Christian metanarrative (as Milbank understands it), one is chained to the wall of Plato's cave. He advocates for the 'Platonic view that reason, to be reason, in some sense knows before it knows'. Thus, 'reason, to be reason, must therefore also be faith'.[48] It is 'only through assent to the realm of eternal unchanging forms, or of the ideas in the mind of God' that one encounters where the 'actual abides'.[49] Only those initiated into the true order of reality hidden behind sense experience might leave the shadows of the cave and enter into the sunlight of reality: 'to reason truly one must be already illumined by God.[50]

In this challenge to the Kantian block, *possibility* of another form of experience is rescued, but only by removing *actuality* from history. The 'actual' is no longer found in social existence, but 'abides' in the 'mind of God'.

## Metaphysical Experience and Theology

Compared to this reaction to the Kantian block, Adorno's approach to theology is less direct and less supportive. But it is also more appreciative of present historical existence, and so is both more promising and helpful for confronting the challenges facing contemporary theology. Adorno's perspective follows from his interpretation of Kantian philosophy, and is motivated by the following concern:

> Certainly a *ratio* that does not wantonly absolutize itself as a rigid means of domination requires self-reflection, some of which is expressed in the need for religion today. But this self-reflection cannot stop at the mere negation of thought by thought itself, a kind of mystical sacrifice, and cannot realize itself through a 'leap': that would all too closely resemble the politics of catastrophe.[51]

In this statement, Adorno locates the contemporary 'need for religion' in the effort of reason to resist absolutizing itself. He suggests that theology is related to reason's critique of itself. Furthermore, he connects it with a determination to resist the 'negation of thought by thought itself' – i.e. to a rejection of nihilism. It is also clear in these words that Adorno associates religion with what he calls 'metaphysical experience'. It cannot be stressed enough, however, that this not to say that Adorno thereby advocates a direct 'return to religion' or to a theological ontology. Although he states that metaphysics is 'a reprise, a resumption of theology' in the manner in which it 'points to a world behind *the* world we know', he also argues that it is at the same time a critique of theology.[52] When Adorno claims that rational thought pushes beyond itself, he is in no way hypo-statizing this observation, turning it into a concept capable of contributing to a fundamental theology. That he criticizes science for turning its facts into 'idols'[53] does not lead him to consider it acceptable to turn what he calls 'metaphysical experience' into an idol in its own right.

This is because the 'metaphysical moment' in thought does not amount to a positive grasp of something directly 'in-itself'. Here one can see that Adorno is indeed a student of Kant. For him, metaphysics is not an intuition into the 'true nature of things'; neither does it lead to the sense of some sort of meaning in life. He insists that it is impossible after Auschwitz to posit 'the presence of a positive meaning or purpose in being'.[54] Instead, the metaphysical emerges as a problem when the tension between historical experience and conceptual thinking arises in reflection. 'Metaphysics arises at the point where the empirical world is taken seriously'.[55] As critical second reflection discovers that concepts are inadequate to their object; 'the question whether metaphysics is still possible at all must reflect the negation of the finite which finiteness requires'.[56]

Adorno's argument here is that, as reason vigorously criticizes itself, as it discovers the 'preponderance of the object', it must admit that the object of thought as it is 'in-itself' always surpasses discursive reason. Absolute objectivity exceeds what reason can directly conceive. But Adorno does not understand this recognition of the 'non-identity' between thing concepts and objects to authorize abandoning conceptual thought. At the same time, any denial of the existence of the non-identical, by prohibiting the recognition of what he calls 'metaphysical experience', itself becomes a positive theology, as the existing is absolutized:

> [T]his explains the occasional alliance between positivism and positive religion against metaphysics – against the disintegrating force which they both detect in it. Autonomous thought is a mouthpiece of the transcendent, and is thus always in danger – when it approaches the transcendent through metaphysics – of making common cause with it.[57]

Adorno realizes that any appreciation of a metaphysical moment is perilous at best. Although its destabilizing function is something to be embraced, there always exists a temptation to absolutize its insights, which can only be fragmentary and fleeting. If the 'metaphysical' or the 'transcendent' is mistaken to be a thing-in-itself, then one escapes from one ideological perspective only to replace it with another.

For Adorno, the individual subject plays a central role in overcoming its own limitations. Since he follows Kant in asserting that 'all our knowledge begins with experience', he suggests that objectivity is in fact 'created by passing through subjectivity'. Although certainly by no means does it 'create' the object, the subject does serve as 'the guarantor of objectivity'.[58] Although Adorno criticizes the Kantian transcendental subject, along with the implied division between subject and object, he nevertheless insists that this distinction cannot be discarded (although it should also not be absolutized, being historically determined).[59] For 'what defines the prior object as distinct from its subjective trappings' can only be comprehended by what conditioned it – the subject. Thus, the 'preponderance of the object' requires 'reflection on the subject and subjective reflection'.[60] Only the subject can overcome the biases and presuppositions that it imposes upon its object, and it can only do this when

> it entrusts itself to its own experience. In places where subjective reason scents subjective contingency, the preponderance of the object is shimmering through – whatever in the object is not a subjective admixture. The subject is the object's agent, not its constituent; this fact has consequences for the relation of theory and practice.[61]

Ironically, the critically self-reflexive emphasis of Adorno's negative dialectics makes it much more open to the preservation of an 'eschatological reserve' than Milbank's more positively motivated reaffirmation of the Christian metanarrative. Although Milbank is reacting to similar concerns regarding the limitations of Enlightenment rationality and of modern society and culture, his project limits the effort to reconcile broken human experience to the boundaries of the Christian tradition. His strong form of communitarianism confines reconciliation within the boundaries of his ecclesiology. Adorno's attempt to reconcile the gulf between subject and object is more perilous, perhaps, but it is also more relational. It searches for the symptoms of both hope and suffering within the brokenness of actuality, while Milbank must look beyond the given to find evidence of an 'Other City'.

Despite this rejection of Milbank's strong form of communitarian concern for the formative power of local narratives and practices, his warnings against underestimating the seductive power of contemporary global capitalism do challenge the central role that Adorno grants to the individual subject. As Gillian Rose has astutely noted, Adorno's thought 'is haunted by [a] ghostly missing agency'.[62] He both denies the efficacy of the subject, due to its implication in commodity culture and instrumental rationality, while at the same time making the subject the agent of an attentive eschatological reserve. This attempt – in the words of Espen Hammer – to 'affirm the subject in its moment of involuntary annihilation' is ambitious, to say the least.[63]

Adorno's critics frequently dismiss negative dialectics for this very reason. Lyotard interprets his defence of the subject as a hopeless commitment to a totalizing narrative.[64] Jürgen Habermas argues that Adorno cuts off the limb he is standing on, committing a 'performative contradiction' that employs reason and the subject in a circular and groundless critique.[65] Hans Jürgen Krahl, a radical student of Adorno's, came to view negative dialectics as a recipe for a resigned pessimism, leaving the political subject directionless and silent.[66]

If Adorno's critical theory is to continue to be an important resource for contemporary social theory and theology, as well as an alternative path from that of Milbank's Radical Orthodoxy, then it must prove to be more than a melancholy science that ends in a resigned pessimism. If the subject is to play a role in keeping open an appreciation for metaphysics at the moment of its fall, then Adorno's theory of subjectivity requires more thorough elaboration. Attention to this issue will resume in Chapters 5 and 7.

What this chapter has clarified, however, is why Adorno remains interested in theology. It has shown that he relates it to the 'metaphysical experience' that he thinks the Kantian block alludes to, but also prevents philosophy from taking seriously. Theology's pursuit of a truth that cannot be reduced to the fashions of the *status quo* serves as a resource for holding open a conceptual space that allows human beings to imagine the possibility that the brokenness of contemporary life might be otherwise. And as the comparison to Milbank's critique of Kant demonstrated, he does this without falling behind Kant's distinction between reason and knowledge, and without distracting his attention away from the immediacies of human suffering found in the actuality of history.

One issue that emerged in the comparison with Milbank must now be addressed more directly. In his critique of Kant, Milbank argued that knowledge of true actuality is only received through faith and revelation, and thus knowledge can be said to rest on an ungrounded vision that has been shaped by its participation in the divine mind. Adorno's reaction to Kant is clearly opposed to Milbank's, but his own position is often criticized for itself resembling a non-foundational and Platonic attitude towards knowledge. For this reason, Chapter 3 now turns to a consideration of his treatment of the relationship between truth and knowledge as it relates to his view of modern science. It explores how, in a heated debate with Karl Popper, Adorno's thought is dismissed for being 'crypto-theology'. The analysis of his response to such a charge offers further clarifications and insights into his understanding of the important function of theology.

Chapter 3

# Social Science and Metaphysical Experience: Negative Dialectics as Crypto-Theology?

*It might be said that what purports today to be sociology's resistance to the allegedly theological inclinations of theoretical thinking is really nothing other than the gesture of the knowing wink, which implies that for sociologists, because everything is conditioned by social interests, no such thing as truth exists at all.*[1]

The previous two chapters have outlined how Adorno's critical philosophy intends to establish a very difficult balance. His work challenges a simplistic faith in the self-evident nature of material reality while maintaining a deep commitment to dialectical materialism. It also seeks to uncover alternative possibilities contained within actuality without abandoning the centrality of concrete historical existence. These are commitments that are difficult to hold together, and they involve many theoretical perils. The comparisons between Adorno's thought and that of Milbank and Tillich have demonstrated some of these issues, but numerous other epistemological questions remain to be explored. On what basis does Adorno claim to recognize 'possibility' within present social forms? As his work seeks to illuminate how nature is actually 'second nature', what replaces the proceduralism of instrumental rationality?

Adorno's critics frequently accuse his writing of implying some privileged access to knowledge, which only he, the prophetic critical theorist, is in possession of. Such detractors suggest that critical theory can be reduced to a learned form of 'mumbo-jumbo' that relies on a revolutionary *deus ex machina* rather than critical reasoning. Given such dismissals, one must ask: what is the nature of Adorno's alternative access to truth? How does this relate to modern science? Does his epistemology suggest some form of romantic and intangible grasp of reality or, in theological terminology, an otherworldly revelation?

In issues such as these, critical debates over the legitimacy of Adorno's project overlap with challenges facing contemporary Christian theology. As Nancey Murphy recalls, epistemological changes during the early modern period resulted in an understanding of knowledge that eroded the credibility of theology as a rational discipline. Descartes attempted to defend theism from scepticism by securing it on a firm foundation established by deduction. In Locke's thought, reason becomes understood as the guarantor of revelation by serving to support established knowledge based on miraculous signs. By the time of David Hume, however, such a foundation came to be thought of it terms of sense experience, which Hume used to demolish the traditional philosophical proofs for God's existence. Uniform experience became the ground for trusting that knowledge rested upon recurring events in the world.[2]

Jeffrey Stout observes that the development of probable reasoning leaves theology with only two directions from which to choose. It can accept Hume's sceptical criticism of metaphysics and seek to ground theology in position located outside of foundational reason; or it can ignore the changes in modern rationality and seek to carry on as before. In either case, theology is left with an air of absurdity compared to the standards for legitimizing modern knowledge. Taking Hume's position for granted, Kant and Schleiermacher sought to separate religious thought from scientific knowledge. Kant relocated theology to the sphere of morality and practical reason, while Schleiermacher moved it to the realm of feeling. But after concluding that Schleiermacher's liberal theology only leads to Feuerbach, Karl Barth, like Kierkegaard before him, described theology as a paradox, which stands outside the possibility of rational apologetics entirely.[3]

The difficulty Christian theology experiences in legitimating its truth claims in modernity highlights issues found in Adorno's critical theory. Perhaps Lorenz Jäger's harsh judgment presents the problem most bluntly: 'the history of critical theory may be summed up as follows: the more the assumptions of Marxism came to seem implausible, the more its shrinking body of ideas was believed capable of explaining an ever increasing number of social phenomena'.[4] Just as theology is accused of making ungrounded truth claims compared with the certainties of the modern understanding science, Adorno's critical philosophy is frequently dismissed for similar reasons, to the point of being labelled a 'crypto-theology' by his critics.

To illustrate the issues involved in such a criticism, and to explore Adorno's response, this chapter revisits the so-called 'Positivist Dispute' that followed a meeting between Adorno and the philosopher of science Karl Popper. What is particularly noteworthy about this debate is that both Adorno and Popper accuse each other of being 'closet' or 'crypto' theologians. While Popper argues that Adorno's resistance to the authority of established scientific procedures resembles an irrational and subjective Gnosticism, Adorno counters by suggesting that Popper's faith in science is exactly that – an ungrounded faith in the *status quo* – which remains blind to the ideological nature of reality as it presents itself. Each accuses the other of epistemological heresy, and this confrontation illuminates the concepts of theology that Adorno both dismisses and claims as his own. The image of critical theory that emerges out of this analysis is that it is a discipline that cannot be established on a firm logical foundation, but which involves what Popper calls a 'moral attitude' and what Adorno refers to as a 'metaphysical moment'.

To set the confrontation between Adorno and Popper in context, the chapter begins with a brief summary of the environments out of which their particular perspectives emerge: Adorno's critical theory develops out of the early work of the Institute of Social Research, and Popper's critical rationality as a response to the Vienna School of Logical Positivists.

## Critical Theory and Positivism

In Kant's *Critique of Pure Reason*, philosophy continues to maintain a privileged position in relation to science. From philosophy's transcendental perspective, science is understood as representing one category of possible knowledge. In the Kantian view, knowledge is encompassed by not only theoretical reason, but also practical reason and aesthetic judgment. By the second half of the nineteenth century, however, knowledge became increasingly identified with science. In the 1920s and 30s an articulation of this position was developed by a movement centred in Vienna, among a group known as the Circle of Logical Positivists.[5] They sought to purify philosophy of its metaphysical elements and restructure it according to the logic of empirical science and mathematics. This association of scholars distanced themselves from philosophical inquiry into the knowing subject, and focused exclusively on the propositions and rules through which empirically meaningful statements could be formed and tested. As Albert Blumberg and Herbert Feigl argued, 'the purpose of philosophy is the elimination of . . . meaningless pseudo-propositions'.[6]

Rudolph Carnap contributed to the circle's agenda by arguing that the elimination of metaphysics from logical empiricism was to be carried out at the level of language analysis. Rejecting Kant's notion of synthetic *a priori* judgements, Carnap (following Bertrand Russell and Alfred Whitehead) considered symbolic logic and mathematics to be purely analytic and *a priori* (independent of any experience). These analytic truths could be contrasted with empirical observations or synthetic judgements *a posteriori*; but some statements, standing outside these forms of judgement, were to be regarded as meaningless. For Carnap, such 'metaphysical' sentences, beyond the scope of logic or empirical observation, were beyond any realm of experience, and thus could not be considered knowledge.[7]

It is precisely such a position that the members of the Frankfurt School opposed. Challenging the reduction of knowledge to the results of the empirical sciences, Horkheimer argues that 'traditional theory', or the perspective of the positivists, fails to acknowledge the social location of its assumptions. He locates their understanding of science in the context of a bourgeois society dominated by techniques of industrial production, focused solely on eliminating contradictions and the technical control of nature. Adorno and his colleagues argue that the natural sciences represent but one form of possible knowledge. The contradictions between the rational concept of society and the human experience of suffering, or between the attempt to control one's natural environment and the experience of powerlessness, are for them evidence of the irrationality of society and the incompleteness of scientific knowledge. The programme for a critical theory of society, therefore, 'is a theory dominated at every turn by a concern for reasonable conditions of life'.[8]

Unlike the positivists, critical theory does not demand absolute value neutrality, for it asserts that 'truth . . . must be decided not in supposedly neutral reflection but in personal thought and action, in concrete historical activity'.[9] Thus Adorno and his collaborators sought to establish an interdisciplinary approach to social research, one which would bring philosophy and scientific method together, so that both the rational concept of society and empirical reality could be unified.

## The 'Positivist Dispute'

A confrontation between two versions of these traditions erupted following a meeting of the German Sociological Association in 1961. Though a critic of the Vienna School himself, Popper spoke in defence of the objectivity of science and its separation from all value claims and metaphysical concerns. In his presentation, Popper maintains that a disciplined scientific methodology safe-guards sociology from dialectical 'mumbo-jumbo'.[10] The dispute which emerges with Adorno is over different conceptions of how society and social experience should be studied. Popper argues in favour of a strictly 'sociological' theory that operates according to his understanding of scientific method. Adorno also defends the importance of sociological research – what he calls 'empirical research' – but insists that the results of such analysis must be examined as part of a critical self-reflection, or a 'social theory', in order to compensate for the possibility that a strictly sociolo-gical theory may be influenced by unacknowledged biases and social forces.

Zygmunt Bauman's distinction between 'social theory' and 'sociological theory' helps to clarify what is at stake here. He suggests that 'sociological theory' signifies empirical social science. Its methodology explains social phenomena on the basis of causal laws. 'Social theory' employs such empirical research, but also incorporates a philosophical element that includes ethical analysis, a concern with human freedom and motivation, and a reflexive analysis of the results of more explicitly 'sociological' research. Like Adorno, Bauman states that 'sociological theory' denies its own philosophical presuppositions when it repudiates the validity of 'social theory'. It is such a 'denial of the moral significance of non-technical issues', Bauman argues, that permitted modernity's ideals to become reduced to the horrors of the Holocaust. The 'rules of instrumental rationality are singularly incapable of preventing such phenomena'.[11]

## Conjecture and Refutation or Dialectics?

The conference at Tübingen began with Popper's paper, 'The Logic of the Social Sciences', in which he summarized his position on the philosophy of science in 27 theses.[12] The central points he presents include the following:

(i) knowledge does not start from perceptions or observation, but from problems[13]

(ii) the method of the social sciences, as in the natural sciences, 'consists in trying out tentative solutions to those problems from which our investigations start'[14]

(iii) proposed solutions are then subjected to criticism that attempts to refute the conjecture

(iv) if a proposed hypothesis withstands the criticism, the proposal may be temporarily accepted, and subjected to further discussion and criticism

(v) social science thus proceeds through 'trial and error'

(vi) this critical method establishes sociology's objectivity, along with the 'logical instrument of criticism' – the logical contradiction

(vii) there is no 'positive justification' for social theories, as scientific knowledge consists simply of provisional and tentative solutions.[15]

Thus, 'we cannot justify our theories rationally and cannot even prove that they are probable', but, 'we can criticize them rationally. And we can distinguish better from worse theories'.[16]

Popper concludes that 'there is a *purely objective method* in the social sciences'. It remains independent of all subjective or psychological ideas and seeks to explain the actions of a person in terms of the context or situation in which the action occurs. Such an approach uncovers how an action was 'objectively *appropriate to the situation*'.[17] This permits the social scientist to understand actions 'in an objective sense', and be able to state that 'had I been placed in his situation thus analysed . . . then I, and presumably you too, would have done what he did'. Sociological theory constructs explanations of social action that resist being reduced to biological, psychological or behaviourist understandings, as well as avoiding the opposite error that Popper calls 'methodological holism', which provides a functionalist account of human action through whole social processes or institutions. He argues elsewhere that,

> it is the central point of situational analysis that we need, in order to 'animate' it, no more than the assumption that the various persons or agents involved act *adequately*, or *appropriately*; that is to say, in accordance with the situation . . . we assume no more than that . . . they 'work out' what was *implicit* in the situation.[18]

In the paper Adorno delivers after Popper's, he states that his position shares 'numerous substantive points of agreement'.[19] One commonality is the assertion that a theory of society is distinct from psychologism or functionalism: 'the more strictly the psychological realm is conceived as an autonomous, self-enclosed play of forces, the more completely the subject is drained of his subjectivity. The objectless subject that is thrown back on himself freezes into an object'.[20] But although Adorno, like Popper, emphasizes the agency of the subject, he is not as optimistic about the individual's ability to accomplish this independently of the influence of societal pressures, nor does he think Popper's method can successfully uncover *objective* explanations for such action.

Adorno argues that all social action is to be understood in the context of the societal 'totality'. The actions of individual subjects, the social role of institutions, and the data collected by the scientist in order to arrive at social 'facts', are all thoroughly mediated by this totality; 'system and individual entity are reciprocal and can only be apprehended in their reciprocity'.[21] Adorno is careful to assert that he is not advocating a relativistic 'sociology of knowledge' position, similar to that of Karl Mannheim.[22] As observed in Chapter 1, he criticizes Mannheim for being unable to consistently maintain the distinction between truth and falsehood. Mannheim, in Adorno's opinion, suggests a relativistic approach to social analysis; that what *is* in social reality is true – the best one could ask for or hope for. The existing society is simply accepted as given, without investigating the constitutive role of consciousness in creating society. Thus Adorno concludes that, 'Mannheim's use of the concept of the societal totality serves not so much to emphasize the intricate dependence of men within the totality as to glorify the social process itself as an evening-out of the contradictions in the whole'.[23]

This is why Adorno accuses Mannheim and Popper of being 'positivists'. In his opinion, both are guilty of a similar error: of taking social phenomena as givens, and then classifying them according to general concepts, at the price of glossing over contradictions that reveal social antagonisms produced by the social whole.[24] When Popper suggests that social 'facts' may serve as effective falsifiers for scientific hypotheses, Adorno argues that he effectively resigns himself to the *status quo* and fails to provide adequate safeguards to prevent sociological theory from being reduced to an ideological support for an unjust society.

Adorno illustrates his point with reference to two arguments presented by Popper. The first is the latter's defence of the objectivity of science, not on the basis of the individual scientist who is subject to personal biases and limitations, but on the collective efforts of the scientific community and its ongoing processes of trial and error. Adorno replies,

> When Popper criticizes the fact that the objectivity of science is confused with the objectivity of the scientist, he seizes upon the concept of ideology which has been degraded to a total one, but does not apprehend its authentic conception. The latter implied the objective determination of false consciousness.[25]

In other words, Popper recognizes that ideology, prejudice, or similar subjective biases often impose themselves on the individual scientist, but he believes that because his conception of science is based on inter-subjective self-criticism within the scientific community, the methodology of science is safeguarded from social manipulation. For Popper, the issue of objectivity is simply an epistemological one, involving the overcoming of individual subjectivism. Adorno replies that it is not merely the individual scientist that is influenced by society, but also the scientific community as a whole, as well as the very methodological process that it is based upon. In his contribution to the debate, Jürgen Habermas adds that Popper's 'belief' in rationalism amounts to a 'confession of faith', which rests solely on a decision over which 'basic statements' will serve to guide his methodological observations.[26]

A second illustration Adorno draws from Popper's essay is the latter's recollection of a conference he attended in which scholars from different disciplines debated the relationship between science and humanism. Near the end of the conference, an anthropologist, who had contributed nothing to this point, informed the group that he had been observing the behaviour of the participants, rather than attending to the content of their debate. Popper quotes the anthropologist's explanation that he had done this in order 'to look at such social phenomena from the outside and from a more objective standpoint'. When challenged with the question whether he believed that it is possible for someone to argue for impersonal reasons, or whether arguments could be valid or invalid, the anthropologist replied that he had not followed the arguments, because to do so might have endangered his objectivity.[27]

In Popper's position, Adorno observes 'formulations which reside in dialectical thought'. What the anthropologist was suggesting, Adorno argues, is that one's scientific method can be independent of reality and of the object under consideration – that the theorist can completely remove her or himself from the context studied. The anthropologist's example denied the significance of the environment in which he was located. This leads Adorno to 'go further than he [Popper] would approve'.[28] For Adorno, the object of sociology – society – involves a dynamic more complex than a contrast between knowledge and ignorance, or the overcoming of logical contradictions. For the problem that presents itself to sociology is itself contradictory: 'society, which keeps itself and its members alive but simultaneously threatens them with ruin, is a problem in an emphatic sense'.

It is in this 'emphatic sense' that society contains contradictory elements within it – elements that elude epistemological resolution through sociological research – that is at the core of the methodological dispute between Adorno and Popper. Adorno argues that society contains a drive to preserve life but at the same time itself hinders this very intention. He therefore asserts that the starting point for sociology is not merely an empirical problem or a logical contradiction demanding resolution, but is instead a concept of society, which, although it does not elude rational knowledge, also resists merely 'conjuring away' contradictions.[29] To Adorno, this recognition demands a dialectical theory of society, as opposed to a more limited 'trial and error' approach to problem solving. It requires a 'social theory' rather than the narrower perspective of 'sociological' research. As such, it is Adorno's concept of 'social totality', as well as his different understanding of 'reason', that distinguishes his argument from that of Popper.

## Totality and Reason

Adorno argues that the project of Enlightenment rationality intends not only to perceive, classify and calculate what is; it also implies that social constraints based on tradition and myth can be overcome by measuring present reality against the idea of a better, more reasonable form of life. This second element of the Enlightenment has been lost, Adorno states, since scientific rationality, when reduced to an instrumental control of nature, dominates what is understood to be 'rational thinking'. This no longer serves the larger goal of freedom – which was part of the project of the Enlightenment – but merely the quest for control and domination based on a mechanical understanding of the world.

Adorno asks how the object might be perceived and constituted by the knowing subject in such a way that the object is not simply distorted and colonized in order to fit it into some theoretical system. Adorno's critique of positivism is based largely on his dissatisfaction with how it treats this issue. Positivism, he argues, does not recognize the active power of subjective thinking in creating what is claimed about the world. In opposition to this, Adorno argues that,

> the separation of subject and object is both real and illusory. True, because in the cognitive realm it serves to express the real separation, the dichotomy of the human condition, a coercive development. False, because the resulting separation must not be hypostasized, not magically transformed into an invariant.[30]

Both subject and object are understood to be mutually mediated. To encourage such recognition, Adorno argues for the 'preponderance' (*Vorrang*) of the object.[31] This highlights the relative character of distinctions between subject and object. It recognizes that,

> What is known through consciousness must be something; mediation aims at the mediated. But the subject, the epitome of mediation, is the How – never the What, as opposed to the object – that is postulated by any comprehensible idea of its concept. Potentially, even if not actually, objectivity can be conceived without a subject; not so subjectivity without an object.[32]

The subject is also an object; 'if it is not something . . . [it] is nothing at all'. This is not to say that subjectivity could be done away with; 'since the preponderance of the object requires reflection of the subject and subjective reflection, subjectivity . . . becomes a moment that lasts'.[33] While the subject inevitably colonizes its object through 'identarian thought', it is also capable of 'rend[ing] the veil it is weaving around the object'.[34] Through ongoing self-criticism – and by analysing how both the process of inquiry, as well as the object under consideration, are mutually mediated – rational thought is able to uncover its hidden biases and misperceptions. Thus, despite being the principle of domination, the subject – including its use of rational identity thinking – is also capable of resistance as it anticipates freedom; 'it contains the potential of sublating its own rule'.[35]

It is with such a philosophical perspective that Adorno approaches social theory and its relation to empirical research. Although, *like* Popper, he emphasizes the rationality of the acting subject in society, *unlike* Popper, Adorno argues that one cannot assume that such agents simply 'act out' rationally what was 'implicit to the situation'. Rather, for Adorno,

> The irrationality of the rational system emerges in the psychology of its trapped subjects. The doctrine of rational behaviour leads into contradictions. Just as the demands made on the individual by the rationality of the system are immanently irrational in so far as the totality of everyone's economically expedient actions furthers, together with the reproduction of society, its disintegration, so, conversely, the absolute *telos* of rationality, fulfilment, would transcend rationality itself.[36]

Adorno warns, therefore, that 'having broken its pledge to be as one with reality or at the point of its realization, philosophy is obliged ruthlessly to criticize itself'.[37] In his writings on society, Adorno proceeds in a similarly dialectical fashion. Modern society, with the ongoing disparities in distribution of wealth, access to education and health care, is to be considered irrational:

> By calling this society irrational I mean that if the purpose of society as a whole is taken to be the preservation and the unfettering of the people of which it is composed, then the way in which this society continues to be arranged runs counter to its own purpose, its *raison d'être*, its *ratio* . . . [The] irrationality of institutions, and the irrational moments in our society, are to be understood only as functions of continuing irrationality. While the means used by society are rational, this rationality of the means is really . . . only a means–ends rationality, that is, one which obtains between the set ends and the means used to achieve them, without having any relation to the real end or purpose of society, which is the preservation of the

species as a whole in a way conferring fulfilment and happiness. That is the reason not only why irrationalities survive, but why they reproduce themselves even further.[38]

If this is the case, then Adorno argues that Popper's conception of critical rationalism, by limiting itself to the abolishment of logical contradictions, brushes over the irrationality of society, filling in the cracks with an epoxy of 'basic statements' that mask structures that encourage social inequalities.[39] The instrumental nature of scientific reasoning that is characteristic of the natural sciences 'ignores the *Telos* which lies in the concept of instrumentalism' and thus becomes 'its own sole purpose', forfeiting knowledge of society for the mere furtherance of technical control over human beings.[40] This is to say that 'sociological research' and scientific method suggest a *telos* of their own: the instrumental control of nature.

Adorno argues that, 'only insight into science's inherent societal mediations contributes to the objectivity of science'.[41] Social theory requires more than the 'trial and error' procedures of falsification. Instead, it 'seeks to give a name to what secretly holds the machinery together'. From the perspective of the natural sciences, such reflection 'is viewed as a mere waste of time'.[42] But, if the concept of society and its present expression in social reality are to be understood, Adorno argues that a theory of the *social totality* is necessary, for 'reflections upon society as a whole cannot be completely realized by empirical findings'.

For Adorno, a 'positivist' approach to society locates objectivity in its methods, not in what is investigated, and ignores 'societal objectivity' – the object of sociology itself.[43] Thus, Popper's claim that 'objectivity rests solely upon criticism'[44] – meaning the process of conjecture and refutation within the context of a critical tradition – remains insufficient. It ignores the preponderance of the object – the manner in which the very society that is under investigation also influences the procedures and methods that are employed to understand it. While the procedure of falsification helps to overcome the subjectivism of individual scientists, it in fact remains a subjectivist position by only reflecting upon the subjective actions of human agents, but not upon the objective structures that are both produced by human actions and at the same time shape human action. If sociology concerns itself only with relationships between human beings without attending to their 'objectified form', it acts as if 'everything really depended on these interpersonal relationships', and not on larger social mechanisms. 'What thus disappears from sociology is not only the decisive element whereby social activity is able to maintain itself at all, but also knowledge of how it maintains itself, with what sacrifices, threats and also with what potentialities for good'.[45]

This speculative element that Adorno considers to be a necessary component of social theory leads him to employ philosophical terminology that Popper rejects. A dialectical theory of society, he argues, seeks to grasp the 'totality' of society, or 'society as a thing-in-itself'.[46] Because the concept of the social totality is not an affirmative statement but merely a 'critical category', it is untestable in the sense of Popper's criterion of falsifiability. But for Adorno, only the category of totality allows for social theory to uncover the 'essence' of social phenomena.

Popper argues that the use of concepts like 'totality' and 'essence' reduces social theory to something metaphysical and politically dangerous. In his contribution to the debate, Popper's student Hans Albert suggests further that, because the dialectical concept of the whole exceeds formal logic, it represents an 'immunization strategy which is based on the expectation that whatever recoils from analysis will escape criticism'.[47] From the perspective of Popper and Albert, a dialectical approach to reason and social theory, with its use of concepts such as 'totality', amounts to a 'fetish which serves to allow arbitrary decisions to appear as objective knowledge'.[48] Criticism and rational argumentation are effectively undermined, while unfalsifiable concepts are upheld. This results in a position that represents to them a 'revolt against reason' that can only suggest totalitarian political implications.[49]

## Value Freedom and Crypto-Theology

Popper's accusation that a dialectical theory of society has totalitarian implications is met in kind by Adorno. The unquestioned authority granted to natural science and instrumental reason is charged with aligning itself with the forces of social domination.

Adorno argues that, 'sociology's abandonment of a critical theory of society is resignatory: one no longer dares to conceive of the whole since one must despair of changing it'.[50] In his opinion, this results in regressive and politically conservative implications, for although Adorno expresses some appreciation for the validity of Popper's approach to pragmatic problem-solving and 'piecemeal social engineering', a demand for the criticism of society and for a change in the social totality 'arises from the situation, from its analysis in all its dimensions'. For example, 'if there is still starvation in a society in which hunger could be avoided here and now . . . then this demands the abolition of hunger through a change in the relations of production'.[51] In Adorno's eyes, Popper's approach to sociology prohibits such a demand. It might be able to recognize the fact that starvation exists, along with the social effects that result, but to criticize these conditions or society itself trespasses against the value freedom that Popper's scientific method insists upon.[52]

Popper argues that the ideal of value freedom in the study of society is the only rational manner with which science can resolve disputes. Anticipating the view of Richard Dawkins and other 'New Atheists', he insists that *critical reason is the only alternative to violence so far discovered*'.[53] An argument that restricts itself to the rules of logical reasoning is presented as the only means available to mediate between conflicting value systems. To permit value statements – which cannot be proven or falsified scientifically – into scientific method undermines its project. Hans Albert echoes this position, asserting that 'science is only possible where there are social spheres in which cognitive interest emancipates itself from . . . elementary needs'.[54]

Both Popper and Albert support their position with reference to the sociologist Max Weber, who argues that, 'whenever the man of science introduces his personal value judgment, a full understanding of the facts ceases'. Science is dependent upon 'facts that are inconvenient for . . . [political] party opinions'.[55] Weber continues,

> Science today is a 'vocation' organized in special disciplines
> in the service of self-clarification and knowledge of
> interrelated facts. It is not the gift of grace of seers and

prophets dispensing sacred values and revelations, nor does it partake of the contemplation of sages and philosophers about the meaning of the universe.[56]

Relating this understanding of science to theology, Weber adds, 'All theology represents an intellectual *rationalization* of the possession of sacred values'. It is never free from presuppositions, for all theology assumes 'that the world must have a meaning'.[57] In Weber's view, then, theology does not represent a form of knowledge, but rather a 'possession' of some faith in meaning. One cannot be both scientific and theological, for the two forms of viewing the world rest upon entirely different cognitive perspectives.

From such a position, Albert accuses Adorno of defending a 'restricted rationality', because he attempts to 'unite normative orientation and technical directions' by advocating that sociology must include a critique of society.[58] For him, any claim that the limitations of technical rationality must be complemented by a hermeneutical understanding amounts to a theological position.[59] It is guilty of presenting a circular argument when it intends to question the norms and rules uncovered by empirical social research on the basis of some conception of the social totality. For Albert, Adorno's position introduces a *deus ex machina* into sociology, based upon insights that emerge from 'who knows where'.[60] As such, it is, he says, a 'crypto-theology'. Popper echoes this argument, adding that there exists little difference between a defence of the existence of God and Adorno's concept of the social whole. Both positions refuse to accept the limitations of logical reasoning and scientific methodology.

Adorno does not deny that the social theorist is vulnerable to false presuppositions and bias. What rational thought must do, therefore, is criticize itself – seeking to 'rend the veil' its weaves around its objects – in order 'by way of the concept, to transcend the concept'.[61] This goal is, in fact, assisted by the concepts themselves, for, as Gillian Rose observes, the German term *Begriff* may mean the referent of a predicate or what in English is called a 'property'. Thus, the statement that 'an object falls under a concept' is equivalent to saying that 'an object has a property'.[62] What Adorno refers to as 'identity thinking' mistakenly assumes that its concept *is* identical to its object. 'Non-identical thinking', however, seeks to maintain the awareness of its contingency. It does not simply discard the ideal of identity, nor does it locate it in any specific metanarrative or transcendent absolute. Instead, thought is to recognize that 'living in the rebuke that the thing is not identical with the concept is the concept's longing to become identical with the thing'. In *Negative Dialectics*, Adorno refers to the example of freedom to illustrate what he means: 'Emphatically conceived, the judgment that a man is free refers to the concept of freedom'. But, 'the concept of freedom lags behind itself as soon as we apply it empirically'. Such a confrontation forces the concept to contradict itself, as the particular individual seeks to be free, but must also diminish what the concept of freedom implies practically 'for utility's sake'.

Dialectics is the form of thinking that Adorno considers necessary to wrestle with this problem. The contradiction between the concept of freedom and particular experiences of social unfreedom is not simply to be resolved in thought. Instead, 'the potential of freedom calls for criticizing what an inevitable formalization has made of the potential'.[63] The tension that arises because of the concept's unrealized *potentiality* results in a criticism of its *actuality*. Dialectical thinking, then, is the ongoing self-critical movement that results from the contradiction. It is not 'the mere projection on the thing of a concept formation that miscarried nor a metaphysics running amuck'. Nor is it an 'irrationalist intuition'. Instead, 'Dialectics is a protest lodged by our thinking against the archaicisms of its conceptuality'.[64] It is the recognition of the mediated nature of all knowledge, and of the contradictions contained within human thought and society.

## On the Necessity of a Normative Foundation

It is noteworthy that some critics who reside closer to Adorno's perspective also raise concerns about his conceptualization of critical theory. Agnes Heller criticizes what she considers to be the 'prophetic' tone within Adorno's writing. She argues that his suggestion that philosophy 'missed its moment of realization' is 'frivolous', because it implies a postulation of an absolute truth, while at the same time depicting contemporary consciousness as wholly corrupt.[65] Hauke Brunkhorst makes a similar accusation when he describes the philosophy of history implied by Adorno's position as 'metaphysical', 'fundamentalist', 'dualistic', and 'elitist'.[66] Rüdger Bittner adds that *Dialectic of Enlightenment*'s lament over reason's lost potential can only be made from a 'religious viewpoint', for the book's vision of a return to the fullness of rationality and reconciliation with nature comes only in the form of a 'promise', not a foundational argument.[67] Such a view leads Axel Honneth to describe Adorno's social critique as an intellectual artefact: 'it cannot really justify what makes the ideals from its own culture chosen to be a reference point normatively defensible or desirable in the first place'.[68]

James Gordon Finlayson challenges such accusations that Adorno's thought suffers from a 'normative deficit'. He notes that Honneth's position shares Habermas' view that communicative action and the theory of 'discourse ethics' provides a normative foundation for critical theory. But Finlayson adds, perceptively, that Habermas' rational reconstruction of morality is not the same thing as a first order foundation for normative knowledge.[69] For example, even though Habermas' theory emphasizes inter-subjective communication as the source of normativity, the consensus achieved in such moral debate is rather a different conception of legitimation than what Popper's demands through the falsification of hypotheses in science.

More to the point, however, it is not that Adorno neglects to consider the problem of foundations; rather, it is precisely this demand for foundational logical deduction that his negative dialectics rejects. Consider this statement from *Negative Dialectics*:

> One ought not to torture: there ought to be no concentration camps . . . These sentences are true only as impulses, when it is reported that somewhere torture is taking place. They should not be rationalized. As abstract principles they lapse into the bad infinity of their derivation and validity.[70]

Finlayson helpfully emphasizes that it would be a mistake to interpret a statement like this as implying that Adorno thinks the principles of morality are self-evident.[71] But Adorno is arguing

73

that moral imperatives are not theorems. For him, philosophy 'does not have answers to everything, but responds to a world that is false to its innermost core'.[72] When actions (or situations) are causing human suffering, he argues that this is sufficient ground to oppose them. Adorno's critical theory aims to reveal such limitations in social life, which, for him, is ground to demonstrate why change is needed:

> The undiminished persistence of suffering, fear, and menace necessitates that the thought that cannot be realized should not be discarded. After having missed its opportunity, philosophy must come to know, without any mitigation, why the world – which could be paradise here and now – can become hell itself tomorrow.[73]

Adorno's philosophy is grounded on a protest against what ought not to be. It is reacting to an objective situation in the world. It is misleading, therefore, to suggest that Adorno criticizes existing society from the vantage point of some pure absolute. Adorno does not claim to have seen 'the promised land'. Rather he points to concepts and presuppositions contained within society, and employs these same concepts and values 'against themselves' when they result in contradiction.

The reality of human suffering is, for Adorno, an indication why such unrealized possibilities should not be surrendered – possibilities that Adorno argues can be observed in a fragmentary form within unjust society itself. Social theory must probe 'the wounds which this order has and which, above all, it inflicts on us', so that those mechanisms that support domination might be unmasked and challenged.[74] In the urge to transcend the bonds that dominate the subject, and in the search to uncover the causes of suffering, a glimpse of freedom is achieved, along with a trace of objective truth: 'the need to lend a voice to suffering is a condition of all truth. For suffering is objectivity that weighs upon the subject'.[75] In this critical process of reflecting upon existing social conditions for the sake of rescuing for the present what is repressed and veiled by these conditions, Adorno states that everything must be viewed in light of a possible future. Suffering is understood to reveal that a just society is not presently found in existing social conditions.

By way of rebutting the accusation that this commitment amounts to an unscientific and irrational position, Adorno highlights Popper's own admission that scientific objectivity and value freedom are, in fact, themselves 'values'.[76] They incorporate 'extra-scientific interests', as Popper himself recognizes, although he considers it a simple matter to distinguish between 'interests which do not belong to the search for truth' from 'the purely scientific interest in truth'.[77] Science demonstrates, in his mind, the validity of such value assumptions by the very fact that it has proven to successfully provide causal explanations for natural phenomena.

For Adorno, however, Popper's admission is not unimportant. To illustrate his point, he notes that Popper recognizes that the scientist cannot be cleansed of 'his partisanship without also robbing him of his humanity, nor can we suppress or destroy his value judgements without destroying him as a human being *and as a scientist*'.[78] To Adorno, this recognition highlights the fact that the 'objective concept' of science is itself endangered by an overly rigid division between *means* and *ends* in rational thinking. For example, without the absence of social violence, the scientific community cannot function properly. Furthermore, in a society that places a high value on technological innovation and profitability, the 'value freedom' of science becomes difficult to maintain, for 'the concept of value is formed in the exchange relationship – a being for another'. If the experiences and human needs of individual scientists become a matter of indifference to technical reason, then even the machinery of technical reason will cease to function, since the very existence of its servants is threatened.

Adorno seeks to clarify here that every judgement is constituted 'in relation to the whole which is contained within it'. What something *is* and what something *should be* are not completely distinct ideas.[79] This was illustrated earlier in the discussion of the concepts of 'freedom' and of 'society'. It is from this perspective that Adorno argues that, 'Society, the knowledge of which is ultimately the aim of sociology if it is to be more than mere technique, can only crystallize at all around a conception of the just society'.[80]

Adorno insists, against Popper, that his problematization of the concept of value freedom, along with his dialectical approach to society, does not amount to a positive theological position or the abandonment of science. The categories of totality and essence do not refer to a system abstracted from empirical reality, functioning as a version of a Platonic ideal form. They are not 'infinite', 'absolute', or 'organically united' in any sense, but represent a recognition of the mediation of all social facts by the interconnected social network that they are a part of.[81] The 'essence' of society, insists Adorno, 'is not identical with meaning, is not a positivity *sui generis*, but is the context of entanglement or guilt in which everything individual is entwined, and which manifests itself in every individual entity'.[82] It is not a 'mere fantasy, but a category of mediation'.[83] 'Social totality' is a critical category that seeks to prevent 'sociological research' from being satisfied with documenting the social *status quo*, without also being attentive to those forces that shape it.

The same is true of Adorno's use of concepts like 'justice', 'reconciliation' and 'redemption'. These are not fully formed blueprints for an alternative society. In fact, they are without any positive content, but are conceived merely as the mirror image of the injustice, conflict and unresolved suffering present in the world. Reason can emphatically grasp them through reflection, but cannot generate them positively. What Adorno's position shares with theological concepts are the ungrounded nature with which it is presented, and the difficulty of legitimating such commitments. What distinguishes these same concepts from Christian theological doctrines is the lack of positive content that Adorno proscribes to them.

## Social Theory and Empirical Research

Where does this debate with Popper leave Adorno in terms of empirical research? What he seeks is a 'combination of empirical investigations with theoretically central questions'.[84] Whereas

Popper insists that social science be limited to the 'explanation' (*Erklären*) of social action, and more humanistic approaches like that of Dilthey emphasize hermeneutical 'understanding' (*Verstehen*), Adorno describes his own position as an 'elucidation' (*Deutung*) of the relation between the underlying processes of society (the totality) and the particular cultural forms and individual opinions found within social life (appearance).[85] He explains his position as follows:

> In sociology, *elucidation* [*Deutung*] acquires its force both from the fact that without reference to totality − to the real social system, untranslatable into any solid immediacy − nothing societal can be conceptualized, and from the fact that it can, however, only be recognized in the extent to which it is apprehended in the factual and the individual. It is the societal physiognomy of appearance. The primary meaning of '*elucidation*' [*Deutung*] is to perceive something in the features of totality's societal givenness.[86]

Adorno understands his method of 'elucidation' as a critical second reflection upon empirical social research. It neither rejects scientific methodology nor accepts it at face value. Although there is no 'truth set apart from the mediated, from the facts', he criticizes any sociology that relies upon 'unreflected facticity'.[87] If methodological problems are made 'falsifiable in an unreflected manner', then scientific research gets reduced to eliminating variables to accommodate the demand to resolve logical contradictions, which only serves to manipulate the object of science into a controlling model that masks the truth about social experience.[88] Instead, a critical theory of society represents an ongoing elucidation of the mediated character of society and of all social action − including the study of society itself. By holding the concept of society (its ideals, general assumptions and practices) in tension with particular social events and situations, Adorno argues that social theory may achieve fragmentary and partial glimpses of the objective truths about society.

Such elucidation can only arrive at fragmentary insights in the process of an ongoing negative critique. The demand for firm foundations represents, in his opinion, a perspective driven by an 'ontological need'. As he states in his inaugural address at the University of Frankfurt,

> philosophy persistently and with the claim to truth, must proceed elucidatively [*deutend*] without ever possessing a sure key to elucidation [*Deutung*]; nothing more is given to it than fleeting, disappearing traces within the riddle figures of that which exists and their astonishing entwinings.[89]

Adorno in no way assumes that his theoretical position provides access to the object 'in-itself' any more than he intends to abandon the pursuit of such knowledge. Instead, his work seeks to prevent critical thought from permitting the existing conditions of society to become naturalized. By resisting the impulse of theoretical thought to resign itself to imperfect solutions and compromises, Adorno's critical theory – or 'negative dialectics' – keeps open the question of the possibility that the existing might be otherwise in the future. In this way, it 'points beyond itself'.[90]

Yet his critics might again ask: from what source do such insights emerge? If it is not necessarily the process of 'trial and error' that elucidates the complex nature of society, what does? Adorno's answer is the dialectical movement between empirical research and theory, but his explanations of this often remain incomplete and undeveloped. In his lectures at the Institute for Social Research, Adorno himself hints that there is a problem in this regard. He argues that 'it is possible to know the object from the inside in a quite different way [from the natural sciences] . . . [T]he method of sociology must stand in a living relationship to this subject matter and must, as far as possible, be developed from it'. But, after making this point, he is compelled to add, 'I would ask you to bear in mind that such a demand *should not be interpreted unreasonably*'.[91]

Adorno recognizes that the tensions he is seeking to hold in balance are difficult to sustain, and that his methodology leaves open the possibility that the theorist could slip into a biased and self-serving subjective approach to the object of study. This is precisely why he insists on a non-foundational *negative* dialectics;

one which consistently remembers that its grasp of the non-identity of the object is always incomplete. To help keep this space of attentive humility open, he employs a concept from Jewish thought: the prohibition on images, or *Bilderverbot*. He employs a theological concept in the service of social science's attention to its object of study.

Adorno's use of this concept will be explored in detail in the next chapter. At present, it is important to underline how this approach avoids what Adorno's critics worry is implied by such a position: a utopian vision that is antithetical to a 'follower of the Enlightenment', because a prophet believes himself to be in possession of a single truth.[92] Adorno does not to claim to possess an intuitive revelatory insight into a mysterious absolute reality behind appearance. As Gillian Rose observes, for him, 'Utopia is another way of naming the thesis that non-dialectical thought is closed thought, because it implies that the object is already captured. To see that the object is not captured is to see utopia'.[93]

There is one point in the debate between Adorno and Popper where the latter appears willing to grant some ground in this direction. He admits that his commitment to critical rationalism is not based on a proof, and could thus be called a 'belief'. He notes that only an 'uncritical reason' – one that demands a 'comprehensive' grasp of reality – demands that it can accept only what can be defended by means of argument. Furthermore, 'since all argument must proceed from assumptions', he acknowledges that 'it is plainly impossible to demand that all assumptions should be based on argument'. Thus, Popper concedes that the rationalist attitude can be described as 'an irrational *faith in reason*'.[94]

This being the case, he is confident that there exist good reasons to choose critical rationalism over the alternative of adopting some more extreme form of irrationalism. It is not simply 'an intellectual affair', but 'a moral decision'.[95] Abandoning critical rationality effectively amounts to the denial of the necessity of making one's personal subjective beliefs accountable to public scrutiny and criticism. Furthermore, the use of reason in scientific methodology has demonstrated that science leads to theories that actually work. Popper does not claim that the technical success of scientific rationality proves its validity, but he certainly considers this fact to permit the claim that one's 'belief' in reason is a decision made with 'open eyes'.

For Popper, a 'moral attitude' is one that recognizes that 'we owe it to other men to treat them and ourselves as rational'. Taking rational argument seriously implies that one must grant the possibility that 'I may be wrong and you may be right'. It serves as a check on individual biases and assumptions. This being the case, Popper concludes that, 'the link between rationalism and humanitarianism is very close'.[96]

This view that rationalism leads one to respect the freedom and opinions of other human beings, and the recognition that it is adopted on the basis of a moral decision, also suggests to Popper the following implication:

> a demand for the rationalization of society, for planning for freedom, and for its control by reason; *not by 'science'*, not by a Platonic, a pseudo-rational authority, *but by that Socratic reason which is aware of its limitations*.[97]

Such an understanding of 'Socratic reason' is not unlike Adorno's demand for a form of thought that surpasses 'means-ends rationality'. Popper is describing *reason* in a manner that suggests that it points beyond itself. It implies a demand for the 'rationalization of society' based, not on the technical demands of science, but upon a 'moral attitude' which is inherently related to the 'decision' to adopt critical reasoning in the first place – the resistance to human suffering, and a respect for the 'other'. This emphasis is not incompatible with Adorno's argument that the concept of society implies by its very nature the idea of a just society. This is not to say, in a simplistic manner, that Adorno and Popper 'mean the same thing' when they are speaking about critical reason, but it does demonstrate that their positions are not as divergent as is often assumed.

For when Popper identifies an intimate link between the intellectual and moral decision in favour of rationalism, and 'what we call our imagination',[98] he is very close to describing what Adorno calls the 'speculative moment' in rational thought. Rational thinking points beyond itself, as is testified to by the fact that it cannot itself be grounded upon a logical foundation, and finds itself dependent upon an 'irrational' decision in its favour, which must be continually nurtured by creative imagination if it is to avoid becoming a rigid and self-absorbed worldview that resists criticism. Adorno calls this recognition a 'metaphysical experience'.[99]

Adorno's critical theory and approach to social science is indeed non-foundational in such a manner, but this by no means results in the theoretical dead-end which his critics accuse him of. As Espen Hammer observes, Adorno's position is related to his view that language is aporetic. Although identity thinking seeks to ignore this reality, all human knowledge of the world is open-ended and incomplete.[100] Language, like rational concepts, involves a necessary failure, given the metaphysical gap between human symbolic constructs and the reality they intend to point to. This is precisely the recognition that Adorno is trying to defend in his debate with Popper, and in his attacks against positivism. Rationality itself often forgets this 'block' between subjective experience and the thing-in-itself, and so other devices are required to help defend the boundary. For Adorno, theology has a significant contribution to make here, if only to provide concepts that help describe and hold a place open for metaphysical experience; a haven for the idea of truth beyond the fragmented nature of contemporary life.

This recollection of the dispute between Adorno and Popper not only highlights the distinctive approach to social research that the Frankfurt School sought to develop; it also brings into view the role that theological concepts serve in Adorno's thought. Adorno recognized, indeed he was harshly criticized for, the manner in which his concepts of the 'essence' and 'totality of society' rested on unclear philosophical foundations. For this reason, many dismissed his thought as irrational, unscientific, or even the product of elitist pomposity. But because of his insistence that the reality of social suffering points beyond itself, and that reason produces concepts like freedom, which imply a demand that existing conditions be transcended, Adorno is convinced that forms of thought dismissed by modernity as 'metaphysical' or 'theological' not only remain legitimate, but are indeed required to challenge an increasingly irrational world. The next chapter thus turns directly to an analysis of this understanding of theology, and explores how his dialogue with the Jewish and Christian theological traditions plays a central role in his philosophical project.

# Chapter 4

# Inverse Theology: *Bilderverbot* and the Illumination of Non-identity

The account of Adorno's approach to dialectical materialism in the previous chapters makes it possible to decipher his unusual references to the role of theology in his critical philosophy. Beyond the influence that his interpretation of Marxian philosophy had on his interest in religion, Adorno's relationship with Walter Benjamin shaped his understanding of 'theology'. This chapter analyses Adorno's use of the term, particularly as it emerges in dialogue with Benjamin's work, and in reference to the writing of Franz Kafka. For Adorno, theology is closely related to the concept of truth, which he thinks requires protection against the structures of technical knowledge. Guided by a commitment to the Jewish concept of *Bilderverbot*, he develops what he calls an 'inverse theology' to challenge identity thinking and the domination of the object by the thinking subject. Neither a positive nor a negative theology, it maintains a negative and dialectical analysis of the contradictions within social existence.

The chapter explores how Adorno associates theology with a form of critical thinking that sustains counter-cultural social action. After a discussion of various interpretations of his use of the term 'theology', it demonstrates that his position rejects any reliance upon an established tradition or positive revelation. For in Adorno's view, only an 'inverse theology' is able to maintain the attention of human thought and action on the brokenness of present life, and prevent it from escaping to the consolations of sentimentality or ideology.

## Astrology and the Return to Religion

In a short paper from 1957 entitled 'Reason and Revelation', Adorno comments on what he perceives as a turn towards 'positive religion' in Western society at that time. He suggests that the revived interest in a form of divine revelation that communicates positive content is related to an experienced need. He argues that people were turning to religion for a sense of guidance, for confirmation of dearly held views, or out of a longing for resolute decision. His point is that the resurgence and new enthusiasm for traditional religion is in no way due to a discovery of new supporting evidence for its truth claims, or in response to a wave of admirable praxis on the part of religious communities. Rather, his diagnosis of this return to religion is that it is a product of subjective desire.[1] In this regard, his view of religion is not unlike that of Sigmund Freud, for whom religious longing is the result of a psychic need for reassurance and a sense of security.[2]

Adorno follows Freud on this point, and similarly understands this dynamic to be inherent to religion throughout human history. However, he considers this pattern of projected desire to be particularly problematic in modern societies. In his view, the religious expressions undergoing a revival were displaying 'a tendency toward obscurantism' that he finds far more politically dangerous and psychologically regressive than the 'restrained orthodoxy of the earlier period'. Why? Because, in his view, the new religious attitude 'does not completely believe in itself'.[3] It is not the product of intellectual consideration, nor does it challenge the dominance of scientific rationality or the economic structures of society. Such a turn to religion is simply the result of emotional need, which leaves the existing structure of society unchallenged. It is not, in other words, attentive to alternative possibilities inherent within society, but merely seeks consolation or escape from history. And so, when such adherents encounter something that appears to contradict or inhibit their religious commitment, it might well result in an over-reactive defensiveness, or even violence.

Adorno's concern is further clarified in a study he conducted of the astrology column in the *Los Angeles Times*. Building on the diagnosis of 'instrumental reason' articulated in *Dialectic of Enlightenment*, Adorno suggests that 'the world appears to most people today more as a "system" than ever before'. The result is a greater sense of helplessness and dependence in the face of an anonymous market system. In such a situation, 'people even of supposedly "normal" mind are prepared to accept systems of delusions for the simple reason that it is too difficult to distinguish such systems from the equally inexorable and equally opaque one under which they actually have to live out their lives'.[4] In an environment of 'feeling caught', astrological columns offer advice and guidance to people, assisting them to make clear decisions. Adorno does not think readers of such columns are stupid or irrational; nor does he suggest that they are somehow intellectually tricked or deluded as to the merits of astrological advice. What he finds particularly intriguing is that 'many followers of astrology do not seem quite to believe but rather take an indulgent, semi-ironical attitude towards their own conviction'.[5] Practitioners of astrology, Adorno suggests, both believe and disbelieve in the efficacy of the advice they receive.[6] People cling to the newspaper columns out of psychic need and a desire for clarity, and often no amount of evidence that contradicts the astrological advice will be sufficient to break their reliance upon it. Often, they will even make fun of the columns, or admit that they doubt the efficacy of the astrological advice, and yet continue to read and discuss the material with enthusiasm.

Beyond the desire and need for reassurance, Adorno identified an additional factor to account for the dynamic of believing unbelief. He observes a considerable emphasis in these newspaper columns, as well as in apologetic literature on astrology, on defending the claims made as being authentically scientific and measurable. The cosmology that astrology implies is one in which the world is ruled by mechanical laws. Astrological advice helps reveal these laws in order to assist one to live in conformity with them. In this manner, part of astrology's attraction is the way in which it complies with the general societal drive to control one's life through instrumental reasoning. As is the case with his reading of the Odysseus story, however, Adorno argues that such intellectual cunning is often misdirected against the self, rather than serving to motivate change in social life. The advice columns encourage the individual 'to find fault with oneself rather than with given conditions'.[7] The implied ontological structure of life is, therefore, one that affirms the society already known by the readers. It is not a vision which disturbs the *status quo*; 'astrology mirrors exactly the opaqueness of the empirical world and implies so little transcendent faith'. Effectively, 'the cult of God has been replaced by the cult of facts'.[8]

This critique of astrology would initially appear to undermine any serious interest in theology. But in the study, Adorno makes an important distinction: 'Astrology, although it sometimes pretends to be chummy with theology, is basically different from religion'.[9] Unlike a belief in a divine being or personal God, the source of causation and control – the stars – 'is not only kept remote, but is also treated as impersonal and thing-like'. Those who want to survive in such a universe are encouraged to accept 'the verdict of the stars' rather than to 'penetrate them by thinking', or to appeal to a divine other who might change an unjust situation. Although the atheist Adorno rejects the existence of God, and any possibility that a divine being will intervene in history, he recognizes that theology is a significant form of *thought* which can maintain a sense that unjust social life should and can be otherwise. Astrology is not theology because it lacks this critical element. While it might appear to be metaphysically meaningful, astrological advice implies no real appeal to an absolute or unrecognized potentiality. Unlike the case of theology, 'the mystery celebrated by astrology is empty'.[10]

## Adorno and Theology

Although Adorno is highly dismissive of much that is found within religious traditions and communities, and articulates some savage critiques of theology as an academic enterprise, he continues to appreciate that, in both religious traditions and theological discourse, one can still find elements that protest against the existing conditions of society. Theology does not consider any so-called self-evident 'facts' before it to represent the fullness of reality. It pushes beyond the existing state of things. Adorno associates theology with the 'metaphysical moment' in thought, as well as with attention to unrealized possibilities in the midst of actuality. This is not to say that he considers theology to be the best or only form of such experience and reflection, as he observes that religion is often as ideological as all other forms of culture, and as prone to mere identity thinking and instrumental reasoning. And yet, for him, theology has been able to sustain within it a utopian vision of a better world. For this reason, Adorno links theology with a concern for truth and with an attention to the concealed realities of life.

The previous chapter highlighted how Adorno suggests that tensions in social life testify to unresolved contradictions; 'suffering is objectivity that weighs upon the subject', and so 'the need to lend a voice to suffering is the condition of all truth'.[11] He conceives of theological discourse as a key expression of these wounds and suffering. Thus 'metaphysical experience' is described as being related to theology. For Adorno, conceptual thought, along with human experience, 'has the curious characteristic that, although itself entrapped, locked inside the glasshouse of our constitution and language, it is nevertheless able constantly to think beyond itself and its limits, to think itself through the walls of its glasshouse'.[12] It offers an opportunity to examine experiences that might 'reflect the negation of the finite which finiteness requires'.[13] Theological discourse thus challenges the foreclosure of the present on itself.

This view is also found in the work of his friend and colleague Max Horkheimer, who argues that religion has provided Western culture with an invaluable inheritance:

> [Human]kind loses religion as it moves through history, but the loss leaves its mark behind. Part of the drives and desires which religious belief preserved and kept alive are detached from the inhibiting religious form and become productive forces in social practice . . . In a really free mind the concept of infinity is preserved in an awareness of the finality of human life and of the inalterable aloneness of [human beings], and it keeps society from indulging in a thoughtless optimism, an inflation of its own knowledge into a new religion.[14]

The legacy that Horkheimer points to in this statement is religion's relation to the concept of objective truth. He acknowledges that throughout history religious thought has also been intertwined with myth and illusion, so that, gradually, reason 'aspires to replace traditional religion'.[15] Although he appreciates this shift, he also laments it, for Horkheimer observes that rationality often gets reduced to instrumentality and calculation. And so he writes, 'the divorce of reason from religion marked a further step in the weakening of its objective aspect'. This is to say that what the Enlightenment 'killed was not the church but metaphysics and the objective content of reason itself'.[16] Human suffering continues, and so individuals and communities continue to express it, sometimes in the form of theological discourse and religious practice. But what becomes increasingly difficult to articulate, in Adorno and Horkheimer's view, is the hope for a better world, and an understanding of society that probes beneath the presuppositions of the current age.

Adorno consistently makes this point: 'certainly a *ratio* that does not wantonly absolutize itself as a rigid means of domination requires self-reflection, some of which is expressed in the need for religion today'.[17] He also warns, however, against trying to use this reality as a tool to advocate for a return to a religious or theological worldview. He observes that such a conclusion is often employed for apologetic or ideological reasons, but this only evaporates theology's relation to its truth content, and reduces it to a product of psychic need. This dual-perspective is paradoxical, in that it implies an appreciation for the contribution of theology, but also a deep suspicion of it, and a rejection of how it is often understood. Adorno never fully resolved this tension in his own position, or clarified the extent to which this materialist and atheistic appreciation of theology opens the door to the traditions and discourses of Christianity or Judaism.

## The Prohibition on Images: *Bilderverbot*

At the end of 'Reason and Revelation' Adorno concludes that any revival of revealed religion will likely dissolve; 'I see no other possibility than an extreme ascesis toward any type of revealed faith, an extreme loyalty to the prohibition of images, far beyond what this once originally meant'.[18] It is clear that he is not imagining that the content of Christian and Jewish theology will have any substantial role in his critical philosophy. But this quotation does invoke a particular concept from Judaism. The reference to a 'prohibition of images' refers to the Jewish notion of *Bilderverbot*: the view that any concrete representation of the divine, even the speaking of its name, is idolatry. In Jewish tradition, the Hebrew name for God, 'Yahweh', is not to be written or spoken: 'You shall not make for yourself an idol, whether in the form of anything that is in heaven above, or that is on the earth beneath, or that is in the water under the earth. You shall not bow down to them or worship them, for I the Lord your God am a jealous God'.[19] In *Dialectic of Enlightenment*, Adorno and Horkheimer invoke the *Bilderverbot* as a potential form of ideology critique:

> The Jewish religion brooks no word which might bring solace to the despair of all mortality. It places all hope in the prohibition against invoking falsity as God, the finite as the infinite, the lie as the truth. The pledge of salvation lies in the rejection of any faith which claims to depict it, knowledge in the denunciation of illusion.[20]

The *Bilderverbot* is one of the most frequent concepts that Adorno borrows from theology. It clearly resonates with his criticism of 'identity thinking', his defence of potentiality against a rigid adherence to actuality, and his development of a 'negative dialectics'. But it is precisely at this point that interpretations of Adorno's work diverge. A concept so central and significant for Adorno's work remains elusive and frequently misunderstood. Does this block on imaging the divine, as well as on conceiving absolute truth or positive content for utopian longing, reduce his philosophy to a resigned silence? Furthermore, given his assertion of an 'extreme loyalty' to the *Bilderverbot*, why does Adorno continue to discuss theology at all? His readers offer a variety of diverse answers to these questions.

## Interpretations of Adorno's References to Theology

One prominent interpretation of this aspect of Adorno's thought places him in the category of a negative theologian. Despairing of the barbaric course of human history, and refusing to identify any solid foundation for hope or consolation, Adorno is described as being left with nothing but a vague longing for a 'wholly other'. This 'message-in-a-bottle' view is popularized by such prominent philosophers as Jürgen Habermas and Albrecht Wellmer. A similar interpretation is presented, with a different intention, among theologians like Matthew Lamb and Ulf Liedke, the latter of whom argues directly that 'Negative Dialectics is negative theology'.[21] A variant of this interpretation is developed by Michael Theunissen, who argues that in Adorno, the negative 'holds the positive within itself', which returns his thought to metaphysics.[22] Unlike its usage among philosophical critics, these theologians do not consider the label 'negative theology' a dismissive accusation. Such theological interpretations are intended to suggest that Adorno's philosophy implies the need for a theological grounding, which is only indirectly hinted at in his work.

A second interpretation of Adorno's remarks on theology suggests that his negative critique of rationality serves to illuminate the 'other of reason' that is hidden within, but remains integral to, rationality. Such a view shares much in common with those who label Adorno as a negative theologian, although it pushes his work in directions distinct from that tradition. This approach suggests that Adorno's thought needs to be supplemented or corrected beyond his overwhelming negativity, while challenging or neglecting some of his explicit references theology. Such an interpretation is developed in the work of philosopher Hent de Vries (whose position will be explored further below).[23] Theologians of a similar view, like Charles Davis, push this interpretation further, and argue that the deep pessimism implied by Adorno serves to point towards the need for a more positive notion of the Absolute (which Adorno's own work fails to provide). Wayne Whitson Floyd, Jr, in contrast, suggests that Adorno prepares the way for a 'theology of otherness'.[24]

A third noteworthy reaction to Adorno is one which suggests that his work contains a problematic nihilism. Among theologians, the primary point to be gleaned through this charge is that his work implies the liquidation of theology. Helmut Peukert argues this view rather pointedly: 'For Adorno, the Old Testament's prohibition of images not only forbids the mention of God's name', but also that 'Theology is then precisely what ought not to be thought'.[25] For many theologians, Adorno's negativity towards tradition and positive identity dissolves any possibility that his work might serve as a useful conversation partner for theology. This position is the theological variant of the view found among those philosophers and social scientists who dismiss Adorno for granting any attention whatsoever to theology. In such a position, any serious consideration of theology corrupts the integrity of rational thought. Gerrit Steunebrink does not go so far as this. He argues instead that, far from implying a negative theology, Adorno's thought ends in a nihilism that crushes all finitude. His philosophy, Steunebrink argues, can be characterized as resembling what Hegel calls an 'unhappy consciousness' and a despairing asceticism.[26]

There remains another way to interpret Adorno's references to theology, and it is that which this chapter will explore in detail. Adorno's own description of his position is that it suggests an 'inverse theology'. The discussion that follows will show that this position is both distinct from, and more appropriate than, the three general interpretations of Adorno's theology just outlined. Before wrestling with the fragmentary descriptions that he offers of this perspective, it is instructive by way of contrast to first clarify what he does not think an inverse theology is, as well as explore why he uses the word 'theology' in the first place.

## A Negative Theology?

Susan Buck-Morss' groundbreaking study of the relationship between Adorno and Walter Benjamin sheds considerable light on Adorno's philosophical instincts. She concludes that Adorno's 'inverse theology' is largely equivalent to a 'negative theology'.[27] Admittedly, it is not difficult to understand why his philosophy is frequently casually classified in such a manner.[28] Adorno's critique of totality and 'identity thinking' might be taken as sharing in negative theology's aversion to asserting positive claims about the absolute, while continuing to posit the usefulness of the category of ultimate truth.

Negative theology is a tradition with roots in late antiquity. It flourished in Neoplatonic philosophy in the third century BCE, and experienced a high point among the mystics of the late Middle Ages. If much of the Greek philosophical tradition (in Parmenides in particular) emphasized that Being and thought are one, negative theology argues to the contrary that the divine is ultimately mystery. In this school of thought, God is unknowable and completely transcendent of the existing world, so that the only way to approach the divine is negatively: through denials and clarifications of what God is *not*. The thirteenth-century German mystic Meister Eckhart wrote with such an emphasis: 'God is nameless, because no one can say anything or understand anything about him'.[29] This tradition is frequently concerned with opposing anthropomorphism in theology, along with rigid doctrinal boundaries, and in their place emphasizes mysticism and experiential access to the divine mystery.

At the core of negative theology is a prominent concern with what could be called, in contemporary terms, a de-centred subjectivity. The tradition frequently stresses the notion that, through an encounter with the divine, the self's claim of self-importance and control are radically shaken, along with the presumption that its knowledge accurately captures the fullness of divine truth. Negative theology typically suggests that, by following the path of a *via negativa*, the subject may experience an intense spiritual reformation.[30] The divine, experienced as *mysterium tremendum*, shatters the presumptions of mere human beings and reveals the incomplete, if not erroneous, nature of existing beliefs or actions. Divine transcendence interrupts as 'Wholly Other', completely beyond the range of human experience.[31]

Some philosophers and theologians argue that contemporary continental thought is witnessing an intriguing turn towards negative theology. Much is made, for example, of Jacques Derrida's acknowledgement that one can legitimately suggest a 'family resemblance' or 'tenable analogy' between negative theology and 'every discourse that seems to return in a regular and insistent manner to this rhetoric of negative determination'.[32] Derrida himself denies that his understanding of deconstruction can be so assimilated, arguing that 'What *différance*, the *trace*, and so on "mean" . . . is "before" the concept, the name, the word, "something" that would be nothing, that no longer arises from Being'.[33] He is concerned that negative theology involves an onto-theological re-appropriation of thought, in the sense that even an apophatic discourse that looks to something 'beyond being' continues to operate in a manner determined by the very categories it seeks to escape.

Labelling Adorno's philosophy a 'negative theology', however, is complicated by his care to avoid suggesting that the categories of thought can be set aside. Furthermore, he held particular scorn for theologians who, in response to the doubts or despair of unbelievers over the state of their existence, 'gradually come to intone their Te Deum wherever God is denied, because at least his name is mentioned'.[34] For Adorno, to affirm a negative theology is ultimately to affirm the eventual identity of subject and object in a divine being who is Absolute Identity. In other words, one would have to draw Adorno's thought much closer to Hegel's. The latter proposed an ultimate resolution of the dialectic between subject and object in his philosophy. These would be reconciled and brought together without remainder in Absolute Spirit. For Hegel, 'the True is the whole'.[35] Adorno's rejection of any positive progression and development emerging out of dialectics suggests to him the opposite view: 'The whole is the false'.[36] Although Hegel was by no means a negative theologian, to suggest that Adorno's perspective accepts the ultimate achievement of an elusive reconciliation, and that it amounts to a negative theology, is to imply that, ultimately, his position accepts the divine source and identity of existence.

Furthermore, the tradition of negative theology emphasizes an access to truth beyond reason, through some form of mysticism, spirituality, or alternative form of consciousness. As Elizabeth Pritchard observes, Wellmer and other critics who associate Adorno with negative theology wrongly suggest that 'Adorno's adherence to the *Bilderverbot* entails his renunciation of the only tool, i.e. discursive reason, with which one might construct an alternative praxis'.[37] Such an accusation neglects the fact that, despite articulating an aggressive criticism of the limits of rational concepts, he also argues that philosophy has no other source for knowledge. Adorno's thinking against thought is not a rejection or despairing over thought; rather, his work is determined to show that reason 'must strive, by way of the concept, to transcend the concept'.[38] Furthermore, although his emphasis on the 'preponderance of the object' is meant to humble and interrupt the presumptions of the thinking subject, he also warns that 'it is not the purpose of critical thought to place the object on the royal throne once occupied by the subject. On the throne the object would be nothing but an idol. The purpose of critical thought is to abolish the hierarchy'.[39]

This emphasis stands in contrast to that found in negative theology, particularly in the form which makes apophantic discourse its focus. As Derrida remarks,

> Once the apophantic discourse is analysed in its logical–grammatical form, it is not merely sterile, repetitive, obscurantist, mechanical, it perhaps leads us to consider the becoming theological of all discourse. From the moment a proposition takes a negative form, the negativity that manifests itself need only be pushed to the limit, and at least resembles an apophantic theology.[40]

Adorno's references to theology are not so preoccupied with language analysis, nor with negativity. The limits he is concerned primarily with are those imposed by social existence, not grammar. This gives his interest in theology a significantly different tone to that generally found among negative theologies.

## Negative Dialectics as a 'Minimial Theology' of the Trace?

Another stream of interpretation of Adorno's *Bilderverbot* is closely related to the understanding of his work as a negative theology. An important articulation of this view is developed by Hent de Vries. De Vries argues that the philosophy of Adorno unveils the 'other of reason' that is hidden in, but remains integral to, modern rationality. He suggests that such a 'trace' of the absolute, which he equates with what Adorno calls the 'non-identical', inhabits reason as a 'stowaway'.[41] This trace serves as a 'placeholder' for an emphatic sense of rationality, and it implies a 'minimal theology'. Such a 'minimal theology' refers to 'an interpretive concern with the other . . . for which the religious tradition and its intellectual archives still offer the most promising concepts, arguments, rhetorical figures'. De Vries quotes the following statement by Adorno in support of this interpretation: 'Seen from the point of view of science and scholarship (*Wissenschaft*), an element of the irrational enters, as a moment, into philosophical rationality itself'.[42]

The limitation of this reading of Adorno is the manner in which de Vries' terminology and emphasis suggest a positivity to this notion of the 'trace'. He helpfully links Adorno's references to an inverse theology with an emphatic concept of reason, but when he argues that Adorno's prohibition of images is intended to 'guarantee respect for the fragile other of reason', there is a sense in which the *Bilderverbot* is being employed in the service of some positive object that is waiting to be acknowledged.[43] Such an emphasis gives the sense that some concrete 'other of reason' is being neglected by philosophy, and Adorno is now seeking to raise it to prominence. This problem emerges, even though de Vries helpfully describes Adorno's concern as resembling a 'para-doxical endeavour to circle around natural history's "secret" in as rational a way as possible'.[44] But the meaning of this position is subsequently equated with Derrida's statement that 'the "theo-logical" is a determined moment in the total movement of the trace'.[45] The concept of 'the trace' is employed here as if it is in possession of a positive property. The 'trace' has a lingering presence; it can be experienced; and it represents 'ab–solute difference'.[46]

Given the close association between possibility and theology in Adorno's thought, the nuance and tone of this interpretation is problematic. Adorno's concept of possibility is not a 'trace'. It is not some positive reality, absent energy, or constrained pressure waiting to be released or disclosed; nor is it absolute difference. Rather, Adorno's emphasis is on a negative critique of existing life, motivated by a concern for utopian potentialities for existence. It does not involve grasping a positive but absent reality, nor does this potentiality have the power to draw thought or experience to itself. The impulse towards possibility is a negative one. What thought might discern to be missing has no concrete form or content; it is only a negative mirror image of what presently is, but ought not to be. A negative criticism of existing 'damaged life' briefly illuminates a glimpse of the possibility that life could be otherwise, but only in a momentary flash of insight. Adorno consistently emphasizes that this glimpse is brief, and that 'the non-identical is not to be obtained directly, as something positive on its part, nor is it attainable by a negation of the negative'.[47] The concept of the 'trace' has the connotation of a spectre lurking beneath the surface of experience, pushing and prodding thought for attention. In de Vries' rendering, it begins to take on an agency of its own, which places it in considerable contrast to Adorno's negative stance. Rather than a focus on thought seeking to transcend its present limitations, de Vries reverses the movement into a vertical momentum: the philosopher perceives a 'trace of the transcendent'.[48]

This subtle nuance in de Vries' book pushes against his own intentions. He states at the outset of the volume that 'The other is not to be had or captured'.[49] This is indeed that case, for there can be no static actuality to the 'non-identical' or 'absolute difference' in Adorno's conception. The 'non-identical' cannot be identical with itself. For Adorno, 'non-identity' is a dialectical and relational concept. It refers to the recognition that subject and object do not resemble each other. They cannot be exchanged without remainder. Thus, they are non-identical. In de Vries' rendering, however, this relational dynamic is diminished by equating non-identity with a 'trace'. The concept becomes undialectical. The trace retains a 'relation without relation'.[50] De Vries rejects dialectics for reducing the absolute to its conceptual representation. Thus, despite the prior disclaimer against capturing the absolutely other, by uncoupling Adorno's concepts of the non-identical and the other from his critique of particular historical manifestations of social experience, de Vries' notion of the trace becomes abstract. His interpretation of Adorno's remarks on theology becomes detached from the latter's concern with a critique of historical suffering, and for a utopian impulse toward a changed society. This is perhaps due to the fact that de Vries faults Adorno for the way in which 'motifs of utopian redemption seem to hold sway' over his work, rather than an exploration of a trace of the transcendent.[51] The subsequent analysis of Adorno's concept of an 'inverse theology' will demonstrate that these very 'motifs' of redemption are crucial to his entire project.

## An 'Inverse Theology'

Given the emphasis that Adorno places on the *Bilderverbot*, it may still remain unclear why he would concern himself with other theological concepts like redemption or the messianic. Why would he continue to use the term in his writing? The explanation for this question does not lie in his understanding of philosophy or reason (i.e. due to some essential 'lack' in knowledge or some pressing 'trace' of the non-rational), but is due to his elucidation of the present conditions in human society:

> Once upon a time the image ban extended to pronouncing the name; now the ban itself has in that form come to evoke suspicions of superstition. The ban has been exacerbated: the mere thought of hope is a transgression against it, an act of working against it.[52]

In bourgeois European society, and subsequently in the aggressive capitalist environment of the postwar era, Adorno argues that the *Bilderverbot* was being adapted and deployed by motivations very different from his own. As society was increasingly becoming subject to the narrow confines of instrumental rationality, the ban on divine images had been rendered ideological. *Bilderverbot* has been extended and exacerbated to such an extent that, not only is the name of God prohibited, but also concepts like justice, freedom, equality, and solidarity. The ban is no longer defending thought against the prejudices of identity thinking; rather, its purpose has been reversed: it has become an instrument of the *status quo*. The *Bilderverbot* now functions to shut out possibility from actuality; it stifles metaphysical experience and dismisses any discourse which evokes a hope for a transformed world as a 'crypto-theology'. Although the critique of myth, theology, and tradition served an emancipatory role during the Enlightenment era, in the instrumentalized society of the contemporary age, such 'demythologization devours itself'. The radicality of the secular 'recoils into the mythus; for the mythus is nothing else than the closed system of immanence, of that which is'.[53]

With such an understanding, it is now possible to grasp what Adorno means by an 'inverse theology'.[54] He presents the basic articulation of his understanding in a letter to Walter Benjamin on 17 December 1934. He writes:

> it seems to me doubly important that the image of theo-
> logy, into which I would gladly see our thoughts dissolve,
> is none other than the very one which sustains your
> thought here – it could indeed be called an 'inverse'
> theology. This position, directed against natural and
> supernatural interpretation alike . . . strikes me as utterly
> identical with my own.[55]

What his reference to an 'inverse theology' implies is not immediately self-evident. The most direct indicators in this statement are in the negative mode. An inverse theology is neither a 'natural' or a 'supernatural' elucidation of reality. It is clear that a *natural* interpretation would resemble the positivism Adorno challenged during his dispute with Karl Popper: a focus on this-world causation, developed on the basis of empirical facts and measurable outcomes. A *supernatural* interpretation would be one founded on extra-historical causation of events, and which involved the sacrifice of reason, or of some 'leap' or 'decision' that withdraws thought from human history. As Chapters 2 and 3 have demonstrated, Adorno considers both such stances to be forms of identity thinking, and so he argues that an 'inverse theology' can be neither of these options.

## Adorno and Benjamin on Kafka

In Adorno's letter to Benjamin, the specific matter under discussion is an essay the latter had written on Franz Kafka. Benjamin views Kafka's work as 'prophetic'. Although Kafka's stories often focus on striking 'oddities of life', everything 'he describes makes statements about something other than itself'.[56] To Benjamin, this prose reminds him of the Jewish *Haggadah*: the text which sets out the Passover Seder, and emphasizes fulfilling the biblical commandment to pass on to children the Exodus story of the liberation of the Jewish people from slavery in Egypt. The consistency and clarity of this form of truth, Benjamin writes, has now been lost, and Kafka demonstrates this 'sickness of tradition'. His *Haggadah* does not 'modestly lie at the feet of doctrine', but at the same time, his tales are like 'parables' that point beyond themselves.[57] Though the world of Kafka's narratives is bleak and bizarre, 'his stories are pregnant with a moral to which they never give birth'.[58] In Benjamin's view, no other writer has been more faithful to the *Bilderverbot*.[59]

Susan Buck-Morss has demonstrated the extent to which Adorno's position is influenced by Walter Benjamin, who 'approached profane objects with a religious reverence', and whose work emphasizes mystical concepts found in literature and art, rather than in theological texts.[60] This is clearly evident in Adorno's response to Benjamin's interpretation of Kafka. He echoes the tone of Benjamin's reading, suggesting that Kafka 'represents a photograph of our earthly life from the perspective of a redeemed one, one which merely reveals the latter as the edge of black cloth'.[61] By presenting troubling stories of humans who have turned into insects ('Metamorphosis'), or who inhabit surreal nightmarish worlds ('The Trial'), Kafka both articulates the dehumanizing aspects of present social existence, and protests against them. This is the crucial element of his stories, Adorno argues, when 'men become aware that they are not themselves – that they themselves are things'.[62]

To understand Adorno's perspective, it is useful to note that he is carefully seeking to resist certain directions in materialist politics and interpretations of Kafka's writing. In his letters to Benjamin, Adorno urges his friend to remain tied to the 'theological content' in his reading of Kafka, in order to steer clear of any resemblance to Bertolt Brecht.[63] Adorno was concerned that Benjamin might eventually be persuaded by the charismatic and influential playwright to adopt an approach to art and literature that sought to reduce them to immediate political statements and utility. Contrary to Brecht, Adorno did not believe that cultural forms – even plays motivated by Marxian ideals – could be treated as if they were free of dominating forms of thinking. An 'inverse theology', then, is invoked by Adorno as something that resists a 'Brechtian atheism', which dismisses traditional religion while imagining that it can then develop a 'committed art' to communicate political truth to the masses.[64] Besides neglecting the ideological nature of all forms of culture, Brecht's perspective, relies on a abstract and false theory of the proletariat, which serves as a *deus ex machina* to deliver redemption to society.[65]

Adorno also presents his concept of an 'inverse theology' as being distinct from existentialist interpretations of Kafka's work. That approach emphasizes the 'Sisyphean labours' of Kafka and his characters, as if to say that 'man had lost the possibility of salvation or that the way to the absolute was barred, that man's life is dark, confused, or . . . "suspended in nothingness"'.[66] Such an interpretation mistakenly turns Kafka's writing into realistic symbolism for the world as it truly is, and suggests that readers are pressed into accepting their own agency through a decision to act. In Adorno's view, Kafka's stories do not strive for symbolism, but allegory. They communicate 'not through expression but by repudiation, by breaking off. It is a parabolic system, the key to which has been stolen'. What Kafka's work illuminates is not the existential reality of existence, but 'the obscurity of the existent'.

One of the principal elements Adorno appreciates about Benjamin's early work is his concept of allegory. In *The Origin of German Tragic Drama*, Benjamin suggests that the role of allegory in these theatre plays was not to arbitrarily represent some idea it was seeking to communicate; rather, the allegory was an expression of the material foundations of the idea. It is not an 'illustrative technique', nor is it a 'plastic' symbol which would be destroyed and vanish when some *deus ex machina* resolves the drama's dilemma. By contrast, in allegory the observer confronts 'a petrified, primordial landscape'.[67] Allegory reveals history in the form of ruins. It suggests that, beneath the 'second nature' of reality as it presents itself, 'first nature' is suffering. Allegory, therefore, interrupts the way in which material existence has taken on the appearance of a mythological permanence. In allegory, the relationship between signified and signifier is arbitrary, and Benjamin is interested in showing how the manner in which the two have come together is a product of the historical environment.

Such is the approach Adorno develops in his reading of Kafka, and it is one that he thinks liberates that latter 'from the shackles of an existentialist theology and free[s] him for a different theology'.[68] This inverse theology understands Kafka's stories, not as scripture, but as a 'relic' or 'prolegomenon of scripture'.[69] What is meant by this can be explained by referring to Benjamin's reading of 'Sancho Panza'. Benjamin suggests that, for Kafka's characters, study is the gate to justice. But in the context of modern life, he did not imagine that this meant remaining close to an authentic tradition, like the study of Torah. Rather, Kafka's characters 'have lost their house of prayer; his students are pupils who have lost their Holy Writ'.[70] An inverse theology is thus a way of approaching social existence that does not reduce it to what is immediately obvious or measurable; nor does it identify hidden signs or symbols within society that point to an absolute truth hidden within it. An inverse theology is attuned to the suffering and incompleteness of what lies before it. It is alert to the reality of a hidden possibility, of an unknown truth, of the incompleteness of understanding, but it cannot articulate what these are fully or clearly. There is no way to access these elusive things in an unmediated fashion. An inverse theology has no revelatory scripture; it is merely aware of its need for one, and feels the pain of its absence.

For example, Benjamin describes the manner in which Kafka employs figures that are distorted in some way (e.g. in 'Metamorphosis', Gregor becomes an insect; other stories present a half-lamb/half-sheep, even the recurring habit of men who constantly sit with their heads bowed to their chests). He argues that these distortions signify unknown guilt, 'being loaded down', and particularly the act of forgetting. The prototype of these figures, he continues, is the figure of the hunchback. He refers to a folksong called 'The Little Hunchback, which ends with the following lines:

> When I kneel upon my stool
> And I want to pray,
> A hunchbacked man is in the room
> And he starts to say:
> My dear child, I beg of you,
> Pray for the little hunchback too.

Benjamin suggests that this image captures the function of distorted forms in Kafka's writing, and what they accomplish: 'In his depth, Kafka touches the ground which neither "mythical divination" nor "existential theology" supplied him with'. He demonstrates that he possesses 'the natural prayer of the soul: attentiveness'.[71]

In a letter to Benjamin, Adorno expresses a great enthusiasm for this definition of attentiveness as 'a historical figure of prayer'.[72] It echoes Adorno's understanding of the preponderance of the object and of 'metaphysical experience' and connects both with theology. The distortions in Kafka's writing represent, to Adorno, the weight of objectivity that hangs over the subject. Given that, for Adorno, all reification results from the act of forgetting,[73] being 'attentive' to one's own distortion, and to how one distorts the object – by probing 'the wounds which this order has and which above all, it inflicts on each of us'[74] – serves the cause of freedom for both the subject and object: 'If thought really yielded to the object, if its attention were on the object, not on its category, the very objects would start talking under the lingering eye'.[75] The subject's attentiveness to the 'hunchback' of the other permits the possibility that it might 'make up for what it has done to non-identity'.[76]

## Inverting Feuerbach, Beyond Marx

A consideration of what it means to 'invert' a concept will allow this discussion to progress beyond the interpretation of Kafka that Adorno employs to describe his approach to theology. In the nineteenth century, Ludwig Feuerbach argued that theology is effectively anthropology. He suggested that the attributes described of God by Christian theology actually represent the highest potential of human beings, which they have projected away from themselves and onto the idea of a divine being. Feuerbach argues that theology thus 'inverts' the relationship between the subject of religion and its predicate. The divine is an abstraction of human thought, which alienates human beings from themselves. Feuerbach sought to correct this projection and restore to humanity an understanding of its proper 'essence'.[77] The relationship between humanity and God was thus 'inverted'.

Karl Marx adopted Feuerbach's criticism of religion and pushed it still further. He agreed that theology was an 'inverted world consciousness', which alienated human beings from themselves.[78] He rejected, however, Feuerbach's idea that a concept of human 'essence' could be rediscovered upon escaping the delusion of religious projection. Contrary to Feuerbach, Marx argues that human nature is shaped by social relations, and is the product of history and material conditions. Furthermore, Marx suggests that Feuerbach fails to appreciate that religion is a social product. The latter neglects the fact, for example, that once it is recognized that 'the earthly family is discovered to be the secret of the holy family, the former must then itself be criticized in theory and revolutionized in practice'.[79] Having unmasked the human self-alienation that he considered theology to be, Marx suggests that the task of critical thought is subsequently to focus directly on history and politics, and to shift from 'the other world of truth' to the 'truth of this world'.[80] Such is the perspective that leads to his declaration: 'the *criticism of religion* has been largely completed; and the criticism of religion is the premise of all criticism'.[81]

Adorno is sympathetic with Marx, but this is not what he means by an 'inverse theology'. As observed in Chapter 1, Adorno agrees that the criticism of religion is the premise of all criticism, but as he observed the preponderance of dogmatism within the social movements of his age, and as he witnessed the decline of emancipatory utopianism in the face of the growing dominance of pragmatic science, he became convinced that Marx had been incorrect to conclude that the criticism of religion was complete. Since capitalism and one's relationships to the means of production were the origins of mystification and commodity fetishism, then religion *as such* is not the cause of superstition or false consciousness. Marx himself would grant this point, but Adorno was dismayed over the extent to which *Marxist* 'scientific socialism' began to resemble the same crude loyalty to empirical facts that was found within scientific positivism, and he could not accept that the criticism of religion could come to a successful end in some sort of 'Brechtian atheism'. Thus, whereas Feuerbach sought to invert Hegel's philosophy, and Marx worked to complete this development, Adorno intends a subtle inversion of Marx.[82] Marx thought his inversion had moved philosophy from the other world of truth to the truth of this world, but Adorno laments that this truth of the world remains elusive. Philosophy has failed to 'realize itself', and so he argues it must go beyond Marx, though certainly still in solidarity with Marxian thought, and 'ruthlessly criticize itself'.[83]

This inverse of Marx is 'theological' because it calls into question the subject, who was the ground of Marx's philosophy, and emphasizes a renewed attention to the elusiveness of the object of thought. This perspective is not based on the claim to be able to grasp concrete materiality better than Marx; rather, it seeks to view the incompleteness and suffering of society from the perspective of a utopian vision. Adorno accomplishes this by calling on theological concepts. Feuerbach had argued that theology had mistakenly projected the attributes of the subject onto the object, and so inverted the relationship. Marx deepened this inversion to focus attention on how the subject was shaped by its environment, but he imagined that the subject could then be in control of itself and these surroundings. Adorno argues that the presumptuousness of this priority of the subject has to be interrupted by a new inversion, which radicalizes Marx's important attention to the influence of the social environment on the subject, while at the same time demonstrating that the revolutionary subject is also other to itself. Marx's materialism had sought to grasp the thing-in-itself in its entirety, but Adorno suggests that 'it is only in the absence of images that the full object could be conceived . . . At its most materialistic, materialism comes to agree with theology'.[84] This position intends to avoid a philosophy which merely composes a new form of identity thinking, and encourages attention to the residue left repressed, hidden, or ignored by such dominating forms of thought.

An 'inverse theology' is not a negation of Marx's criticism of religion, which would imply a return to positive religion: 'to negate a negation does not bring about its reversal; it proves, rather, that the negation was not negative enough'.[85] Adorno is not seeking to diminish Marx's materialism or his focus on social analysis. His inverse theology remains primarily a critical analysis of historical existence, only, rather than being grounded in an independent subject (who is actually shaped by the 'damaged life' around and within it), it is developed from a perspective located beyond the immediate. This standpoint allows the fallenness of the world to come into sharper focus, and encourages attention to as yet unrealized potentialities. Such is the meaning behind this statement from *Minima Moralia:*

> The only philosophy which can responsibly be practiced in the face of despair is the attempt to contemplate all things as they would present themselves from the standpoint of redemption. Knowledge has no light but that shed on the world by redemption, all else is reconstruction, mere technique. Perspectives must be fashioned that displace and estrange the world, reveal it to be, with its rifts and crevices, as indigent and distorted as it will appear one day in the messianic light.[86]

Adorno considers this standpoint to be necessary because thought depends on the possibility that subject and object can be reconciled if it is to be anything more than merely the identity thinking of system-building, or the repetition of the language games from one's local context. Thus, Adorno appreciates the manner in which theology, like metaphysics, seeks to rise above immanence. In fact, he considers a defence of this element of theology to be as important as a defence of such an aim in philosophy, for, in a cultural environment dominated by instrumentality, metaphysical concerns suffer from the same abuse and dismissal as is the case for theology.[87] The fate of both theology and philosophy are tied together, since it is the very concept of a truth beyond the *status quo* which is at stake.

As Adorno conceives of it, theology seeks to discover and articulate a coherent and meaningful world. This aim, once freed from the boundaries of religious tradition, migrated into philosophy in the form of a rational system. Although Adorno clearly considers such a project to be a problematic form of identity thinking, he appreciates how the 'idea that phenomena are objectively interconnected' lingers in this form of thought. Just as a creator God was conceived as being intimately linked to its Creation, all components of a philosophical system were structured in logical connection to each other. Negative dialectics seeks to maintain this attention to interconnection in an environment that prefers to ignore how the social totality shapes experience and thought. Adorno does not imagine that his philosophy can recapture a systematic grasp of totality, but he does argue that thought should continue to be motivated by this quest for understanding. In his view, a form of thinking that is alert to the dangers of identity thinking, and is attentive to the preponderance of the object, might 'aspire to be authoritative without system', and thus might let 'itself be guided by the resistance it encounters'. Rather than force reality to conform to its system, such a philosophy explores 'the coercion that material reality exercises over the thought'.[88] This is the inversion of the impulse of the system, which encourages attention to, and criticism of, particular details of reality. Such an analysis of individual phenomena harnesses and liberates the power formerly celebrated about philosophical systems, for it enables such objects, now recognized as 'non-identical with their own concepts as they are, to become more than themselves'.[89]

## Positive Religion and Judaism

Although Adorno establishes a connection between metaphysics and theology, he also identifies a key difference between them. Whereas metaphysics is developed on the basis of reason, theology is founded on revelation. The complexity of Adorno's understanding of an 'inverse theology' is due to the fact that it does not involve a preference for a non-historical source of knowledge in the form of divine revelation over the processes of human reasoning. It is thus inaccurate to describe his work as being a positive or negative theology. His emphasis on reason sets his work apart from other Jewish thinkers based in Frankfurt at the same time of his writing, including Gershom Scholem. Scholem considered the concept of the messianic to be particularly compelling, given its emphasis on the apocalyptic interruption of human history. In his influential study, *The Messianic Idea in Judaism*, he argues that 'Jewish Messianism is in its origins and by its nature . . . a theory of catastrophe'.[90] It calls into question every historical moment. The redemption brought about by the messianic age is not the product of previous history or human achievement; rather it is 'transcendence breaking in upon history, an intrusion in which history itself perishes'. This is precisely that part of Judaism which 'rational religion' had marginalized, as the modern age had sought to remove the 'apocalyptic thorn'.[91]

This apocalyptic emphasis on 'catastrophe' was picked up by Benjamin. In his 'Theses on the Philosophy of History', an angel is described as looking back at the world and seeing only 'one single catastrophe which keeps piling wreckage upon wreckage and hurls it in front of his feet'. This image challenges any faith in human progress, and any theodicy which suggests that present sufferings serve some purpose. The task of the historical materialist, Benjamin continues, 'is to brush history against the grain'.[92]

There is much in this vision that resonates with Adorno's work, and it recalls emphases found in his interpretation of Kafka. But Adorno is increasingly concerned that his friend's reading of history, and his conception of theology, are becoming apocalyptic in the sense of implying that redemption could only arrive from a source beyond history. This was also how he viewed Scholem's position. While Adorno applauds Benjamin's 'intention to mobilize the power of theological experience anonymously within the realm of the profane', he warns against incorporating 'explosions' of Jewish mysticism which might 'sink the whole ship' of materialism.[93] Although Benjamin's work by no means involves a return to the orthodox Jewish tradition, an over-emphasis on apocalyptic, Adorno suggests, threatens to make his thought undialectical.[94]

## Constellation and Revelation: Adorno and Barth

Adorno's reservations about theology were particularly directed against the 'theology of crisis' movement which emerged in Christian thought in the inter-war period. A principal figure in this development was the Swiss theologian Karl Barth. Barth was troubled by the support his liberal professors publicly gave to the German declaration of war in 1914. In a letter to a friend, he lamented, 'The unconditional truths of the Gospel are simply suspended for the time being and in the meantime a German war-theology is put to work, its Christian trimmings consisting of a lot of talk of sacrifice and the like . . . it is truly sad'.[95] Barth became convinced that liberal theology, which sought to translate Christian beliefs into modern terms, and accepted the authority of science and historical research, had shown itself to be corrupt. His criticism of what he viewed to be a Christian church that had been culturally assimilated by its environment drew heavily from the thought of Søren Kierkegaard. Like Kierkegaard, Barth characterizes Hegel's work as amounting to a 'philosophy of self-confidence' in which the 'self-movement of truth is identical with the self-movement of the thinking human subject'. As such, Hegel's God 'is actually the living man', before 'whom real man would stand before as before an idol'.[96]

There are a number of intriguing parallels here with concerns found in Adorno's work. Ralf Frisch suggests that there is a substantial overlap between the critique of modernity developed by both Adorno and Barth.[97] Barth is concerned with the interweaving of religion and ideology, the expanding influence of natural science over social norms and values, as well as the limits of Hegel's treatment of subjectivity. He argues that Feuerbach's philosophy is the inevitable outcome of any theology that begins with human subjectivity. Barth is thus convinced that faith ought not to be understood as the development of beliefs based upon external facts observed within history. Rather, his theology emphasizes trust and confidence in the God who reveals Godself to human beings.[98]

In *Epistle to the Romans*, Barth argues that the Christian Gospel confronts human society with a crisis, interrupting its assumptions about itself and calling it into question. He distinguishes between 'religion' and God's divine Word to establish a sharp contrast between human culture and divine transcendence. Religion, he argues, is a creation of human beings. It is not in itself holy or sacred, but is limited by human ambitions and biases; 'above all the occurrences of human life there hangs a smoke-screen or religion, sometimes heavy, sometimes light'.[99] His criticism of religion's ideological potential is as scathing as that of Marx: 'Religion . . . acts . . . like a drug which has been extremely skilfully administered. Instead of counteracting human illusions, it does no more than introduce an alternative condition of pleasurable emotion'.[100]

Like Adorno, Barth's argumentation proceeds in a dialectical fashion, and so in his criticism of religion, he does not imagine that the problem he identifies is easily avoided: 'We do not escape from sin by removing ourselves from religion and taking up with some other superior thing – if indeed that were possible'. Similar to Adorno's recognition that thought cannot think without concepts, Barth argues that theology cannot exist without historical religion in its pursuit of the divine. This is part of the crisis in which he thinks human beings find themselves: 'The veritable KRISIS under which religion stands consists first in the impossibility of escape from it *as long as* a man liveth.'[101] What Barth intends to make clear is humanity's complete dependence upon God for knowledge of truth, justice, and similar ideals. Everything else is human folly. One cannot achieve knowledge of God through philosophy, science, historical evidence, or reason. Instead, God must reveal Godself to human beings. And so he writes, 'religion must die. In God we are rid of it'.[102]

There is a clear distinction between Adorno's conception of 'inverse theology' and Barth's theology of crisis. Although Barth's criticism of his age has some resemblance with that of Adorno, and despite the fact that the 'crisis' Barth identifies resonates to some degree with Benjamin's sense of 'catastrophe', Adorno is not prepared to resolve this dilemma by identifying a positive way out of it. In Barth's theology, the reality of a divine wholly other is affirmed; a God who acts, intervenes, and interrupts corrupt human society. This Adorno denies. In an essay on Kafka, he contrasts his interpretation of the author with that of the dialectical theology of Kierkegaard and Barth. In Kafka's stories, 'ambiguity and obscurity are attributed not exclusively to the Other as such but to human beings and to the conditions in which they live'.[103] Thus, although 'Karl Barth . . . detected the fateful intertwinement of metaphysics and culture with that against which they abstractly protested', he then denies himself the fruits of his insights by remaining 'trapped in a subjective position'. After recognizing the self-deception of culture and the decay of metaphysics, rather than probing the contradictions within society that this illuminates, Adorno argues that Barth escapes from history by invoking a mythological form of the absolutely other God:

> What can be said about this concept of the absolutely other is that either it remains entirely indeterminate and abstract, so that it cannot perform what it is supposed to perform; or it takes on determinants which are themselves subject to the criticisms of these theologians, since they are determinants of immanence; or, finally . . . this content is summoned up from outside, in a dogmatic and arbitrary leap, so that the dialectic which forms the core of this theological standpoint is at the same time revoked by it.[104]

One cannot, Adorno insists, simply return to the traditional words and structures of theology in contemporary society. Doing so can only be accomplished by means of a leap outside of history. Or, more precisely, a confident shift of attention to a divine agent serves to distract critical thought from penetrating further into the contradictions of present life. Adorno rejected such a move in his criticisms of Kierkegaard's philosophy, arguing that the 'leap of faith' abandoned the mediations of dialectics, and thus reduced thought to 'simple creaturely immediacy'.[105] In a review of Adorno's Kierkegaard book, Benjamin suggests that Barth's theology tries to withdraw behind Kierkegaard's existentialism, and return to the 'enchanted circle' of idealism. Adorno's philosophy, by contrast, takes Kierkegaard's critique of idealism 'forward'. Rather than turning back to the resolution of theological dogma, it probes deeper into the paradox of social existence.[106] For Adorno, the essential problem with positive revelation is that it relieves the pressure on human thought and action. Human subjects must abandon themselves to a fate determined by an outside force, which in his view is an ideology no structurally different from positivism's assertion that scientific knowledge describes the world as it fundamentally is. Leaving the *status quo* to run its own course, Kierkegaard's philosophy 'develops the cult of sacrifice with such tenacity that it finally becomes a gnosis'.[107]

Adorno's inverse theology, then, does not rest upon a revelation of hidden truth beyond the world. It does not assume that the critical theorist has some inner access to truth that can be subtly accessed with the proper attitudinal attention. The closest Adorno comes to describing a correlative to Barthian revelation is the concept of the 'constellation'. Although philosophy must renounce its ambition to grasp the 'totality' of identity thinking, and likewise theology must accept the loss of positive dogmatic content, this does not leave an 'inverse theology' helpless before the 'factual' immediacy of the world. The task of critical thought, 'does not meet up with a fixed meaning which already lies behind the question [it asks], but lights it up suddenly and momentarily, and consumes it at the same time'.[108] There is, then, an appreciation for sudden insight in Adorno's writing, and it is not simply the product of a specific method or technique. One might, therefore, see some structural similarity in this view with that of Barth's view of a revelation which interrupts and challenges the presumptions and prejudices of human knowledge. While the insights that erupt from Adorno's constellations are 'momentary', might the same be said of Barth's descriptions of the 'Word of God'?

The difference is that, for Adorno, any insights his inverse theology achieves cannot serve as a new foundation for knowledge; no system can be constructed upon them; no hidden agent guarantees their arrival. Furthermore, no 'scripture' is able to either house such revelation or even serve as the place of its arrival. After issuing his rejection of liberal theology, Barth constructs a sophisticated systematic theology, employing traditional Christian concepts. Adorno's constellation, by contrast, is merely a 'changing trial combination' or grouping of differing cultural elements and experiences, which, when assembled together, might serve as the occasion to briefly achieve a moment of insight.[109] Bringing together seemingly different phenomena, however, may illuminate how one or more of them are shaped by the social totality, while simultaneously giving a flash of 'the "more" which the concept is equally desirous and capable of being'. Benjamin describes the constellation in the following manner:

> The idea is best explained as the representation of the
> context in which the unique and extreme stands alongside
> its counterpart. It is therefore erroneous to understand the
> most general references which language makes as concepts,
> instead of recognizing them as ideas . . . Just as a mother is

seen to begin to live in the fullness of her power only
when the circle of her children, inspired by the feeling of
her proximity, closes around her, so do ideas come to life
only when extremes are assembled around them . . . [Ideas]
remain obscure so long as phenomena do not declare their
faith to them and gather round them.[110]

The task of a constellation in thought is to gather phenomena
together so that the relationships between them might be noticed,
or some unrecognized process be suddenly exposed: 'As a constellation, theoretical thought circles the concept it would like
to unseal, hoping it may fly open like the lock of a well-guarded
safe-deposit box: in response, not to a single key or a single number,
but to a combination of numbers'.[111] Because concepts are
incomplete, exploring them through the contrasts that emerge
out of a constellation might help expose the contradictions and
non-identity within them.

This understanding of a constellation lies at the heart of Adorno's
understanding of his work as an 'inverse theology'. Guided by
a stubborn commitment to the *Bilderverbot*, his position is concerned to challenge identity thinking and the domination of the
object by the thinking subject. Neither a positive nor a negative
theology, an inverse theology maintains a negative and dialectical
analysis of the contradictions within social existence. With an
almost prayerful attention to the particularity of phenomena in
the world, Adorno's work seeks to illuminate concealed possibility
and non-identity, and to prevent finite human thought from
grasping onto some seemingly obvious or self-evident facts, and
building an ideology upon them.

While Barth criticizes the human tendency to instrumentalize
subjective ideas about God and thereby turn religion into ideology, his proposed antidote to the problem is to emphasize the
content of positive revelation, in order to urge human attention
and thought to the transcendence of the 'Wholly Other' God.
Adorno's critique of religion directs him in the opposite direction. He denies positive revelation, and directs human attention
to the scrutiny of historical reality. For it is only by immersing
oneself in the immanence of present existence that he thinks a

negative image of that which surpasses immanence might be momentarily perceived.

Having established an understanding of why Adorno refers to his work as an inverse theology, and what this implies, some additional pressing matters can now be addressed. What are the implications of this perspective for political action? How might it give shape to the academic study of religion in social life? What more, if anything, is there to say of theological traditions, and the communities from which such discourse emerges? It is to such matters that subsequent chapters now turn.

# Chapter 5

# Politics, Liberation and the Messianic

*In my view, the difference between the 'idealists' among the fascists and Marcuse is almost negligible.*

Karl Popper[1]

*Materialism comes to be the very relapse into barbarism which it was supposed to prevent. To work against this is not the most irrelevant among the tasks of critical theory . . . once the revolution has suffered the same fate as the Second Coming . . .*

Adorno[2]

At the core of the ethical impulse behind Adorno's critical social theory is Marx's eleventh thesis on Feuerbach: 'the philosophers have only *interpreted* the world, in various ways; the point, however, is to *change* it'.[3] This concern was clearly evident in the description of the Institute for Social Research in earlier chapters of this book. Horkheimer captures this vision with his insistence that the truth of society 'must be decided not in supposedly neutral reflection but in personal thought and action, in concrete historical activity'.[4] Adorno's commitment to a new categorical imperative, 'to arrange . . . thoughts and actions so that Auschwitz will not repeat itself, so that nothing similar will happen', is also a call to engaged action.[5] A central component of the Frankfurt School's programme is the Marxian emphasis on *praxis*, a unity of theory and practice focused on supporting concrete activity aimed at changing the world for the better. Or, at least, this is frequently how Adorno's position is understood. The matter is rather more complicated than this.

This chapter explores the implications of Adorno's inverse theology for conceiving political action. It begins with a recollection of a controversy that erupted in the 1960s between Adorno and the German student movement, which resulted in denunciations against him for a perceived political 'resignation'. This leads to consideration of Adorno's view of the relationship between theory and practice, which is then contrasted with a form of Christian theology that is often associated with the Frankfurt School: Latin American Liberation Theology. An immanent critique of the thought of Gustavo Gutierrez and Juan Luis Segundo will illuminate contradictions in their attempt to bring Christian theology and sociology together, which raises the question of the extent to which liberation theology implies the dissolution of theology entirely. The manner by which Adorno's thought takes up this question will then be explored through consideration of his use of the concept of messianism. His interpretation of this element of Jewish tradition is explored in relation to the treatment of the same by Giorgio Agamben, who faults Adorno for being overly dialectical. This challenge to Adorno's understanding of the messianic involves a return to a debate over the legacy of Walter Benjamin's writing. The resulting analysis demonstrates that Adorno's inverse political theology constantly refuses to abandon the mode of negative critique in favour of a positive affirmation of any particular agenda.

## Adorno and the Political

It is perhaps not surprising that Adorno's philosophy is frequently criticized for its political implications. As Espen Hammer observes, 'Adorno's work seems to resist every effort to categorize and define it'.[6] What is striking, however, is the extent to which Adorno is accused of very different and contradictory failings. As the opening quotation above demonstrates, Karl Popper argued that he and the other Frankfurt School theorists sanctioned anarchic violence by challenging the value-freedom of social science and calling for the transformation of society. On the other side of the spectrum, Adorno's reluctance to adopt clear positions on the political controversies of his age led many on the Left to accuse him of being apolitical or politically resigned to the *status quo*. Perhaps the most well-known denunciation of this sort was penned by Georg Lukács, who berated Adorno for having 'taken up residence in the "Grand Hotel Abyss . . . a beautiful hotel, equipped with every comfort, on the edge of an abyss, of nothing-ness, of absurdity"".[7]

Such accusations resonate with the charge that Adorno's philosophy retreats into a pessimistic negative theology. This suggests that the nature of his inverse theology stands at the heart of debates over the legacy of his thought as a whole. The political philosopher Leo Strauss has argued that the 'theologico–political problem' – or the question of the relationship between reason, revelation, and political authority – is the key issue for political philosophy. In his own reflection on the problem, Strauss concluded that,

> The genuine refutation of orthodoxy would require the proof that the world and human life are perfectly intelligible without the assumption of a mysterious god; it would require at least the success of the philosophic system: man has to show himself theoretically and practically as the master of his human life.[8]

In the face of the Holocaust and other catastrophes of the twentieth century, Adorno is no longer prepared to assume the success of the philosophic system, nor imagine that human beings are the masters of their lives. Although he is by no means concerned with religious 'orthodoxy' in the sense Strauss mentions, he has also lost confidence in many of modernity's traditional ideals, including any faith in the revolutionary potential of mass social movements in the traditional Marxian–communist model. A consideration of his own engagement with such a model of politics in the 1960s will help begin to clarify the nature of his inverse theology and how it relates to contemporary debates over how to conceive of 'political theology'.

## Reason or Revolution? The German Student Movement

In the midst of the turbulence of the 1960s in post–war West Germany, numerous university students who were well versed in critical theory began demanding that theoretical critique be turned into practical political action. Demonstrations and occupations of institutional buildings at the University of Frankfurt became a frequent occurrence. In the midst of these events, tensions began to develop between the student protesters and the critical theorists of the Institute for Social Research themselves. In May of 1964, Adorno initiated legal proceedings against a group for using quotations from his writing on subversive posters.[9] This set off a long series of denunciations against Adorno by student leaders, accusing him of promoting theory for theory's sake, and refraining from any meaningful political activity. In January of 1969, these tensions came to a head when one of Adorno's doctoral students, Hans-Jürgen Krahl, attempted to occupy the sociology department with a group of demonstrators. Finding it locked, they moved instead into the Institute for Social Research. Adorno, in his capacity as co-director of the Institute, called the police and 76 students were arrested. As Krahl was forcefully removed, he screamed abuses at his former mentor.[10] The media responded by publishing photographs of Adorno raising a chair to defend himself against a group of students, along with the following quotation: 'I proposed a theoretical model for thought. How could I suspect that people would want to realize it with Molotov-cocktails?'[11]

In Adorno's later writings, in response to the student movement's protests, he seeks to clarify that social theory's criticism of society, and its insistence upon the need to change unjust social conditions, does not simply imply radical (and violent) political action. In response to being accused of 'resignation' because of such a clarification, Adorno replies, 'the much invoked unity of theory and praxis has the tendency of slipping into the predominance of praxis'. He argues that Marx's demand for the 'ruthless criticism of everything existing' needs to be understood in the context of the same Marx who mocked Bruno Bauer and the young Hegelians for their 'critical critique'.[12] The 'criticism' of such thinkers, Marx argued, transformed itself into a 'transcendent power' by not recognizing the historical conditions in which it operated, while imagining itself above history and society.[13] Adorno also states that Marx's 'Theses on Feuerbach' cannot be understood severed from the historical context in which they were written;

> They take on their meaning only in the context of the expectation of an immanent revolution which existed at that time; without such an expectation they degenerate into mumbo-jumbo. Once this given possibility failed to be realized, Marx spent decades in the British Museum writing a theoretical work on national economy.[14]

Action driven merely by anxiety or rage, Adorno argues, serves only as a 'substitute satisfaction, elevating itself into an end itself'. In an immediate and unreflective form, the demand for practical activity simply remains trapped within the very system of assumptions it intends to overcome:

> If the doors are barricaded, then thought more than ever should not stop short. It should analyse the reasons and subsequently draw the conclusions. It is up to thought not to accept the situation as final. The situation can be changed, if at all, by undiminished thought. The leap into praxis does not cure thought of resignation as long as it is paid for with the secret knowledge that that really isn't the right way to go.[15]

With such a clarification and warning, Adorno's critical social theory acquires a tone not unlike the 'critical rationalism' of Popper. Practical action for activity's sake, or social transformation for change's sake, is meaningless when detached from ongoing critical thought. Furthermore, although at times he criticizes the restriction of social theory to a focus on 'piecemeal social engineering', Adorno later refines this position:

> I think . . . we should be more sparing with the accusation of so-called reformism . . . How one views reform depends in part on how one evaluates the possibility of total structural change, and as this possibility no longer manifests itself with the immediacy it had in the middle of the last

century, the question of reform is also seen in quite a different perspective.[16]

Adorno's reaction to the reception of critical social theory among the more radical leaders of the German student movement serves to defuse some of the incensed rhetoric that the participants in the so-called 'Positivist Dispute' directed against one another. Both feared the extreme implications of the other's position (embodied in the right-wing politics of the Vienna Circle and in extreme elements within the German student movement in the 1960s) and read their opponents in the debate through the lens of these fears. This is not to suggest a simple convergence of their views exists underneath the misunderstandings, but it does highlight the importance of a greater dialogue between these two schools of thought in the effort to develop a more adequate social theory.[17]

## Theory and Practice

Among the criticisms levelled against Adorno by Krahl, is that 'Adorno was incapable of transforming his private compassion toward the "damned of the earth" into an organized partisanship of theory engaged in the liberation of the oppressed'.[18] This accusation brings together many elements of the problems involved in clarifying the relationships between the ethical imperative to reduce human suffering, rational thought, as well as religious tradition. Krahl's statement suggests that there is a distinct separation between one's 'private compassion' and practical activity aimed at 'liberating' the object of this compassion; but he also assumes that it is a simple matter to link the two together.

In Adorno's view, however, there is no immediate and obvious way to bring a theoretical position into an immediate relation with social practice. This was hinted at in the previous chapter, in his resistance to the political theatre of Bertolt Brecht. It was not Brecht's political orientation which concerned Adorno; rather, it was his assertion of the utility and 'political' nature of his committed dramas. What is missed by such an approach is the manner in which all thought and action are mediated by the social totality. Brecht hoped that the shock his plays could produce in his audience would spur them into action. In Adorno's view, however, any immediate demand to decide, to take sides, bears too close a resemblance to 'the Nazi slogan that "only sacrifice makes us free"'.[19] Furthermore, the shock-effect may also neglect the disturbing possibility that images of 'people beaten to the ground with rifle-butts' may actually contain 'the power to elicit enjoyment', so that what was meant to be 'consciousness-raising' is reduced to perverse entertainment.[20]

For Adorno, immediacy in politics is no more progressive than immediacy in thought. Identity thinking meets its practical equivalent in simplistic demands for action. 'Do-it-yourself' political activity might rightly be initiated by anger at an unjust society, but spontaneity is no guarantor that such practice is anything more than vented rage.[21] Such a tendency also frequently thinks in dualistic terms, as if all injustice and suffering is caused by some other outside force, so that the 'pure' activist collective is not complicit in any way. In Adorno's view, this is an error: 'The society that impenetrably confronts people is nonetheless these very people'.[22] The immediacy of political slogans are contained within the social totality, and so critical politics needs to take account of this problem; 'false praxis is no praxis'.[23]

Although he does not intend to diminish the importance of practice, Adorno places a priority on the practical significance of thought. Theory, he insists, 'speaks for what is not narrow-minded'.[24] It is what pushes beyond the boundaries of seemingly unquestionable assumptions and structures. There can thus be no simple dichotomy between theory and practice. An 'act of thought about reality is . . . always a *practical* act'.[25] Running counter to existing trends, reflection begins to uncover alternative possibilities for living and acting. This careful and considered approach to political action is not the product of fear, ivory-tower arrogance, or pessimism. Rather, Adorno is concerned with the capacity of practical activity, as with rational reflection, to sabotage itself. In *Dialectic of Enlightenment*, he demonstrated how instrumental reason can turn against and oppress the rational subject. The same is true of demands to act. Just as rationality is linked to self-preservation, the same is true of action. This, of course, is not problematic in itself, but, given free reign, active self-preservation can become aggressive domination of others. Adorno does not imagine that this implies the need to adopt a passive and quietistic subjectivity, nor does it necessitate disengagement from the struggles of public political life. It does, however, suggest the need to maintain a distanced and rigorous critical analysis of the immediacies and demands of such activity. He writes, 'Through self-preservation the species indeed gains the potential for that self-reflection that could finally *transcend the self-preservation* to which it was reduced by being restricted simply to a means'.[26]

Theory and practice which 'transcends' being reduced to mere self-preservation in this way is achieved through a form of reflection which 'catches its breath'.[27] As Marianne Tettlebaum observes, Adorno is concerned that political activism must limit itself to what is possible in a given moment, rather than on what ought to be.[28] As such, without critical reflection, political activity can only be defined according to the mechanisms of the *status quo*. Perhaps the course of some social activism will achieve a different balance of 'winners' and 'losers', but the rules of the game will have remained the same. The Christian theologian Miroslav Volf makes a similar point in an analysis of the dialectic between justice and oppression. He argues that the 'categories of oppression and liberation provide combat gear . . . they are good for fighting, but not for negotiating or celebrating'.[29] Engaging in politics in such a manner thus remains 'ill-suited to bring about reconciliation and sustain peace between people'. The grand narrative of freedom from oppression threatens to become a mere 'injustice-with-role-reversal'.[30]

This perspective helps explain the concerns that Adorno brings to his remarks on politics, and they illuminate why his approach is negative, as well as interested in an inverse theology. The tone of his negative approach is captured in a lecture on the definition of freedom. Alert to problems such as those Volf raises, Adorno proposes a 'remedy' from his 'medicine chest'. Rather than focus on constructing a systematic theory of freedom, he asks his audience to imagine having their homes invaded by the Gestapo in the early hours of the dawn. In such a situation of impending threat, 'freedom' would mean having the capacity to invoke the right of *habeas corpus* or some similar legal security.[31]

Here one observes the relationship Adorno conceives between theory and practice. The criticism of what ought not to happen or exist is a practical act. It should not be that people can be dragged from their homes without legitimate cause and the protection of legal rights. This impulse is a progressive support for politics and critical philosophy. What it does not provide, however, is a blueprint for a social order. Nor does the negative stance present a clear alternative way of life. A desire for these, though understandable, is what drives identity thinking in Adorno's view. This is why he suggests that critical thought must continue to challenge simplistic calls for political activism.

## Adorno and Liberation Theology

These reflections on the relationship between theory and practice bring Adorno's thought into some tension with a form of Christian theology that his work otherwise resonates with. Latin American Liberation theology seeks to bring together Christian thought and Marxian social theory, in order to oppose ideological thinking and oppressive social structures. A brief examination of two of the leading figures of this movement sheds further light on the nature of Adorno's inverse theology and its relation to politics.

The Peruvian Roman Catholic theologian Gustavo Gutierrez outlines the principal programme of liberation theology in *A Theology of Liberation*. He argues that Marx demonstrated that the human being 'is an agent of history, responsible for his own destiny'. In the secular modern world, which has broken away from 'the tutelage of religion', theology must come to terms with a new understanding of humanity and of its relationship to God.[32] Gutierrez argues that theology is not merely concerned with extra-worldly existence or a form of salvation only to be experienced in heaven; for him 'there is only one human destiny'.[33] If the locus of salvation and of humanity's encounter of God is found in the experience of liberation from oppression within historical action, Gutierrez concludes that the action of Christian communities is not to be derived from theological premises: 'Theology does not produce pastoral activity; rather it reflects upon it'. This implies that the primary concern of liberation theology is human well-being; 'Theology *follows*; it is the second step'.[34]

This emphasis on liberative praxis raises issues that Adorno considers problematic. Gutierrez upholds an ideal of '*orthopraxis*' – or correct practice – which a theology of liberation must focus on in order 'to modify the emphasis, often obsessive, upon the attainment of an orthodoxy which is often nothing more than fidelity to an obsolete tradition or a debatable interpretation'.[35] A primary emphasis of the liberation movement in South America is on being 'converted to the poor' and learning from the marginalized. Since the poor are closest to and most affected by the unjust structures of society, Gutierrez suggests that one can speak of the 'epistemological privilege' of the oppressed.

A perspective informed by Adorno's thought might appreciate how Gutierrez is criticizing the form of identity thinking often found within systematic theology. Yet, this invocation of right-practice, and the corresponding defence of an epistemological privilege of the marginalized, are vulnerable to Adorno's concern with the capacity of the social totality to distort all spheres and activities in society. Gutierrez is seeking to ground a liberative praxis on a solid foundation: the experiences of the poor, which are correlated with certain themes found in Christian theology (the Exodus liberation from Egypt, the love of neighbour taught by Jesus of Nazareth, and the denunciation of poverty and oppression among the Hebrew prophets). An immediacy between theology and practice is on display here, which recalls, at least in its formal arrangement, the style of political engagement that Adorno finds problematic in Brecht.

Juan Luis Segundo is perhaps the liberation theologian whose work seeks to develop the most extensive theoretical articulation of the interdisciplinary task of bringing together theology and Marxian social science. Admitting that those who proclaim themselves to be Christians are found both among the oppressed and the oppressors, and that motives for human behaviour often remain hidden, Segundo argues that theology requires an instrument to help identify how 'ideology has *de facto* infiltrated the edifice of our faith', and to assist in discovering 'a way of deideologization'.[36] In order to 'rescue theology from its impotence' in these matters, he believes that it needs to incorporate the methodologies of the social sciences. Otherwise, 'the unconscious element' contained within all theological discourse will remain unrecognized, and the interpretation of biblical texts and doctrines will be employed 'by and large at the service of domination'.[37] To prevent this, theology must use the social sciences as it once relied on philosophy.

In the latter period of his work, Segundo becomes increasingly critical of other liberation theologians for not recognizing the methodological significance of the social sciences for theology, and for not consistently employing them. He suggests that in the 1980s a shift occurred within the movement as a response to the opposition of the Vatican. This resulted, he claims, in a retreat from the use of social theory among theologians in Latin America, as they sought to adhere more uncritically to traditional orthodox positions. In the face of a concern that the growth of the movement was being outstripped by conservative Protestant evangelical groups, Segundo argues that the shift was also motivated by a desire to become more attractive to popular religion. He insists, however, that the shift from social analysis to a focus upon a celebration of the poor and popular piety defeats the goals of liberation itself: 'I observe that we are becoming less and less critical when it comes to the power of ideology victimizing our people, even in the religious elements transmitted to them by their culture'.[38] Segundo concludes that this shift effectively abandons social theory and returns to a dependence upon philosophical reflection as a means for developing a theological rationale for celebrating and incorporating popular piety while being 'converted by the poor'.[39] In other words, liberation theology is charged with becoming increasingly concerned with Christian apologetics and adherence to traditional religious teachings, and less focused on social analysis and the liberation of human beings from oppressive social structures.[40]

The theologian Alasdair Kee comes to a similar conclusion. He cites an account by Clodovis Boff of a six-month work period he undertook in a rural area on the Brazilian-Bolivian border. Boff describes the religiosity of the rubber-gathers there as representing 'Christianity pure and hard'. Although the people cannot recite the Lord's Prayer properly, Boff is impressed by a prayer for curing toothaches, which invokes the saints and the Virgin Mary. In Kee's words, 'he copies it down like a recipe'. Troubled by what he considers to be Boff's sentimental celebration of his experiences in Santa Caterina, Kee adds:

> Boff arrives among these primitive people like a being
> from another world . . . He wishes them to enter more
> fully into that mythological religious world from which all
> modern people are in practice entirely alienated . . . There
> is no hint of the crisis which will come when with the
> advent of a dentist the prayer for curing toothaches will
> be obsolete. Immediately [after] Boff returned to the city
> he went into hospital to be treated for vivax malaria.
> Some demons can only be cast out by penicillin.[41]

Kee's concerns resonate with Adorno's criticism of immediate linkages between theory and practice. This brief summary of the early development of liberation theology serves to illustrate once again a number of problematic issues faced by theology as it reflects on its relation to political action, and particularly when it seeks to implement Marx's eleventh thesis in a direct or immediate fashion. The romanticization of the poor of Latin America criticised by Kee resembles the celebration of the proletariat that Adorno seeks to challenge in his early work, and subsequently in his engagement with the German student movement. Moreover, another issue is illuminated when liberation theology is drawn into this constellation with Adorno. This has to do with the fate of positive theology in the writing of a theologian like Segundo.

Liberation theology is frequently criticized for bringing Christian theological discourse together with social action in a simplistic manner. But in this instance, the criticism is presented from the perspective of systematic theology rather than politics. Dennis McCann argues that a result of Segundo's methodology 'is a theology without a substantive norm save the process of liberation itself'.[42] If human liberation is the primary norm, does anything inherently 'theological' remain to distinguish Segundo's theology from a 'secular' humanistic social theory? Marsha Hewitt suggests that,

> It can be reasonably argued, that in Segundo's hands,
> liberation theology reveals itself as containing the seeds
> of its own negation *as theology*, which is inevitable when
> politics becomes an ontological category, and when history
> is posited as the sole locus of human freedom.[43]

Since the focus of theology becomes liberating human life from domination, and humanity, rather than doctrinal claims, serves as both 'the historical subject and object', Hewitt asks, 'is Segundo a theologian or is he more of a critical social theorist?'[44] McCann asks a similar question: 'is liberation theology still recognizable as theology?'[45]

This debate continues to rage within subsequent interpretations of liberation theology. Bryan Stone disagrees with Hewitt that Segundo should push the implication of his methodology to its logical completion, which would effectively negate theology and evolve into a critical social theory. He suggests that Segundo's limitations can be corrected through the insertion of a metaphysical component into his methodology. Stone argues that the language of faith implies existential claims which function metaphysically and provide the necessary presuppositions for human activity that Segundo's methodology lacks.[46] Thus, in opposition to Hewitt, he states,

> As I see it, the more basic problem is not that affirming
> a thoroughly historical context for understanding the
> meaning and value of human praxis yields fundamentally
> anti-theological results, but rather, especially with regard
> to christological method, that the necessarily historical
> context in which we find ourselves can hardly provide, in
> and of itself, any indication of why our praxis is to be taken
> as authentic.[47]

Basically, Stone asks: why does Segundo claim that human liberation is a good thing? What leads a human being to prefer some values as opposed to others? In order to answer such questions, he continues, a metaphysical description of what is 'ultimately real' is required, which can provide the foundation necessary to understand the significance of human action.

## A Foundational Ground for Political Theology?

As this debate shifts from a concern over political tactics and emphases, to a concern for normativity and metaphysics, the plane of argumentation moves from the realm of political action to the nature of political theology. In contradistinction to Adorno's work, Stone argues that an effective politics requires a firm foundational ground. The 'values' required for liberative practice must be rooted in a clear metaphysical system. Another recent interpretation of liberation theology takes a different view of the matter, although it arrives at a similar conclusion. Ivan Petrella agrees with Hewitt's view that liberation theology withdrew from critical social science in the 1980s and became a more traditional form of theological discourse. Unlike Stone, however, he suggests that this should be corrected by a greater focus on concrete and 'practical' historical 'projects'.[48] This is argued in opposition to a position which only enables a negative critique of existing oppression and injustice; 'We cannot remain satisfied with denouncing, we must also announce'.[49]

This is a compelling challenge to Adorno's defence of a negative dialectical politics. It recalls the accusation of the German students against Adorno that mere negativity leaves the world's present structures undisturbed. But Adorno's refusal to advocate for a positive political programme was not due to a failure to appreciate the urgent desire for social change that the German students, as well as Petrella and Segundo, articulate so passionately. His reluctance to adopt a political blueprint is based on his similar resistance to system-building in metaphysics and philosophy: such thought, in order to satisfy its desire for totality and completeness, must shut out and ignore what does not conform to its model. The demand for a firm foundation for thought and practice, he argues, can only end in identity thinking. The problem is the same one he criticized in the practice of astrology explored in the previous chapter: employing either a metaphysical system or a

clear 'historical project' to heal the contradictions within liberation theology can only be the product of a desire for a coherent
totality, rather than the achievement of a more accurate or effective position. It would be an achievement of instrumental reasoning, not truth. As such, these attempts to suture the contradictions
in theological method get reduced to identity thinking, as well
as end up serving to mask the roots of the contradiction in the
present conditions of social existence.

In the face of such dilemmas in political praxis, Adorno argues
that 'only thinking could find an exit, and moreover a thinking
whose results are not stipulated'.[50] This is to say, that politics ought
not to be reduced to the desire for immediate effect nor for a
coherent programme. For, in Adorno's view, thought motivated
only by these goals cannot point beyond itself. In order to achieve
the closure necessary to establish firm foundations, thought must
ignore the non-identity of its other. The cost of a clear course of
revolutionary political activity is that the thinking subject 'must
abolish itself so that it may be blessed with the grace of being
chosen by the collective'. Thus, the security 'is purchased with the
sacrifice of autonomous thinking'.[51]

Adorno's conception of an inverse political theology intends to
nurture and support a form of 'open thinking' that can resist the
tempting impulse to cling to identity thinking. This is not to say
that he intends human beings to smother any desire to help those
in need or to challenge oppressive structures. Far from it; 'it is not
possible to think a right thought unless one *wills* the right thing'.[52]
But his approach depends on an ongoing negative critique of
existing society, along with an elucidation of its contradictory
state, rather than the construction of foundational positive programmes. Political action, in Adorno's view, can only be occasional
and context specific; any particular strategic actions will have to
be subject to ongoing critical analysis and revision. No one source,
technique, or particular actor can serve as an infallible foundation
upon which to build the perfect political movement.

Adorno's concept of *Bilderverbot* is that element of his inverse
theology which prevents critical thought from foreclosing on
itself and becoming mere instrumental thinking. In what follows,
a second concept from Jewish theology that Adorno employs
will be explored in more detail, for it serves to focus the will and

desire he refers to in the quotation cited above. For in Adorno's inverse political theology, the concept of the messianic serves to keep thought seeking for signs of possibility for a transformed existence.

## Messianism and Political Theology

Joseph Klausner makes a distinction within Jewish theology between 'messianic expectation' and 'belief in the Messiah', which may serve as a helpful initiation clarification. The former perspective involves hope for the end of the present age, and anticipation of political freedom and moral perfection for all people. Belief *in* the Messiah represents a similar hope, but this achievement is the result of the power and spirit of a 'strong redeemer'.[53] When Adorno refers to the messianic, he does so only in the mode of a 'messianic expectation'. He does not intend to identify himself directly with either the Jewish or Christian theological traditions. What he does seek to accomplish through the deployment of the messianic is to interrupt and challenge the domination of oppressive structures shaping society, thought, and the course of history.

Adorno suggests such a vision in the final aphorism of *Minima Moralia*; 'Perspectives must be fashioned that displace and estrange the world, reveal it to be, with its rifts and crevices, as indigent and distorted as it will appear one day in the messianic light'.[54] This vision has recently been challenged by Giorgio Agamben, and his alternative approach thus merits attention. Agamben suggests that Adorno's aphorism is ultimately empty, amounting to 'nothing other than an aestheticization of the messianic in the form of the *as if*'.[55] He is concerned that Adorno's articulation represents a mere negative condemnation of reality, which fails to interrupt the destructiveness of the dialectic of reason. Thus, Agamben argues that Adorno's 'negative dialectics is an absolutely non–messianic form of thought'.[56] It fails to nurture any new possibilities for experience or society, but remains trapped in a dialectical entanglement with the faulty mediations of existing life. For Agamben, the messianic brings dialectics to a 'standstill'.

At the centre of this challenge to Adorno's work are differing interpretations of Walter Benjamin's philosophy. Agamben draws from Benjamin particularly while developing his concept of biopolitics with reference to Carl Schmitt's theory of sovereignty. In *State of Exception*, Agamben explores a concept which he argues inhabits an obscure location between politics and the law. The term refers to those rare moments in Roman, German and French legal history when the political sovereign found it necessary to suspend the law in order to defend the existing political order against a threat to its stability. This discussion concerns Agamben because, in his view, what was once a rare and extreme measure 'tends increasingly to appear as the dominant paradigm of government in contemporary politics'.[57] In a post–9/11 world order, the 'indefinite detention' of individuals occurs outside of any juridical status covered by the Geneva Convention, resulting in the production of a 'legally unnameable and unclassifiable being'. The 'state of exception' does not possess the status of a law because it effectively suspends the juridical order. It is, rather, a 'threshold', a 'zone of indifference' that is neither external nor internal to law.[58] Furthermore, although the 'state of exception' suspends the existing legal norm, it is done for the sake of making the application of the norm possible (e.g. the sovereign breaks the law to punish those who fail to obey the law, in order to defend the law). The central task of Agamben's argument is to differentiate the juridical from the non-juridical, particularly by challenging Carl Schmitt's insistence that the 'state of exception' is actually grounded in the administration of law. In *Political Theology*, Schmitt intends to unite sovereignty and the state of exception through the concept of *decision*. This conceptualization is developed on the basis that it is precisely due to the sovereign's ability to decide on whether a situation is normal or exceptional that sovereignty is manifest. The law applies, of course, only in a situation of normalcy, but Schmitt argues that the exception is included in the law through its very exclusion.

Agamben draws from Walter Benjamin's essay 'Critique of Violence' to challenge Schmitt's claim that the 'state of exception' remains bound to the law, for it is not a 'state of law' but a 'space without law'.[59] Agamben appreciates Benjamin's insistence that one can locate the possibility of a 'pure violence' outside of the law, as he understands this intent to coincide with its counterpart 'pure being' or 'pure existence'. This is to say that *being* is conceivable beyond the confines of the juridical order. To accept otherwise is, in Benjamin's view, tantamount to chaining being and politics to the limits of the existing *status quo*. This is particularly alarming to Agamben, given his belief that the 'state of the exception' is no longer a rare state in contemporary existence, but is increasingly the norm and the 'dominant paradigm in government'.[60] When this occurs, 'the juridico-political system transforms itself into a killing machine'.[61]

What is of primary concern here is Agamben's suggestion that the way to escape this dilemma is neither to attempt to erase the law, nor to endlessly deconstruct it, since both options end up re-inscribing the exclusion–inclusion dynamic he wishes to avoid. In his view, what is necessary is to reclaim a politics that escapes the nexus between violence and law. This relationship remains in place when the political is conceived in terms of constituent power that focuses on harnessing means to establish a desired end. In Benjamin's concept of 'pure violence', Agamben sees the figure of a 'paradoxical "mediality without ends"', which approaches *means* in a way that achieves a different relationship to *ends*. Here the intention is, through some form of immediacy, to deactivate the force of law. What the 'biopolitical machine' has constructed – the distinctions between life and law, anomie and *nomos* – is 'disenchanted'. This process will not reveal a purity of 'life' in its 'original state', but it does offer 'the possibility of reaching a new condition'.[62] What all this means is rather unclear and unformulated by Agamben. The achievement of a state of action based on pure means, in which the force of law has been deactivated (i.e. freed from all sovereignty and discipline) is only hinted at. It is compared with visions of children playing creatively with obsolete objects, and to a question that confronts the Apostle Paul in the early Christian movement: 'What becomes of the law after its messianic fulfilment?'[63] The path down which Agamben is heading is considerably hazy, but in this reference to Paul one gets a glimpse of how he will make his way.

Adorno's thought, as previous chapters have shown, is influenced by Benjamin's work to a considerable degree. He is particularly attracted to Benjamin's concept of allegory as it is developed in *The Origin of the German Tragic Drama*. For Benjamin, allegory is of interest for the way it enables him to rethink Kant's distinction between cognitive knowledge and noumenal truth, and challenge the manner in which the knowing subject serves in Kantian philosophy to establish objectivity through synthetic activity. Although for Benjamin, as in Kant, the Absolute remains elusive to direct intuition, he suggests that a momentary grasp is possible through representation of ideas in 'constellations' – or clusters – of concepts and images. He develops this with an emphasis on attending to the particular and the fragmentary, as opposed to the general and universal. In the melancholic vision of the tragic dramas he analyses, Benjamin suggests that understanding history as catastrophe, as opposed to immanent progress, allows thought to break free of the standardized and ideological version of the past. Instead, the allegorist looks to uncover the 'intentionless being' that lies buried beneath the authorized version of history. Adorno echoes this perspective appreciatively, and suggests that it implies that Benjamin's work 'consists in treating profane texts as though they were sacred'.[64] Adorno describes 'the secret coded character of our theology' as being comparable to looking at broken and damaged life from the perspective of a redeemed existence.[65]

Although Adorno's work owes much to Benjamin, he does nevertheless raise some pointed concerns against his friend, and these criticisms directly challenge Agamben's interpretation of Benjamin. Adorno is concerned that Benjamin's concept of 'pure violence' is in danger of leading his thought in a quietist direction. On occasion, he suggests that Benjamin's work becomes 'undialectical' when it creates such bleak images of the present that only a source from outside of history could be conceived as bearing the possibility of a better life. For Adorno, the concept of redemption cannot be located outside of historical existence. Although appreciative of the general emphases of Benjamin's method, he is concerned when it becomes a 'dialectics at a standstill', which stresses the polarities of myth and reconciliation to such an extent that his philosophy becomes 'inhuman'.[66] He sees this in Benjamin's later work on the *Arcades Project*, in which his aesthetic constellations appear to Adorno to imply an immediate grasp of an image of the absolute. He argues that any 'restoration of theology . . . would simultaneously require the utmost intensification of the social–dialectical and indeed economic motifs'.[67] Because Benjamin's concept of a 'dialectical image' is increasingly, in

Adorno's view, becoming more like a 'dream' for consciousness, it has become thoroughly undialectical.[68]

In his writing, Agamben frequently leaps to defend Benjamin against Adorno, and when he does so, the focus of his disagreement turns on their differing use of the concept of the messianic. Agamben's deploys the messianic to challenge the ontological boundaries of inclusion and exclusion established by political sovereignty. He argues that, as politics constitutes itself through exclusion, it also binds the two sides of the caesura together. His work, therefore, seeks to articulate an alternative conception of human existence from that which is diagnosed in *Homo Sacer*. In *The Open*, Agamben articulates such an alternative foundation. He turns to perhaps the most basic distinction of existence: that between human beings and animals. The human being is only defined in comparison to its other – the animal. And yet, the life of a human being (*bios*) is not so easily separated from the life of the animal (*zoe*). Agamben suggests that a dynamic of exclusion-inclusion exists at one of the core metaphysical foundations of western culture and politics. In this case, the 'animal' in human beings functions in the same way as the *homo sacer* does in Roman law: excluded from the law and subject to the whims of a sovereign power. The concept 'life' remains largely undefined in Western culture, but it is repeatedly articulated 'through a series of caesurae and oppositions that invest it with a decisive strategic function'.[69]

In contrast to this dilemma, Agamben points to archaic artworks where human beings have animal heads, and to images of eschatological animals possessing the features of both man and beast. He recalls an idea from the Talmud which suggests that, in the messianic kingdom, animal nature will be transformed. All of these observations serve as a suggestive possibility that, 'on the last day, the relations between animals and men will take on a new form, and that man himself will be reconciled with his animal nature'.[70] To avoid the violence and instrumentality that Agamben sees as invariably implicated in biopolitical sovereignty, an attitude and identity must be nurtured that does not encourage the mastery of nature by the human, nor the human by nature. What also must be avoided is a dialectical synthesis of these tensions by a third term. Instead, 'what is decisive here is only the "between", the interval'. Instead of allowing the production of the human through a contrast with or control of the animal, the 'anthropological machine' is to be rendered 'at a standstill'.[71]

Just as Benjamin's philosophy served as a resource in *State of Exception* to conceive of a 'pure violence' that remains external to the juridical order, in *The Open* his work serves as a support for Agamben's articulation of a 'letting be' of the animal, which results in conceiving of it as 'outside of being'. It is not a more authentic or accurate relationship with animality that is sought, but rather a 'Shabbat of both animal and human', which reaches for 'a way in which living beings can sit at the messianic banquet of the righteous without . . . setting the anthropological machine into action'.[72]

One way of understanding Adorno's criticism of Benjamin is that he is concerned that his friend is losing the capacity to see any possibility of a different society within the actualities of history. A similar concern might be raised here regarding the direction of Agamben's messianism. As Alastair Morgan observes, Agamben conceives of an opening of experience through pure possibility, which exists prior to actuality.[73] A new form of 'being' is required, if the biopolitical machine is to be escaped. Possibility, therefore, cannot be actualized within existing history. For Agamben, the problem is to determine how one moves from possibility to actuality without it becoming corrupted by the human will. He reasons that 'pure potentiality' includes the potential *not to be*. This, he argues, is the origin of human power.[74] Thus, just as a 'pure being' is theorized beyond the juridical order in *State of Exception*, in *The Open*, 'boredom' is the trope deployed to describe the human distinction from the animal. Unlike animals, who are captive to their environments, the human 'is simply an animal that has become bored, it has awakened *from* its captivation *to* its own captivation'.[75] Possibilities for human action remain at a standstill, for fear of being contaminated by actuality.

Adorno consistently resists separating possibility and actuality in this manner, as Chapter 2 made evident in an analysis of his criticism of Kant's prohibition on metaphysics. Adorno's *Negative Dialectics* attempts to resist foreclosing on the possibility of a new form of experience; one not based on mere self-preservation or control of the other. This effort does not amount to the consoling assertion that reconciliation between subject and object will inevitably occur in the future, nor that a 'new way of thinking' can be found to lead the way. Rather than emphasizing the 'possibilities of being', his philosophy is directed 'at the existing itself in its concrete historical definition'. One must, he insists, 'criticize the separation of the real and possible from the point of view of reality'.[76]

At this point, the key difference between the references to the messianic by Agamben and Adorno comes into view. For Agamben, the messianic represents a deferral, a suspension, a declaration that 'I prefer not to'. In the concept of the messianic, the possibility of a life beyond the tentacles of biopolitical power is upheld in its purity, far from the entanglements of actuality. Political theology is brought to a standstill, to prevent it from being corrupted by limited historical mediations. Adorno's messianic serves as a negative contrast against the already existing. It helps the philosopher recognize what ought not to be. Although the possibility of a better life remains elusive for Adorno, he insists that signs of it are to be sought, not beyond history, but through attention to the cracks and fissures of damaged life itself. The concept of the messianic is meant to focus attention on the actualities of history, not to distract thought from it.

Agamben's position is most clearly articulated in his reading of Paul's 'Letter to the Romans'. For Agamben, the opposition that the Pauline paradigm interrupts is not that which opposes *being* and *event*, but rather that established between the *norm* and the *exception*. The revolutionary potential of the Pauline vision is thus not its capacity to offer a new form of identity or ground for action. Instead, what Agamben calls the 'messianic' renders inoperative the law and its power over 'bare life'. This is accomplished, not by cancelling divisions in the social order (such as between Jew and Gentile), but by inserting further divisions in between the troublesome binaries.

Agamben describes this shift of emphasis by referring to the story of the Greek painter Apelles who succeeds in overcoming his rival Protogenes by successfully dividing the fine lines his competitor had drawn with even finer lines, cutting them in half. Agamben perceives this 'cut of Apelles' throughout the Pauline corpus: in Gal. 3.28 ('neither male nor female, slave nor free'); and in Rom. 2.28 (Jew 'according to the flesh' and 'according to the Spirit'). The political legacy of Paul is thus his capacity to offer a perspective that dislodges antiquated approaches to identity politics. His vision reveals that 'the people is neither the all nor the part, neither the majority nor the minority. Instead, it is that which can never coincide with itself'.[77] This figure does not present the achievement of a new identity, nor does it correspond to the possession of certain attributes or capacities. Instead, it is the result of a new messianic condition, a division – not between binaries – but between the divisions of binary distinctions. Like the cut of Apelles, the messianic contests the boundaries of biopolitics, not through erasure or confrontation, but by an even sharper act of dislocation. In Paul's vision, the messianic vocation corresponds neither exclusively to the Jew, nor to the non-Jew. Instead, the space opened up by messianic time is for the 'non-non-Jew', a 'division of divisions' that 'forces us to think about the question of the universal and particular in a completely new way, not only in logic, but also in ontology and politics'.[78]

This messianic event achieves something that corresponds to the possibility of a 'pure violence' that is external to the state of exception, and resembles that which was described as a 'Shabbat' between the human and the animal. At the core of Agamben's political theology, then, is an appreciation of 'the neutralization that divisions of the law and all juridical and social conditions in general undergo as a consequence of the messianic event'.[79] It is important to recognize that Agamben describes this shift as something distinct from transcendence, a positive possession, a right, or a stabilizing identity. It is an 'immobile dialectic' which can be used, but not possessed.[80] Instead of living under the form *as-if*, like Adorno (which he argues remains chained to exclusion-inclusion), it operates according to a state of inhabiting an *as-not*. Instead of living in anticipation of some utopian future, which effectively excludes the merely present, the messianic in-between time – the 'time that remains', is a space that renders the existing grinding biopolitical forces inoperative. The remnant 'make[s] salvation possible', and, as such, 'is the only real political subject'.[81]

When set against Adorno's alternative vision, one might begin to ask Agamben some pointed questions; particularly: *who* is this *real political subject* that is being invoked here? The remnant, like Agamben's conception of potentiality, does not appear to have any actual place within history. It is instructive to return to Adorno's aphorism from *Minima Moralia*, and to Agamben's dismissal of this position as empty pessimism in the form of an '*as if*'. The limitation of this criticism of Adorno is illuminated by asking whether taking refuge in the messianic might represent a flight from the problem that Agamben has so powerfully articulated. Agamben's own contrasting of himself against Adorno's '*as if*' does raise the question as to whether his messianic '*as not*' suggests problematically that the subject can undermine and render 'inoperative' the destructive biopolitical system without replacing it? The confession of 'faith' that is celebrated in *The Time that Remains* produces salvation within itself. It is an 'experience of being beyond existence and essence', which Agamben compares to the state of being in love.[82] But here his understanding – not only of love but also political resistance – becomes romanticized. When he states that, 'the words of faith rise forth to go beyond the denotive relation between language and the world, toward a different and more originary status of the word', the implication is that the anthropological machine of exclusion–inclusion is overcome by a change of attitude in the subject, rather than a changed relationship with the other.[83] This is verified when it is suggested 'that in messianic time the saved world coincides with the world that is irretrievably lost'.[84] The world does not appear to change, but only the subject's attitude toward it.

As the first section of this chapter explored, Adorno himself was sometimes criticized for articulating a seemingly pessimistic and resigned political vision. And so, the question might well be asked: is Adorno vulnerable to the same criticisms he levels against Benjamin, and, by extension, to those raised here against Agamben? At this point, a key difference between his inverse theology and the political theology of Agamben becomes significant. Although Adorno himself admitted that his own level of engaged praxis sometimes came to a standstill, he insisted that his thought, in the form of a negative criticism of identity thinking and social oppression, did not. What he lamented about Benjamin, however, was his impression that, in Benjamin's deployment of a messianic vision that left history behind, Benjamin's critical thought had suspended dialectics and had itself come to a standstill. By weakening attention on how thought is mediated by the social totality of damaged life, Benjamin's work was becoming idealistic and insufficiently dialectical in a materialist sense. The same can be said of Agamben's thought in a way that is not the case in Adorno's work.

When Agamben defends Benjamin against Adorno's charge that the former lacks sufficient attention to historical *mediation*, Agamben responds, 'Praxis is not, in fact, something which needs a dialectical mediation'.[85] What is suggested here is a political practice as pure immediacy, or, possibly, politics as permanent deferral. As seen above, Adorno's thought is painfully alert to how all forms of reason and action are mediated by a corrupting social totality, but he consistently resists any suggestion that such historical mediation can be avoided. For him, the concept of the messianic serves as a negative interruption of history, which illuminates the incompleteness and injustice of damaged life. For Agamben, the messianic serves to evade these mediations entirely. The messianic appears to suspend life altogether, in order to achieve some form of pure otherness that is untainted by social interaction. As such, when Agamben articulates his alternative vision, with its emphasis on an immediate 'now' that neither looks to the future nor intends to change the existing in any particular way, he abandons any attention to the work of mediation, which anything resembling a 'politics' requires.

Agamben's messianism is not a politics of the state, of relationship, nor even of the subject. Salvation simply arrives in the midst of the immediate 'now'. Though his work offers a powerful portrait of the brokenness of the world, the healing he offers does not go *through* these experiences of suffering, but merely *eludes* them. The salvific event has no site, no institution, no community, and so effectively occurs nowhere. The 'as not', having no material substance, cannot be corrupted by biopolitics, but neither can it intervene in what is normally called 'the political'. This being the case, the possibility of 'performing' the faith of Agamben leaves its preconditions unexplored, which is exactly the concern Adorno raised against Benjamin's work. Agamben himself frequently alludes to this critique only to quickly reject it, yet Adorno's caution bears further reflection: 'Materialist determination of cultural traits is only possible if it is mediated through the *total social politics*'.[86] Thus, when at the end of *The Open* Agamben suggests that, 'Perhaps there is still a way in which living beings can sit at the messianic banquet of the righteous *without taking on a historical task*' a position informed by Adorno's thought would do well to suggest: *there isn't*. A politics that abandons the brokenness of history is no politics at all.[87]

This chapter has highlighted the nuanced reflection Adorno offers on the relationship between theory and practice. It observed a connection between his critique of ideology, and Segundo's view that the social sciences are required by theology to help interrupt its capacity to support injustice and domination. Finally, the discussion contrasted Adorno's concept of the messianic with that of Agamben, demonstrating how, for Adorno, the messianic serves as a negative contrast against existing society, helping philosophy to recognize what ought not to be. Unlike Agamben's undialectical notion of a space 'in-between' the subjects and objects of history, Adorno maintains that it is crucial to focus attention on how thought is mediated by the social totality of damaged life. This examination of how Adorno's inverse theology shapes his attitude towards politics illustrates the importance that attention to social life has in his work. This recognition merits a return to his approach to the study of society, to which the next chapter turns. As it will demonstrate, any discussion of the relationship that positive religious discourse has with an inverse theology must consider how Adorno considers it to be embedded within the complex dynamics of what he calls the 'culture industry'.

## Chapter 6

# Religion and the Culture Industry: Spirituality, Rational Choice and the Theology of Correlation

*Religion is on sale, as it were. It is cheaply marketed in order to provide one more so-called irrational stimulus among many others by which the members of a calculating society are calculatingly made to forget the calculation under which they suffer.*[1]

This warning remains as prescient today as it was when Adorno wrote these remarks in 1945. He was concerned that an emerging enthusiasm for a 'return to religion' after the Second World War was being driven more by an emotional need for reassurance, as well as some ideological agenda, rather than being the product of a renewed search for moral and intellectual truth.

The contemporary scepticism towards the theory of secularization has encouraged a new version of a 'return to religion' in academic circles.[2] Chapter 1 demonstrated that Adorno shares some level of scepticism about the independence of reason and secularism from mythology and irrationality. And yet his nuanced view on such matters stands in sharp contrast with current discourses on the concept of 'spirituality', and with the manner in which some sociological treatments of religion account for religion's ongoing influence and growth in certain areas of the world. This chapter explores how Adorno's inverse theology contrasts with two common deployments of 'post–secular' theory by theology. The first approach responds to recent criticisms of the secularization thesis by emphasizing that the rising interest in 'spirituality' demonstrates that religion is an important aspect of life. A second trend develops as a curious enthusiasm among church growth theorists for the rational choice approach in the sociology of religion. In both cases, Adorno's work offers an important critical corrective to the temptation for theology to embrace such trends simply because they initially seem to strengthen its status and significance in contemporary society. Adorno's distinct understanding of 'spiritual experience' encourages a more cautious approach to these developments, while his theory of the 'culture industry' serves to warn how ideology can function through any cultural expression or medium, including theology and religion.

The chapter demonstrates that Adorno's approach to theology and society suggests an *inverse* correlation. He does not look to society to discover the questions about existence, which theology then answers. Rather, Adorno inverts the ordering of Tillich's theology of correlation. In his work, theological concepts like redemption, justice, the messianic, and the fullness of reason (in its 'emphatic sense') confront society with questions. Human beings are then pressed to pursue the answers to the questions, through critical thought and committed social engagement.

## 'Spirituality'

With the growth of so-called 'New Age' movements, alternative health therapies, and multiple variants of new religious groups and philosophies, numerous scholars of religion and sociologists suggest that Western society is seeing a startling increase in expressed yearning for a reconstituted interior life. For some religious leaders and theologians, such trends are seen as evidence for the 'spiritual' nature of human beings, and illustrate the deep inner needs that all people have for the divine. 'Spirituality' is now frequently used to replace 'religion' as a universal category. In such a formulation 'religions' are viewed as particular traditions and institutionalized forms of piety, whereas 'spirituality' is a universal aspect of human life, often an interiorized or psychological state. One observes a variety of versions of this trend: the 'spirituality of sport', 'spirituality in the workplace', and even a 'spirituality of food'.[3] Linda Woodhead defines 'spirituality' as follows,

> I shall use the word . . . to refer both to the belief/aware-
> ness that there is some reality more real, more valuable,
> more important and more extensive than that revealed by
> science, and to the practices by which people hope to get
> in touch with this reality. I understand it as a rather more
> personal and individualistic notion than 'religion' which
> I generally use to refer to a system of more institutionally
> embodied beliefs and practices.[4]

Although Adorno certainly argues that reality is more extensive than what is revealed by science or empirical observation, his
concern is not to imply that this broader context of life is some
positive 'reality' with which people should 'get in touch' in a personal and intimate manner. He considers many expressions of
'spirituality' to be vulnerable to the manipulations of ideology or
psychological need. They may offer consolation to those living
within modern society, but they can also serve as a support for,
rather than a challenge to, the *status quo*. Thus celebration of
'spirituality' is vulnerable to the same critique that Adorno develops against astrology (explored in Chapter 4). Although it may
'feel' more personally relevant or more immediately 'useful' than
traditional theology, the concept of spirituality often does so at the
expense of losing any critical element or any direct connection
to the pursuit of truth.

In *Selling Spirituality*, Jeremy Carrette and Richard King
suggest that popular discourses about spirituality 'tend to displace
questions of social justice, being increasingly framed by the individualist and corporatist values of a consumer society'.[5] Echoing
the concerns that both Marx and Adorno raise about the possibility that religion can function as an 'opiate for the people', the
authors warn that, with its focus on individual private experience
and choice of lifestyle orientation, 'religion is rebranded as 'spirituality' in order to support the ideology of capitalism'.[6]

Roger Foster has recently demonstrated that the concept of
'spiritual experience' is an important concern in Adorno's philosophy. So Adorno does not simply brush away the idea or treat

it as inherently meaningless. As Foster argues, 'Adorno's negative dialectics [i]s a theory of spiritual experience'.[7] But this form of experience is rather different than what is often meant by slogans such as 'spirituality of sport' or 'spirituality in the workplace'. It is not some positive or energizing internal feeling; rather, for Adorno, 'spiritual experience' is what his inverse theology seeks to make a place for. It is more an experience of coming up short, or of making an 'outbreak attempt', than a grasping of some specific orientation. Whereas many Christian spirituality programmes emphasize concepts like 'integration', 'wholeness', or 'meaning', Adorno's concern is to prevent one's understanding of life from masking its disintegration, brokenness and lack of meaning.

Adorno emphasizes that, contrary to the view that the world of experience should be restricted to 'brute facts', intellectual life, and the reflective mode of behaviour 'always contains the possibility of what might be called a spiritualization of the world'. Such experience goes beyond immediate sense experience, turning 'the object of experience into something spiritual'. This concern surpasses the reduction of life to the cold calculations of instrumental rationality, and in this regard, Adorno has some sympathy for the sensitivities behind the contemporary enthusiasm for 'spirituality'. There is an 'essential element of play' in philosophy, he argues; 'there is no rationality without this intrinsic element of irrationality'.[8]

But even as he invokes his own notion of spiritual experience, Adorno emphasizes the dangers inherent to the 'built-in tendency' of this approach. One can easily be tempted, he observes, to over-identify with one's own intuitions and fail to be sufficiently reflexive when exploring such experiences.[9] If spiritual experience might be said to be in pursuit of the 'depth' behind immediate appearances, 'it cannot mean something like the sort of retreat into inwardness that evidently exercises a kind of inextinguishable attraction'.[10] Discovering spiritual 'depth' does not involve immersion of the subject, but comes from 'the strength to externalize oneself'. Not being satisfied with the immediate surface experience, critical intelligence breaks through the façade of the seemingly self-evident. While this is nurtured by expressive rhetoric, artistic creation, or playfulness, such experiences cannot be simply accepted as pure givens. If explored self-reflexively and critically, spiritual experience may enhance understanding; but when it is hypostasized or regarded as a grasp of immediate truth, it may be reduced to little more than 'dangerous forms of bleating', which reproduce the ideology of the social totality.[11]

Carrette and King's suggestion that the current shift of emphasis away from 'religion' or 'theology' to the concept of 'spirituality' often serves to provide an accommodationist orientation towards the ideology of global capitalism resonates with Adorno's concerns. In the face of the present enthusiasm for the idea of spirituality in North Atlantic societies, his exploration of the relationship between culture and capitalism remains an important resource. This is developed most directly in his theory of the 'culture industry'.

## The Culture Industry

During his ten years in the United States, Adorno wrote extensively on popular culture. For him, cultural entertainment and commercial advertising are not neutral forces or trivial matters. He employs the term 'culture industry' to clarify that he is not simply describing folk or mass culture, but an aspect of social life that encourages a certain kind of subjectivity; 'the culture industry intentionally integrates its consumers from above'. Adorno is concerned with the manner in which the ideology of the social totality − primarily the capitalist system − shapes the human subject according to the priorities and values of the market. It encourages a consumer to conform to a certain way of life, resulting in the development of a weak ego, acceptance of authoritarian power structures, and dependency behaviour. Although American culture celebrated individuality and freedom, in Adorno's view, it was actually the culture industry that was shaping what individuality and freedom were understood to be; 'The consumer is not the king, as the culture industry would have us believe, not its subject but its object'.[12]

Adorno's position is rooted in an analysis of capitalism, as he adapts a number of Marx's concepts: the theory of commodity fetishism, the concept of alienation, and his understanding of ideology. Marx argues that material objects manufactured within a capitalist system become 'commodities'. His labour theory of value draws from a distinction found in Aristotle between a practice that arises out of need (like that found in household management) and an economic practice in which the intended outcome is an abstract object like money. A commodity is the product of the latter form of practice. An object that satisfies a basic need has a specific use value; but what the capitalist system is based upon is the exchange of different commodities according to their 'exchange value'. This is not necessarily a problematic dynamic; many material artefacts produced by human labour are extremely useful. All such objects require a certain amount of socially necessary time and labour to produce. This required effort is subsequently converted into abstract concepts like 'exchange value' and money to facilitate the sharing of goods to meet diverse human needs.

Marx's criticism of the capitalism system is rooted in his understanding of what happens to this dynamic between human labour and its exchange value. When the market is based on the abstraction of money, which forgets the concrete processes of human labour required to produce a commodity, exchange value is determined by the relationship between supply and demand. Individuals and their labour become valued solely according to the flow of the market. The injustice of capitalism is that the manner in which commodities are valued loses all connection to the actual labour that went into producing them. This results in labourers not being paid according to the true cost to them of producing the object. The commodity develops a 'surplus value' that surpasses the value given to the labour that human beings put into it. As a consequence, human beings become disconnected from the products of their labour, and 'alienated' from the actual value of their work.

The significance of this general perspective for theology is twofold. First, Marx identified 'commodity fetishism' as being the outcome of disconnecting a material object from the concrete labour that produces it. This concept refers to the abstract belief encouraged by the capitalist system that value resides within the commodity itself; that it produces value, not the labour of human beings. This is an illusion, or, as Marx often writes, a 'mystification' of the commodity. In anthropology, the concept of a fetish describes how a humanly created material object is treated as if it has sacred powers. Marx argues that, in capitalist economies, commodities take on a similar aura when it appears that they possess an inherent value that radiates independently of any history of production. Effectively the commodity develops an otherworldly aura to it, which, abstracted from any connection to its history of production, parallels the problem Marx criticizes about religious discourse. Concrete historical existence is masked by an abstract concept whose properties transcend the material world, and so the commodity is revealed to be 'a very strange thing, abounding in metaphysical subtleties and theological niceties'.[13]

The second point Marx makes with regard to the relation between theology and the commodity is his accusation that there exists 'a conspiracy of the Church with the monopoly of capital'.[14] For Marx, a society's primary motive force is the economic sphere, so that all forms of culture are shaped accordingly in the service of the principal mode of production. As part of the 'superstructure', Marx suggests that the Church serves as an instrument in support of the capitalist system and the interests of the social class who owned the means of production.

Adorno's approach to the culture industry is indebted to both of Marx's concerns. He argues that the culture industry enhances the process of commodity mystification and strengthens the hold that ideology has upon all members of society. This includes a capacity to shape the form and content of theological discourse and the spiritual inner lives of individuals in an ideological manner. But Adorno also seeks to correct and supplement Marx's theory of capitalism through attention to other material forces beyond the economic system of production. He also draws from elements of Freud's psychoanalytic theory, particularly the theory of drives – or instincts – which he understands as additional material forces that influence culture and society.[15]

Whereas some Marxian theorists argue that culture is merely an element of a superstructure produced by the economic base, so that progressive thought should focus solely on changing the economic system, Adorno argues for the importance and relevance of cultural criticism. This practice intends to analyse how 'all culture takes part in society's guilty coherence', while at the same time demonstrating that culture also resists the limitations of instrumental reason.[16] Exploring this tension illuminates not only the presence of the social totality at work, but also the potentiality that society could be otherwise. Adorno's nuanced treatment of culture, therefore, suggests that merely lamenting the distortion of culture's 'purity' by consumerism is itself a form of ideology. For such a stance often implies that culture is essentially a distinct form of life without being rooted in the economic structures of social life. The same attitude holds for his view of theology: to simply dismiss it for its failings (its mimicking of ideology, sentimentality, faulty reasoning, etc) would be to miss its attempt to grasp the truth behind appearance.

## Rational Choice Theory and the Scientific Study of Religion

Adorno's perspective on the culture industry not only challenges the contemporary enthusiasm for 'spirituality' as a concept; it also stands in rather dramatic contrast with the contemporary application of rational choice theory in the study of religion. This trend in the sociology of religion has been adopted by numerous theologians and church leaders interested in promoting 'church growth'. It is not uncommon for those interested in 'church planting', evangelistic mission, or 'congregational development' to refer to the work of scholars like Rodney Stark and Lawrence Iannaccone, for they offer concrete and practical observations about the behaviour of churchgoers, which can be adapted to specific strategies to attract new members.[17] But from the perspective of Adorno's critical theory, the assumptions made by rational choice theory are highly problematic. Contrasting his work with that of Stark and Iannaccone reveals that, although they may immediately offer some instrumentally useful suggestions to church leaders, they also imply some philosophical assumptions about human beings, which these same leaders would not normally accept. Intertwined in these debates are even more far ranging disputes over social scientific methodology, not unlike those discussed in relation to Adorno's debate with Karl Popper.

The advocates of rational choice theory intend to overcome a perceived 'disparity in development' that exists between natural and social science by adopting mathematical models from economic theory and applying them to the analysis of social action.[18]

This approach is understood to bypass metaphysical assumptions about human nature and behaviour, as well as holistic theories about the nature of society at the macro level, by focusing on strategic and instrumental decisions by individuals in social interaction. The perspective develops a voluntaristic theory of action, emphasizing the role of calculation and the achievement of expected outcomes in human behaviour. Rational choice theory argues that intended consequences motivate human choice in social interaction, more than environmental conditioning, repetition of custom or essential attribute.

A key element of this model emerges out of game theory, a mathematical approach to analysing conflict and cooperation. Game theory employs mathematical principles and equations to analyse situations where two people make decisions that influence each other. This perspective has been adopted particularly by economic theory, where it is employed to both explain and predict patterns of interaction between rational agents. This perspective on human life emphasizes two things Adorno is highly critical of: a positivistic approach to studying human behaviour; and a concept of an abstract rational subject who acts independently of its objects and the social totality in which it is located. To illustrate the assumptions behind this approach, it is illuminating to analyse a more popular exposition.

## A Beautiful Mind?

The Academy Award winning film *A Beautiful Mind* is based loosely on the life of John Nash, one of the developers of game theory.[19] In an early scene, the main character John (a student at Princeton) is sitting in a bar with his friends, searching for both female companionship and a topic for his doctoral dissertation. When a group of women enters the room, the men begin to boast and tease each other over who has the best chance to attract the most desirable of the women (stereotypically enough, the blonde). One of the men, referring to Adam Smith, states that in this competition, it is 'every man for himself'. Implied in this chauvinistic bravado is the sense that only one man will 'win' the prize, while the others will have to be content with the 'leftovers'; 'those who strike out are stuck with her friends'.

The situation results in an intellectual breakthrough for John. He insists that, 'Adam Smith needs revision'. He explains as follows:

> If we all go for the blonde, we block each other. Not a single one of us is going to get her. So then we all go for her friends, but they all give us the cold shoulder, because nobody likes to be second choice. But what if no one goes for the blonde? We don't get in each other's way, and we don't insult the other girls. It's the only way to win.

The apparent lesson that the viewer is supposed to derive from this scene is that the best resolution to this competition, the most rational choice when faced with this situation, is for the group of men to coordinate their actions with each other so that their own private interests are furthered. The Nash character determines that this insight proves that Adam Smith's conclusions about human self-interest were incorrect:

> Adam Smith said that the best result comes from everyone in the group doing what is best for himself. Right? Incomplete. Because the best result will come from everyone in the group doing what's best for himself *and* the group.

This analysis of the situation facing the men in the bar resembles what game theorists call a 'coordination game'. The group of individual (male) agents are situated within a static environment in which they are confronted with a choice of action. They then develop a strategy to achieve a desired end that takes into account the responses of the other agents in the room. The fictional Nash character calculates the different consequences of all possible actions and selects that which maximizes the expected desired outcome. Unlike his rivals, however, he argues that it is more beneficial for all the men involved to strategize collectively so as to ensure that they each individually achieve the desired goal (a woman).

Such a 'rational' choice calculation results in what is known as a 'Nash–equilibrium', the product of a game in which each player adopts a strategy that is the best reply to the actions of others. The result is a stable outcome, given that none of the players has a better strategy than his rivals. The insight derived by game theorists from such a model is that players have a mutual interest in coordinating their actions. The nature of social cooperation and interaction becomes something that one can explain as emerging from the individual choices of rational agents.[20]

This example serves to illustrate the basic presuppositions of game theory, which have a principal role in rational choice theory. There are two primary assumptions involved in this game model. The first is that a decision–maker is 'rational', which is defined narrowly as meaning that the individual 'makes decisions consistently in pursuit of his own objectives'. It is presumed that each player's objective is to maximize the expected value of any reward earned in the course of the game. The second premise is that the decision–maker is 'intelligent'. A player is considered to be so when he is in possession of complete information about the game and is aware of all relevant data about the given situation. This is to say that the agent is not vulnerable to hidden factors, or is deprived of information available to any competitors.[21]

There is much to question about these presuppositions generally, but for the moment, it is instructive to apply them to the bar scene as presented in *A Beautiful Mind*. For the Nash character's argument to work, the following assumptions must be granted:

- the blonde woman is the most desirable (*all* the men would usually pursue her);
- the blonde will not be interested in any of the men in particular;
- the other women will be interested in the men;
- the particularity of each individual woman is largely irrelevant in terms of her desirability for the men (i.e. any woman is better than none).

These presumptions are difficult to relate to the complexities involved in inter-personal relationships of dating. Why should one assume that any of these assumptions can be granted? In this example, the male participants in the game assume they know how the women will behave. The men 'strategize' based upon their own (questionable) assumptions about 'female behaviour'. How the women will respond to the attention of the men cannot be so simply predicted. Even more importantly, it is clear that the actual end of this competition is left outside the field of rationality. What is considered 'rational' amounts to two limited concerns: strategic instrumental calculation, and maximizing personal gain. What is 'rational' about the choice in no way involves determining which woman one might actually be compatible with. Any woman, it appears in this situation, represents maximizing self-interest. What is 'rational' about that? It is precisely such assumptions that Adorno's criticism of positivism calls into question.

## The Presuppositions of Rational Choice Theory

Although it has recently risen in prominence, the deployment of rational choice theory in the study of religion often resembles this fictional analysis of partner selection depicted in *A Beautiful Mind*, repeating many of its flaws. In their study of religion, both Rodney Stark and Lawrence Iannaccone assume the following premises about human activity:

(a)  human beings act rationally, weighing the costs and benefits of actions, and making choices with the intention of maximizing the benefits of their actions;
(b)  the ultimate human preferences (or needs) used to assess costs and benefits do not vary much;
(c)  the interaction of individual choices and actions result in a social equilibrium.[22]

In a manner similar to the way in which the assumptions made about women in the bar scene from *A Beautiful Mind* are simplistic and reductive, these premises are problematic. They are presuppositions asserted at the outset of theorizing; they are not proven or derived out of empirical study of social action. And yet, these assumptions subtly outline a very precise theory of human nature and rationality, which are based, as will become evident, on a not-so-subtle economic ideology.

The first premise reduces rationality to the calculation of costs and benefits. Thinking, in this view, is limited to what Adorno calls 'instrumental reasoning', and it is this reductive understanding of reason that he criticizes positivism for fostering. Chapter 3 demonstrated how he draws on Max Weber's distinction between value and purposive social action to defend a broader and more nuanced understanding of rationality. As Horkheimer writes, 'When the idea of reason was conceived, it was intended to achieve more than the mere regulation of the relation between means and ends; it was regarded as the instrument for understanding the ends, for determining them'.[23] In the presuppositions of rational choice theory, there is no place for the determination of ends; reason's sole purpose is to employ the means at hand to achieve whatever particular end is desired. Adorno considers such a divorce of thought from practice and context to be an abstract form of unthinking irrationality, which leaves the human subject vulnerable to the manipulations of ideology and impulse. By confining an understanding of rational thought to the task of purposive calculation, without submitting existing presuppositions or desired ends to self-examination, Adorno argues that 'instrumental thinking' becomes ideological and blind to unrecognized (and quite possibly erroneous) assumptions.

A rational choice theorist might try to reply that non-maximizing choices are in fact 'irrational'. What Adorno argues in his interpretation of rationality, however, is that it is purposive (or 'instrumental') rationality that becomes 'irrational' once it loses sight of the ends towards which it was initially employed. Calculating a way to attract *any* woman in a bar, regardless of whether one is compatible with her, is not necessarily rational, just as deciding *not to pursue* any of the women in the bar due to a preference based on values, taste, or other considerations is not necessarily irrational. This being the case, the assumptions made by Stark and Iannaccone regarding what constitutes a 'rational choice' are clearly problematic.

While the first presupposition employed by both Stark and Iannaccone reduces rationality to the cost–benefit calculations of economic exchange, their second premise is vulnerable to issues that Adorno criticizes regarding the 'culture industry'. As rational thought is limited to instrumental calculation, and ends become separated from means, Adorno argues that this results in the impoverishment of human preference and discernment. Aesthetic and moral concerns such as taste, individuality, ethics, and culture become susceptible to 'fabricated need'.[24] This perspective presents two challenges to the rational choice premise that human preferences do not vary much. First, the question arises whether this assumption can be taken to be universal and constant? Given the scope of human diversity and cultures, it is difficult to accept that everyone assesses and weighs costs and benefits on exactly the same scale. Such a presumption is not unlike the suggestion that every man in the bar scene of *A Beautiful Mind* desires the same woman, while simultaneously agreeing that any woman will suffice. Second, even if it can be shown that many human beings desire and value the same things, the concept of 'fabricated need' alerts the scholar to the possibility that critical analysis will uncover that apparent similarities among human preferences are by no means 'natural', but are rather the construct of concealed social forces and dynamics operating prior to individual decision. Should this be the case, it would be difficult to call such preference a rational 'choice'.

From the perspective of Adorno, the limitations of these first two premises are rooted in the third presupposition of the rational choice theorists regarding social 'equilibrium'. The notion that existent society and social forms represent the stable outcomes of the different strategic actions of individual agents is challenged by Adorno's concept of the social 'totality'. If the study of social action concerns itself only with the interactions between human beings without attending to their 'objectified form', it acts as if 'everything really depended on these interpersonal relationships', and not on larger social mechanisms. 'What disappears from sociology is not only the decisive element whereby social activity is able to maintain itself at all, but also knowledge of how it maintains itself, with what sacrifices, threats and also with what potentialities for good.'[25] For Adorno, the social whole cannot simply be reduced to the sum of its parts.

This speculative concept of 'social totality' intends to suggest a dialectical theory of society, in order to maintain a notion of 'society as a thing–in–itself'.[26] As such, it serves to 'give a name to what secretly holds the machinery together'.[27] The concept provides a way to appreciate Marx's critique of ideology in socio-logical method, and it prevents treating social structures and experiences as 'natural' or *a priori*. Adorno argues that 'positivist' empirical studies of social action fail to attend to the ways in which objective social structures shape the subjective actions of human agents. To ignore this is to ignore the mediated nature of all knowledge and experience, and the contradictions contained within human society.

Thus, while rational choice theorists might observe how some individuals behave, and then apply this to their analysis of religious behaviour, Adorno's critical perspective insists that such an approach represents only one element of the study of religion. A critical theory of religion includes analysing, and perhaps even criticizing, the seemingly 'rational choices' that individuals make, in order to determine the manner and extent to which their subjectivity is shaped by the larger social whole.

## Religion as Compensation

Both Stark and Iannaccone apply the above three presuppositions to their analysis of religion in North Atlantic societies. For Stark, the first premise of rational choice theory regarding the nature of rationality implies the assumption that human beings seek rewards and avoid costs. Thus, any 'rational' choice will be guided by this preference, and his interpretation of religion emerges out of this perspective. He argues that, because some desired rewards are in limited supply, or remain beyond the capacity of certain people to achieve, individuals often substitute a 'compensator' for a reward. A compensator is an explanation or proposal for an alternative manner to obtain a desired reward, often through elaborate and lengthy methods. Religion serves to provide com-pensators in the absence or unavailability of certain rewards, principally the longing for immortality. Stark writes, 'it usually is necessary to enter into a long-term exchange relationship with the divine and with divinely inspired institutions, in order to follow the instructions' on how to achieve the desire goal over the longer term. He concludes, 'churches rest upon these underlying exchange relationships'.[28]

From this premise, Stark deduces axioms such as the idea that less powerful people will be more likely to accept compensators. He also suggests that, when a religious organization weakens its emphasis on supernaturalism and an afterlife, it inevitably weakens itself, due to a diminished ability to offer the promise of powerful compensators. This explains, he concludes, why liberal mainstream Christian churches are in decline. It is noteworthy that this analysis leads Stark to challenge rather than support the secularization thesis. Instead of expecting a general decline of interest in religion, spurred on by the spread of modernity and scientific knowledge, he argues that secularization is a self-limiting process. Although some people might abandon their religious traditions, Stark suggests that their children will likely be religious. While major religious denominations may decline, new faiths and traditions will emerge that offer more compelling and supernatural compensators.[29] The general logic behind Stark's argumentation against secularization is that access to desired rewards will always be limited, and so compensators will continue to be required in order to pacify disappointed or frustrated desires.

Some of the language Stark employs to describe this approach to religion reveals the extent to which macroeconomic theoretical models inform the assumptions of rational choice theory. Religious communities are referred to as 'firms'. Those that 'specialize' will flourish in the 'religious economy'. Those that fail to offer a compelling enough compensator will decline. He argues that, 'Religious economies are like commercial economies in that they consist of a market of current and potential customers, a set of firms seeking to serve that market, and the religious 'product lines' offered by the various firms'.[30] He continues, 'to the degree that a religious economy is competitive and pluralistic, overall levels of religious participation will tend to be high'. In other words, as the 'monopoly' of mainline Christian churches declines, the emerging pluralistic and 'free' religious market will result in increasing 'religious' activity and exchange, as individual 'religious investors' diversify what Lawrence Iannaccone calls their 'religious portfolios'.[31] It is suggested that, in a 'free market', flexible institutions will prosper.

From a perspective informed by Adorno's work, there are numerous problems with this approach to religion, but two will be highlighted in particular: its reliance upon the concept of 'compensators', and its roots in 'supply-side' economic theory.

In terms of its logical argument, it is difficult to see how an explanation will necessarily substitute for an immediate reward. A compensator is, in fact, not a reward at all – only a substitution for one. Yet both Stark and Iannaccone often treat these deferred rewards as concrete 'products' delivered by the religious 'firm'. Surely a step is omitted in this analysis, however, for the religious 'compensator' can only function as such when an individual is somehow convinced that what is on offer can substitute for an immediate reward. This process of how and why certain concepts or practices are able to function in this way remains largely unexamined in the theory of compensators.

Furthermore, why should the scholar of religion conclude that accepting the promise of a better life after death, in the face of a life of suffering, represents a 'rational choice'? Again, it is instructive to refer to *A Beautiful Mind*. As the Nash character sits in the bar, he might decide that he should avoid the blonde woman he truly desires, and accept the 'compensation' of whatever other woman accepts his attention. Conceivably, he might also be inspired by a sign on the wall that reads 'good things come to those who wait'. There are many possible courses of action available to him. The question is: why should a social theorist label a decision to accept the compensation of a generic 'woman', or of the sentimental cliché on the wall, 'rational' behaviour? Why should one conclude that the end result of his decision serves to satisfy the actual 'reward' he desires? One might equally suggest that his shyness or insecurity is 'irrational' and that it deprives him of the 'reward' of a possible relationship. The reduction of human decision-making to the basic currency of this concept of 'compensation' is based upon assumptions whose logic is tenuous at best.

Stark's conceptualization of human desire is narrow and highly materialistic. His approach reveals how the behaviour models developed by game theory contain subtle assumptions about human nature. The concept of compensation, for example, focuses on immediate material benefits (wealth, power, health, immortality), but displays little attention on other important, though less empirically measurable values, such as relationships, identity, meaning, etc. It does not attend in any significant way to examining its own methodological presuppositions, but often describes basic human motivations as if they are self-evident and 'natural'. The implied understanding of human beings is rather opposed to the Christian vision of moral life and the purpose of ecclesial community. But those theologians who draw on rational choice to orient church growth strategies generally fail to note the baggage such understandings of religion bring with them.

It is at the level of its core presuppositions that the rational choice model of religion is most problematic and bears the closest resemblance to the reductive treatment of relationships in *A Beautiful Mind*. The conclusions of these theorists echo the free market assumptions of contemporary neo-conservative economics. Simplifying secularization once again, Stark argues that state-funded clergy work less hard, which is why their churches are in decline.[32] In other words, government civil servants are lazy, while the entrepreneur is successful; 'religious professionals, *like anyone else*, do not exert themselves unless they need to do so – in the absence of eager competitors, religious organizations will be lax and inefficient'.[33] Stark is comfortable asserting that *all* human beings are only motivated by threat and competition. The diversity and complexity of human behaviour is swept aside by this assertion, and it noteworthy that such a statement resembles the rhetoric often found in criticisms of the welfare state and Keynesian economics.

Similar assumptions can be found in Iannaccone's writing. He credits greater 'efficiency' for the strength of more doctrinally conservative and morally strict Christian churches in the United States. For Iannaccone, religion is a 'commodity' produced collectively. In a voluntaristic and less rigid community, some individuals are able to benefit from the services of a church, without contributing significantly. Such 'free riders' effectively 'take more than they give'.[34] Since he assumes that time is money, Iannaccone argues that churches with higher average salaries have a shorter worship service, and that shared-faith marriages result in a higher level of church attendance than 'mixed' denominational marriages because 'partners of the same religion can produce religious commodities more efficiently'. Why? Because they benefit from economies of scale: 'The same car drives everyone to church; there is no question as to how time and money contributions will be allocated to different religions'.[35] But imaging that couples agree to practice the same religion because it saves on travel expenses is about as profound as suggesting that, if the men in the bar avoid the more attractive blonde woman, they can have their pick of any other 'grateful' mate.

The unflinching embrace of the compensatory role of religion is startling from a position informed by Marx's criticism of the ideological nature of religion as 'the opium of the people'. For Marx, the promise of consolation in the afterlife all too easily becomes reduced to decorating the chains of unjust social relations with flowers. The critical principle implied in this perspective is the argument that discourse which fails to acknowledge that it is shaped and produced by its historical context is abstract and naïve. In the theories of religion developed by Stark and Iannaccone, little attention is given to analysing present social conditions, or how people respond to these conditions.

Adorno's critique of positivism challenges a social scientific method that relies upon such entrenched assumptions. It insists that social theory has to become more self-reflective about what shapes and informs it, but it also pushes reflection and analysis still further. For, even if the rational choice theorist's description of existing patterns of social behaviour is accurate, Adorno challenges the presumption that this description can be considered a complete grasp of social reality. For him, social theory cannot presume that observed patterns of behaviour are 'natural' or illustrative of social 'laws'.

The debate for Adorno is not over whether to study religion scientifically, nor is it over the appropriateness of employing empirical research or analysing patterns of behaviour. As Adorno notes, 'social regularities do self-evidently exist'. Social science will thus seek to uncover such patterns through empirical research. What Adorno criticizes are sociological theories that fail to acknowledge the historicity of these social patterns – that they are produced and are subject to change; 'there is, indeed, a very strong tendency to amputate the historical dimension altogether'.[36]

By this, Adorno suggests that a perspective which treats its object as a static fact, without exploring how it is socially constructed in history and remains subject to ongoing development, effectively reifies what it intends to study. He argues that, not only does this attitude result in faulty theoretical conclusions, it also serves to canonize the *status quo*. It suggests that existing society is unalterable and is the best of all possible worlds. And so, the behaviour of the men in *A Beautiful Mind* can be considered to be an accurate and universal portrait of relationships between the genders, and the observations of Stark and Iannaccone regarding some American Protestant churches can be taken as an explanation of different forms of 'religion'. By neglecting to appreciate the constructed nature of all social phenomena, such an approach 'causes its object to congeal into something solid while at the same time "momentizing" it. That which is nothing other than "here and now" hardens and solidifies'.[37]

Even though Stark's approach to religion is certainly aware of historical changes and developments in different religions, from the perspective of Adorno, his rational choice model stops short of analysing and explaining the social patterns he observes among religious adherents. Adorno argues that such phenomena need to be examined and explained in the context of the larger social totality – in order to determine how society is shaping and constructing the very patterns being studied, along with the observing theorist himself. Without a dialectical concept of society, he suggests, one cannot distinguish between a society's actuality and its potentiality. The *status quo* will be taken to be society's only possible form.

## From *A Beautiful Mind* to the 'Beautiful Soul'

This is to say that, even if the methodology of Stark and Iannaccone resulted in some helpful initial empirical data (which Adorno's perspective might well challenge), without a broader concept of society – one more attentive to particularity and open to the critical sense of a different *potentiality* – their social theory risks ignoring internal social contradictions, exceptions, and diversity, while simply serving to support the established state of affairs:

> The process which supports life, which sociology has as its essential subject matter, is indeed the economic process, but the economic laws already stylize this process in accordance with a conceptual system of strictly rational actions, which asserts itself all the more insistently as an explanatory schema, the less it is actualized in the real world. Sociology is economics only as political economy, and that requires a theory of society.[38]

Examining rational choice theory on religion through the lens of Adorno's criticism of positivism demonstrates that the explication of human relations narrated in *A Beautiful Mind* amounts to what Hegel calls the 'beautiful soul', who, 'in order to preserve the purity of its heart . . . flees from contact with the actual world'.[39] The 'beautiful soul' is a consciousness that has withdrawn into itself, certain of its own validity, and unwilling to let the objectivity of the outside world threaten its self-certainty. The fictional male characters can walk out of the bar, confident in their new insights, without actually pausing to talk to the women in order to verify whether their assumptions about them are accurate.

Ignoring the differences in and between distinct religious communities and traditions, the rational choice model proves to be based upon ideological presuppositions about human nature and social action. External concrete differences between different religious traditions and social locations receive little to no attention in its statistical analyses. Furthermore, the society in which the object of their study is found, particularly the dominant political economy of the United States, is subjectively unquestioned. Existing social forms are naturalized, ignoring the objectivity of what Adorno calls the broader social totality.

## Adorno on Religion

The different theoretical basis of the critical theory Adorno embraces results in a very different approach to the study of religion from that of rational choice theory. Whereas Stark and his colleagues define religion exclusively as being concerned with the supernatural, Adorno understands religion as being related to the concern for objective truth. This is not to say that he is uncritical of the frequent tendency of members of religious traditions to cling to supernatural and otherworldly ideas and aspirations. But unlike Stark and Iannaccone, he also opposes any appreciation for 'compensation' or, in their language, 'consolation'. Horkheimer insists that such ideas are illusions, 'the suffering of past generations receives no compensation'.[40]

On this point, then, Adorno's scrutiny of religion's connection to compensation and suffering takes his analysis further than that of Stark and Iannaccone. As Horkheimer phrases it, 'religion as consolation means more than might occur' to a religious leader or theorist. For, 'it is not the truth of religion that dawns on the person in need, it is the need that constitutes its truth, not only individual, but social need as well'.[41] Adorno approaches religious traditions in a similar spirit. Religion is for him a particular form of social expression that reveals in a unique way the inherent tensions and contradictions among individuals and communities in their social context. It is therefore the task of the study of religion to explain why people require and depend on 'compensators'. A critical theory of religion intends to resist the temptation to conclude that the existence of these virtual rewards is itself an 'explanation' for religious behaviour. From the perspective of Adorno, theorists like Stark and Iannaccone reduce religion to a theory of compensators, without probing into the conditions that make compensators necessary. This is exactly the approach to social analysis that Adorno accuses of 'amputating' attention to historicity and the social totality.

Adorno's approach to the issue of 'consolation' is noteworthy for the fact that, although it certainly emphasizes the cognitive aspect of religious *belief*, it in no way limits itself to a cerebral understanding of 'religion' to the same extent that rational choice narrowly restricts it to belief in immortality. Adorno recognizes that the identity and experience of religious adherents involves far more than cognitive beliefs, but also emotional, social and psychological aspects of relation. For, although the metaphysical beliefs of the various religious traditions are considered to be illusions, he understands these same traditions are intimately linked to human aspirations, which, as they push beyond given social conditions, connect them to a longing for a better world, and for a connection to objective truth.

This is the starting point for the study of religion offered by Adorno; one that represents a marked contrast to the model presented by rational choice theory. For Adorno, 'certainly a ratio that does not wantonly absolutize itself as a rigid means of domination requires self-reflection, some of which is expressed in the need for religion today'.[42] But by this he does not advocate a return to a religious or theological worldview. Rather, Adorno argues that part of the motivation behind religious practices, expressions, and longings, is to be understood as a longing for a better world, and for an objective truth. Because of this, the study of religion offers critical theory a rich site in which to analyse social contradictions and tensions. Thus, although far from advocating a 'return to religion', Adorno calls for a return to the criticism of religion, and for greater critical attention to the social conditions in which religious traditions function. For, in Horkheimer's estimation, a philosophy that seeks to be anything more than 'scientism' is itself entangled with the same dilemmas as theology: 'Knowledge is ultimately governed by purposes. Theology wants to be free of earthly ends. It is both lower and higher than any form of knowledge'.[43] The problem with a rigid positivism is that, forgetting its own historicity, it clings to its narrow grasp of its object, which effectively reduces the object to an irrational myth based on subjective presuppositions, and results in a theory no more reliable than the metaphysical beliefs it seeks to escape.

To be sure, neither Adorno or Horkheimer were able to develop thorough studies of particular religious communities in their lifetime. Adorno completed a few very sketchy examples, neither of which encompasses the more detailed empirical work that he advocates in his methodological writings.[44] The failure to put forward a developed research programme was partially the result of their deepening despair over what they saw as the domination of social science and rationality by instrumental reason. Horkheimer in particular grew increasingly pessimistic in his later years about the possibility of resisting the snare of technical rationality's 'iron cage'. In a late aphorism, he writes, 'to the extent that philosophy wants to be more than directions that can be confirmed, i.e. science, it disregards speaker and listener and posits itself as absolute. Language in the emphatic sense, language which wants to be truth, is chattering silence'.[45]

This tone in his later writing is unfortunate, for it distracts from the strong emphasis throughout both his own writing and that of Adorno on the analysis of concrete particular manifestations of social experience. As his work increasingly focused on responding to the Holocaust and the challenges of post-war reconstruction, along with the emerging domination of technology and consumer advertising, Adorno gradually set his interest in empirical social research and the study of religion to one side. Given the promise of his particular approach to an interdisciplinary social theory, along with the limitations of rational choice theory demonstrated here, a return to the perspective he develops towards religion will bear considerable fruit. What is required, in contrast to rational choice theory, is attention to the complex particularity of distinct communities that shape and are shaped by contemporary social and economic forces. A critical theory of religion challenges the slippage that leads from *A Beautiful Mind* to the 'beautiful soul'. As Adorno urged,

> What is called for is not only the assimilation of the mathematized market economy into sociology; economics, in its turn, is called upon to do precisely what it fails to do: to translate the economic laws back into congealed human relationships.[46]

## Correlation, Ideology and Damaged Life

If Adorno's concept of the culture industry brings his approach to religion into sharp contrast with rational choice theory, it also implies a considerable challenge to a prominent methodology employed by Christian theology to engage with contemporary culture. In the first volume of his *Systematic Theology*, Paul Tillich develops what he calls a method of 'correlation'. Arguing that 'God in his self-manifestation to man is dependent on the way man receives his manifestation', Tillich suggested that contemporary society presents the *questions* to theology and the theological tradition is subsequently examined for *answers* to these questions.[47] Responses to such questions are shaped by the Christian tradition, which might sometimes require some revision based on contemporary experience. In Tillich's existentialist approach, he suggests that the questions are 'implied in human experience', and belong to humanity's 'essential being'; 'Man is the question he asks about himself, before any question has been formulated'.[48] The analysis of the present situation and its questions is, for Tillich, a philosophical task, which may also draw from psychology, sociology, and a close study of human cultural forms, such as literature and art. This theoretical perspective proceeds as follows:

> Whenever man has looked at his world, he has found
> himself in it as a part of it. But he also has realized that
> he is a stranger in the world of objects ... And then he
> has become aware of the fact that he himself is the door
> to the deeper levels of reality, that in his own existence
> he has the only possible approach to existence itself ...
> [T]he immediate experience of one's own existing reveals
> something of the nature of existence generally.[49]

In Tillich's view, once an analysis of humanity's 'essential nature' is completed, along with the questions that such an examination raises about existence (finitude, etc.), the Christian theologian can then demonstrate how the symbols of the Christian tradition provide answers to these questions.

Adorno's philosophy challenges Tillich's presumption of a common human essence that is rooted in a concept of finitude: recall Chapter 1's summary of his criticism of Tillich's religious socialism. But more generally, Adorno's analysis of the culture industry, and its roots in the social totality, prevent any methodological presumption that present experience might serve as a foundation for either a philosophical or theological ontology. For, in the context of damaged life, why should the theologian presume that the 'questions' posed by a specific social situation represent an accurate or undistorted perspective that one can accept at face value? In *The Jargon of Authenticity*, Adorno criticizes Martin Buber's existential analysis of a society for supplying human beings with 'patterns' for being human 'which have been driven out of them by unfree labour'.[50] If the social totality shaping human existence is producing unjust relationships and ideological cultural forms, then it would be misguided to construct a positive theology on the basis of its prominent 'questions'. The method of correlation, drawing as it does from Heidegger's philosophy, is vulnerable to Adorno's criticisms of this tradition: the approach neglects the reality that human existence is caught up in a determining objectivity. It ontologizes present forms of damaged life. What Adorno considers to be signs of social alienation and distorted consciousness, Tillich identifies as evidence of the ontological need for, and truth of, theology. But such a method takes distorted 'second nature' as evidence for an ontological given.

With this refusal to accept the existing social structures and cultural forms as 'given' or unproblematic, Adorno's methodology represents a challenge to any theology of correlation. It is interesting to note, by contrast, the manner in which Adam Kotsko has recently suggested that Slavoj Žižek's critical theory can be understood as a variation on Tillich's method.[51] Žižek draws to a degree from the Frankfurt School, while supplementing it with the psychoanalytic theory of Jacques Lacan. Like Adorno, Žižek is concerned to develop a sophisticated critique of contemporary culture. His work similarly intends to expose contradictions within social existence. But Žižek criticizes Adorno's readings of culture – particularly his deployment of Freudian psychoanalytic theory – for taking a merely negative approach to the psychology of ideology. Adorno, he argues, treats ideology as something that operates within the inner lives of human beings 'behind their back'. This implies, Žižek continues, that irrational forces are at work beyond the control of the conscious subject. In his rendering, Adorno's aim is to emancipate the human being from the rule of his unconscious, which effectively represents a view of 'a subject without psychology'.[52]

The general thrust of this criticism is to say that Adorno's negative stance goes too far. Cannot some elements of present experience and culture serve as a positive support for progressive thought and practice? There is some real substance to this concern, as will be explored more fully in Chapter 7. If one recalls

Adorno's analysis of astrology columns, however, it is difficult to support Žižek's more specific claim: that Adorno's theory of ideology suggests that human beings are controlled like puppets by a hidden manipulative mechanism. Recall that Adorno describes practitioners of astrology as demonstrating clear signs that they do not fully believe in the predictions they read. They both disbelieve and believe in the columns at the same time. Adorno does not crudely suggest that the minds of such individuals are simply being manipulated and controlled by ideology. To the contrary, their own desires and felt needs 'prepare the minds of people for astrology'.[53] These are not subjects without a psychology; rather, it is their psychological needs which construct and support the ideology. The emphasis in these columns on being vulnerable to the fate of the stars is shown by Adorno to be shaped by the subjects themselves. He argues:

> What drives people into the arms of the various kinds of 'prophets of deceit' is not only their sense of dependence and their wish to attribute this dependence to some 'higher' and ultimately more justifiable sources, but it is also *their wish to reinforce their own dependence*, not to have to take matters into their own hands.[54]

Thus, the followers of astrology 'do not seem quite to believe' in their practices (due to considerable empirical evidence against these acts) but they do act *as if* they believe. Žižek himself makes a similar observation about the nature of belief. He suggests that, in the cynical and sophisticated cultural environment of contemporary society, most people keep any firm commitments at a distance. He illustrates this by referring to the film *Unbreakable*, the story of a 'regular guy' who becomes a super-hero when he discovers that he is invincible to pain. When the man attempts to avoid accepting the responsibility his new found powers confront him with, Žižek argues, 'it is difficult, properly traumatic, for a human animal to accept that his or her life . . . is in the service of a Truth'. Rather than accept the reality of a situation, many human beings seek to carry on *as if* the world is the way they want it to be. This is what Žižek thinks our ideological environment has made of belief: 'We perform our symbolic mandates' without 'taking them seriously'. Our culture tends to 'make fun of our beliefs, while continuing to practice them'.[55]

Žižek laments this situation, and his recent work had turned to evaluate theology positively. He looks to those moments where religion encourages people to act decisively for the 'truth', appreciating in particular 'Christ's famous words about how he has come to bring the sword and division, not unity and peace'.[56] In St Paul, he sees a call to 'commit ourselves to an excessive intensity which puts us beyond "mere life"'.[57] Such an understanding serves as a model for what Žižek calls an 'event' or 'radical Act'. This is characterized by an action that breaks the cycle of ideological positions that shape an existing situation.

This stance is compared with Pascal's wager, which suggests that, faced with uncertainty, it is better to 'wager' a belief in God than it is to be an atheist. While the gain one attains if one is correct is very high, non-belief promises nothing at all but would have tragic consequences if the reality of God was true. Believing, Pascal concludes, is thus much more advantageous than not believing. In similar fashion, Žižek calls his concept of the 'radical Act' a 'Pascalean wager'.[58] One cannot prove that an 'Act' will be successful or that it will make the situation better. But in an antagonistic world of dualistic ideological options, Žižek argues that it is more advantageous to risk an 'Act' than it is to merely 'go with the flow' or to sit at a cynical distance from the rest of society.

This challenge to Adorno's treatment of ideology, with its alternative proposal of an 'Act', revisits issues that were raised in Chapter 5 over Adorno's supposed political resignation. For Adorno's criticism of Brechtian decisionism, as well as his caution against political activism done for the sake of acting, represent a challenge to Žižek's treatment of 'belief'. As Adorno argues against Kierkegaard, when 'right living is defined entirely in terms of decision', a form of subjectivity is implied that suggests 'the absolute disposal of the individual over himself, without regard to the fact that he is caught up in a determining objectivity'.[59] Rather than developing this comparison between Adorno and Žižek in further detail, however, this constellation with Tillich's and Žižek's approaches to theology and culture is sufficient to illuminate the nature of Adorno's inverse theology.

## Inverse Correlation

Adorno's inverse theology does not engage in correlating present problems with theological themes, in the manner developed by Tillich, and perceptively observed by Kotsko in Žižek's work. In Adorno's view, connections to the theological tradition based on trends or anxieties in present social experience are symptoms of damaged life, not traces of divine presence. In a similar manner, he argues that the need for political action cannot in itself ground progressive action. By contrast then, Adorno's approach to theology and society suggests an *inverse* correlation. He does not look to society to discover the questions about existence, which theology then answers. The examples of rational choice theory, as well as Adorno's own study of astrology and the concept of spirituality, demonstrate that the priorities of religious practitioners are often driven by a psychic need for consolation and comfort. For such reasons, Adorno inverts the ordering of Tillich's theology of correlation. For Adorno, theological concepts like redemption, justice, the messianic, and the fullness of reason (in its 'emphatic sense') confront critical thought with questions about society. It is, then, human beings, within their social situation, who are charged with constructing the answers to the questions. An inverse theology is thus not a top-down imposition of idealist concepts; rather, the theological element in Adorno's work is employed to crack open existing life; to make room for new insights.

Adorno consistently argues that theology possesses 'truth content', and that religions like Christianity have on occasion supported emancipatory reason and progressive challenges to unjust social conditions. What Adorno's *Bilderverbot* prohibits, however, is any attempt to harness this potential and employ it in a utilitarian manner. This is what some theologians seek to do when they enthusiastically and uncritically embrace the contemporary interest in 'spirituality', or the conclusions of rational choice theory for developing church growth strategies. Such efforts, from the perspective of Adorno, easily become reduced to identity thinking. No cultural phenomenon is so free from the cultural industry that it may perform such a function. It will be the task of the next chapter to explore the nature of this inverse correlation in more detail, through an exploration of Adorno's engagement with art and music.

# Chapter 7

# Hymns to the Silence

*When I'm away from you, I just have to sing, my hymns. Hymns to the silence.*

*Van Morrison*[1]

| | |
|---|---|
| *Gelobt seist du, Niemand.* | *[Praised be your name, no one.* |
| *Dir zulieb wollen* | *For     your     sake* |
| *Wir blühn.* | *We     shall     flower.* |
| *Dir* | *Towards* |
| *Entgegen.* | *you.]* |

*Paul Celan*[2]

The previous chapter brought together various elements of Adorno's inverse theology that had been identified over the course of this book: his understanding of the entwinement of myth and rationality, the central role of the *Bilderverbot*, his critique of identity thinking and positivism, and the association he establishes between 'metaphysical experience' and theology. It demonstrated how this perspective contrasts with the contemporary interest in 'spirituality' and with the rational choice understanding of religion. A central conclusion of this discussion was to show how Adorno's inverse theology establishes an inverse correlation with damaged life.

This final chapter draws these various strands together, and contrasts this interpretation of Adorno's perspective on theology with other theological engagements with his work. By comparing these readings with Adorno's aesthetic theory, some fragmentary aphorisms on the nature of love, and his enthusiasm for the poetry of Paul Celan, this examination demonstrates that Adorno's interest in theology is not a marginal aspect of his writing, but that it lies at the very core of the moral impulse that motivates his work. For in his view, without the critical distance opened up on the brokenness of life that is achieved by assuming the perspective of an inverse theology, the complete abandonment of theology surrenders life to the sufferings of the *status quo*. While Adorno insists that one must remain silent about God, he also argues that one must at the same time continue to search for the possibility that has been silenced within damaged life and might still be found beyond the limits of actuality.

## Adorno among Christian Theologians

It is noteworthy that Christian theologians do not frequently engage with Adorno's thought. His rejection of foundational ontology and his resistance to positive systems often makes him an unattractive conversation partner for systematic theologians. Those who do draw from Adorno's philosophy appreciate the intensity of his moral vision, but then proceed to argue that his position requires a more solid foundation, which only a more positive theology can provide. A brief survey of some different theological engagements with Adorno's thoughts will illustrate a sample of the more prominent directions that have been developed to date. Although these theological readings of his work offer a number of interesting insights into and challenges to his thought, it is more fruitful to allow his work to resist simply being assimilated or 'repaired' by Christian theology, and to appreciate how his work warns against the tendency of the system to close in on itself. For although Adorno's philosophy contains a number of limitations and paradoxes, it is his insistence on preventing thought from foreclosing on itself that represents his most promising challenge to the theological tradition.

Although Jürgen Moltmann's 'theology of hope' does not draw significantly from Adorno (but rather from Ernst Bloch), his concern with historical praxis, as well as the emphasis he places on the interruption of an eschatological future, resonates with the concerns of Adorno's 'inverse theology'. Moltmann criticizes present actuality on the basis of a future possibility. He argues that the task of theology is not to interpret the world, but to change it, and suggests that the work of reconciliation in history is enlivened and enabled by the hope that God will redeem the world in the enfolding of the future.[3]

Despite this emphasis on historical praxis and protest against injustice, the focus of Moltmann's positive theology – hope – is a concept that Adorno finds problematic. To him, 'hope' is easily reduced to something abstract and ideological. Although he acknowledges that 'without hope, the idea of truth would be scarcely even thinkable', because otherwise thought merely accepts the misery of the *status quo*, over-emphasizing hope easily gets reduced to a preoccupation with consolation and redemption. Such slippage takes the pressure off a negative stance towards existing reality.[4] Adorno argues that it is illogical to root signs of hope in a broken world, 'because the situations in which people are forced to think "positively" simply in order to survive are themselves situations of compulsion'.[5] He insists that the greatest danger and potential misunderstanding of both theology and metaphysics occurs when 'hope is mistaken for truth'. Lacking any real possibility rooted within existing social conditions, and withholding the potential for a greater experience of freedom, embracing hope can resemble 'reconciliation under duress'.[6] One cannot hypostatize hope simply because suffering human beings may find temporary comfort in it.

Lambert Zuidervaart defends a closer affinity between Adorno and Moltmann than is suggested here. He argues that if 'one interprets "the hope of salvation" as a hope for fundamental transformation in society, then the apparent dilemma of either salvation or historical transfiguration disappears'.[7] While there is indeed a resonance between Moltmann's hope for a better world and Adorno's critical theory, the difference between them remains rather deep: Moltmann's position is grounded in a positive ontology of God, for which the existence of suffering becomes, almost despite his own intentions, an apologetic support. For Adorno, the idea of a crucified God implies that suffering is the secret meaning of being.

Edgar Thaidigsmann interprets Adorno's work as a form of hope by bringing his thought into dialogue with Moltmann and particularly Karl Barth. By focusing on Adorno's emphasis on possibility, Thaidigsmann suggests that it implies a transcendental horizon for thought. This manner of thinking, Thaidigsmann continues, is both testimony to, and defence of, an idea of promise [*Versprechen*].[8] He points to aphorisms on childhood from *Minima Moralia* as evidence for this view, suggesting that Adorno understood them as 'bearing a promise'. The aphorisms present children as having a particular openness to experience, over which they seek neither dominance nor self-control. Vague memories of visitors to the family home, or of the excitement of Christmas, for example, bring to a child 'an epiphany of the everyday beyond'.[9]

Thaidigsmann's discussion helpfully teases out of such stories the manner in which Adorno conceives the truth in theology and religion as being in their attempt to articulate and reflect on an expanded concept of experience. And yet, Thaidigsmann's interpretation stresses how a positive element is contained in such elusive experience, which is not really the emphasis of Adorno's writing itself. Thaidigsmann writes of the Christmas memories, for example, 'through different rituals, one can see the time of celebration, a special time, as separate from the rest of time', and suggests that, for Adorno, such experiences result in the 'expectation that such moments full of promise are possible and can happen always and everywhere'.[10] To push Adorno's reflections in such a direction is not unlike Agamben's proposal to replace Adorno's 'as if' with the more existential 'as not'.[11] For Adorno, the experiences that point beyond the limitations of present life don't interrupt the given moment in a positive way; their contribution is to point to the possibility of a different life, not deliver it.

In the aphorism under consideration here, when Adorno recalls that the presence of guests 'promises the child a world beyond the family home, reminding him that it is not ultimate', there is indeed a sense that such an experience opens up an awareness of alternative possibilities for life.[12] But the experience points to such possibility; it does not provide assurance of its arrival. In this moment, 'the child's whole being is waiting'. Adorno then adds, however, that the adult must learn 'to be able to wait who does not forget what is best in childhood'. There is a prominent anamnestic tone to this reflection, for he is concerned with the particularity of the object prior to its reification into an exchangeable commodity. But the experiences being remembered, at least in his view, cannot serve as a foundation upon which to build an alternative way of life; nor can they be retrieved. For Adorno, such experiences are more fleeting, and less frequent, than Thaidigsmann's reading implies. Instrumentalizing celebratory rituals as the generator of metaphysical experiences effectively commodifies them, according to Adorno, which thereby robs them of their capacity to momentarily illuminate that the world could be otherwise.

The subtle nuance here comes clearly into view when dealing with the issue of translating Adorno's well known phrase '*Es gibt kein richtiges Leben im falschen*'. Edmund Jephcott renders this as 'Wrong life cannot be lived rightly'.[13] Finlayson observes, however, that it is more accurate to translate this as, 'The false life cannot be truly lived'.[14] This shift away from concepts like 'right' and 'wrong' clarifies Adorno's concern to maintain a negative engagement with present social existence. Within 'damaged life', what it means to 'truly live' cannot even be thought. It is only the falseness of present reality that can be concretely pointed to. And so, while the memories of childhood may indeed represent for Adorno moments when he experienced the possibility of happiness, they do not in themselves contain the 'promise' of such an achievement. Indeed, more often than not, his references to childhood point to the 'nightmare' that has come true.[15]

Thaidigsmann's close reading of these texts does nevertheless help capture the general tone of Adorno's inverse theology. While it may be going a bit too far to suggest that his negativity 'mirrors the promise of the Sabbath',[16] Adorno's use of the childhood memory of returning from holiday to the initial peacefulness of the home does indeed serve as a brief glimpse of what it might mean to imagine a world 'no longer under the law of labour'.[17] What his thought resists, however, is any sense of taking consolatory refuge in such memories. To longingly dwell on them risks bringing thought 'to a standstill'. It is thus not hope or promise to which Adorno's inverse theology points; rather it involves the 'spiritual experience' of thinking the 'last extreme of horror' and being prepared to confront it.[18] Thaidigsmann's analysis does tease out, however, that there are brief and fragmentary references to positive experience in Adorno's writing, which sit somewhat uncomfortably alongside his stronger concern with negativity. This tension will be explored in more detail at the end of this chapter.

An alternative theological approach to Adorno's thought is developed by Wayne Whitson Floyd, who brings it into a constellation with the theology of Dietrich Bonhoeffer.[19] For Floyd, the former's work represents an 'anti-systematic theology'. He argues that Adorno's concept of the preponderance of the object establishes a 'dialectics of otherness'. This suggests the 'otherness of theology' based on a recognition of the 'non-identity of God'.[20] Kenneth Surin offers a similar consideration of Adorno's work in dialogue with Bonhoeffer's theology.[21] For Surin, Adorno's immanent critique of society implies a criticism of secularism and disenchantment. Although it is indeed correct to argue that Adorno 'seek[s] to "demystify" social reality' and reveal it to be 'second nature',[22] Surin suggests that such a critique points beyond the limitations of history, opening up a space for an affirmative theology resembling something like Karl Barth's concept of revelation.[23]

Although these discussions identify notable resonances between some basic concerns that Adorno shares with Bonhoeffer, these discussions do not uncover moments of deep connection. Moreover, such interpretations of Adorno's work occasionally resemble what he might describe as the hypostasizing of non-identity. These appear when the location of 'the non-identity of non-identity' is described as the 'wholly other' of the divine. Although there are indeed moments when the bleak vision through which Adorno views the world might be called 'apocalyptic', and Floyd's book can be commended for drawing attention to this element, it is clear that Adorno is also at pains to warn against the Christian tendency to make a virtue out of the tragedy of the world.

For Adorno, speaking of a God 'wholly other' to human history is unacceptable. In his view it turns the divine into an abyss. The non-identity of non-identity is, for him, nothing objective or determinate. Having no specificity of its own, the concept is simply filled by the projections of the subject via 'a dogmatic and arbitrary leap'.[24] Such a way of speaking, as he argues in a letter to Paul Tillich, makes 'common cause with the logical positivists', for the language serves only to 'replace the subject'.[25] Any experience of otherness, in his view, must have its own objectivity, and can only be mediated through historical experience. Although Barth and Bonhoeffer seek to emphasize the concrete particularity of the person of Christ, for Adorno, their positions are at once too concrete and not concrete enough. The positivity given to the image of God too closely resembles mythology. Furthermore, having criticized and uncovered the ideological entwinement of

German Protestantism and German culture, and having thereby insisted upon the absolute transcendence of God, neo-orthodox theology nevertheless 'continued to use the traditional words of theology without interruption'.[26] Thus, in his view, the roots of this traditional theological language in the brokenness of human history are not submitted to sufficient concrete analysis.

Ralf Frisch seeks to overcome this gap between Adorno's and Barth's perspectives by emphasizing the centrality of artwork as the place of theology 'at the moment of its fall'. Frisch reads the final aphorism of *Minima Moralia* – with its reference to contemplating the present from the standpoint of redemption – as a 'Medusan-messianic' gaze, which is most properly located in the form of a modern artwork.[27] He interprets moments in *Aesthetic Theory*, such as when Adorno writes, 'The spirit [Geist] of artworks is their immanent mediation . . . [in which] every element in the artwork becomes its own other',[28] as pointing to a 'theological more', a moment in which the artwork transcends the realm of immanent causality.[29]

Frisch's attention to Adorno's aesthetics is a helpful contribution, for it is in such work that Adorno articulates most directly a vision of the possibility of reconciliation between culture and nature. In a society traumatized by war and Auschwitz, he argues that traditional aesthetic categories like 'beauty', 'taste' and the 'sublime' have become problematic. In order for art to present the 'truth' of the brokenness of reality, it must somehow portray the world in its unreconciled state. But the pursuit of such a task erodes art's coherence and capacity to communicate. The artwork's mimesis of the fragmented reality before it threatens its ability to represent that world.

Whereas Kant's aesthetics focuses on the subjective reception of the artwork, while Hegel explores the aesthetic object itself as objective, Adorno seeks to overcome this opposition. He argues that modern art, by resisting the fashions of culture (which reduce it to the functional role of commodity), demands an intense and almost devotional attention from the observing subject. The modern artwork resists subjective consumption, so that, in a way, the subject observing the work is itself consumed. But the dialectic does not cease there, for not only is the subject changed by this engagement; so too is the artwork. While a false relation to art treats it as a possession, the individual who has a genuine engagement with art's 'enigmaticalness', in which he himself vanishes, finds that 'art is not an object'.[30] It has its own autonomy, and its very form resists immediate 'meaning' or purpose; 'Artworks that unfold to contemplation and thought without any remainder are not artworks'. For as the work of art begins to be 'unpuzzled' and opened up, 'it reveals itself as a question and demands refection'. But under such scrutiny 'the work vanishes into the distance, only to return to those who thought they understood it, overwhelming them for a second time with the question "What is it?"'.[31]

A more adequate analysis of Adorno's aesthetic theory is beyond the scope of this study, although some further discussion of his treatment of modern music follows below.[32] This brief sketch simply provides the background to Frisch's suggestion that, for Adorno, art serves as the 'view of God, as well as God's [own] view'.[33] It is the locus of his vision for the reconciliation of subject and object. In art's protest against the brokenness of the world, it points toward that same world's affirmation. Frisch argues that art's 'suffering' thus points to a theology of the cross. Adorno's own treatment of this dialectic, Frisch continues, is not sufficiently guarded against succumbing to a 'necrophilic longing for death'.[34] He intends to rectify this by bringing Adorno's aesthetic vision into a constellation with Barth's theology, so as to highlight how death's overcoming is entwined in the death of the artwork.

The problem raised by Frisch's interpretation is the question of whether Adorno's work actually implies or requires this move from critique to affirmation, from death to resurrection, or whether making such a move actually requires the abandonment of Adorno's philosophy altogether. Adorno certainly understands art to have a utopian dimension. The artwork seeks to articulate or represent truth, and thus reaches beyond itself. But is it helpful to argue that this implies, or necessitates, speaking of this achievement as being divine or serving as an analogy for God? In Adorno's rendering, the achievement of the artwork is found more in its protest against its own failure to represent truth. The modern artwork resists its own identity as a cultural commodity – a fate it cannot escape – so that its primary witness is less to an absent absolute, but rather to the brokenness of society in its current form. For Adorno, the 'theological' dimension here is more an inverted critique of the existing, than it is the consolation offered by a theology of the cross. To argue more than this would be to leave the core commitments of Adorno's thought behind, and so Frisch's interpretation is not simply a supplement or a repair operation on behalf of Adorno's own vision.

Andreas Pangritz also argues that Adorno's philosophy requires a more positive theological supplement. In his study, he astutely emphasizes that Adorno's social philosophy is not itself a theology, but suggests that it raises questions that are themselves theological.[35] This view is certainly compatible with the interpretation of Adorno's inverse theology developed in Chapter 4 of this book. But in Adorno's post-war writing, Pangritz argues that Adorno not only mourns for what has been lost, but also communicates the possibility of being saved from destruction. In a provocative interpretation of Adorno's *Philosophy of New Music*, he associates art's opposition and protest against the horrors of history, with the image of the suffering servant in the Deutero-Isaiah biblical text. When Adorno suggests that the atonal form of Schoenberg's modern music 'sacrifices itself' to a meaningless world by shunning melodic convention, he writes that 'it has taken all the darkness and guilt of the world upon itself'.[36] In these words, Pangritz hears literal echoes of Isa. 53.[37] Art, he suggests, bears a burden in Adorno's thought which the biblical poetry of Isaiah surely captures: 'he was wounded for our transgressions, crushed for our iniquities' (Isa. 53.4). The issue with such an interpretation, however, is the christological overtones that the text carries with it. Pangritz himself initially resists this (while criticizing Michael Theunissen for exactly such a reading).[38] He describes critical theory's relationship to theology as being one of questioning and experimentation, and recalls that, in Jewish thought, the suffering servant is the prophet of God, not God himself. But despite acknowledging that Adorno himself does not incorporate a christological structure to his argument, Pangritz argues that the issues and questions his philosophy raises can only be resolved by following a trajectory that leads to the christological tradition.

Such a move crosses a boundary that Adorno does not permit. It inverts his inverse theology. It is not that his thought does not contain the pressures and implied longings that Pangritz describes; rather, Adorno refuses to release this pressure by lifting the lid on broken human history and allowing a positive concept of the Absolute to resolve the dilemma. By pointing to the 'messianic' implications found in thought, Adorno intends to confront his audience with the question of redemption. He does not think an answer to this question is immanent or possible, beyond what human beings are able to achieve in history. He insists that 'metaphysics cannot rise again'.[39] So any 'pledge of redemption' is found only in 'the rejection of any faith which claims to depict it'.[40]

Given the resistance of Adorno's philosophy to positive theological systems, it is not surprising that theological engagement with his work by Christian theologians frequently follows a more Habermasian line of argument. Such theologians accept Habermas' argument that Adorno's critique of reason is guilty of a 'performative contradiction' because it remains ungrounded. They follow Habermas' proposal that critical reason requires a theory of communicative action, but then argue that only theology can provide the ground and full potentiality for such a theory. This strategy is employed in differing ways by Helmut Peukert, Charles Davis, and Rudolph Siebert.[41] Each highlights Habermas' claim that linguistic speech acts between subjects contain within them an implied potential for mutual self-expression and understanding, and that language points toward a reconciliation between differences. The tensions between subject and object that are found within Adorno's philosophy are overcome by making a 'linguistic turn' toward a theory of inter-subjectivity based in language.[42]

The argument that Habermas' theory requires the support of a theological moment in order to be grounded securely is developed in different ways. Davis suggests that what motivates human beings to enter into a discourse that seeks reconciliation is not inherently contained within language itself (as Habermas argues) but requires a religious faith and openness.[43] Peukert supplements this argument by emphasizing that Habermas' communicative action only offers a possible reconciliation for subjects who are still alive. Habermas' theory, in its secular form, forecloses on the reconciliation of all the suffering that has ever existed by shutting out those who have already died. When this is recognized, Peukert argues, one realizes that justice is not achieved until those who were wronged in the past also participate in reconciliation.

179

If communicative action is to truly lead to a reconciling consensus, he continues, it must open itself up to a solidarity that 'also includes the dead and the generations to come'.[44] Siebert argues in a similar fashion that Habermas' theory requires the Christian theological doctrine of resurrection as its proper foundation:

> In such faithful communicative action the possibility is given to the survivor to find a new identity in the face of the death of the innocent other and of his or her own death to come in the future . . . It is . . . an identity which develops out of the experience of liberation into an unlimited, universal solidarity.[45]

Such theological engagements with critical theory demonstrate a tendency to attempt to restore traditional theological concepts to prominence, after having initially accepted a theory that rejects importing knowledge and concepts from outside of history. In his response to his theological critics, Habermas observes this same point:

> My theological dialogue partners . . . choose the indirect procedure of apologetic argumentation and attempt to force the secular opponent into a corner by way of an immanent critique such that the opponent can find a way out of the aporias demonstrated only by conceding the theologically defended affirmations.[46]

There is a sense in which these Habermasian theological projects aim to out-do Habermas at his own game. Habermas is himself concerned to fully ground his theory of communicative action, and criticizes Adorno for failing to legitimize his positions on a firm normative foundation. An Adornoian rebuttal is to raise the question of whether Habermas' insistence on the logical completeness and reliability of communicative action is itself guilty of being dogmatic. As many critics have argued, his theory of language establishes one form of discursive procedure as authoritative.[47] Adorno himself was reluctant to place complete confidence in language, for there are 'no words which cannot be used in the service of lies'.[48] In a commodified world, communication easily succumbs to advertising, or simply to the pragmatic demands of instrumental utility. For this reason, he argued that 'direct communicability is not a criterion of truth. We must resist the all but universal compulsion to confuse the communication of knowledge with knowledge itself'.[49]

The reluctance among theologians to follow the direction of Adorno's inverse theology is understandable, for in his view, 'rescue attempts' on behalf of traditional theology are not possible. This, of course, calls into question theology's coherence, which is all the more troubling in a cultural environment already hostile to the discipline's legitimacy. But Adorno's motivations are not rooted in any inherent antagonism against theology. His position is based on his view that submitting to the temptation to secure rationality (or theology) on a firm foundation, forfeits the search for truth and slides into identity thinking.

In *Perseverance Without Doctrine*, Mattias Martinson argues that approaching theology from the perspective of Adorno's thought implies that 'theology must speak without making strong truth-claims that refer to a fundamental theological framework or a non-foundational doctrine'.[50] Martinson suggests that theological reflection 'must be realized as perseverance without alternative doctrine', and adds that theology is motivated by a hope for a 'true communicative relationship between subject and object'. He describes his own project as a 'modelling theology', one that proceeds without a prototype, but

> still *wants* to have one, since one has the capacity to
> imagine something of how good it would be to have
> such a prototype. Constructive modelling means not
> to conjure up such a prototype, but to proceed in the
> consciousness of the *lack* of prototype.[51]

This is a thoughtful articulation of a theology generally in keeping with the spirit of Adorno's philosophy. This interest in a prototype, however, is occasionally developed in a way that implies the re-establishment of some foundational commitments, particularly when Martinson describes theology as the academy's 'other'.[52] This latter idea does not suggest a return to Barth's doctrine of revelation, but an ongoing movement between foundational and non-foundational theology, along with theology's endless struggle with its own legitimacy. This disruption of theology as a stable discipline 'leaves us with an utterly sad "something" that we cannot handle without reflecting on precisely that which eludes reflection'. This struggle, which Martinson likens to the work of Sisyphus, 'can be interpreted as a faint notion of salvation';

> If the hubris of human work is shattered in a meaningless wrestling with that which cannot be wrestled down, then, perhaps, the world can heal from the form of ideological and dogmatic humanism, whose idea of progress inevitably leads to regression.[53]

Martinson then adds the following: 'Fundamentally, as a human being today, one has to cry theologically. This makes theology's concern with the problem of legitimacy too important to be left to theologians'. Initially, Martinson appears to be equating theology with what Adorno calls philosophy's 'metaphysical moment', but this subsequent argument begins to leave Adorno's emphases behind; one '*has to cry theologically*'? What is meant by 'theology' here? Martinson appears to mean more than thought's 'metaphysical moment' or an inverse critical perspective on present social life. He continues, 'the problem is grounded in the fact that the human world, in its progressive development, thinks and acts as if God was dead . . . without being able to really convince itself of this circumstance'.[54] What is subtly implied is not only a re-assertion of theology's legitimacy, but also – in a certain sense – its function as 'queen of the sciences'. Theology's problem of legitimacy is presented as revealing '*the*' problem of legitimacy for all forms of knowledge. Martinson's 'modelling theology', in its struggle with the tensions between the traditions of theological doctrines and the academic study of the history of religions, understands itself to be embodying the tensions inherent within the modern academy. It resists the simplistic division between rational knowledge and irrational myth that the academy establishes in its approach to theology, and 'safeguards' the religious system 'from illegitimate subjectivist critique', by pointing out the biased and ungrounded elements ('the mythical elasticity') contained in both science and many forms of theology.[55]

The chief limitation of Martinson's argument here is the manner in which his treatment resembles Tillich's method of correlation. Adorno's contribution, in Martinson's rendering, is to identify a correlation between the present fractured nature of knowledge and identity, and the theological tradition. The dilemmas of contemporary life confront human beings with a *question*, which leads them to 'cry theologically' in a search for an *answer*. To be sure, Martinson does not attribute any positive content to the answer theology is able to provide as a resolution to the questions of the age, but the directionality of his argument, and its preoccupation, are rather distinct from the inverse correlation which Adorno's approach to theology encourages.

## Theology after Auschwitz?

Given the minimalist nature of Adorno's inverse theology, one might understandably ask whether his perspective, rather than implying a theology of the cross or some similar ontological completion, is more accurately described as a negation of theology. To illustrate why this is not so, it is useful to recall a statement from a much discussed essay on literature; 'To write poetry after Auschwitz is barbaric . . . Absolute reification . . . is now preparing to absorb the mind entirely. Critical intelligence cannot be equal to this challenge as long as it confines itself to self-satisfied contemplation'.[56] Given his theory of the culture industry, and in the context of the horror of the Nazi death camps, Adorno appears to dismiss all possibility of articulating anything beautiful, compelling, or truthful. All had apparently become corrupted, so that anything resembling consolation could only be an ideological patch covering over the wounds of society.

This is how Adorno's comment about poetry after the Shoah is often interpreted, and it is clear how such an understanding would support the view that his philosophy ends in pessimism.[57] What often goes unexplored, however, is that when this provocative statement is repeated in *Negative Dialectics*, Adorno *withdraws* it: 'Perennial suffering has as much right to expression as a tortured man has to scream; hence it may have been wrong to say that after

Auschwitz you could no longer write poems'.[58] In a subsequent lecture, he supplements his retraction further and strengthens it;

> I would readily concede that, just as I said that after Auschwitz one *could not* write poems – by which I meant to point to the hollowness of the resurrected culture of that time – it could equally well be said, on the other hand, that one *must* write poems, in keeping with Hegel's statement in his *Aesthetics* that as long as there is an awareness of suffering among human beings there must also be art as the objective form of that awareness.[59]

His reasons for this change are expanded in what follows shortly after this admission:

> Yet one must ask a further question, and this is a metaphysical question, although it has its basis in the total suspension of metaphysics. It is, in fact, curious how all questions which negate and evade metaphysics take on, precisely thereby, a curiously metaphysical character. It is the question whether one can *live* after Auschwitz. This question has appeared to me, for example, in the recurring dreams which plague me, in which I have the feeling that I am no longer really alive, but am just the emanation of a wish of some victim of Auschwitz.[60]

These reflections offer perhaps one of the clearest articulations of the spirit of his inverse theology in Adorno's writing. While the *Bilderverbot* prevents thought from closing in upon itself, theological concepts like the messianic and redemption serve as a critical protest and challenge to unjust domination and oppression in society. The remark against poetry is intended to counter what he calls the desire for a 'resurrected culture', in which the sufferings of the past are swept away or sentimentally resolved. Viewing society from the perspective of the 'messianic light' requires theory of negative correlation. Adorno's utopian vision of what ought to be confronts society with questions, which human beings are then responsible to take up and answer. This dialectic becomes the basis upon which Adorno advocates a return to aesthetic experience. Rather than being rooted in positive childhood experiences, he is motivated by a moral response to a nightmare:

> A new categorical imperative has been imposed by Hitler upon unfree humanity: to arrange their thoughts and actions so that Auschwitz will not repeat itself, so that nothing similar will happen.[61]

This commitment is determined, *not* by an argument, but by what even Karl Popper supports in the form of an imaginative visualization of 'the consequences which are likely to result from the alternatives between which we have to choose'.[62] It is not 'otherworldly' or the product of any secret Gnosticism. Rooted in reason and critical thought, Adorno's utopian vision is attentive to the possibilities for society which remain unrealized, but more directly on the tragic realities of human suffering.

This revision of his prior valuation of aesthetic experience also leads Adorno to return to metaphysics, although 'it . . . survives only negatively'. This emerges in those experiences that lead to the question, 'is that all?'[63] After Auschwitz, Adorno argues for the ongoing existence of the 'metaphysical experience', but acknowledges that it 'can no longer be anything other than a *thinking* about metaphysics', which 'presupposes a kind of critical self-reflection of thought, in the sense that . . . one asks oneself whether thought and its constitutive forms are *in fact* absolute'.[64]

This retention of a metaphysical moment remains firmly in the mode of the idea that 'the false life cannot be truly lived'. The significance of Adorno's reference to his nightmare that only death remains after the Final Solution is illustrated by highlighting a distinction between two well-known cinematic comedies that deal with the Holocaust. The difference between the two films clarifies how his vision does not require or draw from a positive ontological foundation.

In Radu Mihaileanu's *Train de Vie* ['Train of Life'], a small Jewish village organizes a fake Nazi deportation train in order to fool the authorities and make their escape to Palestine.[65] The story is full of mischievous comic tricks, and ultimately ends in success. The film concludes, however, with the audience discovering that the narrator who is telling the tale is doing so from within a Nazi death camp. The vision is one that longs for a better resolution to history; but the narrative itself does not pretend that the catastrophes of life can simply be evaded.

Roberto Benigni's Academy Award winning *La Vita è bella* ['Life is Beautiful'] stands in sharp contrast to Mihaileanu's film. It is the story of a man who is able to mask from his young son the reality that they are prisoners in a death camp, which he accomplishes by pretending that the whole experience is a game.[66] While *Train de Vie* can be understood as a view of damaged life from the perspective of redemption, Benigni's film is a rather sentimental celebration of the victory of the 'human spirit', regardless of its social location. The latter movie possesses a direct metaphysical moral, and an implicit christological interpretation (the father dies in the process of saving his son). By contrast, Mihaileanu's film hints at metaphysical experience, but it is in the mode of an inverse theology. The longing for redemption is not itself sufficient for the erasure of the horrors of historical existence, but its deployment serves to illuminate and protest against what ought not to be.

## The 'Metaphysical Moment' and Theology

In his essay 'Reason and Revelation', Adorno offers a glimpse of how his attitude towards poetry after Auschwitz relates to theology. He locates the contemporary 'need for religion' in the effort of reason to resist absolutizing itself;

> Certainly a *ratio* that does not wantonly absolutize itself
> as a rigid means of domination requires self-reflection,
> some of which is expressed in the need for religion today.
> But this self-reflection cannot stop at the mere negation
> of thought by thought itself, a kind of mystical sacrifice,
> and cannot realize itself through a 'leap': that would all too
> closely resemble the politics of catastrophe.[67]

This statement suggests that theology is related to reason's critique of itself. Furthermore, religion is associated with an avoidance of the 'negation of thought by thought itself' – i.e. it is connected to the rejection of nihilism. It is clear by these remarks that Adorno associates religion with what he calls 'metaphysical experience'. It also demonstrates that he resists any reduction of critical thought, including his own philosophy, to mere negativity. Adorno's negative dialectics is not developed out of some ludic enjoyment of nihilism, or pessimistic collapse in the face of catastrophe. Rather, its relentless negative critique of all that is exists is a form of practice that is committed to supporting the possibility of a better world. If Pangritz's image of the suffering servant is in any way appropriate, it is found only in the figure's prophetic witness against the sufferings and tragedies of history.

This is not to say that Adorno advocates a return to a positive theological position. Although he states that metaphysics is 'a reprise, a resumption of theology' in the manner in which it 'points to a world behind *the* world we know', he also argues that it is at the same time a critique of theology.[68] When Adorno claims that rational thought pushes beyond itself, he is in no way hypostatizing this observation, turning it into a concept capable of contributing to a fundamental theology. That he criticizes science for turning its facts into 'idols' does not make it acceptable to turn what he calls 'metaphysical experience' into an idol in its own right.[69]

This is because the 'metaphysical moment' in thought does not amount to a positive grasp of something. It is not an intuition into the 'true nature of things', nor does it lead to the sense of some sort of meaning in life. Adorno insists that it is impossible after Auschwitz to posit 'the presence of a positive meaning or purpose in being'.[70] Instead, the metaphysical emerges as a problem when tensions develop between historical experience and conceptual thinking. 'Metaphysics arises at the point where the empirical world is taken seriously', for, as observed when examining Adorno's contributions to the 'Positivist Dispute', critical second reflection discovers that concepts are inadequate to their object.[71] In *Negative Dialectics* he writes: 'the question whether metaphysics is still possible at all must reflect the negation of the finite which finiteness requires'.[72] This is distinct from Thaidigsmann's suggestion that Adorno recognizes that humanity is 'promised' a reconciled existence, but it certainly supports the contention, that, for Adorno, the theological 'refuses to align itself to what actually exists, always seeking transcendence'.[73]

Adorno's argument is that, as reason vigorously criticizes itself, as it discovers the 'preponderance of the object', it must admit that the object of thought as it is 'in–itself' always surpasses discursive reason. At the same time, the denial of the existence of the non–identical, by prohibiting the recognition of what he calls 'metaphysical experience', becomes itself a positive theology, as what presently exists is absolutized:

> this explains the occasional alliance between positivism and positive religion against metaphysics – against the disintegrating force which they both detect in it. Autonomous thought is a mouthpiece of the transcendent, and is thus always in danger – when it approaches the transcendent through metaphysics – of making common cause with it.[74]

Adorno suggests that any appreciation of a metaphysical moment is perilous at best. Although its destabilizing function is something to be embraced, there always exists a temptation to absolutize the flash of momentary insight, which can only be fragmentary and fleeting. If the 'metaphysical' or the 'transcendent' is mistaken to be a *thing*-in–itself, then one escapes from one ideological perspective only to replace it with another.

Just as a fleeting experience of freedom is contained within metaphysical thinking 'at the time of its fall', the same is true of theology at the moment of theology's fall. Such a view explains Adorno's continued use of theological concepts and his own description of his work as an inverse theology. The most that can be said about such a theology, however, is that it amounts to working 'one's way through the darkness without a lamp, without possessing the positive through a higher concept of the negation of the negation, and to immerse oneself in the darkness as deeply as one can'.[75]

This does not imply the negation theology. As Horkheimer notes, 'humanity loses religion as it moves through history, but the loss leaves its mark behind'.[76] What remains is that impulse towards 'attentiveness' that is the 'historical figure of prayer'; the ongoing 'groping' on the part of subjective experience 'for the preponderance of the object'.[77]

## Theology and Aesthetics

As is evident in the responses by numerous Christian theologians to his thought, Adorno's remarks on theology are closely linked to his treatment of aesthetic experience. In 'On Lyric Poetry and Society', he maintains that works of art are able to 'give voice to what ideology hides. Their success moves beyond false consciousness'.[78] The lyric poem is 'the subjective expression of social antagonism', thus making it an important object of sociological reflection.[79] It serves as an important resource for society, acting as a medium through which individuation is accomplished. As such, poetry serves an anticipatory role, similar to the act of viewing all things from the perspective of reconciliation: 'lyric speech becomes the voice of human beings between whom the barriers have fallen'.[80]

Adorno is less optimistic that theology in the modern world can serve the same role (although he implies that it once did).[81] He argues that the status of religious symbolism has largely deteriorated into 'mere embellishment' of what is 'actually of this world'. He states that one must do 'away with any pretension to the ultimate validity of . . . religious theses . . . [that] glorify religion because it would be so nice if one could believe again. Religion is on sale, as it were'.[82] In this remark, Adorno suggests that religion is frequently little more an ideological function in contemporary society. Elsewhere he adds that, because of the tendency for religion to succumb to dogmatism, 'I am unwilling to attach a metaphysical experience to religious experience'.[83] And yet, he often says much the same thing about art as well. Art in modern society can no longer serve to convey a positive message 'of human solidarity, brotherly love, all-comprising universality'. Art, philosophy, and theology – together – have 'all become identical, or at least reconcilable with each other, as "cultural goods" which are no longer taken quite seriously by anybody'. Thus, he concludes that, 'Art that wants to fulfil its humane destination should not peep at the humane, nor proclaim humanistic phrases'.[84] Metaphysical thinking cannot have anything apologetic about it. It must cease 'pointing to something one can hold onto and never lose'.[85]

In the similar way that Adorno's injunction against writing poetry becomes an imperative for the importance of such poetry, one might add – albeit in a highly qualified sense – his injunction against employing theological language sublates into a recognition of the need for such language. Of course, such a recognition can only imply a form of theological reflection focused on present historical experience. Adorno is clear that any positive theses offered by metaphysical – and especially theological – speculation can only be considered 'blasphemies'. Those who despair over this reality and 'take refuge in theology' by establishing a doctrine of the 'wholly other' nature of the divine 'effectively demon[ize] the absolute'.[86] He insists that, 'After Auschwitz there is no word tinged from on high, not even a theological one, that has any right unless it underwent a transformation'.[87]

## The Weight of Objectivity: Theology as an Empty Shell

Adorno's inverse theology does not encourage a return to doctrinal orthodoxy or even to a 'modelling' that locates a 'theological moment' within the troubled status of reason within the 'postmodern' academy. Instead, the contribution of his work is his emphasis on the importance of focusing critical reflection upon the 'weight of objectivity' that the study of society and human suffering illuminates. Theology 'at the moment of its fall' – when it is realized that as a discipline it does not possess the resources it requires to fulfil its own demands (love of neighbour, etc.) – must be content to ruthlessly criticize itself. To a large extent, this might appear to negate theology as it has traditionally existed. Rather than providing a positive foundation, it serves as critical reflection motivated by the call to alleviate human suffering and furthering happiness and freedom, rather than serving an apologetic role.

Adorno's inverse theology does not sit comfortably, however, with the notion of a positive negation of a tradition like theology. In his essay 'On Tradition', he confronts the question of how modern culture is to deal with the bourgeois cultural traditions of the Enlightenment after they have lost their former authority. He rejects the simple dismissal of such older cultural forms, for in a world that threatens to foreclose against any new possibilities, human society 'must seek support from the very irrationality [i.e. tradition] it eradicates, it must turn to tradition'. This is not to say that traditional aspects of culture should be 'idolized as relics', which would reduce them to 'elements of ideology'. Instead, these traditions are treated seriously because within them can be found historical experience in a congealed form; 'having lost what tradition guaranteed – the self-evident relation to its object, to its materials and techniques – it must reflect upon them from within'.[88]

Adorno is concerned to show that one cannot begin theorizing about society – or any critical endeavour – from nowhere; 'whatever imagines itself from nothing, unadulterated by history, will be the first victim of history unconsciously and thus fatefully'.[89] The traditions of modernity, of science, and of theology have all failed human beings in many ways, but this realization cannot be considered sufficient reason to discard them as if one can 'start all over again'. Instead, the careful study of these failures can help reveal the dynamics that caused their breakdown, and to point to what resources these traditions contain within them that may help point the way forward.

This position, as Adorno articulates it, implies that one is 'not to forget tradition and yet not to affirm it'.[90] He thus advocates once again a 'second reflection' upon all elements of human culture, with the intention of elucidating how social experience and history have influenced their present forms. In *Minima Moralia*, this perspective is summed up in the following manner: 'One must have the tradition in oneself, to hate it properly'.[91] The sense of hating tradition 'properly' opposes any ongoing conformity or orderliness based on deference or nostalgia. A proper critical engagement approaches a tradition's own claims with an attentiveness to the history congealed within it, in order to demonstrate how it points beyond itself – how it cannot in and of itself achieve its own promise.

A tradition's failures, in other words, point towards what is missing from, or preventing, its realization. Such limitations and contradictions reveal elusive possibilities. The theological traditions of Christianity and Judaism have included within them the expressed intention to care for other human beings and to bring the fullness of justice into the world. These unrealized goals remain. Critical reflection upon these traditions can help to uncover the ways in which these utopian goals were prevented from being achieved: what elements within the traditions themselves have blocked their realization? In what ways have the larger social and historical forces in which Christian communities are found contributed to their failure? Furthermore, in a social environment that tends to deny that 'something is missing' or that knowledge can point beyond itself, theological tradition serves as a reminder that actuality does not exhaust possibility, and that the concept of society already suggests the hope for a just society. As Adorno states in a discussion with Ernst Bloch,

> unless there is [a] kind of trace of truth in the ontological proof of God, that is, unless the element of its reality is also already conveyed in the power of the concept itself, there could not only be no utopia but there could also not be any thinking.[92]

This is how Adorno's inverse theology relates to theological tradition. It supports an attentiveness to the 'weight of objectivity' that is contained in the protests against suffering, and in the recognition that thought points beyond itself. Adorno describes his philosophy as being 'utterly opposed to the idea of philosophy as a basic overarching science'. It is, in other words, a 'shell'.[93] The same might be said of his inverse theology: it is the shell that remains of the theological tradition, after it has relinquished its tendency towards ideological support of the *status quo*, the impulse towards identity thinking, and the psychic desire for consolation.

## Thinking with One's Ears: Hymns to the Silence

While Adorno's philosophy focuses on an inverted gaze upon the world 'as indigent and distorted as it will appear one day in the messianic light', it is in his aesthetic theory that some anticipatory elements of what he refers to as 'redemption' can be found.[94] As a contrast to the philosophical *Bilderverbot*, for example, 'Music is the imageless art and was excluded from that prohibition'.[95] In music, Adorno perceives a form of subjective experience that takes the subject out of and beyond itself. Although the source of musical composition is simply the composer and the material of music-making (instruments, air for sound to travel through, human ears to receive the sound, etc.), once a musical score begins to take shape, 'the purity of the procedure aims to eliminate whatever the individual has added to it externally'.[96] The music begins to take on a shape of its own; it has its own logic, which transcends that of subjective intention and use. In Adorno's view, the musical composition thus has an intimate connection to truth; 'The absolute which this music sets out to make real . . . it achieves as its own idea of itself'. This gives it, he concludes, a 'theological dimension'.[97]

Although a fuller discussion of Adorno's complex philosophy of music cannot be developed here, recognizing the motivations that fuel his passion for modern classical music provides further nuance to the nature of inverse theology.[98] Whereas in instrumental reasoning subjective thought is driven to master nature, which serves only to dominate the other and thus separate it further from the subject, in musical experience, the subject's grasp over its object is considerably weakened. Adorno acknowledges that, like any form of cultural production, music is vulnerable to manipulation by ideology and the culture industry, and yet, because the origin of music is rooted in human bodily experience even more intimately than spoken language, it has the capacity to emancipate itself more readily from instrumentality. Adorno suggests that 'the emancipation of music today is synonymous with its emancipation from the language of words'. It reaches beyond intentionality and control, because it is more 'akin to crying', and 'music and crying open the lips and bring delivery from restraint'. In such experiences, he observes the possibility of achieving reconciliation between subject and object. His appreciation of this vision is worth quoting at length:

> The man who surrenders to tears in music that no longer resembles him at the same time allows the stream of what he himself is not – what was dammed up back of the world of things – to flow back into him. In tears and singing, the alienated world is entered . . . [T]his is the gesture of music. The gesture of returning, not the feeling of waiting, describes the expression of all music, even in a world worthy of death.[99]

This view leads Adorno to speak of a rational element in music. He describes this dynamic as a 'thinking with the ears'.[100] A foretaste of redemption can be grasped in the flash of a brief moment. This is not so much a 'promise' or foundation, but remains elusive, non-manipulable, and surprising. The possibility of harmony between subject and object is briefly experienced by the thinking subject, whose subjectivity is gripped in a far deeper manner than linguistic discourse is typically capable of. More frequently, however, the most music can achieve, as it resists the pressures and temptations of the culture industry, is to model its own determinate negation, becoming atonal in its quest to break from the consolations of sentimentality or the rigidity of melody. And yet, music possesses the capacity to stand 'in tensed opposition to the horror of history'.[101]

## Reconciliation: From Autonomy to Love

This emphasis on the reconciliation between subject and object is found throughout Adorno's aesthetic theory. It stands in sharp contrast to those critics who accuse him of remaining within a paradigm of the Enlightenment individualist subject, remaining elitist, pessimistic, and obsessed with autonomy. Some recent interpretations highlight how Adorno's attention to non-identity, and his intention to illuminate the inter-connection of subject to its object, suggest a much more relational model of subjectivity. His critique of the culture industry, as well as his interest in autonomous art, are influenced by his rejection of a naïve celebration of the independent and autonomous will. In *Minima Moralia*, he argues, 'He who stands aloof runs the risk of believing himself better than others and misusing his critique of society as an ideology for his private interests'.[102] As has emerged in previous chapters, Adorno's subject is deeply immersed in a society shaped by ideology and oppression. There is no pure and isolated ground upon which to stand. He writes, 'There is no way out of entanglement', and so there is no such thing as private existence.[103] Because of this view, Adorno can neither accept Kierkegaard's ideal of authenticity, nor Nietzsche's defence of the genuine. Such notions not only prove false in themselves, but they also result in a denunciation of all that falls short of the privileged concept.[104]

Despite this strong emphasis in his work, it is striking that Adorno struggles to find examples of such reconciliation outside of models drawn from music or autonomous art. These latter examples, though interesting, are in fact rather limited, for the capacity of a work of art to serve as the social antithesis of reified society 'depends on its relative independence from the rest of society'.[105] But when Adorno refers to human relationships, there is little evidence that he is able to locate resources that hint at other possibilities for human connection with other human beings. This absence in Adorno's work is a significant limitation.

One can, however, identify some fragmentary allusions to recon-ciliation that are more inter-subjective in nature when he refers to love. Adorno suggests that, 'Love is the power to see similarity in the dissimilar'.[106] As Eva Geulen observes, for Adorno, 'Any self always owes itself to an other. But only in love is this truth acknowledged'.[107] Far from idealizing love, Adorno is alert to the way romantic sentimentality is manipulated by the culture industry. Furthermore, his Freudian lens suggests to him that erotic desire often serves to reify the object of desire. Indeed, Adorno himself occasionally advances chauvinistic and stereotypically patriarchal views about women.[108] Scattered fragments in his writings, how-ever, offer illuminating commentary on relationships of love which enhance the power of his conception of an inverse theology.

One noteworthy image occurs in the following aphorism: 'Now that we can no longer pluck flowers to adorn our beloved – a sacrifice that adoration for the one atones by freely taking on itself the wrong it does to all others – picking flowers has become something evil'.[109] The dilemma here is similar to the one identi-fied by Freud in *Civilization and its Discontents*, when he suggests that loving one's neighbour as oneself robs the loved one of the privileged treatment that she or he deserves.[110] The giving of love to one person implies a preference for that individual over others. In Adorno's image, the desire to express love for the beloved results in the killing of a flower. This highlights the sacrifices and limitations which social life imposes on human beings. Favouring one person often prevents assisting another. The fullness of love demands reconciliation to otherness that is impossible to fulfil.

As Adorno writes, 'love uncompromisingly betrays the general to the particular in which alone justice is done to the former'.[111]

The problem is more complicated still. Adorno notes that in love, the individual is 'made to feel the untruth of all merely individual fulfilment'. This important recognition can be experienced by the subject as a violent disruption, however, when the other who is loved spurns or disappoints the lover. This violates the sense of the subject's 'right to be loved by the beloved'. The experience of love, then, can both reconcile the lover and beloved, but also result in sacrifice and disappointment. Love calls into question the control of the subject, not only over the other, but also over itself; 'the secret of justice in love is the annulment of all rights, to which love mutely points'.[112]

In her analysis of this aphorism, Eva Geulen is at pains to avoid what she calls a 'theological' reading of this text. Such an interpretation would suggest to her that the sacrifices of love are in need of reconciliation or 'atonement'.[113] For Geulen, the message Adorno intends is 'transience for transience's sake'. In her view, the flowers that are picked for the beloved are not only sacrificed, but the love they are intended to communicate will also wither and die.

This interpretation is modified to a degree by a consideration of Adorno's inverse theology. Clearly, as Geulen suggests, he does not imagine there can be an appropriate 'atonement' for the dilemma of sacrifice found within these aphorisms. Judith Butler argues, however, that Adorno's treatment of love demonstrates that, should one be intent on protecting oneself from being hurt by the beloved, and is 'successful at walling oneself off from injury, one would become inhuman'.[114] She interprets Adorno's reference to love as pointing to the 'annulment of all rights' as a warning against 'treating the other's love as an entitlement rather than a gift'.[115]

In such a perspective, the image of the flower would not imply 'transience for transience's sake', but the importance of self-restraint in the work of love. Given how Adorno's analysis of the dialectic of enlightenment demonstrates that self-preservation and control of the other are intertwined with rationality in a self-destructive manner, self-restraint becomes a crucial moral virtue. To prevent oneself from becoming 'inhuman', Adorno argues that it is important to recognize that, 'true injustice is always to be found at the precise point where you put yourself in the right and other people in the wrong'.[116]

This is not a call for passivity or self-denial, but it is an emphasis on encouraging a form of subjectivity that is alert to its connection to, and dependence on, the other. Furthermore, the point intended by Adorno is not that there exists a pure or perfect way to live which avoids such problems. He is not, in other words, awaiting some positive theological resolution to the painful imperfection of relationships of the sort Geulen is concerned about. But Adorno is suggesting the importance and need for a form of thinking which helps limit and interrupt the subject's 'walling off of itself'. This is not accomplished with a sentimental ideal of love, but is, once again, in the mode of the negative image. He suggests 'that the place of moral philosophy today lies more in the concrete denunciation of the inhuman, than in the vague and abstract attempts to situate man in his existence'.[117] Such is the function of the image of the sacrificed flower. In lamenting what ought not to be, the subject might better learn self-restraint. In achieving a capacity to tolerate such frustrations, the subject may learn to experience the other as a gift. If so, then, in a momentary flash, it might experience the same reconciliation that Adorno analyses in his philosophy of music, 'In tears and singing, the alienated world is entered'.[118] Rowan Williams captures this tone in his own discussion of the cost of relationships, when he observes, 'the suspension or deferrals of gratification are . . . something to do with the expectation of grace: by deferral, by refusing what I conceive myself to want or need, I invite what I don't know, the 'non-existent Other''.[119]

## Inverse Theology as Negative Correlation

This perspective on love, and the manner in which it resonates with Adorno's understanding of music, allows a fuller grasp of Adorno's inverse theology to come into view. In addition to the manner that his engagement with theology establishes a negative correlation with a utopian vision of a reconciled world, the prohibition against idols also serves to press in on the subject's propensity to build walls between itself and the other. It intends, in other words, to try to expand the experience Adorno locates in musical enjoyment into wider social relationships. This is not achieved through the development of positive programmes or models for human relationships, but negatively – through criticism of relationships from the perspective of both what ought not to be, as well as from a utopian vision of subject and object living together in harmony, with their differences preserved; 'Peace is the state of differentiation without domination, with the differentiated participating in each other'.[120]

So long as such relationships remain distant from our world, Adorno's understanding of an inverse theology will be a significant resource for philosophy and theology. Critical reflection on broken relationships will prevent a resigned acceptance of them, and encourage a deeper commitment to work towards a more reconciled form of life. It is the case that Adorno's writings exhibit little confidence in the capacity of human relationships to embody such a way of living, but his inverse theology acts as a 'force–field' against a collapse into pessimism. The brokenness of life is not used merely as a nihilistic weapon against theology; rather, Adorno's prohibition against constructing romantic notions of relationship is developed as a defence for a utopian vision of life, which may interrupt the passivity of human beings and call them into question. Adorno hopes that people will seek to respond.

In some notes that record his own personal dreams, Adorno describes one vision in particular which gave shape to his life and his desire to live despite the horrors he observed in the world. He discovers a deep longing for the reality of an after-life, after dreaming that he and his wife Gretel are in a terrible bus accident while on vacation. Following the impact, Adorno wakes up crying, and says as he looks over to his wife, 'I would so like to have kept on being alive with you'.[121] For Adorno, the utopian hope of eternal life presses him to recognize the significance of the other he meets on a daily basis. His connection to this human being presents to him the question of what kind of partner he intends to be.

## Hymns to the Silence

It is clear that Adorno's inverse theology remains only a 'shell' of the tradition of systematic theology and positive religion. But it is also clear that what remains of the theological has deep roots in Adorno's philosophy, and its impulse serves a key role in his approach to society, politics, and science. The priority Adorno places on the *Bilderverbot* implies that any hymns endorsed by his inverse theology would be largely silent and without positive content. They could not be directed to a positive image of the divine, for no such metaphysical reality is available to him. Yet he does continue to reach for a reconciled relationship with the other, which messianic longing helps to nurture and maintain. While Adorno cannot identify many resources for a renewed society in a world dominated by instrumentality and the culture industry, his inverse theology does not permit him to despair. Like the new music he loved, it continues to 'illuminate the meaning-lessness of the world' while reaching out for its other. The 'true message in a bottle'[122] is not a nihilistic pessimism, but a hymn to the silence of the other.

The poet who convinced Adorno to withdraw his prohibition against art after Auschwitz was Paul Celan. In Celan's work, Adorno finds a use of language that escapes the clutches of instru-mentality. His poetry 'yearns neither for nature nor for industry'. Refusing to pursue either, it avoids the ideological tendency to 'make peace with an unpeaceful world'.[123] Adorno contrasts Celan's difficult and obscure writing with 'hermetic' poetry. The latter style, characteristic of the French symbolist movement, is intentionally self-contained in its obscurity. Immediate sensations or fleeting impressions are expressed, without overt meaning, with the intention of sustaining an air-tight elusiveness. In Celan's poetry, however, Adorno suggests that the hermetic is inverted. Although the meaning of Celan's writing is obscure, his work does not embrace this obscurity or relish in it. Instead, 'Celan's poems want to speak of the most extreme horror through silence. Their truth content itself becomes negative'.[124] It is as if the life-less and the dead protest in his poems through what is not said, and their broken witness exposes the brokenness of present life.

In the poem 'Psalm', Celan mimes some of the words of a theological doxology, but the addressee who is being spoken to and praised is called 'no one' [*Niemand*]. 'No one moulds us again out of earth and clay', and it is toward 'no one' that 'we shall flower'.[125] In this psalm, no god is named and no consolation is promised. What is meant by the strange invocation is unclear. And yet, in this silence, the longing of the author for redemption from the terrors of history is clear, and it is exactly the barbarism of history that is illuminated more fully by leading the reader to invert their view of this world so that it is seen from the perspective of this 'no one'.

Such is the nature of Adorno's inverse theology. The idea of truth, which he associates closely with theology, demands of theology that it turn on itself and criticize its complicity with ideology and identity thinking. This is demanded, not out of rage, a desire for revenge, nor even from disrespect; it is demanded, rather, by the very truth that theology is in pursuit of; 'It is why one who believes in God cannot believe in God'. If this is understood merely as rhetorical flourish, then a tension that is at the very core of Adorno's thought remains unnoticed, and the impulse that drives his critical theory is dismissed from view. For Adorno warns that, if theology is dismissed entirely, should the process of demythologization be content to leave behind 'nothing but what merely is', then thought itself 'recoils into the mythos', and life is reduced to the closed system of instrumentality.[126] Without the critical distance opened up on the brokenness of life by assuming the perspective of an inverse theology, the complete abandonment of God surrenders life to the sufferings of the *status quo*. Adorno thus insists that one must remain silent about God, but one must at the same time sing hymns to this silence.

# Notes

## Introduction

1. Richard Rorty and Gianni Vattimo *The Future of Religion* (New York: Columbia, 2005); Jacques Derrida, *Acts of Religion* (Oxford: Blackwell, 2002); Slavoj Žižek, *The Puppet and the Dwarf* (Cambridge, MA: The MIT Press, 2003).
2. Jürgen Habermas, *Between Naturalism and Religion,* trans. Ciaran Cronin (Polity Press, 2008).
3. Richard Dawkins, *The God Delusion* (London: Bantam Press, 2006); Sam Harris, *The End of Faith* (New York: W. W. Norton, 2004); Daniel C. Dennett, *Breaking the Spell* (New York: Viking, 2006).
4. Theodor W. Adorno and Walter Benjamin, *The Complete Correspondence: 1928–1940*, ed. Henri Lonitz, trans. Nicholas Walker (Cambridge, MA: Harvard University Press, 1999), 53.
5. Ibid., 67.
6. Michael Sullivan, and John T. Lysaker, 'Between Impotence and Illusion: Adorno's Art of Theory and Practice', *New German Critique* 57 (Fall 1992), 87.
7. Habermas, *The Philosophical Discourse of Modernity*, trans. Frederick G. Lawrence (Cambridge, MA: The MIT Press, 1987), 117.
8. For a fuller portrait of Adorno's life, see: Stefan Müller-Dooh, *Adorno: A Biography*, trans. Rodney Livingstone (Cambridge: Polity Press, 2005).
9. See: Rolf Wiggershaus, *The Frankfurt School*, trans. Michael Robertson (Cambridge, MA: The MIT Press, 1994); Martin Jay, *The Dialectical Imagination* (Boston and Toronto: Little, Brown, and Co., 1973).
10. Theodor W. Adorno, and Max Horkheimer, *Dialectic of Enlightenment: Philosophical Fragments*, trans. Edmund Jephcott (Stanford University Press: Stanford, CA, 2002).
11. Habermas, *The Philosophical Discourse of Modernity*, 119.
12. Albrecht Wellmer, *The Persistence of Modernity*, trans. David Midgley (Cambridge, MA: The MIT Press, 1991), 7, 12.
13. Susan Buck-Morss, *The Origin of Negative Dialectics* (New York: The Free Press, 1977), 190.
14. Adorno, *Prisms*, trans. Samuel and Shierry Weber (Cambridge, MA: The MIT Press, 1981), 34.
15. Adorno, *Negative Dialectics*, trans. E. B. Ashton (New York: Continuum, 1995), 362.
16. Ibid., 365.

# Notes

17. Adorno, *Minima Moralia*, trans. E. F. N. Jephcott (London and New York: Verso, 1974), 15.

18. Some examples of the suggestion that Adorno's thought is Gnostic include: Stanley Corngold, *Lambent Traces: Franz Kafka* (Princeton: Princeton University Press, 2004), 170; Willem van Reijen, 'Redemption and Reconciliation in Benjamin and Adorno', *Adorno: The Possibility of the Impossible*, ed. Nicolaus Schafhausen et al. (New York and Berlin: Lukas and Sternberg, 2003), 76.

19. Adorno, *Metaphysics: Concepts and Problems*, ed. Rolf Tiedemann, trans. Edmund Jephcott (Stanford, CA: Stanford University Press, 2000), 110 (emphasis in original).

20. Robert Hullot-Kentor, translator's foreword in: Adorno, *Kierkegaard: Construction of the Aesthetic* (Minneapolis: University of Minnesota Press, 1989), xi.

21. Adorno, *Negative Dialectics*, 18.

22. Paul Tillich, *Systematic Theology*, vol. 1 (University of Chicago Press, 1951), 61.

23. Adorno, 'The Actuality of Philosophy', *Telos* 31 (Spring 1977), 126.

24. Walter Benjamin, *The Origins of German Tragic Drama*, trans. John Osborne (London and New York: Verso, 1977), 34.

25. Adorno, 'Actuality', 127.

26. See: Jonathan Z. Smith, 'Religion, religions, religious', *Critical Terms for Religious Studies*, ed. Mark C. Taylor (Chicago: University of Chicago Press, 1998), 269–84; William E. Arnal, 'Definition', *Guide to the Study of Religion* (London: Cassell, 2000), 21–34.

27. A debate rages over whether Judaism has a 'theology', or if this represents a misplaced use of what is more properly a Christian concept. Gillian Rose argues that there is no Jewish '*logos* of God'. David Novak suggests that, particularly in Medieval Jewish writings, one observes rational accounts of the divine and the Jewish tradition. See: Gillian Rose, *Judaism and Modernity* (Oxford: Blackwell, 1993); David Novak, *Problems in Contemporary Jewish Philosophy* (Lampeter: Edwin Mellen, 1991).

# Chapter 1

1. Karl Marx, 'Contribution to the Critique of Hegel's *Philosophy of Right*: Introduction', *The Marx-Engels Reader*, second edition, ed. Robert C. Tucker (New York: W. W. Norton, 1978), 53 (italics in original).

2. Theodor W. Adorno, *Negative Dialectics*, trans. E. B. Ashton (New York: Continuum, 1973), 205.

3. Philippa Berry, 'Introduction', *Shadow of Spirit: Postmodernism and Religion*, eds Philippa Berry and Andrew Wernick (New York: Routledge, 1992), 3.

4. See: Steve Bruce, *God is Dead: Secularization in the West* (Oxford: Blackwell, 2002).

5. Jay, *The Dialectical Imagination*, 5.

6. Horkheimer, Max, *Dawn and Decline: Notes 1926–1931 and 1950–1969*, trans. Michael Shaw (New York: The Seabury Press, 1978), 62.

# Notes

7. Mannheim, Karl, *Ideology and Utopia: An Introduction to the Sociology of Knowledge*, trans. Louis Wirth and Edward Shils (New York: Harcourt and Brace, 1954).

8. Max Horkheimer, *Between Philosophy and Social Science*, trans. G. Frederick Hunter et al. (Cambridge, MA: The MIT Press, 1995), 129–50.

9. Horkheimer, *Dawn and Decline*, trans. Michael Shaw (New York: The Seabury Press, 1978), 65.

10. See: Engels, 'The Peasant War in Germany', *Marx and Engels on Religion* (Moscow: Progress Publishers, 1976), 86–103.

11. Horkheimer, *Dawn and Decline*, 156.

12. J. J. Bachofen, *Myth, Religion and Mother Right,* trans. Ralph Manheim (London: Routledge, 1967).

13. E. B. Tylor, *Primitive Culture* (London: Murray, 1871); J. G. Frazer, *The Golden Bough* (London: Macmillan, 1922).

14. Adorno, Review of Roger Caillois, *Zeitschrift für Sozialforschung* 7 (1938), 411.

15. Adorno and Horkheimer, *Dialectic of Enlightenment: Philosophical Fragments*, ed. Gunzelin Schmid Noerr, trans. Edmund Jephcott (Stanford; Stanford University Press, 2002), 6.

16. Catherine Bell, *Ritual Theory, Ritual Practice* (Oxford and New York: Oxford University Press, 1992), 216.

17. Adorno and Horkheimer, *Dialectic of Enlightenment*, 43.

18. Ibid., 6.

19. *Dialectic of Enlightenment*, 154.

20. Karla L. Schultz, *Mimesis on the Move* (Berne/NY: Peter Lang, 1990), 97, 26.

21. Adorno and Horkheimer, *Dialectic of Enlightenment*, 6.

22. Ibid., xvii.

23. Horkheimer, *Critical Theory: Selected Essays*, trans. Matthew J. O'Connell (New York: Continuum, 1995), 194, 199.

24. Adorno, *Introduction to Sociology*, ed. Christoph Gödde, trans. Edmund Jephcott (Stanford: Stanford University Press, 2000), 77–82.

25. Ibid., 85.

26. Adorno, *Negative Dialectics*, trans. E. B. Ashton (New York, Continuum, 1995), 192.

27. I draw here from Simon Jarvis' insightful discussion in 'Adorno, Marx, Materialism', *The Cambridge Companion to Adorno*, ed. Tom Kuhn (Cambridge University Press, 2004), 79–95.

28. See: Ellen Meiksins Wood, *The Retreat from Class* (London and New York: Verso, 1986).

29. John Milbank, 'Materialism and Transcendence', *Theology and the Political: The New Debate*, eds Creston Davis, John Milbank, Slavoj Žižek (Durham: Duke University Press, 2005), 395.

30. Ibid., 398.

31. Ibid., 424.

32. Adorno, *Hegel: Three Studies*, trans. Shierry Weber Nicholson (Cambridge, MA and London: The MIT Press, 1994), 8–9.

33. Paul Tillich, *The Socialist Decision*, trans. Franklin Sherman (New York, San Francisco: Harper and Row, 1977 [first German edition, 1933]); *Political Expectation*, ed. James Luther Adams (New York, San Francisco: Harper and Row, 1971). See: Champion, James W., 'Tillich and the Frankfurt School: parallels and differences in prophetic criticism', *Soundings* 69.4 (1986), 512–30; Strum, Erdmann, 'Theodor W. Adorno contra Paul Tillich', *Zeitschrift für neuere Theologiegeschichte* 3 (1996), 251ff.
34. Paul Tillich, 'Man and Society in Religious Socialism', *Christianity and Society*, VIII, No. 4 (Fall, 1943), 13.
35. Tillich, *Political Expectations*, 47–8.
36. Tillich, *Socialist Decision*, 69.
37. Adorno, 'Contra Paulum', *Briefwechsel: Theodor W. Adorno und Max Horkheimer*, vol. 2, ed. Christoph Gödde and Henri Lonitz (Frankfurt: Suhrkamp, 2004), 491.
38. Ibid., 482 (my translation).
39. Ibid., 488.
40. Adorno, *History and Freedom*, ed. Rolf Tiedemann, trans. Rodney Livingstone (Cambridge: Polity Press, 2006), 7.
41. Adorno, 'Contra Paulum', 487.
42. Adorno, *Negative Dialectics*, 17–18.
43. Ibid., 297
44. Adorno, *Philosophische Terminologie*, vol. 2, ed. Rudolf zur Lippe (Frankfurt: Suhrkamp, 1992), 198. Translation by Simon Jarvis in 'Adorno, Marx, Materialism', 82.

# Chapter 2

1. Adorno, *Metaphysics: Concepts and Problems*, ed. Rolf Tiedemann, trans. Edmund Jephcott (Stanford, CA: Stanford University Press, 2000), 2.
2. Adorno, *Kant's Critique of Pure Reason*, ed. Rolf Tiedemann, trans. Rodney Livingstone (Stanford, CA: Stanford University Press, 2001), 6.
3. Adorno, *Negative Dialectics*, trans. E. B. Ashton (New York: Continuum, 1973), 384.
4. The following interpretation of Adorno's reading of Kant is influenced by Simon Jarvis's *Adorno: A Critical Introduction* (New York: Routledge, 1998).
5. Adorno, *Negative Dialectics*, 391.
6. Adorno, *Negative Dialectics*, 188.
7. G. W. F. Hegel, *Faith and Knowledge*, trans. Walter Cerf and H. S. Harris (Albany: State University Press of New York, 1977), 76.
8. Hegel, *Lectures on the History of Philosophy*, vol. 3, ed. Robert Brown (Berkeley: University of California Press, 1990), 441
9. Adorno, *Negative Dialectics*, 388.
10. Adorno, *Kant's Critique of Pure Reason*, 48.
11. See: Immanuel Kant, *The Critique of Pure Reason*, trans. Norman Kemp Smith (New York: St Martin's Press, 1929), 551–2 (A672–4/B700–2).

12. Hegel, *Hegel's Logic*, trans. William Wallace (Oxford: Clarendon Press, 1975), 86 (§52).
13. Kant, *Critique of Pure Reason*, 180–7 [B176–87].
14. Ibid., 183 [B180].
15. See lecture 12 in: Adorno, *Kant's Critique of Pure Reason*, 128–37.
16. Quoted in Jarvis, *Adorno*, 180.
17. Kant, *Critique of Pure Reason*, 181 (A138/B177).
18. Adorno, *Kant's Critique of Pure Reason*, 217 (emphasis in original).
19. Ibid., 131–2.
20. Jarvis, 181.
21. Adorno, *Negative Dialectics*, 183.
22. Ibid., 185.
23. Ibid., 188.
24. Kant, *Critique of Practical Reason*, trans. Lewis White Beck (New York: Liberal Arts Press, 1956), 3.
25. Jarvis, *Adorno*, 185.
26. Kant, *Critique of Practical Reason*, 49.
27. Adorno, *Negative Dialectics*, 231–2.
28. Ibid., 137.
29. Ibid., 236.
30. Adorno, *Negative Dialectics*, 265.
31. Ibid., 392.
32. Wellmer, Albrecht, 'Metaphysik im Augenblick ihres Sturzes', *Metaphysik nach Kant?*, ed. Dieter Henrich and Rolf-Peter Horstmann (Stuttgart: Klett-Cotta, 1988), 773.
33. Adorno, *Negative Dialectics*, 389–90.
34. Adorno, 'The Idea of a Natural History', trans. Robert Hullot-Kentor. *Telos* 60 (sum 1984), 117.
35. John Milbank, *Theology and Social Theory* (Oxford: Blackwell, 1990), 38.
36. Ibid., 151.
37. Milbank, *The Word Made Strange: Theology, Language, Culture* (Oxford: Blackwell, 1997), 9–12.
38. Milbank, *Theology and Social Theory*, 173.
39. Adorno, *Negative Dialectics*, 218.
40. Milbank, *Theology and Social Theory*, 262; 387–8.
41. Milbank, et al., 'Introduction: Suspending the Material', *Radical Orthodoxy*, ed. Milbank, Ward, and Pickstock (London: Routledge, 1999), 5.
42. Milbank, 'Sublimity: The Modern Transcendent', *Religion, Modernity and Postmodernity*, ed. Paul Heelas (Oxford: Blackwell, 1998), 264.
43. Milbank, 'The Politics of Time: Community, Gift and Liturgy', *Telos* 113 (Fall 1998), 51.
44. Ibid., 56.
45. Ibid., 63–4.
46. Milbank, 'The Conflict of the Faculties', *Faithfulness and Fortitude: In Conversation with the Theological Ethics of Stanley Hauerwas*, eds Mark Thiessen Nation and Samuel Wells (Edinburgh: T&T Clark, 2000), 43.

47. Ibid., 45.
48. Milbank, 'The Programme of Radical Orthodoxy', *Radical Orthodoxy?* – *A Catholic Enquiry*, ed. Lawrence Paul Hemming (Aldershot: Ashgate Publishing Ltd., 2000), 34–5.
49. Milbank, 'The Conflict of the Faculties', 45.
50. Milbank, 'Knowledge: The Theological Critique of Philosophy in Hamann and Jacobi', *Radical Orthodoxy*, ed. J. Milbank, C. Pickstock, G. Ward (London and NY: Routledge, 1999), 24.
51. Adorno, 'Reason and Revelation', *Critical Models*, 138.
52. Adorno, *Metaphysics*, 3 (emphasis in original), 88.
53. Adorno, *Introduction to Sociology*, 148.
54. Adorno, *Metaphysics*, 101.
55. Ibid., 18.
56. Adorno, *Negative Dialectics*, 392.
57. Adorno, *Metaphysics*, 7.
58. Adorno, Theodor W., *Kant's Critique of Pure Reason (1959)*, ed. Rolf Tiedemann, trans. Rodney Livingstone (Stanford, CA: Stanford University Press, 2001 [1995]), 28, 33.
59. Ibid., 162–4.
60. Adorno, 'Subject and Object', 503–4.
61. Ibid., 506 (translation modified).
62. Gillian Rose, *The Melancholy Science* (New York: Columbia University Press, 1978), 142.
63. Espen Hammer, *Adorno and the Political* (London and New York: Routledge, 2006), 104.
64. Jean-Francois Lyotard, *The Postmodern Condition*, trans. Geoffrey Bennington and Brian Massumi (Minneapolis: University of Minnesota Press, 1974),
65. Jürgen Habermas, *The Philosophical Discourse of Modernity*, trans. Frederick G. Lawrence (Cambridge, MA: MIT Press, 1987).
66. Hans-Jürgen Krahl, 'The Political Contradictions in Adorno's Critical Theory', *Foundations of the Frankfurt School of Social Research*, eds Judith Marcus and Zoltán Tar (New Brunswick, NJ and London: Transaction Books, 1984), 308.

## Chapter 3

1. Adorno, *Introduction to Sociology*, ed. Christoph Gödde, trans. Edmund Jephcott (Stanford, CA: Stanford University Press, 2000), 11.
2. Nancey Murphy, *Theology in the Age of Scientific Reasoning* (Ithaca: Cornell University Press, 1990), 4–11.
3. Jeffrey Stout, *The Flight from Authority* (Notre Dame: The University of Notre Dame Press, 1981), 128–34.
4. Lorez Jäger, *Adorno: A Political Biography*, trans. Stewart Spencer (New Haven: Yale University Press, 2004), 57.

5. See Oswald Hanfling, *Logical Positivism* (New York: Columbia University Press, 1981).

6. Albert Blumberg and Herbert Feigl, 'Logical Positivism: a New Movement in European Philosophy', *Journal of Philosophy* 28 (1931), 269.

7. See Rudolph Carnap, 'Elimination of Metaphysics Through Logical Analysis of Language', *Logical Positivism*, ed. A. J. Ayer (New York: Free Press, 1959), 60–81.

8. Ibid., 199.

9. Ibid., 222.

10. Karl R. Popper, 'Reason or Revolution? – Addendum 1974: The Frankfurt School', *The Myth of the Framework: In Defence of Science and Rationality*, ed. M. A. Notturno (London and New York: Routledge, 1994) 78.

11. Zygmunt Bauman, *Modernity and the Holocaust* (Cornell University Press, 1989), 18.

12. Popper, 'The Logic of the Social Sciences', *In Search of a Better World*, trans. Laura J. Bennett (London and New York, 1994), 64–81.

13. Ibid., 65.

14. Ibid., 66.

15. Ibid., 67.

16. Ibid., 81.

17. Ibid., 79 (emphasis in original).

18. Popper, 'The Rationality Principle', *Popper: Selections*, ed. David Miller (Princeton: Princeton University Press, 1985), 359 (emphasis in original).

19. Adorno, 'On the Logic of the Social Sciences', *The Positivist Dispute in German Sociology*, trans. Glyn Adey and David Frisby (London: Heinemann, 1976), 105.

20. Adorno, 'Sociology and Psychology (part 2)', *New Left Review* vol. 47 (Jan–Feb 1968), 81.

21. Adorno, 'On the Logic of the Social Sciences', 107.

22. Ibid., 115.

23. Adorno, *Prisms*, trans. Samuel and Shierry Weber (Cambridge: The MIT Press, 1981 [1967]), 38.

24. Adorno, *Prisms*, 37; Adorno, 'Introduction', *The Positivist Dispute*, 5.

25. Adorno, 'On the Logic of the Social Sciences', 115.

26. Habermas, 'The Analytical Theory of Science and Dialectics', *The Positivist Dispute*, 147, 151.

27. Popper, 'The Logic of the Social Sciences', 70–2.

28. Adorno, 'On the Logic of the Social Sciences', 108.

29. Ibid., 106.

30. Adorno, 'Subject and Object', *The Essential Frankfurt School Reader*, eds Andrew Arato and Eike Gebhardt (New York: Continuum, 1997), 498–9.

31. Ibid., 503 (translation modified).

32. Ibid., 502.

33. Ibid., 504 (translation modified).

34. Ibid., 506.

35. Ibid., 508.

36. Adorno, 'Sociology and Psychology' (part 1), *New Left Review* 46 (Nov–Dec 1967), 72.

37. Adorno, *Negative Dialectics*, trans. E. B. Ashton (New York, Continuum, 1973 [1966]), 3.

38. Adorno, *Introduction to Sociology*, 133.

39. Adorno. 'Introduction', *The Positivist Dispute*, 16.

40. Ibid., 18.

41. Ibid., 19.

42. Adorno, 'Sociology and Empirical Research', *The Positivist Dispute*, 68–9.

43. Ibid., 71.

44. Popper, *In Search of a Better World*, 73.

45. Adorno, *Introduction to Sociology*, 142.

46. Adorno, 'Introduction', *The Positivist Dispute*, 12.

47. Hans Albert, 'The Myth of Total Reason', *The Positivist Dispute*, 169.

48. Ibid., 181.

49. Popper, *Conjectures and Refutations*, 335. See also: Popper, *The Open Society and its Enemies*, vol. 2. New York: Harper and Row, 1962), 78–80.

50. Adorno, 'On the Logic of the Social Sciences', 121.

51. Adorno, 'Introduction', *The Positivist Dispute*, 62.

52. Popper, 'The Logic of the Social Sciences', 73–4.

53. Popper, 'Reason or Revolution?' 69 (emphasis in original).

54. Albert, 'Behind Positivism's Back?' *The Positivist Dispute*, 237.

55. Max Weber, 'Science as a Vocation', *From Max Weber*, trans and eds H. H. Gerth and C. Wright Mills (New York: Oxford University Press, 1958), 146–7.

56. Ibid., 152.

57. Ibid., 153.

58. Albert, 'The Myth of Total Reason', 165.

59. Ibid., 178.

60. Ibid., 182.

61. Ibid., 13–15.

62. Gillian Rose, 'How is Critical Theory Possible?' *Political Studies* 24.1 (1976), 70.

63. Adorno, *Negative Dialectics*, 149–51.

64. Ibid., 152–4.

65. Agnes Heller, 'On the New Adventures of the Dialectic', *Telos* 31 (Spring 1977), 134–42.

66. Hauke Brunkhorst, 'The Enlightenment of Rationality', *Constellations* 7.1 (2000), 139.

67. Rüdiger Bittner, 'Does *Dialectic of Enlightenment* Rest on Religious Foundations?' *The Early Frankfurt School and Religion*, eds Margarete Kohlenbach and Raymond Geuss (Houndmills: Palgrave Macmillan, 2005), 168–70.

68. Axel Honneth, *Pathologies of Reason*, trans. James Ingram et al. (New York: Columbia University Press, 2009), 50.

69. James Gordon Finlayson, 'Morality and Critical Theory: On the Normative Problem of Frankfurt School Social Criticism', *Telos* 146 (Spring 2009), 8.

70. Adorno, *Negative Dialectics*, 286.
71. Finlayson, 18.
72. Adorno, *Negative Dialectics*, 31.
73. Adorno, 'Why Still Philosophy', *Critical Models*, trans. Henry W. Pickford (New York: Columbia, 1998), 14.
74. Adorno, *Introduction to Sociology*, 144.
75. Adorno, *Negative Dialectics*, 17–18.
76. Adorno, 'On the Logic of the Social Sciences', 117.
77. Popper, 'The Logic of the Social Sciences', 73–4.
78. Ibid., 74 (emphasis in original).
79. Adorno, 'On the Logic of the Social Sciences', 117–18.
80. Ibid., 118.
81. Adorno, 'Introduction', *The Positivist Dispute*, 37–8.
82. Adorno, *Introduction to Sociology*, 21.
83. Ibid., 46.
84. Ibid., 83.
85. Rose defends 'elucidation' over 'interpretation' as the proper translation of Adorno's use of '*Deutung*'. See Rose, *The Melancholy Science* (New York: Columbia University Press, 1978), 102.
86. Adorno, 'Introduction', *The Positivist Dispute*, 32 (emphasis in original, translation modified).
87. Ibid., 63.
88. Ibid., 32.
89. Adorno, 'The Actuality of Philosophy', *Telos* 31 (Spring 1977), 126 (translation modified).
90. Adorno, 'Resignation', 293.
91. Adorno, *Introduction to Sociology*, 72 (emphasis added).
92. Popper, 'What does the West Believe in?' *In Search of a Better World*, 206–7.
93. Rose, 'How is Critical Theory Possible?', 84.
94. Popper, *The Open Society and its Enemies*, vol. 2 (New York: Harper and Row, 1962), 227–31 (emphasis in original).
95. Ibid., 232.
96. Popper, *The Open Society and its Enemies*, vol. 2, 240.
97. Ibid., 238–9 (emphasis added).
98. Ibid., 233.
99. Ibid., 100.
100. Espen Hammer, 'Minding the World', *Philosophy and Social Criticism* 26.1 (2000), 89.

## Chapter 4

1. Adorno, 'Reason and Revelation', *Critical Models: Interventions and Catchwords*, trans. Henry W. Pickford (New York: Columbia University Press, 1998), 135–42.
2. Sigmund Freud, *The Future of an Illusion*, trans. James Strachey (New York and London: W. W. Norton and Company, 1961), 19–23.

# Notes

3. Adorno, 'Reason and Revelation', 137.

4. Adorno, *The Stars Down to Earth and Other Essays on the Irrational in Culture*, ed. Stephen Crook (London and New York: Routledge, 1994), 115.

5. Ibid., 114.

6. Slavoj Žižek makes a similar point about the nature of 'belief' in *On Belief* (London and New York: Routledge, 2001).

7. Adorno, *The Stars Down to Earth*, 58.

8. Ibid., 116.

9. Ibid., 42.

10. Ibid., 117.

11. Adorno, *Negative Dialectics*, 17–18

12. Adorno, *Metaphysics: Concept and Problems*, ed. Rolf Tiedemann, trans. Edmund Jephcott (Stanford, CA: Stanford University Press, 2000), 68.

13. Adorno, *Negative Dialectics*, 392.

14. Max Horkheimer, *Critical Theory: Selected Essays*, trans. Matthew J. O'Connell et al. (New York: Continuum, 1995), 131.

15. Horkheimer, *Eclipse of Reason* (New York: The Seabury Press, 1974), 12.

16. Ibid., 14, 18.

17. Adorno, 'Reason and Revelation', 138.

18. Adorno, 'Reason and Revelation', 142.

19. Exodus 20.4–5a, *The Holy Bible: New Revised Standard Version* (Nashville: Thomas Nelson Publishers, 1989).

20. Adorno and Horkheimer, *Dialectic of Enlightenment*, ed. Gunzelin Schmid Noerr, trans. Edmund Jephcott (Stanford, CA: Stanford University Press, 2002), 17.

21. Jürgen Habermas, 'Theodor Adorno', *Philosophical-Political Profiles*, trans. Frederick Lawrence (Cambridge, MA: MIT Press, 1987), 107; Albrecht Wellmer, *The Persistence of Modernity*, trans. David Midgeley (Cambridge, MA: MIT Press, 1993), 7; Matthew Lamb, *Solidarity with Victims: Toward a Theology of Social Transformation* (New York: Crossroad, 1982), 34–5; Ulf Liedke, *Naturgeschichte und Religion: Eine theologische Studie zum Religionsbegriff in der Philosophie Theodor W. Adornos* (Frankfurt, Bern, New York: Peter Lang, 1997), 439 (my translation).

22. Michael Theunissen, 'Negativität bei Adorno', *Adorno-Konferenz 1983*, eds Ludwig von Friedeburg and Jürgen Habermas (Frankfurt am Main: Suhrkamp, 1983), 50 (my translation).

23. Hent de Vries, *Minimal Theologies: Critique of Secular Reason in Adorno and Levinas*, trans. Geoffrey Hale (Baltimore and London: The John Hopkins University Press, 2005).

24. Charles Davis, *Theology and Political Society* (Cambridge: Cambridge University Press, 1980), 137; Wayne Whitson Floyd, Jr, *Theology and the Dialectics of Otherness: On Reading Bonhoeffer and Adorno* (Lanham, New York, London: University Press of America, 1988).

25. Helmut Peukert, *Science, Action, and Fundamental Theology: Toward a Theology of Communicative Action*, trans. James Bohman (Cambridge, MA: MIT Press, 1984), 212.

26. Gerrit Steunebrink, 'Is Adorno's Negative Philosophy a Negative Theology?' *Flight of the Gods: Philosophical Perspectives on Negative Theology*, eds Ilse N. Bulhof and Laurens ten Kate (New York: Fordham University Press, 2000), 318.

27. Susan Buck-Morss, *Dialectic of Seeing: Walter Benjamin and the Arcades Project* (Cambridge, MA: MIT Pres, 1989), 249.

28. Other interpreters who suggest that Adorno articulates a 'negative theology' include: Hauke Brunkhorst, *Adorno and Critical Theory* (Cardiff: University of Wales Press, 1999), 119; J. A. Columbo, *An Essay on Theology and History* (Atlanta: Scholars Press, 1990), 152–3.

29. Quoted in Denys Turner, 'Apophaticism, idolatry and the claims of reason', *Silence and the Word: Negative Theology and Incarnation* (Cambridge University Press, 2002), 12.

30. Oliver Davies and Denys Turner, 'Introduction', *Silence and the Word: Negative Theology and Incarnation* (Cambridge University Press, 2002), 2.

31. Merold Westphal, *Transcendence and Self-Transcendence: On God and the Soul* (Bloomington: Indiana University Press, 2004), 3.

32. Harold Coward and Tiby Foshay (eds), *Derrida and Negative Theology* (Albany: SUNY, 1992), 2.

33. Jacques Derrida, 'How to Avoid Speaking: Denials', *Derrida and Negative Theology*, 79.

34. Adorno, *Negative Dialectics*, 372.

35. G. W. F. Hegel, *Phenomenology of Spirit*, trans. A. V. Miller (Oxford: Oxford University Press, 1977), 11(§20).

36. Adorno, *Minima Moralia*, trans. E. F. N. Jephcott (London: Verso, 1974), 50.

37. Elizabeth A. Pritchard, '*Bilderverbot* Meets Body in Theodor W. Adorno's Inverse Theology', *Harvard Theological Review* 95:3 (2002), 293.

38. Adorno, *Negative Dialectics*, 15.

39. Ibid., 181.

40. Derrida, 'How to Avoid Speaking', 6.

41. Hent de Vries, *Minimal Theologies*, 71.

42. Ibid., 56.

43. Ibid., 168.

44. Ibid., 30.

45. Ibid., 31.

46. Ibid., 161.

47. Adorno, *Negative Dialectics*, 158.

48. Vries, *Minimal Theologies*, 529.

49. Ibid., xxv.

50. Ibid., 559.

51. Ibid., 559.

52. Adorno, *Negative Dialectics*, 402.

53. Ibid., 402.

54. Other interpretations of Adorno's use of 'inverse theology' include: Pritchard, '*Bilderverbot* Meets Body in Theodor W. Adorno's Inverse

# Notes

Theology'; René Buchholz, *Zwischen Mythos und* Bilderverbot (Frankfurt am Main: Peter Lang, 1991); David Kaufman, 'Beyond Use, Within Reason: Adorno, Benjamin and the Question of Theology', *New German Critique* 83 (Spring/Summer 2001), 151–73; Willem van Reijen, 'Redemption and Reconciliation in Benjamin and Adorno', *Adorno: The Possibility of the Impossible*, eds Nicolaus Schafhausen, Vanessa Müller, Michael Hirsch (New York and Berlin: Lukas and Sternberg, 2003), 69–84.

55. Ibid., 67.
56. Walter Benjamin, 'Franz Kafka: *Beim Bau der Chinesischen Mauer*', *Walter Benjamin: Selected Writings*, vol. 2, eds Michael W. Jennings, Howard Eiland, Gary Smith, trans. Rodney Livingston et al. (Cambridge, MA: Belknap Press of Harvard University Press, 1999), 496.
57. Benjamin, *Illuminations*, ed. Hannah Arendt, trans. Harry Zohn (New York: Schocken Books, 1969), 143–4.
58. Benjamin, 'Franz Kafka', 497.
59. Benjamin, *Walter Benjamin: Selected Writings* vol. 2, 808.
60. Susan Buck-Morss, *The Origin of Negative Dialectics*, (Hassocks, Sussex: The Harvester Press, 1977), 6.
61. Adorno and Benjamin, *The Complete Correspondence*, 66. For further analysis of Adorno and Benjamin on Kafka, see: David Kaufman, 'Adorno, Benjamin and the Question of Theology, 151–73.
62. Adorno, *Prisms*, trans. Samuel and Shierry Weber (Cambridge, MA: MIT Press, 1983), 255.
63. Adorno and Benjamin, *The Complete Correspondence*, 53.
64. Adorno, 'Commitment', *Aesthetics and Politics*, trans. Ronald Taylor (London and New York: Verso, 1977), 183.
65. Adorno and Benjamin, *Complete Correspondence*, 54.
66. Adorno, *Prisms*, 245.
67. Benjamin, *The Origin of German Tragic Drama*, trans. John Osborne (London and New York: Verso, 1977), 162–3, 166.
68. Adorno and Benjamin, *Complete Correspondence*, 62.
69. Ibid., 67.
70. Benjamin, *Selected Writings*, vol. 2, 815.
71. Benjamin, 'Franz Kafka: On the Tenth Anniversary of his Death', *Illuminations*, ed. Hannah Arendt, trans. Harry Zohn (New York: Schocken Books, 1969), 133–4.
72. Adorno and Benjamin, *The Complete Correspondence: 1928–1940*, ed. Henri Lonitz, trans. Nicholas Walker (Cambridge: Harvard University Press, 1999), 66–7.
73. Horkheimer and Adorno, *Dialectic of Enlightenment*, 230.
74. Adorno, *Introduction to Sociology*, 144.
75. Adorno, *Negative Dialectics*, 27–8.
76. Ibid., 145.
77. Ludwig Feuerbach, *The Essence of Christianity*, trans. George Eliot (New York: Harper and Row, 1957).

# Notes

78. Karl Marx, *The Marx-Engels Reader*, second edition, ed. Robert C. Tucker (New York: W. W. Norton and Co., 1978), 53.

79. Ibid., 144.

80. Ibid., 54.

81. Ibid., 53.

82. For a similar view on this point, see: Pritchard, '*Bilderverbot* meets Body', 309–10.

83. Adorno, *Negative Dialectics*, 3.

84. Ibid., 207.

85. Ibid., 159–60.

86. Adorno, *Minima Moralia*, 247.

87. Adorno, *Metaphysics: Concepts and Problems*, trans. Edmund Jephcott (Stanford, CA: Stanford University Press, 2000), 1.

88. Adorno, *Lectures on Negative Dialectics*, ed. Rolf Tiedemann, trans. Rodney Livingston (Cambridge: Polity Press, 2008), 38–9.

89. Ibid., 40.

90. Gershom Scholem, *The Messianic Idea in Judaism and Other Essays on Jewish Spirituality* (New York: Schocken Books, 1970), 7.

91. Ibid., 10, 27.

92. Benjamin, *Illuminations*, 257.

93. Adorno and Benjamin, *Complete Correspondence*, 249–50.

94. Ibid., 108. Further consideration of Adorno's criticisms of Benjamin will be taken up in Chapter 6.

95. Karl Barth, *Revolutionary Theology in the Making*, trans. James D. Smart (Richmond, VA: John Knox Press, 1964), 26.

96. Barth, *Protestant Thought: From Rousseau to Ritschl*, trans. Brian Cozens (New York: Harper and Row, 1959), 302–3.

97. Ralf Frisch, *Theologie im Augenblick ihres Sturzes: Theodor W. Adorno und Karl Barth* (Wien: Passagen Verlag, 1999).

98. Simon Fisher, *Revelatory Positivism?* (Oxford: Oxford University Press, 1988), 180.

99. Barth, *The Epistle to the Romans*, trans. Edwyn C. Hoskyns (London, Oxford, New York: Oxford University Press, 1933), 230.

100. Ibid., 236.

101. Ibid., 241–2.

102. Ibid., 238.

103. Adorno, *Prisms*, 259.

104. Adorno, *Metaphysics*, 122.

105. Adorno, *Kierkegaard: Construction of the Aesthetic*, trans. Robert Hullot-Kentor (Minneapolis: University of Minnesota Press, 1989), 15.

106. Benjamin, *Selected Writings*, vol. 2, 703.

107. Adorno, *Kierkegaard*, 112.

108. Adorno, 'The Actuality of Philosophy', *Telos* 31 (1977), 127.

109. Ibid., 129.

110. Benjamin, *The Origin of German Tragic Drama*, 35.

111. Adorno, *Negative Dialectics*, 163.

# Chapter 5

1.  Popper, 'Against Big Words', *In Search of a Better World*, 86.
2.  Adorno, *Negative Dialectics*, 205.
3.  Robert C. Tucker (ed.), *The Marx-Engels Reader*, second edition (New York: W. W. Norton and Co., 1978), 145.
4.  Horkheimer, *Critical Theory*, trans. Matthew O'Connell et al. (New York: Continuum, 1995), 222.
5.  Adorno, *Negative Dialectics*, 365.
6.  Espen Hammer, *Adorno and the Political* (London and New York, 2006), 4.
7.  Georg Lukács, 'Preface', *The Theory of the Novel*, trans. Anna Bostock (Cambridge, MA: MIT Press, 1971), 22.
8.  Leo Strauss, *Spinoza's Critique of Religion*, trans. E. M. Sinclair, (New York: Schocken Books, 1982), 30.
9.  Esther Leslie, 'Introduction to Adorno/Marcuse Correspondence', *New Left Review* 23 (1999), 119–20. See also: Wiggershaus, *The Frankfurt School*, 609–35; Wolfgang Kraushaar (ed.), *Frankfurter Schule und Studentenbewegung*, 3 vols (Hamburg: Rogner and Bernhard, 1998).
10. Kraushaar, *Frankfurter Schule*, vol. 1, 398.
11. Leslie, 'Introduction to Adorno/Marcuse Correspondence', 120.
12. Adorno, 'Resignation', *Critical Models*, 290.
13. Marx and Engels, *The Holy Family, or Critique of Critical Criticism*, trans Richard Dixon and Clemens Dutt (Moscow: Publishers Press, 1975), 12.
14. Adorno, *Introduction to Sociology*, 150.
15. Adorno, 'Resignation', 291.
16. Adorno, *Introduction to Sociology*, 28.
17. For commentaries that point to a convergence, see: Robert D'Amico, 'Karl Popper and the Frankfurt School', *Telos* 23 #86 (Winter 1990–1) 33–48; Geoffrey Stokes, *Popper: Philosophy, Politics and Scientific Method* (Cambridge, UK: Polity Press, 1998).
18. Krahl, 'The Political Contradictions in Adorno's Critical Theory', *Foundations of the Frankfurt School of Social* Research, eds Judith Marcus and Zoltán Tar (New Brunswick: Transaction, 1984), 307.
19. Adorno, 'Commitment', *Aesthetics and Politics*, trans. Ronald Taylor et al. (London and New York: Verso, 1977), 182.
20. Ibid., 189.
21. Adorno, *Critical Models*, 291.
22. Ibid., 291.
23. Ibid., 265.
24. Ibid., 263.
25. Adorno, *Lectures on Negative Dialectics*, 46–7.
26. Adorno, *Critical Models*, 273 (emphasis added).
27. Ibid., 274.
28. Marianne Tettlebaum, 'Political Philosophy', *Adorno: Key Concepts*, ed. Deborah Cook (Stocksfield: Acumen, 2008), 140.

29. Miroslav Volf, *Exclusion and Embrace* (Nashville: Abingdon Press, 1996), 103.

30. Ibid., 104, 109.

31. Adorno, *History and Freedom*, ed. Rolf Tiedemann, trans. Rodney Livingston (Cambridge: Polity Press, 2006), 140. I credit Tettlebaum for drawing this example to my attention, *Adorno: Key Concepts*, 131.

32. Ibid., 67.

33. Ibid., 153.

34. Ibid., 11.

35. Ibid., 10.

36. Juan Luis Segundo, 'Theology and the Social Sciences', *Signs of the Times: Theological Reflections*, ed. Alfred T. Hennelly, trans. Robert R. Barr (Maryknoll: Orbis Books, 1993), 7–8.

37. Ibid., 13.

38. Segundo, 'A Note on Irony and Sorrow', *Signs of the Times*, 87. Segundo includes Gustavo Gutierrez and Jon Sobrino on his list of those who have made the 'shift'.

39. Segundo, 'The Shift Within Latin American Theology', *Signs of the Times*, 79.

40. Segundo, *Our Idea of God*, trans. John Drury (Maryknoll: Orbis, 1974), 130–1.

41. Alasdair Kee, *Marx and the Failure of Liberation Theology* (London: SCM Press, 1990), 260–1; Clodovis Boff, *Feet-on-the-Ground Theology* (Maryknoll, NY: Orbis Books, 1987), 21.

42. Dennis McCann, *Christian Realism and Liberation Theology* (Maryknoll: Orbis, 1981), 222.

43. Marsha Aileen Hewitt, *From Theology to Social Theory* (New York, Bern, Frankfurt: Peter Lang, 1990), 14.

44. Ibid., 165.

45. McCann, *Christian Realism and Liberation Theology*, 231.

46. Bryan Stone, *Effective Faith* (Lanham: University Press of America, 1994), 128.

47. Ibid., 147.

48. Ivan Petrella, *The Future of Liberation Theology* (London: SCM Press, 2006), 29.

49. Ibid., 35.

50. Adorno, *Critical Models*, 291.

51. Ibid., 293.

52. Adorno, *Lectures on Negative Dialectics*, 53.

53. Joseph Klausner, *The Messianic Idea in Israel*, trans. W. F. Stinespring (New York: Macmillan, 1955), 9.

54. Adorno, *Minima Moralia*, 247.

55. Giorgio Agamben, *The Time that Remains*, trans. Patricia Dailey (Stanford, CA: Stanford University Press, 2005), 35.

56. Ibid., 38.

57. Agamben, *State of Exception*, trans. Kevin Attell (Chicago: Chicago University Press, 2005), 2.

58. Ibid., 23.

59. Ibid., 60.

60. Ibid., 2.

61. Ibid., 86.
62. Ibid., 88.
63. Ibid., 63.
64. Adorno, *Prisms*, 234.
65. Adorno and Benjamin, *The Complete Correspondence*, 67.
66. Adorno, *Notes to Literature*, vol. 2, trans. Shierry Weber Nicholsen (New York: Columbia University Press, 1992), 228.
67. Adorno and Benjamin, *The Complete Correspondence*, 108.
68. Ibid., 105.
69. Agamben, *The Open*, trans. Kevin Attell (Stanford, CA: Stanford University Press, 2002), 13.
70. Ibid., 3.
71. Ibid., 83.
72. Ibid., 91–2.
73. Alastair Morgan, 'Petrified Life: Adorno and Agamben', *Radical Philosophy* 141 (2007), 23–32.
74. Agamben, *Potentialities*, trans. Daniel Heller-Roazen (Stanford, CA: Stanford University Press, 1999), 182.
75. Agamben, *The Open*, 70.
76. Adorno, *Negative Dialectics*, 117.
77. Agamben, *The Time that Remains*, 57.
78. Ibid., 51.
79. Ibid., 13.
80. Ibid., 26.
81. Ibid., 57.
82. Ibid., 128.
83. Ibid., 134.
84. Ibid., 42.
85. Agamben, *Infancy and History*, trans. Liz Heron (London and New York: Verso, 1993), 119.
86. Ibid., 111.
87. Agamben, *The Open*, 92.

## Chapter 6

1. Adorno, *Notes to Literature*, vol. 2, trans. Shierry Weber Nicholsen (New York: Columbia University Press, 1992), 294.
2. Peter L. Berger (ed.), *The Desecularization of the World* (Grand Rapids: Eerdmans, 1999).
3. Paul Heelas and Linda Woodhead (eds), *The Spiritual Revolution* (Oxford: Blackwell, 2005).
4. Linda Woodhead ,'Post-Christian Spiritualities', *Religion* 23.2 (1993), 117, n.4.
5. Jeremy Carrette and Richard King, *Selling Spirituality* (London and New York: Routledge, 2005), x.
6. Ibid., 17.

# Notes

7. Roger Foster, *Adorno: The Recovery of Experience* (Albany: SUNY, 2007), 197.

8. Adorno, *Lectures on Negative Dialectics*, 89–90.

9. Ibid., 93.

10. Ibid., 106.

11. Ibid., 107.

12. Adorno, *The Culture Industry*, ed. J. M. Bernstein (London: Routledge, 1991), 85.

13. Karl Marx, *Capital: A Critique of Political Economy*, vol. 1., trans. Ben Fowkes (London: Penguin Books, 1976), 163.

14. Marx, 'Anti-Church Movement – Demonstration in Hyde Park', *Marx and Engels on Religion* (Moscow: Progress Publishers, 1976), 111.

15. See: Deborah Cook, *The Culture Industry Revisited* (London: Rowman and Littlefield, 1996); Robert W. Witkin, *Adorno on Popular Culture* (London and New York: Routledge, 2003).

16. Adorno, *Prisms*, trans. Samuel and Shierry Weber (Cambridge, MA: MIT Press, 1981), 20.

17. For example, see: Alan Hirsch, *The Forgotten Ways: Reactivating the Missional Church* (Grand Rapids: Brazos Press, 2007); Duncan MacLauren, *Mission Implausible* (Milton Keynes: Paternoster, 2004); David A Roozen and C. Kirk Hadaway, *Church and Denominational Growth* (Nashville: Abingdon Press, 1993).

18. William Riker, 'Political Science and Rational Choice', *Perspectives on Positive Political Economy*, eds. James Alt and Kenneth Shepsle (Cambridge, MA: Cambridge University Press, 1990), 177.

19. *A Beautiful Mind,* directed by Ron Howard, screenplay by Akiva Goldsman and Sylvia Nasar. USA: Universal Pictures, 2001.

20. For more on equilibrium in game theory, see Roger B. Myerson, *Game Theory: Analysis of Conflict* (Cambridge, MA: Harvard University Press, 1991), Ch. 3.

21. Myerson, *Game Theory*, 1–4.

22. For a brief summary, see: Laurence R. Iannaccone, 'Framework for the Scientific Study of Religion', *Rational Choice Theory and Religion*, ed. Lawrence A. Young (New York: Routledge, 1997), 26.

23. Horkheimer, *Eclipse of Reason* (New York: The Seabury Press, 1974), 10.

24. Adorno, and Horkheimer, *Dialectic of Enlightenment*, 109.

25. Adorno, *Introduction to Sociology*, 142.

26. Adorno, 'Introduction', *The Positivist Dispute*, 12.

27. Ibid., 68.

28. Stark, 'Bringing Theory Back In', *Rational Choice Theory and Religion*, ed. Lawrence A. Young (New York and London: Routledge, 1997), 6–7.

29. Ibid., 18–19.

30. Ibid., 16–17.

31. Iannaccone, 'Voodoo Economics? Reviewing the Rational Choice Approach to Religion', *Journal for the Scientific Study of Religion*, 34.1 (1995), 81.

32. Stark, 'German and German-American Religiousness', *Journal for the Scientific Study of Religion*, 36.2 (1997), 185.

33. Ibid., 191 [emphasis added].
34. Iannaccone, 'Why Strict Churches are Strong', *American Journal of Sociology*, 99.5 (1994, 1183–84.
35. Iannaccone, Religious Practices: A Human Capital Approach', *Journal for the Scientific Study of Religion*, 29.3 (1990), 301.
36. Adorno, *Introduction to Sociology*, 147–8.
37. Ibid., 149.
38. Adorno, and Horkheimer, *Aspects of Sociology*, trans. John Viertel (London: Heinemann, 1973), 28.
39. G. W. F. Hegel, *Phenomenology of Spirit*, trans. A. V. Miller (Oxford: Oxford University Press, 1994), 400.
40. Horkheimer, *Critical Theory*, trans. Matthew O'Connell (New York: Continuum, 1995), 26.
41. Horkeimer, *Dawn and Decline*, trans. Michael Shaw (New York: The Seabury Press, 1978), 177.
42. Adorno, *Critical Models*, 138.
43. Horkheimer, *Critical Theory*, 235.
44. For examples of Adorno's sociological writing on religion, see: Adorno 1994 and 2000c.
45. Horkheimer, *Dawn and Decline*, 178.
46. Adorno, *Introduction to Sociology*, 143.
47. Paul Tillich, *Systematic Theology*, vol. 1 (The University of Chicago Press, 1951), 61.
48. Ibid., 62.
49. Ibid., 62.
50. Adorno, *The Jargon of Authenticity*, trans. Knut Tarnowski and Frederic Will (Evanston, IL: Northwestern University Press, 1973), 17.
51. Adam Kotsko, *Žižek and Theology* (London and New York: Continuum, 2008), 142.
52. Slavoj Žižek, *The Metastases of Enjoyment: Six Essays on Women and Causality* (London and New York: Verso, 1994), 18.
53. Adorno, *The Stars Down to Earth* (New York: Routledge, 1994), 114.
54. Ibid., 114.
55. Žižek, *Welcome to the Desert of the Real* (London: Verso, 2002), 68–71.
56. Ibid., 68.
57. Ibid., 88.
58. Ibid., 153.
59. Adorno, *The Jargon of Authenticity*, 128.

# Chapter 7

1. Van Morrison, 'Hymns to the Silence', *Hymns to the Silence*, disk 2, track 3 (United Kingdom: Polydor records, 1991).
2. Paul Celan, *Poems of Paul Celan*, trans. Michael Hamburger (New York: Persea Books, 1972), 175.

3. Jürgen Moltmann, *Theology of Hope: On the Ground and the Implications of a Christian Eschatology*, trans. James W. Leitch (London: SCM, 1967).

4. Adorno, *Minima Moralia*, 97–8.

5. Adorno, *Metaphysics*, 124.

6. Adorno, 'Reconciliation under Duress', *Aesthetics and Politics*, trans. Ronald Taylor. (London:Verso, 1977), 151–76.

7. Lambert Zuidervaart, *Social Philosophy after Adorno* (Cambridge: Cambridge University Press, 2007), 58.

8. Edgar Thadigsmann, 'Das Versprechen: Metaphysische Erfahrung bei Theodor W. Adorno', *Zeitschrift für Theologie und Kirche* 106 (2009), 119.

9. Ibid., 124.

10. Ibid., 125.

11. For a discussion of this distinction, see Chapter 5.

12. Adorno, *Minima Moralia*, 178.

13. Adorno, *Minima Moralia*, 39.

14. James Gordon Finlayson, 'Morality and Critical Theory', *Telos* 146 (2009), 29.

15. Adorno, *Minima Moralia*, 193.

16. Thaidigsmann, 126.

17. Adorno, *Minima Moralia*, 112.

18. Adorno, *Metaphysics*, 125–6.

19. Floyd, Wayne Whitson, Jr., *Theology and the Dialectics of Otherness: On Reading Bonhoeffer and Adorno.* (Lanham, New York & London: University Press of America, 1988).

20. Ibid., 261–91.

21. Surin, Kenneth, "*Contemptus mundi* and the disenchantment of the world," *The Turnings of Darkness and Light.* (Cambridge University Press, 1989), 180–200.

22. Ibid., 195.

23. Ibid., 198–9.

24. Adorno, *Metaphysics*, 122.

25. Ibid., 183.

26. Ibid., 123.

27. Ralf Frisch, *Theologie im Augenblick ihres Sturzes: Theodor W. Adorno und Karl Barth.* Vienna: (Passagen Verlag, 1999), 128.

28. Adorno, *Aesthetic Theory*, trans. Robert Hullot-Kentor (Minneapolis: University of Minnesota Press, 1997), 87.

29. Frisch, 128.

30. Adorno, *Aesthetic Theory*, 13.

31. Ibid., 121.

32. See: Lambert Zuidervaart, *Adorno's Aesthetic Theory* (Cambridge, MA: MIT Press, 1991).

33. Frisch, 130.

34. Ibid., 95.

35. Andreas Pangritz, *Vom Kleiner- und Unsichtbarwerden der Theologie* (Tübingen: Theologischer Verlag, 1996), 126.

36. Adorno, *Philosophy of New Music*, trans. Robert Hullot-Kentor (Minneapolis: University of Minnesota Press, 2006), 102.

37. Pangritz, 217.

38. See: Michael Theunissen, "Negativität bei Adorno," *Adorno-Konferenz 1983* (Frankfurt: Suhrkamp, 1983), 60.

39. Adorno, Negative Dialectics, 404.

40. Adorno and Horkheimer, *Dialectic of Enlightenment*, 17.

41. Helmut Peukert, *Science, Action, and Fundamental Theology*, trans. James Bohman. (Cambridge: The MIT Press, 1984 [1976]); Charles Davis, *Religion and the Making of Society: Essays in Social Theology.* (Cambridge: Cambridge University Press, 1994); Rudolph J. Siebert, *The Critical Theory of Religion* (Berlin & New York: Mouton Publishers (de Gruyter), 1985).

42. See Habermas, *The Theory of Communicative Action*, 2 vol., trans. Thomas McCarthy. (Beacon Press: Boston, 1984, 1987 [1981]).

43. Davis, Religion and the Making of Society, 188–205.

44. Peukert, Helmut, 'Enlightenment and Theology as Unfinished Projects', *Habermas, Modernity, and Public Theology*, ed. Don S. Browning & Francis Schüssler Fiorenza. (New York: Crossroad, 1992), 62.

45. Siebert, Critical Theory of Religion, 383.

46. Habermas, 'Transcendence from Within, Transcendence in this World', *Habermas, Modernity, and Public Theology.* ed. Don S. Browning & Francis Schüssler Fiorenza. (New York: Crossroad, 1992), 236.

47. See: Seyla Benhabib & Fred R. Dallmayr (eds), *The Communicative Ethics Controversy* (Cambridge, MA: MIT Press, 1990).

48. Adorno, Negative Dialectics, 219.

49. Ibid., 41.

50. Mattias Martinson, *Perseverance without Doctrine* (Frankfurt am Main: Peter Lang, 2000), 353.

51. Ibid., 354 (emphasis in original).

52. Ibid., 341.

53. Ibid., 347 (emphasis in original).

54. Ibid., 346.

55. Ibid, 358–9.

56. Adorno, "Cultural Criticism ajnd Society," *Prisms*, trans. Samuel and Shierry Weber (Cambirdge, MA: MIT Press, 1981), 34.

57. See, for example, Susan Gubar, *Poetry after Auschwitz. Remembering what one never knew* (Bloomington and Indianapolis: Indiana University Press, 2003), 240.

58. Adorno, *Metaphysics*, 110 (emphasis in original).

59. Adorno, *Metaphysics*, 110.

60. Adorno, Negative Dialectics, 362.

61. Adorno, *Negative Dialectics*, 365 (translation modified). German Original: Adorno, *Gesammelte Schriften, vol. 6, Negative Dialektik: Jargon der Eigentlichkeit*, ed. Rolf Tiedemann, et al. (Frankfurt am Main: Suhrkamp, 1997), 358.

62. Karl Popper, *The Open Society and its Enemies*, vol. 2, 232.

63. Adorno, *Metaphysics*, 143.

# Notes

64. Ibid., 99.

65. Radu Mihaileanu (dir), *Train de Vie* (Paramount Pictures, 1998).

66. Roberto Benign (dir), *La Vita è bella* (Miramax, 1999).

67. Adorno, 'Reason and Revelation', *Critical Models*, 138.

68. Adorno, *Metaphysics*, 3 (emphasis in original), 88.

69. Adorno, *Introduction to Sociology*, 148.

70. Adorno, *Metaphysics*, 101.

71. Ibid., 18.

72. Adorno, *Negative Dialectics*, 392.

73. Gerhard Schweppenhäuser, *Theodor W. Adorno: an introduction*, trans. James Rolleston (Durham: Duke University Press, 2009), 35.

74. Adorno, *Metaphysics*, 7.

75. Adorno, *Metaphysics*, 144.

76. Ibid., 131 (translation modified).

77. Adorno, *Negative Dialectics*, 183.

78. Adorno, 'On Lyric Poetry and Society', *Notes to Literature*, vol. 1, trans. Shierry Weber Nicholsen (New York: Columbia University Press, 1991), 39.

79. Ibid., 45.

80. Ibid., 54.

81. Adorno, 'Theses Upon Art and Religion Today', *Notes to Literature*, vol. 2, trans. Shierry Weber Nicholson (New York: Columbia University Press, 1992 [1974]), 292–8.

82. Ibid., 294.

83. Adorno, *Metaphysics*, 139.

84. Adorno, 'Theses Upon Art and Religion', 295–6.

85. Adorno, *Metaphysics*, 115.

86. Ibid., 121.

87. Adorno, *Negative Dialectics*, 367.

88. Adorno, 'On Tradition', *Telos* no. 94 (winter 1993), 76–7.

89. Ibid., 78.

90. Ibid.

91. Adorno, *Minima Moralia*, 52. See the discussion of this statement in: Neil Lazarus 'Hating Tradition Properly', *New Formations* #38 (summer 1999), 9–30.

92. Adorno, Theodor and Bloch, Ernst, 'Something's Missing: A Discussion between Ernst Bloch and Theodor Adorno on the Contradictions of Utopian Longing', *The Utopian Function of Art and Literature*, trans. Jack Zipes and Frank Mecklenburg (Cambridge: The MIT Press, 1996), 16 (translation modified).

93. Adorno, *Lectures on Negative Dialectics*, 57.

94. Adorno, *Minima Moralia*, 247.

95. Adorno., 'Sacred Fragment: Schoenberg's *Moses and Aron*', *Quasi una fantasia: Essays on Modern Music*, trans. Rodney Livingstone (London and New York: Verso, 1994), 230.

96. Ibid., 229.

97. Ibid., 229–30.

# Notes

98. For helpful studies of Adorno's philosophy of music, see: Max Paddison, *Adorno's Aethetics of Music* (Cambridge: Cambridge University Press, 1993); Robert W. Witkin, *Adorno on Music* (London and New York: Routledge, 1998).

99. Adorno, *Philosophy of New Music*, 98–9.

100. Adorno, *Gesammelte Schriften*, vol. 15, ed. Rolf Tiedemann, et al. (Frankfurt am Main: Suhrkamp, 1997), 184.

101. Adorno, *Philosophy of New Music*, 102.

102. Adorno, *Minima Moralia*, 26.

103. Ibid., 27.

104. Ibid., 152.

105. Zuidervaart, *Social Philosophy after Adorno*, 135.

106. Adorno, *Minima Moralia*, 191.

107. Eva Geulen, 'No Happiness Without Fetischism: *Minima Moralis* as *Ars Amadni*', *Feminist Interpretations of Theodor Adorno*, ed. Renée Heberle (University Park, PA: Pennsylvania University Press, 2006), 101.

108. See Marsha Aileen Hewitt, *Critical Theory of Religion: A Feminist Analysis* (Minneapolis: Fortress Press, 1995), 86–105.

109. Adorno, *Minima Moralia*, 112.

110. Sigmund Freud, *Civilization and its Discontents*, trans. James Strachey (New York: W. W. Norton and Co., 1961), 56–7.

111. Adorno, *Minima Moralia*, 164.

112. Ibid., 164–5.

113. Geulen, 'No Happiness Without Fetishism', 109.

114. Judith Butler, *Giving an Account of Oneself* (New York: Fordham University Press, 2005), 103.

115. Ibid., 102.

116. Adorno, *Problems in Moral Philosophy*, trans. Rodney Livingstone (Stanford, CA: Stanford University Press, 2001), 169.

117. Ibid., 175. Quoted in Butler, *Giving an Account of Oneself*, 106.

118. Adorno, *Philosophy of Music*, 99.

119. Rowan Williams, *Lost Icons: Reflections on Cultural Bereavement* (Harrisburg, London, New York: Morehouse Publishing, 2000), 175–6.

120. Adorno, 'Subject and Object', *Constellations*, trans. Henry W. Pickford (New York: Columbia University Press, 1998), 247.

121. Adorno, *Dream Notes*, ed. Christoph Gödde and Henri Lonitz, trans. Rodney Livingstone (Cambridge: Polity Press, 2005), 2.

122. Adorno, *Philosophy of New Music*, 102.

123. Adorno, *Aesthetic Theory*, 219.

124. Ibid., 322.

125. *Poems of Paul Celan*, 175.

126. Adorno, *Negative Dialectics*, 402.

# Bibliography

Adorno, Theodor W., 'The Actuality of Philosophy', *Telos* 31 (1977), 120–33.
—*Aesthetic Theory*, trans. Robert Hullot-Kentor (Minneapolis: University of Minnesota Press, 1997).
—'Commitment', *Aesthetics and Politics*, trans. Ronald Taylor et al. (London and New York: Verso, 1977), 177–95.
—'Contra Paulum', *Briefwechsel: Theodor W. Adorno und Max Horkheimer*, vol. 2, eds Christoph Gödde and Henri Lonitz (Frankfurt: Suhrkamp, 2004), 475–503.
—*Critical Models: Interventions and Catchwords*, trans. Henry W. Pickford (New York: Columbia University Press, 1998).
—*The Culture Industry*, ed. J. M. Bernstein (London: Routledge, 1991).
—*Dream Notes*, eds Christoph Gödde and Henri Lonitz, trans. Rodney Livingstone (Cambridge: Polity Press, 2005).
—*Gesammelte Schriften*, vol. 15, eds Rolf Tiedemann, et al. (Frankfurt am Main: Suhrkamp, 1997).
—*Hegel: Three Studies*, trans. Shierry Weber Nicholsen (Cambridge, MA and London: The MIT Press, 1994).
—*History and Freedom*, ed. Rolf Tiedemann, trans. Rodney Livingstone (Cambridge: Polity Press, 2006).
—'The Idea of a Natural History', trans. Robert Hullot-Kentor. *Telos* 60 (1984), 111–24.
—*Introduction to Sociology*, ed. Christoph Gödde, trans. Edmund Jephcott (Stanford: Stanford University Press, 2000).
—*The Jargon of Authenticity*, trans. Knut Tarnowski and Frederic Will (Evanston, IL: Northwestern University Press, 1973).
—*Kant's Critique of Pure Reason (1959)*, ed. Rolf Tiedemann, trans. Rodney Livingstone. (Stanford, CA: Stanford University Press, 2001).
—*Kierkegaard: Construction of the Aesthetic*, trans. Robert Hullot-Kentor (Minneapolis: University of Minnesota Press, 1989).
—*Lectures on Negative Dialectics*, ed. Rolf Tiedemann, trans. Rodney Livingstone (Cambridge: Polity Press, 2008).
—*Metaphysics: Concept and Problems*, ed. Rolf Tiedemann, trans. Edmund Jephcott (Stanford, CA: Stanford University Press, 2000).
—*Minima Moralia*, trans. E. F. N. Jephcott (London: Verso, 1974).
—*Negative Dialectics*, trans. E. B. Ashton (New York: Continuum, 1995).
—*Notes to Literature*, vols 1 and 2, trans. Shierry Weber Nicholsen. (New York: Columbia University Press, 1991 and 1992).
—*Philosophy of New Music*, trans. Robert Hullot-Kentor (Minneapolis: University of Minnesota Press, 2006).

# Bibliography

—*Prisms*, trans. Samuel and Shierry Weber (Cambridge, MA: The MIT Press, 1981).

—*Problems in Moral Philosophy*, trans. Rodney Livingstone (Stanford, CA: Stanford University Press, 2001).

—*Quasi una Fantasia: Essays on Modern Music*, trans. Rodney Livingstone (London and New York: Verso, 1994).

—'Review of Roger Caillois', *Zeitschrift für Sozialforschung* 7 (1938), 410–11.

—'Sociology and Psychology (part 1)', *New Left Review* vol. 46 (1967), 67–80; part 2 *NLR* 47 (1968), 79–96.

—*The Stars Down to Earth* (New York: Routledge, 1994).

—'Subject and Object', *The Essential Frankfurt School Reader*, eds Andrew Arato and Eike Gebhardt (New York: Continuum, 1997), 497–511.

Adorno, Theodor W. (ed.), *The Positivist Dispute in German Sociology*, trans. Glyn Adey and David Frisby (London: Heinemann, 1976).

Adorno, Theodor W. and Benjamin, Walter, *The Complete Correspondence: 1928–1940*, ed. Henri Lonitz, trans. Nicholas Walker (Cambridge, MA: Harvard University Press, 1999).

Adorno, Theodor W. and Bloch, Ernst, 'Something's Missing: A Discussion between Ernst Bloch and Theodor W. Adorno', *The Utopian Function of Art and Literature*, trans Jack Zipes and Frank Mecklenburg. (Cambridge: The MIT Press, 1996), 1–17.

Adorno, Theodor W. and Horkheimer, Max, *Aspects of Sociology*, trans. John Viertel (London: Heinemann, 1973).

—*Dialectic of Enlightenment*, ed. Gunzelin Schmid Noerr, trans. Edmund Jephcott (Stanford, CA: Stanford University Press, 2002).

Agamben, Giorgio, *Infancy and History*, trans. Liz Heron (London and New York: Verso, 1993).

—*The Open*, trans. Kevin Attell (Stanford, CA: Stanford University Press, 2002).

—*Potentialities*, trans. Daniel Heller-Roazen (Stanford, CA: Stanford University Press, 1999).

—*State of Exception*, trans. Kevin Attell (Chicago: Chicago University Press, 2005).

—*The Time that Remains*, trans. Patricia Dailey (Stanford, CA: Stanford University Press, 2005).

Arnal, William E. 'Definition', *Guide to the Study of Religion* (London: Cassell, 2000), 21–34.

Bachofen, J. J., *Myth, Religion and Mother Right*, trans. Ralph Manheim (London: Routledge, 1967).

Barth, Karl, *The Epistle to the Romans*, trans. Edwyn C. Hoskyns (London, Oxford, New York: Oxford University Press, 1933).

—*Protestant Thought: From Rousseau to Ritschl*, trans. Brian Cozens (New York: Harper and Row, 1959).

—*Revolutionary Theology in the Making*, trans. James D. Smart (Richmond, VA: John Knox Press, 1964).

Bauman, Zygmunt, *Modernity and the Holocaust* (Cornell University Press, 1989).

Bell, Catherine, Ritual Theory, Ritual Practice (Oxford and New York: Oxford University Press, 1992).

# Bibliography

Benhabib, Seyla and Fred R. Dallmayr (eds), *The Communicative Ethics Controversy* (Cambridge, MA: MIT Press, 1990).

Benign, Roberto (dir), *La Vita è Bella* (Miramax, 1999).

Benjamin, Walter, *Illuminations*, ed. Hannah Arendt, trans. Harry Zohn (New York: Schocken Books, 1969).

—*The Origin of German Tragic Drama*, trans. John Osborne (London and New York: Verso, 1977).

—*Walter Benjamin: Selected Writings*, vol. 2, eds Michael W. Jennings, Howard Eiland and Gary Smith, trans. Rodney Livingston et al. (Cambridge, MA: Belknap Press of Harvard University Press, 1999).

Berger, Peter L. (ed.), *The Desecularization of the World* (Grand Rapids: Eerdmans, 1999).

Bernstein, J. M. *Adorno: Disenchantment and Ethics* (Cambridge: Cambridge University Press, 2001).

Berry, Philippa and Wernick, Andrew (eds), *Shadow of Spirit: Postmodernism and Religion* (New York: Routledge, 1992).

Bittner, Rüdiger, 'Does *Dialectic of Enlightenment* Rest on Religious Foundations?' *The Early Frankfurt School and Religion*, eds Margarete Kohlenbach and Raymond Geuss (Houndmills: Palgrave Macmillan, 2005), 168–70.

Blumberg, Albert and Herbert Feigl, 'Logical Positivism: a New Movement in European Philosophy', *Journal of Philosophy* 28 (1931), 281–96.

Boff, Clodovis, *Feet-on-the-Ground Theology* (Maryknoll, NY: Orbis Books, 1987).

Browning, Don S. and Schüssler Fiorenza, Francis (eds), *Habermas, Modernity and Public Theology* (New York: Crossroad, 1992).

Bruce, Steve, *God is Dead: Secularization in the West* (Oxford: Blackwell, 2002).

Brunkhorst, Hauke, *Adorno and Critical Theory* (Cardiff: University of Wales Press, 1999).

—'The Enlightenment of Rationality', *Constellations* 7.1 (2000), 133–40.

Buchholz, René, *Zwischen Mythos und Bilderverbot* (Frankfurt am Main: Peter Lang, 1991).

Buck-Morss, Susan, Dialectic of Seeing: Walter Benjamin and the Arcades Project (Cambridge, MA: MIT Press, 1989).

—*The Origin of Negative Dialectics* (New York: The Free Press, 1977).

Butler, Judith, *Giving an Account of Oneself* (New York: Fordham University Press, 2005).

Carnap, Rudolph, 'Elimination of Metaphysics through Logical Analysis of Language', *Logical Positivism*, ed. A. J. Ayer. (New York: Free Press, 1959), 60–81.

Carrette, Jeremy and King, Richard, *Selling Spirituality* (London and New York: Routledge, 2005).

Celan, Paul, *Poems of Paul Celan*, trans. Michael Hamburger (New York: Persea Books, 1972).

Champion, James W., 'Tillich and the Frankfurt School: parallels and differences in prophetic criticism', *Soundings* 69.4 (1986), 512–30.

Columbo, J. A., *An Essay on Theology and History* (Atlanta: Scholars Press, 1990).

# Bibliography

Cook, Deborah (ed.), *Adorno: Key Concepts* (Stocksfield: Acumen, 2008).

—*The Culture Industry Revisited* (London: Rowman and Littlefield, 1996).

Corngold, Stanley, *Lambent Traces: Franz Kafka* (Princeton: Princeton University Press, 2004).

Coward, Harold and Foshay, Toby (eds), *Derrida and Negative Theology* (Albany: SUNY, 1992).

D'Amico, Robert, 'Karl Popper and the Frankfurt School', *Telos* 23 #86 (Winter 1990–91) 33–48.

Davies, Oliver and Turner, Denys (eds), *Silence and the Word: Negative Theology and Incarnation* (Cambridge University Press, 2002).

Davis, Charles, *Religion and the Making of Society: Essays in Social Theology* (Cambridge: Cambridge University Press, 1994).

—*Theology and Political Society* (Cambridge: Cambridge University Press, 1980).

Dawkins, Richard, *The God Delusion* (London: Bantam Press, 2006).

de Vries, Hent, *Minimal Theologies: Critique of Secular Reason in Adorno and Levinas*, trans. Geoffrey Hale (Baltimore and London: The John Hopkins University Press, 2005).

Dennett, Daniel C., *Breaking the Spell* (New York: Viking, 2006).

Derrida, Jacques, *Acts of Religion* (Oxford: Blackwell, 2002).

Engels, Friedrich, 'The Peasant War in Germany', *Marx and Engels on Religion* (Moscow: Progress Publishers, 1976), 86–103.

Feuerbach, Ludwig, The Essence of Christianity, trans. George Eliot (New York: Harper and Row, 1957).

Finlayson, James Gordon, 'Morality and Critical Theory: On the Normative Problem of Frankfurt School Social Criticism', *Telos* 146 (Spring 2009), 7–41.

Fisher, Simon, *Revelatory Positivism?* (Oxford: Oxford University Press, 1988).

Floyd, Wayne Whitson, Jr, *Theology and the Dialectics of Otherness: On Reading Bonhoeffer and Adorno* (Lanham, MD, New York and London: University Press of America, 1988).

Foster, Roger, *Adorno: The Recovery of Experience* (Albany: SUNY, 2007).

Frazer, J. G., *The Golden Bough* (London: Macmillan, 1922).

Freud, Sigmund, *Civilization and its Discontents*, trans. James Strachey (New York: W. W. Norton and Co., 1961).

—*The Future of an Illusion*, trans. James Strachey (New York and London: W.W. Norton and Company, 1961).

Friedeburg, Ludwig von and Habermas, Jürgen (eds). *Adorno-Konferenz 1983* (Frankfurt am Main: Suhrkamp, 1983).

Frisch, Ralf, *Theologie im Augenblick ihres Sturzes: Theodor W. Adorno und Karl Barth* (Wien: Passagen Verlag, 1999).

Geulen, Eva, 'No Happiness without Fetishism: *Minima Moralia* as *Ars Amandi*', *Feminist Interpretations of Theodor Adorno*, ed. Renée Heberle (University Park, PA: Pennsylvania University Press, 2006), 97–112.

Gubar, Susan, *Poetry after Auschwitz. Remembering What One Never Knew* (Bloomington and Indianapolis: Indiana University Press, 2003).

Habermas, Jürgen, *Between Naturalism and Religion,* trans. Ciaran Cronin (Polity Press, 2008).

# Bibliography

—*The Philosophical Discourse of Modernity*, trans. Frederick G. Lawrence (Cambridge, MA: The MIT Press, 1987).

—*Philosophical–Political Profiles*, trans. Frederick Lawrence (Cambridge, MA: MIT Press, 1987).

—*The Theory of Communicative Action*, 2 vols, trans. Thomas McCarthy (Beacon Press: Boston, 1984, 1987).

Hammer, Espen, *Adorno and the Political* (London and New York: Routledge, 2006).

—'Minding the World', *Philosophy and Social Criticism* 26.1 (2000), 71–92.

Hanfling, Oswald, *Logical Positivism* (New York: Columbia University Press, 1981).

Harris, Sam, *The End of Faith* (New York: W. W. Norton, 2004).

Heelas, Paul and Woodhead, Linda (eds), *The Spiritual Revolution* (Oxford: Blackwell, 2005).

Hegel, Georg Wilhelm Friedrich, *Faith and Knowledge*, trans Walter Cerf and H. S. Harris (Albany: State University Press of New York, 1977).

—*Hegel's Logic*, trans. William Wallace (Oxford: Clarendon Press, 1975).

—*Lectures on the History of Philosophy*, vol. 3, ed. Robert Brown (Berkeley: University of California Press, 1990).

—*Phenomenology of Spirit*, trans. A. V. Miller (Oxford: Oxford University Press), 1994.

Heller, Agnes, 'On the New Adventures of the Dialectic', *Telos* 31 (Spring 1977), 134–42.

Hewitt, Marsha Aileen, *Critical Theory of Religion: A Feminist Analysis* (Minneapolis: Fortress Press, 1995).

—*From Theology to Social Theory* (New York, Bern, Frankfurt: Peter Lang, 1990).

Hirsch, Alan, *The Forgotten Ways: Reactivating the Missional Church* (Grand Rapids: Brazos Press, 2007).

Honneth, Axel, *Pathologies of Reason*, trans. James Ingram et al. (New York: Columbia University Press, 2009).

Horkheimer, Max, *Between Philosophy and Social Science*, trans. G. Frederick Hunter et al. (Cambridge, MA: The MIT Press, 1995).

—*Critical Theory*, trans. Matthew O'Connell (New York: Continuum, 1995).

—*Dawn and Decline*, trans. Michael Shaw (New York: The Seabury Press, 1978).

—*Eclipse of Reason* (New York: The Seabury Press, 1974).

Howard, Ron (dir) *A Beautiful Mind,* screenplay by Akiva Goldsman and Sylvia Nasar. (USA: Universal Pictures, 2001).

Iannaccone, Laurence R., 'Framework for the Scientific Study of Religion', *Rational Choice Theory and Religion*, ed. Lawrence A. Young (New York: Routledge, 1997), 25–44.

—'Religious Practices: A Human Capital Approach', *Journal for the Scientific Study of Religion* 29.3 (1990), 297–314.

—'Voodoo Economics? Reviewing the Rational Choice Approach to Religion', *Journal for the Scientific Study of Religion* 34.1 (1995), 76–89.

—'Why Strict Churches are Strong', *American Journal of Sociology* 99.5 (1994), 1183–4.

Jäger, Lorez, *Adorno: A Political Biography*, trans. Stewart Spencer (New Haven: Yale University Press, 2004).

# Bibliography

Jarvis, Simon, *Adorno: A Critical Introduction* (New York, Routledge, 1998).

—'Adorno, Marx, Materialism', *The Cambridge Companion to Adorno*, ed. Tom Kuhn (Cambridge University Press, 2004), 79–100.

Jay, Martin, *The Dialectical Imagination* (Boston and Toronto: Little, Brown, and Co., 1973).

Kant, Immanuel, *Critique of Practical Reason*, trans. Lewis White Beck (New York: Liberal Arts Press, 1956).

—*The Critique of Pure Reason*, trans. Norman Kemp Smith (New York: St Martin's Press, 1929).

Kaufman, David, 'Beyond Use, Within Reason: Adorno, Benjamin and the Question of Theology', *New German Critique* 83 (Spring/Summer 2001), 151–73.

Kee, Alasdair, *Marx and the Failure of Liberation Theology* (London: SCM Press, 1990).

Klausner, Joseph, *The Messianic Idea in Israel*, trans. W. F. Stinespring (New York: Macmillan, 1955).

Kotsko, Adam, *Žižek and Theology* (London and New York: Continuum, 2008).

Krahl, Hans-Jürgen, 'The Political Contradictions in Adorno's Critical Theory', *Foundations of the Frankfurt School of Social Research*, eds Judith Marcus and Zoltán Tar (New Brunswick, NJ and London: Transaction Books, 1984), 307–10.

Kraushaar, Wolfgang (ed.), *Frankfurter Schule und Studentenbewegung*, 3 vols (Hamburg: Rogner and Bernhard, 1998).

Lamb, Matthew, *Solidarity with Victims: Toward a Theology of Social Transformation* (New York: Crossroad, 1982).

Lazarus, Neil, 'Hating Tradition Properly', *New Formations* 38 (Summer 1999), 9–30.

Leslie, Esther, 'Introduction to Adorno/Marcuse Correspondence', *New Left Review* 23 (1999), 118–23.

Liedke, Ulf, *Naturgeschichte und Religion: Eine theologische Studie zum Religionsbegriff in der Philosophie Theodor W. Adornos* (Frankfurt, Bern, New York: Peter Lang, 1997).

Lukács, Georg, *The Theory of the Novel*, trans. Anna Bostock (Cambridge, MA: MIT Press, 1971).

Lyotard, Jean-Francois, *The Postmodern Condition*, trans Geoffrey Bennington and Brian Massumi (Minneapolis: University of Minnesota Press, 1974).

MacLauren, Duncan, *Mission Implausible* (Milton Keynes: Paternoster, 2004).

Mannheim, Karl, *Ideology and Utopia: An Introduction to the Sociology of Knowledge*, trans Louis Wirth and Edward Shils (New York: Harcourt and Brace, 1954).

Martinson, Mattias, *Perseverance without Doctrine* (Frankfurt am Main: Peter Lang, 2000).

Marx, Karl, *Capital: A Critique of Political Economy*, vol. 1., trans. Ben Fowkes. (London: Penguin Books, 1976).

—*The Marx-Engels Reader*, second edition, ed. Robert C. Tucker (New York: W. W. Norton and Co., 1978).

# Bibliography

—*Marx and Engels on Religion* (Moscow: Progress Publishers, 1976).

Marx, Karl, and Engels, Friedrich, *The Holy Family, or Critique of Critical Criticism*, trans Richard Dixon and Clemens Dutt (Moscow: Publishers Press, 1975).

McCann, Dennis, *Christian Realism and Liberation Theology* (Maryknoll: Orbis, 1981).

Mihaileanu, Radu (dir), *Train de Vie* (Paramount Pictures, 1998).

Milbank, John, 'The Conflict of the Faculties', *Faithfulness and Fortitude: In Conversation with the Theological Ethics of Stanley Hauerwas*, eds Mark Thiessen Nation and Samuel Wells (Edinburgh: T&T Clark, 2000), 39–58.

—'Knowledge: The Theological Critique of Philosophy in Hamann and Jacobi', *Radical Orthodoxy*, eds J. Milbank, C. Pickstock and G. Ward (London and NY: Routledge, 1999), 21–37.

—'Materialism and Transcendence', *Theology and the Political: The New Debate*, eds Creston Davis, John Milbank and Slavoj Žižek (Durham: Duke University Press, 2005), 393–426.

—'The Politics of Time: Community, Gift and Liturgy', *Telos* 113 (Fall 1998), 41–67.

—'The Programme of Radical Orthodoxy', *Radical Orthodoxy? – A Catholic Enquiry*, ed. Lawrence Paul Hemming (Aldershot: Ashgate Publishing Ltd., 2000), 34–5.

—'Sublimity: The Modern Transcendent', *Religion, Modernity and Postmodernity*, ed. Paul Heelas. (Oxford: Blackwell, 1998), 258–84.

—*Theology and Social Theory* (Oxford: Blackwell, 1990).

—*The Word Made Strange: Theology, Language, Culture* (Oxford: Blackwell, 1997).

Milbank, John, Ward, Graham, and Pickstock, Catherine (eds), *Radical Orthodoxy* (London: Routledge, 1999).

Moltmann, Jürgen, *Theology of Hope: On the Ground and the Implications of a Christian Eschatology*, trans. James W. Leitch (London: SCM, 1967).

Morgan, Alastair, 'Petrified Life: Adorno and Agamben', *Radical Philosophy* 141 (2007).

Müller-Dooh, Stefan, *Adorno: A Biography*, trans. Rodney Livingstone (Cambridge: Polity Press, 2005).

Murphy, Nancey, *Theology in the Age of Scientific Reasoning* (Ithaca: Cornell University Press, 1990).

Myerson, Roger B., *Game Theory: Analysis of Conflict* (Cambridge, MA: Harvard University Press, 1991).

Novak, David, *Problems in Contemporary Jewish Philosophy* (Lampeter: Edwin Mellen, 1991).

Paddison, Max, *Adorno's Aesthetics of Music* (Cambridge: Cambridge University Press, 1993).

Pangritz, Andreas, *Vom Kleiner - und Unsichtbarwerden der Theologie* (Tübingen: Theologischer Verlag, 1996).

Petrella, Ivan, *The Future of Liberation Theology* (London: SCM Press, 2006).

Peukert, Helmut, Science, *Action, and Fundamental Theology: Toward a Theology of Communicative Action*, trans. James Bohman (Cambridge, MA: MIT Press, 1984).

# Bibliography

Popper, Karl R., *The Myth of the Framework: In Defence of Science and Rationality*, ed. M. A. Notturno (London and New York: Routledge, 1994).

—*In Search of a Better World*, trans. Laura J. Bennett (London and New York, 1994).

—*The Open Society and its Enemies*, vol. 2 (New York: Harper and Row, 1962).

—*Popper: Selections*, David Miller (ed.) (Princeton: Princeton University Press, 1985).

Pritchard, Elizabeth A., '*Bilderverbot* Meets Body in Theodor W. Adorno's Inverse Theology', *Harvard Theological Review* 95:3 (2002), 291–318.

Riker, William, 'Political Science and Rational Choice', *Perspectives on Positive Political Economy*, eds James Alt and Kenneth Shepsle (Cambridge, CA: Cambridge University Press, 1990).

Roozen, David A. and C. Kirk Hadaway, *Church and Denominational Growth* (Nashville: Abingdon Press, 1993).

Rorty, Richard and Gianni Vattimo, *The Future of Religion* (New York: Columbia: 2005).

Rose, Gillian, 'How is Critical Theory Possible?' *Political Studies* 24.1 (1976), 69–85.

—*Judaism and Modernity* (Oxford: Blackwell, 1993).

—*The Melancholy Science* (New York: Columbia University Press, 1978).

Scholem, Gershom, *The Messianic Idea in Judaism and Other Essays on Jewish Spirituality* (New York: Schocken Books, 1970).

Schultz, Karla L, *Mimesis on the Move* (Berne/NY: Peter Lang, 1990).

Schweppenhäuser, Gerhard, *Theodor W. Adorno: An Introduction*, trans. James Rolleston (Durham: Duke University Press, 2009).

Segundo, Juan Luis, *Our Idea of God*, trans. John Drury (Maryknoll: Orbis, 1974).

—*Signs of the Times*, Alfred T. Hennelly (ed.), trans. Robert R. Barr (Maryknoll: Orbis, 1993).

Siebert, Rudolph J., *The Critical Theory of Religion* (Berlin and New York: Mouton Publishers (de Gruyter), 1985).

Smith, Jonathan Z., 'Religion, Religions, Religious', *Critical Terms for Religious Studies*, ed. Mark C. Taylor (Chicago: University of Chicago Press, 1998), 269–84.

Stark, Rodney 'Bringing Theory Back In', *Rational Choice Theory and Religion*, ed. Lawrence A. Young (New York and London: Routledge, 1997), 3–23.

— 'German and German–American Religiousness', *Journal for the Scientific Study of Religion*, 36.2 (1997).

Steunebrink, Gerrit, 'Is Adorno's Negative Philosophy a Negative Theology?' *Flight of the Gods: Philosophical Perspectives on Negative Theology*, eds Ilse N. Bulhof and Laurens ten Kate (New York: Fordham University Press, 2000), 292–318.

Stokes, Geoffrey. *Popper: Philosophy, Politics and Scientific Method* (Cambridge: Polity Press, 1998).

Stone, Bryan, *Effective Faith* (Lanham: University Press of America, 1994).

Stout, Jeffrey, *The Flight from Authority* (Notre Dame: The University of Notre Dame Press, 1981).

# Bibliography

Strauss, Leo, *Spinoza's Critique of Religion*, trans. E. M. Sinclair (New York: Schocken Books, 1982).

Strum, Erdmann, 'Theodor W. Adorno contra Paul Tillich', *Zeitschrift für neuere Theologiegeschichte* 3 (1996).

Sullivan, Michael, and John T Lysaker, 'Between Impotence and Illusion: Adorno's Art of Theory and Practice', *New German Critique* 57 (Fall 1992), 87–122.

Surin, Kenneth, *The Turnings of Darkness and Light.* (Cambridge University Press, 1989).

Thadigsmann, Edgar, 'Das Versprechen: Metaphysische Erfahrung bei Theodor W. Adorno', *Zeitschrift für Theologie und Kirche* 106 (2009), 118–36.

Tillich, Paul, 'Man and Society in Religious Socialism', *Christianity and Society*, VIII, No. 4 (Fall, 1943), 10–21.

—*Political Expectation*, ed. James Luther Adams (New York, San Francisco: Harper and Row, 1971).

—*The Socialist Decision*, trans. Franklin Sherman (New York, San Francisco: Harper and Row, 1977.

—*Systematic Theology*, vol. 1 (The University of Chicago Press, 1951).

Tylor, E. B., *Primitive Culture* (London: Murray, 1871).

Van Morrison, *Hymns to the Silence* (United Kingdom: Polydor Records, 1991).

van Reijen, Willem, 'Redemption and Reconciliation in Benjamin and Adorno', *Adorno: The Possibility of the Impossible*, Nicolaus Schafhausen, Vanessa Müller and Michael Hirsch (eds) (New York and Berlin: Lukas and Sternberg, 2003), 69–84.

Volf, Miroslav, *Exclusion and Embrace* (Nashville: Abingdon Press, 1996).

Weber, Max, *From Max Weber*, H. H. Gerth and C. Wright Mills (trans. and ed.) (New York: Oxford University Press, 1958).

Wellmer, Albrecht, *Metaphysik nach Kant?* ed. Dieter Henrich and Rolf–Peter Horstmann (Stuttgart: Klett-Cotta, 1988).

—*The Persistence of Modernity*, trans. David Midgley (Cambridge, MA: The MIT Press, 1991).

Westphal, Merold, *Transcendence and Self–Transcendence: On God and the Soul.* (Bloomington: Indiana University Press, 2004).

Wiggershaus, Rolf, *The Frankfurt School*, trans. Michael Robertson (Cambridge, MA: The MIT Press, 1994).

Williams, Rowan, *Lost Icons: Reflections on Cultural Bereavement* (Harrisburg, London, New York: Morehouse Publishing, 2000).

Witkin, Robert W., *Adorno on Music* (London and New York: Routledge, 1998).

Wood, Ellen Meiksins, *The Retreat from Class* (London and New York: Verso, 1986).

Woodhead, Linda, 'Post–Christian Spiritualities', *Religion* 23.2 (1993), 167–81.

Žižek, Slavoj, *On Belief* (London and New York: Routledge, 2001).

—*The Metastases of Enjoyment: Six Essays on Women and Causality* (London and New York: Verso, 1994).

—*The Puppet and the Dwarf* (Cambridge, MA: The MIT Press, 2003).

# Bibliography

Zuidervaart, Lambert, *Adorno's Aesthetic Theory* (Cambridge, MA: MIT Press, 1991).

—, *Social Philosophy after Adorno* (Cambridge: Cambridge University Press, 2007).

# Index

# Index

# Index

gnosticism 6, 7, 58, 185
God 92
    God–human relation 102
    *mysterium tremendum* 92
Gutierrez, Gustavo 115, 132–3

Habermas, Jürgen 1, 2, 5, 54, 64, 73,
    90, 179, 180, 201n. 2, 201n. 7,
    201n. 11, 206n. 65, 207n. 27,
    210n. 21, 210n. 22, 220n. 42,
    220n. 44, 220n. 46
Haggadah 98, 99
Hammer, Espen 54, 81, 115, 206n. 63,
    209n. 100, 214n. 6
Harris, Sam 1, 201n. 3, 204n. 7
Hegel, G. W. F. 5, 15, 30, 31, 32, 40,
    41, 42, 43, 44, 45, 48, 49,
    91, 93, 103, 108, 117, 160,
    176, 184, 202n. 1, 203n. 32,
    204n. 7, 204n. 8, 205n. 12,
    211n. 35, 218n. 39
Heller, Agnes 72, 208n. 65
Hewitt, Marsha 126, 127, 215n. 43,
    222n. 108
historical materialism 20, 22
Hitchens, Christopher 17
Hitler, Adolf 2, 3, 6, 22,
Holocaust, the 6, 61, 116, 163, 185
Homer 25
Honneth, Axel 73, 208n. 68
Horkheimer, Max 3, 4, 5, 19, 20,
    22, 23, 24, 27, 33, 59, 87, 88,
    89, 114, 152, 161, 162, 188,
    201n. 10, 202n. 6, 203n. 8,
    203n. 9, 203n. 11, 203n. 15,
    203n. 17, 203n. 21, 203n. 23,
    203n. 37, 210n. 14, 210n. 15,
    210n. 20, 212n. 73, 214n. 4,
    217n. 23, 217n. 24, 218n. 38,
    218n. 40, 218n. 43, 218n. 45,
    220n. 40
Hullot-Kentor, Robert 7, 202n. 20,
    205n. 34, 213n. 105, 219n. 28,
    220n. 36
Hume, David 38, 39, 57

Iannaccone, Lawrence 147, 151, 152,
    154–9, 161, 217n. 22, 217n. 31,
    218n. 34, 218n. 35
identity thinking 4, 9, 26, 71, 81,
    83, 87, 89, 91, 97, 98, 104,
    105, 106, 111, 112, 120,
    122, 123, 127, 128, 137,
    169, 170, 181, 192, 200
    *see also* inverse correlation
ideology 20, 134, 151–4, 175–7
Institute of Social Research
    (Frankfurt) 3, 4, 17,
    19, 58
inverse correlation 141, 168–9, 170,
    183 *see also* identity thinking
inverse theology 2, 7–8, 12, 13,
    14, 33, 83, 91, 95–101,
    104, 106, 109, 110–14,
    116, 121, 122, 128, 137,
    139, 140, 143, 168, 170,
    171, 174, 178, 181, 183, 184,
    186, 188, 190, 192, 193,
    195–200, 211n. 54
    *see also* negative dialectics
    as negative correlation 197–8
    as negative theology 91–4
    versus political theology of
        Agamben 137
Islam 17

Jäger, Lorenz 57, 206n. 54
*The Jargon of Authenticity* 164
Jarvis, Simon 43, 44, 203n. 27,
    204n. 4, 204n. 44, 205n. 16,
    205n. 20, 205n. 25
Jephcott, E. F. N. 174, 201n. 10,
    202n. 17, 202n. 19, 203n. 15,
    203n. 24, 204n. 1, 206n. 1,
    210n. 12, 210n. 20, 211n. 36,
    213n. 87
Jesus Christ 48, 49, 123, 167
Judaism 11, 16, 18, 21, 88, 89, 106,
    107, 191, 202n. 27
    positive religion and 106–7
    the Talmud 133

# Index

# Index

# Index

praise for **WHAT SHE'S NOT TELLING YOU**

"This book exposes the serious consequences of 'literal listening' and taking what women say at face value and teaches how to do one, not-so-simple thing: getting women to tell the truth. The Just Ask a Woman women have nailed it."

— **CHERYL CALLAN**, SVP, Marketing, North America, Weight Watchers

"The relationship between brands and consumers has changed forever and the quality of your dialogue with them is in direct proportion to how well you understand them. Mary Lou and her colleagues have exposed just how far we still have to go to get to the real truth inside women's heads. Ignore this insight at your peril."

— **MARK BAYNES**, Vice President, Global CMO, Kellogg Company

"Just Ask a Woman is in the forefront of understanding what really motivates women. You will listen more deeply, assess more easily, and engage more meaningfully for insights that lead to powerful marketplace results."

— **DONNA STURGESS**, Founding Partner, Buyology, Inc., and former Head of Innovation, GlaxoSmithKline

"Finally a marketing book that brings new meaning to the term retail therapy! This book puts marketers AND female consumers on the couch to teach how strategic interviewing and analysis can reveal profitable answers."

— **NANCY BERK**, PhD, clinical psychologist, researcher, humorist

"This book 'gets it'! A truly insightful tool that will help marketers better understand what women are really saying! This book is a must if you want to hear the Whole Truth and understand the 'GAMES' women play."

— **REBECCA NOEL**, Associate Director, Market Research, Kao Brands

"Healthcare professionals know that getting women to open up about what's really bothering them is the first step to healing. This marketing book brilliantly teaches how to get under women's skin!"

— **ELLEN S. MARMUR**, MD, Chief, Division of Dermatologic & Cosmetic Surgery, Department of Dermatology, Mount Sinai Medical Center

# what she's ~~not~~ telling you

**not**

## telling you

Why Women Hide
the Whole Truth
and What Marketers
Can Do About It

# Mary Lou Quinlan

*with* **Jen Drexler** *and* **Tracy Chapman**

just ask a
**woman**

Published by Just Ask a Woman Media
New York, NY
www.justaskawoman.com

Distributed by Greenleaf Book Group LLC

For ordering information or special discounts for bulk purchases, please contact
Greenleaf Book Group LLC at PO Box 91869, Austin, TX 78709, 512.891.6100.

Design and composition by Greenleaf Book Group LLC
Cover design by Greenleaf Book Group LLC
Author photo: Stephanie Halmos
Stylist: Mordechai Alvow
Stock photography: Istockphoto

Publisher's Cataloging-In-Publication Data
(Prepared by The Donohue Group, Inc.)

Quinlan, Mary Lou.
   What she's not telling you : why women hide the whole truth and what marketers
can do about it / Mary Lou Quinlan with Jen Drexler and Tracy Chapman.
-- 1st ed.

   p. : ill. ; cm.

   ISBN: 978-0-9823938-0-2

1. Women consumers. 2. Consumer behavior. 3. Women--Attitudes.
4. Marketing. I. Drexler, Jen. II. Chapman, Tracy (Tracy Lee), 1973- III. Title.

HC79.C6 Q56 2010
658.80082                                        2009932968

Part of the Tree Neutral™ program, which offsets the number of
trees consumed in the production and printing of this book by
taking proactive steps, such as planting trees in direct proportion
to the number of trees used: www.treeneutral.com

TreeNeutral

Printed in the United States of America on acid-free paper

10 11 12 13 14   10 9 8 7 6 5 4 3 2

TO THE WOMEN WHO LED US
AND THE MEN WHO ARE BEHIND US

# CONTENTS

# the Whole Truth behind her Half Truth

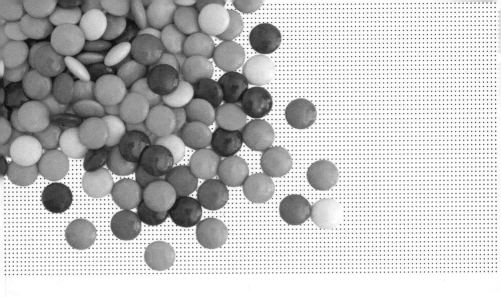

Y ou're in the dark—literally.

It's 11 a.m. but the dim lighting makes it feel like night-time in a hushed room in a nondescript building off an interstate. You're feeling tense as you watch a group of women talk about your new product concepts on the other side of a one-way mirror. It's your third city in three days and you're feeling the pressure to be home, or back at the office, or anywhere but here in focus group hell. You're looking for any shred of hope that you've finally nailed the *big* idea but so far, they hate everything.

You glance furtively at your BlackBerry and munch Peanut M&M's and then continue grimly staring through the glass. Your plans are already over deadline and you can't send the agency back to the drawing board one more time. If this group doesn't like something soon, you're thinking of hurling the M&M's at them. These eight women you've never met are about to destroy your last good idea and you are fit to be tied.

The women, eerily aware of your surveillance, are listening to the last shot you've got. And suddenly one woman perks up. She likes it.

She really likes it. Then a second one chimes in. And another. You're feeling the love. You've got a potential blockbuster on your hands. At last. You can head back home with a win.

*Eight months later . . .*

Your new product is such a flop that the stores are pulling it off the shelves. Why did those women say they loved it when they didn't? Why did they tell you one thing and do another? Were they lying? Were you buying it? Why, why, why?

You're in the dark—literally.

## what your best customers aren't telling you

Women are the most powerful customers on the planet, influencing or purchasing 85% of everything you make, sell, or offer.

They're the voices on your customer service line, the cash at your counter, and the fingertips on your website. Whether you're in consumer packaged goods, retail, service, technology, finance, healthcare, or any category you can name, they're the "It Girls" of your marketing plan and the lifeblood of your sales and profits. Knowing what women want is your ticket to big ideas and big money.

Unfortunately, and this likely shocks or baffles you, women don't always say what they really mean, especially to the marketers who want their money. So we're about to divulge what women aren't telling you. After a decade of listening to women as partners in our strategic marketing firm, Just Ask a Woman, we've detected a critical behavior among female consumers: the tendency to disclose what we call Half Truths (what they are willing to admit) and to hide Whole Truths (what they really believe, do, and buy). These Half Truths, particularly the deadly five that we'll discuss in detail, can undermine your marketing results by encouraging you to throw good money after bad insights.

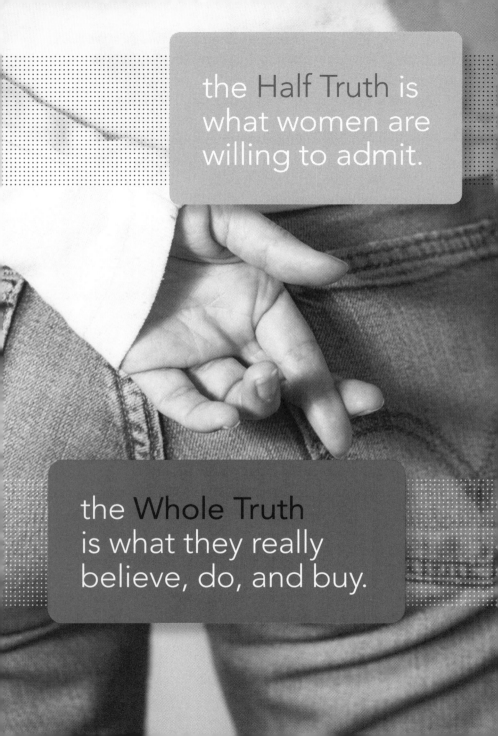

As a marketer, you've probably been a victim of her drive-by duplicity at some point. Have you ever heard a woman swear that she loves your new product and then watch her buy a competitor's product? Ever wonder why women claim your store is their favorite yet rarely visit it? Or have you ever rejoiced as women raved about your ads in research only to discover months and millions of lost dollars later that they've all changed their minds?

With little provocation, the average female respondent can dance her way through a game of mental dodgeball with billion dollar marketers. You may not want to believe that women are hiding the Whole Truth from your brand. But would you know it if they were?

## her Half Truths will cost you

Buying into Half Truths will only get you halfway to your marketing goals: so-so strategies, unremarkable products, mediocre communications, and routine retail experiences. In other words, you may be leaving half the money on the table.

If you're trying to get her attention, her dollars, or her loyalty, you've got to avoid buying into the Half Truths that can undermine your best-laid plans. Only her Whole Truths can save you from a marketing mistake before it's millions of dollars too late.

**Stop throwing good money after bad insights.**

To help you solve this problem, we will be your truth detectors, your insiders in the Half Truth epidemic that you're paying for—not just in billions of wasted dollars in concept development, market research, and creative exploration, but in the marketplace, where it really hurts.

Just ask the leaders at **THE GAP** why they opened and quickly shuttered **FORTH & TOWNE**, a ballyhooed chain of stores for boomer women. They nobly tried to respond to the Half Truth frustration of

women 40 and older, who couldn't find any age-appropriate clothes. Women said they were tired of squeezing into midriff-exposing clothes better suited to the 18-year-olds giggling in the next dressing room.

So Forth & Towne designed what they called "grown-up style" stores, that featured "age appropriate" sizing and styling (even age-appropriate associates!), and dressing rooms with flattering, adjustable lighting. But Gap forgot to ask boomers the most important question that would have led to the Whole Truth: "What age do you consider yourself?" Lots of 50-year-olds would answer, "35," which translates to clothes and stores that balance cool *and* comfort. RIP dowdy Forth & Towne.

You may be wondering if I am telling you that women have been lying to you. Not exactly. What really holds you back is everything women aren't telling you—the Whole Truth. Instead, you're buying her Half Truths.

## what's a "Half Truth"?

We want to be clear upfront that most women are not intentionally dishonest. A Half Truth is not a lie. A Half Truth is true, but it's not a woman's whole story. This Half Truth telling is generally subconscious, instinctual, or learned behavior. But the subterfuge is so ingrained that it can be tricky to detect when and why she's telling Half Truths.

Just ask a woman, "How are you?" Assuming she's a stranger, she's likely to answer with a reflexive, "Oh, I'm fine." And when probed, she recites, "I've got great kids, a good guy, a nice home. I've got my health. Things are okay." Really? Do you honestly believe that?

She's not lying; she's just given you her good enough answer, her Half Truth. She might be fine, but in her debt-ridden, stressed-out world, she's probably not. A woman who tells you "I'm fine" would rather leave it at that, than admit that she's unhappy, unhealthy, or unfulfilled.

Like it or not, Half Truths are a habit. They're survival gear. They cut the conflict and smooth the way. They're an easy way out. "Yes, I like that dress." "No, it doesn't bother me when you snore." "Yes, I'd love to go to your mom's for dinner (*Again!?*)."

If you think, as a marketer, that you're above being conned by Half Truths, consider how often you've nodded approvingly when female consumers say, "I try to be healthy." How many times have you bought into survey results describing how often women exercise, how carefully they watch their weight, how they've quit smoking, how they always use sunscreen, blah, blah, blah? If the majority of women are so darn healthy, then why is it that the average American woman wears nearly a size 14 (girded in spandex), one in five smokes, tanning beds are still hot, and 82% are so uncomfortable with their bodies that they turn the lights out before sex? "I try to be healthy" is a Half Truth.

Here's the Whole Truth: women exercise (when they feel like it), they watch what they eat (sometimes), they don't smoke (too much), and they wear sunscreen (when they remember).

Half Truths lead to "me too" (or is it "she too"?) products and ideas. So if you create advertising based on this Half Truth, prepare

to waste money on a been-there, ho-hum spot featuring yet another yoga-obsessed woman inhaling calcium pills, when in real life she's consoling her hips with six-packs of high-fat granola bars.

## why do women tell Half Truths?

Why do women tell Half Truths? Because they can and because marketers let them.

Despite their desperate need to know what women really want, marketers can actually discourage women from opening up. Most market research and customer feedback techniques run counter to the way women communicate.

Have you ever watched or been part of a group of women when they're with friends? They laugh, tease, touch, share, and generally let it all hang out. Women are amazing communicators, wired to be the more verbal sex. Studies from the book *The Female Mind* have shown that in a typical day, a woman speaks on average 20,000 words while a man speaks on average 7,000. While some scientists argue over the accuracy of the count, it's hard to challenge the everyday evidence. (Plus, it brings to mind the cliché of women's compulsion to ask for directions.) Women ask. Women tell. And women want to be heard.

> The question to ask yourself is, "Am I really listening . . . or just Half Listening?"

Contrast the easy exchange of women talking together to the stilted processes most marketers rely on to learn about their female consumers: rigid questions, the formal moderator, the hidden spycam, the dispassionate recording of responses. These techniques fight women's natural impulses to express themselves. On top of that is the penchant for busy marketers to Half Listen. We'll break down these Half Listening dynamics early on in this book so that marketers can understand just how difficult they're making it for women to speak truthfully.

Women have an instinctive ability to know the answer you're looking for. They've spent their lives tuning in to what other people think and picking up visual nuances, body language, and voice cues, whether it's from a demanding teacher, a needy child, or an approaching traffic cop. Like the trained members of a TV studio audience who laugh on cue, women can tell what answer you want from them. And they know how to give it to you, without you even realizing they're handing you a line. And since they sound sincere and reasonable, you believe them and bake those "insights" into brand strategies that can fail.

We want to repeat, women aren't intentionally deceiving you; their Half Truths are simply shortcuts or shorthand so they can get on with their busy lives. A true but halfway response can be a no-fault way for her to evade a tough question or her best effort to deal with the rhetorical, mundane surveys that don't deserve better. Women will save the Whole Truth for those who respect who she is and what her life is about, who ask smarter questions, and who are honestly intent on hearing her answers.

By the way, you may be wondering, do men tell Half Truths, too? While all our research has been focused on women, our intuitive response is yes, but men don't do it as often and their motivations are

not as layered or complex. Women's relationship-driven natures propel their Half Truth telling, whether it's to please, cajole, repel questioners, or protect herself or her family from emotional intruders, like marketers. And women learn to perfect techniques that can keep you from breaking and entering their "consumer space."

# the five Half Truths that can shortchange your success

Half Truths are easy for a woman to say and difficult for you to detect. And there's more than one kind of Half Truth waiting to shortchange your business.

After ten years of espionage with female consumers, we've detected five universal emotional drivers of Half Truths—across categories and industries—that can compromise your ability to succeed. These five very female factors help explain how and why women withhold the Whole Truth. Women and marketers play both cat and mouse as they dodge each other and go down blind alleys in pursuit of mutual success. The process of truth seeking and truth keeping becomes a high-stakes game with its own road rules, detours, and potholes. That's why we came up with the acronym GAMES to help keep you on course.

$$G = Good\ Intentions$$
$$A = Approval\ Seeking$$
$$M = Martyrdom$$
$$E = Ego\ Protection$$
$$S = Secret\ Keeping$$

**1** **Good Intentions** Good Intentions fuel the tendency of women to make promises and profess big aspirations, even with no plan or commitment to achieve them. Simply stating their vows makes women feel more in control of their out-of-control lives. Some Good Intention stories have been told so many times that women start to believe they are true. Marketers fall for this Half Truth because it often matches what they hope to hear, which results in overengineered products and inflated claims.

2 Approval Seeking Women Seek Approval and know how to get it. They'll give pleasing answers to be liked, not only by marketers but also by other women in order to belong and to be accepted. Marketers bite because the answers feel familiar and validate what they think they know about women. When many women chime in, all saying good things about your product or ad (and all hoping to fit in), you're tempted to believe their unanimous opinions and feel discouraged from digging deeper for insights.

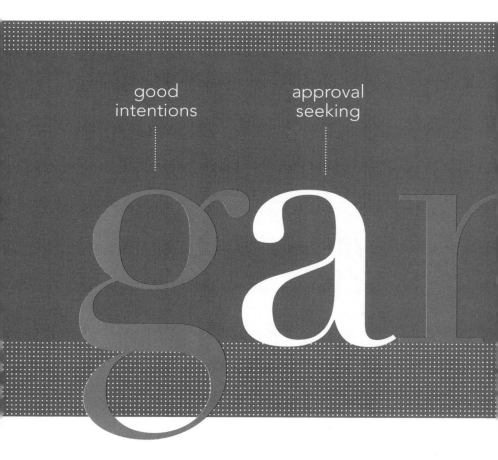

good
intentions

approval
seeking

**3 Martyrdom** Women, often the productive and responsible caretakers of everybody and everything, deserve to complain sometimes. But they also need you to know that they are doing all the hard work, so they express every detail of their daily hardships and inadvertently try to out-martyr each other. Marketers, also stressed, may find themselves in a "stress competition" with women and miss their need to be heard. The result of this stand-off is that women can scare you away from asking them to do anything more, such as buy your product.

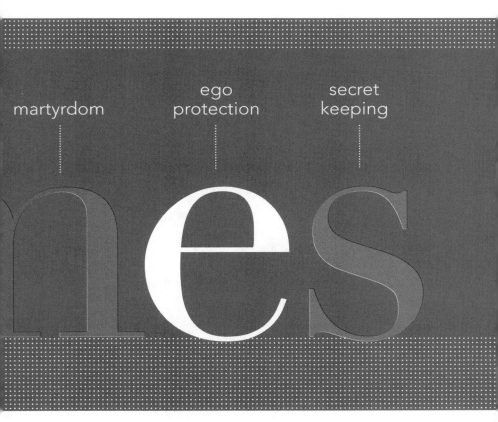

martyrdom

ego
protection

secret
keeping

4 Ego Protection Women will protect their own inadequacies with pretensions of confidence. They'll pretend to read your fine print. They'll describe themselves as younger, smarter, and trendier than they actually are. And you may believe them because it's more satisfying to market and sell to confident, knowledgeable customers than insecure, uninformed ones. This Half Truth spawns products and services that may overshoot most women's aspirations or be too complicated and then be returned or ignored.

5 Secret Keeping Women use cover stories to defend against interlopers, like you, who may want to collect personal information that will seem shameful when spoken aloud. Thanks to her pride and her protective feelings for those close to her, she'll hide information that invites your disapproval, like her penchant for sneaking cigarettes or even her kids' bad behavior. You won't discover her Whole Truth because you may feel too embarrassed

to ask. And she'll hide some secrets from you that she whispers happily to others as a form of social currency.

Making Half Truth detection even trickier, a simple response can straddle several of the five Half Truths, depending on the question, the setting, and the woman. For example, let's return to the "I try to be healthy" Half Truth. It's a classic Approval Seeking response. But women can also fall back on this Half Truth for totally different reasons.

If you're a healthcare or fitness marketer, "I try to be healthy" is grounded in Good Intentions ("I'm planning to start exercising any day now . . ."). If she's surrounded by a group of fitness buffs but is overweight, a woman might hide behind the Secret Keeping Half Truth ("I've been on Weight Watchers!") rather than admit her yo-yo dieting and exercise habits. And if she senses you're selling appearance-related products, "I try to be healthy" is an example of her Ego Protection kicking in ("If I don't say I'm trying, you'll think I've given up").

Missing or ignoring any of these Half Truths can send you down the wrong strategy or execution paths. In later chapters, we will dismantle the emotional drivers behind these Half Truths, one by one, so you can keep them from sabotaging your new product or ad campaign, as well as your customer service, product development, or retail plans.

## how can I get to the Whole Truth?

With all these decoy answers, how can you know what she *really means* and whether she's telling you the *Whole Truth*?

The question to ask yourself is, "Am I really listening . . . or just Half Listening?"

It seems as though it would be easy to listen. But dedicated, single-minded listening is hard to do and hardly anyone does it well. How many times have you simultaneously chatted on a conference call while checking emails, eating a sandwich, and rolling your eyes at your colleague across the desk? That proud multitasking degenerates into chronic nonlistening. (And you wonder why women don't open up to you!)

Deep, engaged listening takes time, which is always in short supply, as well as heart, hard work, and a lot of nerve. That's why we do what we do, so our clients don't have to. Face it, even you, the most conscientious marketer, are reluctant to doggedly pursue the elusive Whole Truth because you'll have to ask women questions that you're afraid to ask. You'll also have to pay attention to her every word, gesture, and reaction like your job depends on it, because it does or it will.

You have to earn your way to her Whole Truth. That starts with listening differently, with all of your senses, as well as your persistence, curiosity, intuition, and, yes, patience, because a woman saves her Whole Truth for the person she trusts. Sometimes, the Whole Truth may be so deeply held that she may not even confess it to herself and may need help untangling what she feels.

This book will open your eyes to a new way of Power Listening to women. We'll help decode what she's hiding and what it means for your strategies so that you can build your brand on Whole Truths for more success and distinction. Once you learn to listen differently, you'll begin to hear what she's not telling you.

## why we can tell the Whole Truth and nothing but

If women are so hard to decipher, why should you believe that they've told *us* the truth? For the past decade, Jen, Tracy, and I have refined emotional forensics that defy the "safety net" of the one-way mirror. We've gone one-on-one with women, from Gen Y to seniors, from the shy to the outspoken, from the flip and outrageously funny to the deeply sad and scared.

We engage in emotional forensics.

As partners in Just Ask a Woman, we have listened, eavesdropped, and obsessed over what women think, feel, and buy. Thousands and thousands of female consumers have confidentially confessed their personal stories so that we could help some of the world's biggest brands market and sell better to women.

Leading marketers, manufacturers, retailers, service providers, and media outlets, including **KRAFT**, **GLAXOSMITHKLINE**, **WESTIN**, **BLOOMINGDALES**, **IKEA**, **KAO**, **LIFETIME TELEVISION**, and dozens of others, have commissioned us to be their eyes and ears in the women's marketplace. What we've uncovered has helped these companies make a ton of money and deepen their relevance with their most valuable customers.

We discovered these Half Truths after tens of thousands of hours of interviews and after researching nearly every major product category and most industries (many, multiple times). We began to notice patterns of thinking that were powerful and universal among women, no matter the subject or their income, education, geography, or lifestage. While all women are unique, they also share traits in the way they communicate, make decisions, and react.

For whatever reason, marketers often like to focus more on women's differences, preferring fine-toothed segmentation and consumer algorithms that split hairs instead of commonalities that can actually be marketed to. We think they're missing the forest for the trees. Indeed, there *are* many commonalities, even if these similarities vary slightly from woman to woman or brand to brand, that can help you listen differently, sort through marketing decisions, and better understand why women say what they do and what they really mean when they say it.

These insights emerged from years of qualitative work. In earlier research, we identified female characteristics like otherness (women's affinity for taking care of everyone else first), deliberate decision making (a sometimes slow, but always thorough way of coming to the right answer or purchase), and the predilection for turning to a circle of trusted advisors, a "board of directors," for confirmation of plans and beliefs.

In this research, we looked to build on that knowledge, seeking patterns in the way women communicate their feelings and desires. The result is this analysis of five underlying, universal emotional drivers that can help you decode what women really mean and what they really want.

You might also wonder if these Half Truths differ by age or lifestage. We believe that as women mature, they get craftier about hiding from marketers. Where a young woman may withhold information, it's more about her uncertainty than gamesmanship. Moms in their 30s and 40s are so seasoned from dealing with kids that they can conceal on cue. And boomers have been telling some of their Half Truths so long that they will be expert at convincing you, too.

While mining for women's truths, we've also heard some real whoppers and disclosing them could seem like talking out of school about women. But we're coming clean so that you can be more successful. (And, coincidentally, sharing their Whole Truths will help women get what they really want.)

We offer this note to marketers, particularly women, who may be offended that women are even categorized as Half Truth tellers: Don't take this as an affront to your own honesty. And anyway, this isn't about you, though you might find yourself doing a little silent self-analysis as you read. Rather than vet this book as a Rorschach test of your own truth telling, let yourself take this in and see if this new approach to marketing with women helps simplify and illuminate some blockages with your consumers. And, if you get some insights on your personal life, male or female, then it will be a bonus!

At Just Ask a Woman, we had an ingoing advantage: we're marketers and communicators ourselves and, yes, we're all women. But gender's not enough, since plenty of high-flying female executives will admit that their female consumers can lead them astray (or maybe they don't even realize how their own lifestyles and beliefs may be coloring what they hear from their customers).

What makes us different is the *way* we listen. As you'll learn, we question pretty much every rule of research. We immerse ourselves in women's real worlds every day by devouring their media, reading over their shoulders, snooping in their closets, and road testing the way they shop.

We believe in marketing *with* women, not *to* them as if they were a target to be tapped when you need some cash. By putting women

## We believe in marketing *with* women, not *to* them as if they were a target to be tapped when you need some cash.

on our clients' side and engaging them in new ways, we are able to break through to startling, surprising Whole Truths that lead to successful new ways to market with them. Throughout the book we'll share some of these eye-opening techniques for getting women to open up so that you can detect and avoid the Half Truths before it's too late.

Soon, you'll stop asking, "What do women want?" You'll start asking, "What does she really mean by that? Am I accepting a Half Truth . . . or is there a bigger Whole Truth to be found and a bigger innovation or market opportunity waiting for me?"

Next, we'll dig into a case of two well-known marketers: one who bought a Half Truth and stumbled, one who doggedly pursued the Whole Truth and won.

# a case of pretty lies

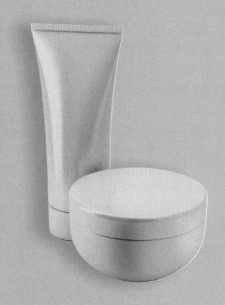

H ow are Half Truths born and believed? How can women hide the Whole Truth even from the smartest marketers? This is a story about two leading beauty brands, one that pursued the Whole Truth and reaped the rewards and one that was lured into a Half Truth that snowballed into a dead end. Let's begin on a high.

A few years ago, the **DOVE** team at **UNILEVER**, in an effort to expand the brand from bar soap to skin care, turned the beauty business on its ear by launching the "Campaign for Real Beauty," a salute to the natural and unique beauty of women.

Dove decided to break every one of the "road rules" of the cosmetics business. In an about-face from the industry formula of perfect faces, pouty looks, and legs up to there, Dove changed the game. They photographed a half dozen unretouched, clean-scrubbed, slightly overweight women happily wearing nothing but their plain white undies, and then they plastered the pictures on bus kiosks and highway billboards. TV commercials, magazine ads, and Web banners blanketed the country.

The surprising appearance of the Dove "un-models" in fashion magazines and high-impact outdoor media immediately drew controversy for putting "fat women in their underwear" on exhibit and then kudos as the first honest cosmetic ad campaign. (Ironically, the models were actually still thinner than the majority of American women, but no one was owning up to *that* Whole Truth.)

Dove invited consumers to vote online for what real beauty looked like and millions did. The brand introduced the Dove Self-Esteem Fund, a feel-good grassroots program to raise awareness of the link between inflated beauty ads and self-esteem and to educate young women to a wider definition of beauty. One of their later efforts, a viral film called *Evolution*, which graphically showed how images of supermodels are airbrushed and altered, drew nearly nine million hits on YouTube.

Women fell in love with Dove. They hailed Dove as the modern brand built on how women really feel about the beauty industry: disillusioned, disengaged, and dissed.

The verdict was in: finally, someone "gets" what women really want!

## realbeautypalooza

When the Campaign for Real Beauty kicked off, newspapers, radio shows, TV news features, and the blogosphere were all over it. Women weighed in with buzz that broke the bank.

Talk shows went crazy. Even Oprah (who, let's face it, has done her share of makeovers) had the Dove women on the show. (Note that the brand was reported to have spent more than $49 million in advertising on Oprah's TV, print, and Web properties over a four-year period.)

The PR value of the "real beauty" campaign was unparalleled, with Dove gaining more than 650 million impressions in the summer of 2005, thanks to coverage on 62 national television programs, devoting the equivalent of four hours of broadcast time, including more than 10 minutes on *The Today Show*. An early skeptic, I was invited to go on *The Today Show* to provide a marketing counterpoint, face-to-face with one of the supernice regular gals from the billboards. I was kind of relieved that I was out of town and unable to do it because I couldn't imagine facing off with someone so universally beloved without seeming like a shallow jerk in front of millions of smitten viewers.

At first, Dove brand's sleepy worldwide sales woke up. (After spending kazillions of dollars, we would hope so!) Even the usually jaded and hardheaded creative ad community genuflected to this heartwarming campaign. They honored "Evolution" with two Grand Prix awards at the Cannes festival of the world's best advertising. Dove received two Grand Good awards at the annual Advertising Women of New York's Good, Bad, and Ugly Awards. And, in tribute to their marketing effectiveness, the campaign won the Grand Effie, the highest industry award for ads that work.

Dove fever was contagious as CMOs everywhere caught Dove envy. (Do you know how many brand managers have said to us, "We want to be the Dove of sneakers/sodas/finance?") You can still go to any conference on women's marketing and hear speakers gush about how they love the way Dove loves women.

The cosmetic kumbaya was complete, except for one little problem: Looking like yourself every day is no reason to buy beauty products. Dove bought into the Half Truth that women want to feel good about their natural looks. It's true, they do. But the Whole Truth is that they really want to look better than they do and that's why they spend $7 billion a year trying.

## caught in a Half Truth trap

As women publicly cheered, Dove's second year sales started to slow and then eventually flatlined as the months went on. According to *Advertising Age*, Dove's well-funded 2005 growth of 12.5% fell to 10.1% in '06 and to 1.2% in '07, and the trickle of new products in '08 are a giveaway to the limitations of this platform (not to mention, new rounds of ads that were traditional cookie-cutter, product-as-hero spots).

### WE ASK **IMPERTINENT** QUESTIONS

At Just Ask a Woman, we don't mind asking impertinent questions (so our clients don't have to!) because they crack open Half Truths. A beauty-related question we've asked is, "If you were going to your high school reunion, would you rather be told you look gorgeous or look happy?" Although about 60% of women in our poll answered "happy," 40% is a lot of women admitting that they'd rather get a "Wow!" And I'll bet the "happy" ones would be even happier if an unrequited teenage love made a pass.

While the "real beauty" positioning made strategic sense for basic Dove soap-and-water products, the big money and margin in the skin care category goes to innovations with fancy ingredients and packaging. So, by defining the brand as "you're great the way you are," Dove was hard-pressed to convince women they needed multiple SKUs and the latest science.

How did Dove get in this jam? Because they didn't ask the ugly follow-up questions that would have revealed the Whole Truths, such as "If you like the way you already look, then why do you bother buying beauty products?" Or, "Yes, you feel good about who you are inside, but if you had the choice to look a little better or to look exactly the same, which would you choose?" Sure, those probes would have been a buzzkill in the backroom but they would have saved Dove a bundle.

While Dove's early payoff was a ton of goodwill and fresh awareness for an old-fashioned brand, a huge victory in itself, this Half Truth would make for a short and costly honeymoon. And from a business perspective, it would eventually amount to a very expensive public service campaign about positive self-image.

## credit and blame to go around

We were only observers of the Dove story, but I have to believe that plenty share the credit and the blame.

The Dove brand team, confined for years to a simple "¼ moisturizing cream" claim on a cake of soap, must have been excited to see women react so viscerally to the Real Beauty concept. From a strategic perspective, the Dove team was justified in aligning with "Everywoman" based on the brand's heritage as a low-priced soap that's so gentle, it's almost neighborly. At last, the Dove brand, trusted but rusty, had a big idea to hang its hat on.

The marketing team deserves huge credit for boldly supporting the real women idea and moving what must have been a mountain of big-company resistance to change the game. Most companies side with safe rather than risk a renegade strategy.

Likewise, Ogilvy, Dove's ad agency, must have leapt at the chance to shoot a groundbreaking campaign without the stereotypical scaffolding of beauty advertising. Creative directors who make their living pushing cosmetics know the three casting ground rules they're stuck with: skinny, gorgeous, and young. Men and women in those jobs get bored with the same young, same young.

In this rush to real, the team was tempted into believing a lovable (but limiting) series of Ego Protection Half Truths.

- "She looks friendly and normal, not like a scary, perfect model."
- "I'm sick of those airbrushed 18-year-old faces selling me wrinkle cream."
- "I like her because she's regular, just like me."

But there's a difference between making nice and making money. Dove didn't bank on three financial realities.

1. Women want beauty products that make a difference, whether they spend $5 or $500. Dove marketers should have pushed harder for improved results, as well as self-esteem.

2. Skin care and hair care profits hinge on the ability to sell more premium-priced products. Was this "everyday" platform up to that reality?

3. When the heavy spending faded, women could see through the ruse. ("If you tell me I look great the way I am, then why are you still selling me more stuff?")

"She looks friendly and normal, not like a scary, perfect model."

"I'm sick of those airbrushed 18-year-old faces selling me wrinkle cream."

"I like her because she's regular, just like me."

(AT THE RISK OF SOUNDING POLITICAL, SOME WOMEN'S RESPONSES TO VICE PRESIDENTIAL CANDIDATE SARAH PALIN DURING THE 2008 REPUBLICAN NATIONAL CONVENTION WAS VERY AKIN TO THIS: "I LIKE HER BECAUSE SHE'S A REAL HOCKEY MOM, JUST LIKE ME.")

## HOW OLD DO **YOU** LOOK?

Women love to believe that they look younger than they do. In research we did on haircolor and aging, Tracy asked women to confess what age people took them for. One woman, who was clearly 50 years old or older, said without a shred of guile, "Well, I can pass for 35, maybe 33." If she says so.

And what was the lesson learned? Ask the hard questions, even when you're enamored of "The Truth." Instead, Dove did it again in 2008. Doubling down against that Half Truth would come back to bite them.

## fifty-something flop

Year two, the brand stumbled when they transported the real beauty Half Truth into dangerous boomer territory with the introduction of **PRO-AGE**, a line of higher-tech skin care products featuring nude, wrinkled, 50-plus women thrilled to look older. (Get it? Pro-Age instead of Anti-Age? As in "Hooray, gravity's working!")

We've got to believe that Unilever spent a bundle doing research for Pro-Age. But after listening to women wax poetic about their newfound midlife wisdom, did Dove or their agency probe, "Since you are feeling so great about midlife, do you wake up each day and say, 'Wow, I am so glad I look my age today?'"

There's probably no more annoying "compliment" that mature women hear than this hateful line: You look good *for your age*. And Dove was now saying it right to their faces. Dove confused women's pride in their accomplishments ("I've earned every one of these wrinkles") with their acceptance of their looks as they age.

Showing 30-something women's unclad, imperfect bodies is one thing. Letting it all hang out on a 60-year-old woman in a beauty ad is another. (Hey, we know this isn't politically correct and the idea might work in yogurt or insurance or even home furnishings; but like it or not, this is a category of hope.)

The underlying Whole Truth is that women older than 40 see themselves as much younger than their age. So, the candid imagery of models content to look every ounce and line of their years wasn't what consumers wanted to see in their own mirrors.

Dove gave them no reason to hope for better than what they already had. As cosmetic industry consultant Suzanne Grayson said in an interview with *Advertising Age*, "What they're (Unilever) saying is that (Pro-Age) is for people who are giving up." So, boomer dollars went to beauty brands that delivered improvement, along with respect.

**The Whole Truth hurts.**

Lesson learned (again!): The Half Truth of real beauty flies in the face of the Whole Truth of women's hidden vanity and thwarts Dove's long-term brand growth. Although today's women are more confident and self-accepting, they haven't stopped aspiring to be more, especially if they're paying for it.

The Whole Truth hurts.

## marketing to her Whole Truth

Like Unilever's Dove, **PROCTER & GAMBLE'S** (P&G) **OIL OF OLAY** was once a low-end, one-horse product, a watery, pink lotion that great aunt Jenny used to keep her skin soft. In the late 80s, Olay broke

emotional category ground with its famous tagline, "I don't want to grow old gracefully, I want to fight it every inch of the way," an interesting counterpoint to Pro-Age's implied "I am old, hear me roar."

Olay realized that it was important to cast models who looked attractive without being intimidating and to speak in language that didn't overpromise. But, as they picked up steam in the 90s, they didn't pitch status quo efficacy. Instead, they marketed Olay to the Whole Truth that women want beauty products that really work.

The Olay product line, with millions invested in product research and packaging innovation, skipped past Dove's Half Truth of Ego Protection and barreled all the way to the Whole Truth. Olay launched Regenerist, marketed as an alternative to invasive cosmetic surgery and billed as the biggest skin care launch in the mass market.

Today, Olay's Regenerist brand and its sisters, Olay Total Effects, Definity, and Complete, own the beauty aisle in pretty much every drug store, with more SKUs than you can shake a stick at. The Olay powerhouses trounced Pro-Age by acknowledging the Whole Truth that women want the results available through professional intervention, but they don't want to spend the money on it or, even more importantly, be judged as artificial.

In 2009, P&G launched Olay Professional Pro-X at department store–level pricing ($69 for a three-product starter set) with the performance promises to back them up. Focusing on the Whole Truth, Olay built an authority platform with sustainable growth and room for innovations that command big bucks. This "results you can see" Whole Truth has propelled the Olay brand to global leadership and dizzying profits, yet they're still perceived as a brand that's on women's side.

Listening to what women say is important. But falling too easily for pretty lies is a mistake. And it all comes down to the way you listen in the first place.

# CHAPTER TWO

# are you half listening?

H alf Listening, the tendency of busy marketers and retailers to give women their "half attention" and to hear what they want to hear, is rampant and lethal. Whether you're conducting the interviews or analyzing the feedback, if you Half Listen to women, you're building your brand on a shaky foundation.

Every day women are telling you what they love by laying down their hard-earned money and staying loyal to your brand. They tell you what they hate by withholding their wallets, but also by ranting to your 800 lines, blogging about what they don't like, and dressing down a nasty salesperson. And every year, hundreds of thousands of female consumers troop into focus group facilities to be paid for two hours of their in-person feedback. But if you're Half Listening, prepare to get the Half Truths you deserve.

Listening is a tough and demanding job and even the best marketers, under job and deadline pressures, can lapse into settling for convenient Half Truths.

You may have experienced this yourself. You skip out on the research session early, promising to watch the video later, but never do. You're so keen on the idea you are testing that you ignore the women's protests and defend until you win. You gather customer feedback forms but file them under "Later."

Whether we chalk up this Half Listening epidemic to Marketing ADD, a reliance on the same tired questions, or blind adherence to cliché consumer insights, the danger is that you won't hear the Whole Truths you need to succeed.

Most marketers spend as if they have the best intentions as far as listening to consumers—more than $6.7 billion is spent on market research annually in the United States alone. Add to that the cost of hours devoted to reviewing surveys, checking customer satisfaction scores, or training associates in customer care, as well as the millions of air miles and overnights on the road just to "listen," and the dollars

## A 50/50 CHANCE

Do you know that many women don't think you are listening at all? One of the saddest questions I ever heard came from a woman at the end of a particularly stimulating videotaped discussion. As I shook her hand goodbye, she looked at me and said, "Do you think that the people who sell this product will even look at this tape of what we said?" I promised her they would, but I have to admit, I'd lay odds at 50/50.

are astronomical. Given that investment, isn't it time to reexamine the fundamental listening practices that are shortchanging success with women?

# why focus groups fuel half listening

We lay the blame for Half Listening on the dirty little secret of focus groups, a covert technique of spying on women who are paid to pour their hearts out.

**Focus groups rate an F in listening.** At Just Ask a Woman, we've dubbed focus groups the F word of marketing, for the literal questions, the stilted dialogue, the monopolizing "talker" in every group, and worst of all, the hostile nonlistening environment in the backroom. Focus groups are like imprisoning women in your own worst meeting.

When a woman who is stuck in one of these stale sessions starts worrying about her endless to-do list and the cost of a babysitter, why would she pour her heart out? It's as if the deck is stacked against getting the Whole Truth. Here's a menu of what's wrong.

## The Teflon Moderator

In an effort to engender candor, many moderators will introduce themselves by saying, "I have nothing to do with what I am about to share with you, so you can tell me anything." Imagine whether you'd open up to someone who admits she's the disengaged hired help. It's kind of like going to dinner at someone's house and being told, "Hey, I didn't cook it, I'm just serving it, so if it's lousy, no dirt on me!"

In traditional research, moderators are coached to stay at arm's length from their subjects rather than risk "leading the witness." But in the real world, women open up to people they trust, especially other empathetic listeners who are like them—and ideally, who actually like them.

In contrast to the impartial persona honed by most moderators, Tracy, Jen, and I adapt to the distinct differences of each group. With a group of moms, you can bet Jen will mention her twins. If they're boomers, I manage to let my age slip or use an insider reference that telegraphs our joint experience. Tracy makes sure to dress in a way that is relatable. (You might think this is obvious, but in sessions with middle-class moms, some clients arrive wearing Prada shoes and Gucci pants and then wonder why the women give them the once over.) There's no reason to alienate consumers from the get-go.

## The Bugged Room

Another staple of focus groups is the one-way mirror concealing the clients. Don't you think it's weird and disconcerting to be observed by unseen strangers? Women do.

But the moderator lets them know anyway. "Before we begin," the moderator confides, "I need to tell you this room is bugged (our word!). There's a microphone and there are people behind that mirror. They can see you, but you can't see them, but just relax and share with me the story of your incontinence."

No wonder women fall back on telling Half Truths in focus groups just to get through and get out. But the roadblock to Whole Truths isn't the hardworking, long-suffering moderator in the front room. The real problem lies in the backroom. Don't believe us? Come on back.

## The Half Listening Lounge

Backrooms are designed for Half Listening, from the food and the amenities to the surveillance and the separation from women.

The focus group facility industry caters to bad behavior, literally. The food and environment are getting fancier by the day. While the consumers out front share a meager plate of packaged cookies, the backroom is cooking up an entirely different menu. Perhaps a hot meal awaits from the cool Asian fusion place in town with chilled Riesling to wash it all down. (We've actually seen respondents sniff the air, noting the aroma of a better meal somewhere just out of sight.)

One facility touts "four kitchens, a full-time chef onsite, available for any dietary needs and culinary requests. At (blank) Research, superior cuisine and high-quality research go hand-in-hand. *Bon Appétit!*"

We've heard of facilities with treadmills for clients to pass the time while listening. One has an ice cream bar in the back, another, a corporate masseuse. Our favorite descriptor came from a big-city facility, where "clients can kick their feet up next to their very own cozy fireplace or gaze out at the skyline . . . like a home away from home." In fact, this facility is delighted to crow that "clients can have breakout meetings and conduct business, all while monitoring ongoing focus group activity on plasma monitors." (Obviously, there's no point in watching for body language or facial expressions that belie her words. Just have a simultaneous meeting and "listen.")

The biggest problem with the backroom is that it's designed to keep marketers and women apart. No wonder Half Truths slip right through.

## Talking with Women . . . or About Them?

Once the moderator starts the interview, everyone behind the glass starts to assess the lucky eight women out front who have been recruited, approved, and paid for. You'd think they'd be riveted to every word these women speak.

### THE 5 WORST BACKROOM COMMENTS ABOUT WOMEN

1. She can't be our customer.
2. She's fat/ugly/old/dressed like a nightmare.
3. She's not smart since she's not even getting our idea.
4. She doesn't look like she has enough money to shop with us.
5. She can't even give a straight answer. Can we ask her to leave?

Jen's gone as far as keeping a jar where offending commentators are required to drop a dollar every time they insult the women—no kidding.

Instead, the backroom battle begins as soon as the women enter the observation room. Rather than listen, marketers start to talk. Some criticize the respondents with annoyed outrage: "She's heavy/doesn't even wear makeup/doesn't look like *our* customer!" Some blame the market researcher and become defensive: "Why is *she* here? Why would we select *her?*"

The best listeners don't make assumptions. You never know which woman will give you the insight that will make your idea better. That woman who may not be central casting for your brand may just have the answer you need.

But stereotyping women—assuming the pretty ones are smart, making negative judgments about the unattractive ones before they even speak—is a common mistake. And once you've decided she's not worth listening to, you're bound to miss or ignore the next gem that comes out of her mouth.

But more often, marketers admit that they are passing notes, talking to each other, and even yelling at the mirror when the women don't "get" their idea. Jen has heard some complain that women aren't comprehending the concepts, as if it's the women's fault. "Do women have to have a PhD in your chemistry in order to buy a $4 lotion?" she wonders.

## backroom Whole Truths

Are we being hard on focus groups? Rather than be naysayers, we asked 150 leading marketers and strategists about their experiences in backrooms and here's what they told us.

The majority of respondents had ten or more years experience in marketing, ranging from brand manager/director and ad agency account managers to account planners and independent consultants and researchers. And most had attended at least 25 or more focus

## BACKROOM **BEHAVIOR**

Once when forced to show concepts in a focus group facility, I could hear the clients whooping it up over everything the women were saying. So I took one of the big idea boards and scrawled on the back, SHUT UP! I raised the board above my head in clear view of the one-way mirror. My message was heard loud and clear in the backroom.

groups in their careers, with 19% saying they had attended "more than they could count."

With that kind of time and money investment, you'd think that they'd be paying attention. Why else would you fly to a city, recruit the perfect group of women, and pay tens of thousands of dollars?

Well, it seems that there's a lot more than listening going on. First of all, they were eating. Rather than listening, they were talking, emailing, or tweeting. And a surprising number of these dedicated listeners weren't even in the room! Focus group attendees admitted to playing online games, cleaning out their purses/wallets, sharpening their resumes, generally zoning out, and even napping. (See all the details and stats on the next page.)

As part of this survey, we segmented a group of 50 marketers who attended the 2009 M2W conference, a blockbuster gathering of marketers and communicators dedicated to female consumers. We thought that, as advocates for women, this group would listen better, but their scores were no different than the national average. We asked them to not only rate their own listening behavior but also to comment on what they'd seen their colleagues do. Newsflash! They've seen "others" behave even worse, with 80% seeing others leave early, 36% watching colleagues fall asleep, and 41% cringing while others yelled at the women through the glass. Seems that the only thing most folks are listening to is the sound of their own voices.

So, while women out front are supposedly spilling their guts, the backroom is in a communications free-for-all. Any moderator who's ever visited the backroom to ask her clients if there are any more questions and hears the frustrating comment, "You didn't ask X" and responds, between clenched teeth, "Yes, I did . . . we talked for ten minutes about that!" knows we are telling the Whole Truth here.

Another behavior that respondents confessed is actually something they brag about. Almost 60% said that they are rewriting the

# THE HALF LISTENING EPIDEMIC

What were marketers doing in the backroom?

**They were eating:**

**84%** ate a catered meal

**79%** ate M&M's

**36%** drank wine

**They were talking:**

**73%** passed notes to colleagues

**67%** sent emails

**33%** talked office politics

**27%** made a call in the backroom

**2%** tweeted

**And a surprising number of these dedicated listeners weren't even in the room:**

**67%** left to take a call

**46%** left early to head home

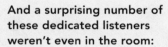

**Of those who stayed:**

**40%** daydreamed

**12%** took a nap

ideas being tested while the women are talking. This could be saluted as a case of proactivity or multitasking, but the fact is that writing while listening assumes there's nothing new to be learned by paying attention. True, if women have trashed what you're showing; premature, if she's just telling you a Half Truth reason that you are accepting too quickly.

## what are you asking?

In advance of research, it's pretty standard to develop a discussion guide of questions. But why are those questions often self-serving or just phrased in "marketing speak"?

### CAN YOU TYPE AND LISTEN?

Tracy once worked with a company whose marketers resisted the idea of being face-to-face with the consumers. "Why don't you want to be in the room with the women?" Tracy asked. "Because we want to be revising the concepts while they talk," they responded. Why would they start writing before they had heard the whole story and how could they truly listen when their fingers are tearing across a computer keyboard?

For instance, a packaged goods company recently announced a new logo and proudly described their in-depth research. They asked women, "How do you engage with a food company?" I can imagine women scratching their heads and answering, "By eating?"

No wonder women have started to swat back with the same jargon that plagues corporate life, such as "this copy doesn't grab me."

The best consumer research probes for feelings and beliefs and attitudes, not for final verdicts. But pressured marketers try to milk qualitative research beyond its bounds, even if the responses aren't projectable. Asking women whether they would buy something that's been "sold" to them for the past two hours isn't something to bank on. Asking for a show of hands so that you can take a number of "hoorays" back to headquarters isn't valid, even if it sounds good.

Rather than forcing rankings from women in a conversational environment, try to probe for conviction and relevance and passion.

Try these questions as wrap-ups instead: "When you leave tonight, how would you describe what we discussed to your best friend?" "If you looked into the eyes of the people who run this company and could tell them what you really want, what would you say?" Get ready for ideas you can use.

## Power Listening and why it matters

Honestly, most businesspeople seem to prefer the anonymity of the backroom and to leave the asking and listening to someone else. Getting close to women who are judging your ideas is uncomfortable (even for many gregarious marketers), as is listening without commenting, wincing, or criticizing.

But we believe that the Whole Truth emerges face-to-face, with no mirror to hide behind. We pretty much forbid our clients to sit in a backroom—in fact, we hold our sessions in nice hotels where there aren't secret hiding places with one-way mirrors.

## The 5 Questions That Beg for Half Truths

1. **"Would you buy this if you saw it on the shelf?"** (Beware total fib attack, answer inadmissible in a marketing courtroom.)
2. **"If this commercial ran on TV, would you stop to watch it?"** (Note: she almost *never* stops to watch a commercial.)
3. **"Is this product for someone like you?"** (If she says, "My sister-in-law would like it," kiss it goodbye.)
4. **"Raise your hand if you think this is something important."** (This is the easiest thing for them to do, and the stupidest thing for you to count on.)
5. **"Let's take a head count of how many of you would buy this idea?"** (A copout for the uncertain woman who will absently nod.)

After sitting next to consumers for the first time, one of our clients said she had never worked so hard to listen.

As testament to the truth-generating power of getting up close and personal, we've noticed that women will approach our clients with personal questions before they leave the sessions. They'll even suggest to clients what "we" need to do to figure out a brand problem. That personal interface is so much more powerful for clients than hiding behind the glass.

Get rid of the conference table when you talk to customers. Retailers can invite a handful of their customers into the store after hours to chat over coffee about how to improve things. Offer to shop along with key customers or take a morning walk with them. We've done it and it's a great way to get the truth *and* a workout.

At Just Ask a Woman, we stretch and reinterpret pretty much every rule of consumer research that we can. We get personal—very personal.

Once when I was asking women about whether they'd consider a particularly gruesome surgical procedure, a skeptical woman asked, "Mary Lou, would *you* do this?" First, I tried the psychologist's twist: "This isn't about me; it's about you." But she shut down, and as I tried to move on, I could feel the question linger in the air. On the spot, I decided to share a story of a medical procedure I had elected to go through. "That was my decision at that point in my life," I said. "Now it's your turn to decide." The room exhaled. The truth flowed.

We challenge women who try to fake us out or tell us what they think we want to hear. We are hands-on, eyes open, and totally female-centric. We have fun. We call them by name, as they do us, and we remember every word they say. (There's nothing more shocking to a woman than when someone remembers what she said a half hour ago.)

We ask the un-askable questions and out them when we feel the Half Truth coming on. And we aren't afraid to laugh with them, cry with them, or admit when we screw up.

The point of Power Listening is to open your mind to her way of thinking, not the other way around. But so often, when we start sessions with some simple conversational openers about what's happening in her life, marketers ask, "Why do we have to waste time on this? Let's get right to talking about our brand." That's not listening; that's selling.

We know women are more open in our formats because when they leave, we've been told more than once by the "pros" (the focus group veterans) that "I really earned my money tonight!" Often, they are relieved to have been so honest. And sometimes, they just thank us for really listening.

That's why women tell *us* the Whole Truth.

# what's holding you back from hearing the Whole Truth?

Just as women hide the Whole Truth, you can be guilty of behaviors that block your ability to hear what she has to say. Here are a few examples.

**You're drinking your own Kool-Aid.** You believe your product is super, so when consumers play that back to you, you pile on. But you may be forcing the consumers to agree with you by asking "Do all these improvements make you reconsider X product?" "Now that you've heard about this new technology, would you be willing to pay more?" It's a big effort for a woman to say outright, "I would never buy this" or "It's not worth the money." You're making it easy for her to fudge.

**Women are worn out from being overresearched, so their tiniest indication of enthusiasm sounds like yes to you.** We always start our sessions by asking women to raise their hands if they've been in research before. Unless we're in a super remote market, nearly every hand is in the air. When women are listless research veterans, you may be too quick to latch on to any positive response, even if it's just the Half Truth. You've got to resuscitate women out of focus group lethargy with fresh methodologies in order to tap their energy for your product.

**Your management loves what you're doing now—or hates it.** If your management is tied to an existing idea or restless for a new one, you may feel the pressure to accept a Half Truth before taking the time to get to the Whole Truth. Tight budgets may be driving decisions and squashing long-term initiatives. Today, no one wants to hear about "long term"; "now" is really the only acceptable timeframe. But jumping to the wrong answer won't make your boss love you more.

**Your ad agency is really pushing their idea hard.** We've repeatedly been in research alongside ad agency folks who become distraught when their idea isn't liked. Are they worried that they can only bring a yes back to the office or that they don't have a backup idea? When

## IMAGES ARE POWERFUL

Before conducting research for a dangerous, sexually related health condition, Tracy suggested that the ad agency's sample photos of models representing afflicted women would be a turn-off. Despite Tracy's protestations that the pictures might hurt their idea, the agency resisted, saying they absolutely could not find any pictures of women that were appropriate. "It's just swipe," they said. "It's not what we really mean the end product to be." It wasn't until the consumers in the testing session said that the women looked so "slutty" that they seemed to deserve the sexually transmitted disease that the agency finally backed down.

you feel an agency digging in, you may be tempted to cave and take a Half Truth and run. But female consumers won't care that the agency is getting their way. She's all about her.

If you're honest with yourself, your behavior may also be driven by Half Truths, for instance,

**Approval Seeking** Have you ever pushed women to say how great your brand is, just so you have it on tape for the higher-ups?

**Good Intentions** Have you ever insisted on a description of your target customer that is much more intelligent, self-assured, and attractive than she really is, just because you wish it to be so?

**Ego Protection** Have you ever found yourself describing your commodity product in Nike-esque terms, such as "We're not in the mayonnaise business, we're actually lubricating life?" Get real. It's fat in a jar.

## start Power Listening

Let's say you are not behaving in any of the horrid ways we just nailed. But are you a *master* listener? What differentiates the Black Belt Whole Listener from the hobbyist is the ability to listen with your entire mind, body, and spirit.

Power Listening starts with shutting up and shutting down the tech and the voices of your colleagues. Power Listening calls on your eyes, your ears, and your ability to pick up the tiniest variations in someone's voice and body language. And more than that, Power Listening starts with the humility to know what you don't know and the willingness to subvert your opinions for a moment and let women speak.

The best marketers admit they're not the smartest ones in the room. They're not. She is. And if you're not careful, you might accept any one of the five Half Truths that drive her answers. We'll break them down in the following chapters, one by one, so they won't break you.

# CHAPTER THREE

# good intentions

Anyone who's ever stepped on a scale, tried not to light up, or remade the same resolution they broke last New Year's knows what Good Intentions are all about. "I'll get that report finished early." "I'll hit the gym at lunchtime." "I'll lose ten pounds after the holidays." The Half Truth of Good Intentions gives us all reason to hope.

Female consumers are veterans at these vows of self-improvement. Whether their intentions are as small as daily flossing or as big as scheduling mammograms, women are addicted to these mantras of their "wannabe better" selves (even if, like us, they rarely follow through). Women are optimists at heart who continue to believe that if they say what they intend, someday it will be.

Of course, retailers of quick-fix fitness chains and designers of skinny jeans have gotten rich getting women to pay for promises they don't keep. But for the most part, facing the fact that women's well-meaning wishes are sometimes just wishes will keep you from being left at the altar of her Good Intentions.

If you can't detect the difference between a commitment and a pipedream, it's time for a remedial workshop on this Half Truth. This chapter will examine the difference between women's wishful intentions and their real-life behaviors. We'll look at brands that have detoured around women's vaporware vows and succeeded with stealth strategies, reverse psychology, even flat-out fib protection. We'll share stories of marketers who've learned to accept and then circumvent the reality that a woman may pledge more than she will actually do or buy.

You'll learn how to ask yourself if she means what she says or if she says it to feel good or because she wishes it to be so. Is there code buried in her resolutions that can be leveraged to a great idea? Can I market to the Half Truth of her Good Intentions, even when we both know she has no intention of being that good? In other words, if the road to hell is paved with good intentions, how can I keep my marketing plans from following right behind?

## once upon a time, i was on a diet . . .

Let's begin with the example of losing weight, the chart topper of every New Year's resolution list.

When it comes to their waistlines, women are pros at making promises. But they're even better at finding reasons not to keep them: "Last night I said to my husband, 'I'm going to start walking every night.' Tonight, will I go walking? Probably not, but . . ."; and "I have this mentality of working all week and then on Friday I end up eating a lot of food. A couple of weeks later, 'Whoops!'"

It's not that women intentionally cheat or profess they're on a diet they never started; it's just that life gets in the way.

# a simple truth detector

Women talk a good game of sticking to promises, even if they don't actually follow through. They really do hope to organize their lives, stay on top of their finances, and take control of the unbelievably large amount of time they spend online. So how can marketers capitalize on their Good Intentions without getting shortchanged?

In face-to-face research, the first simple step to eliciting a woman's Whole Truths rests with a one-word question: "Really?" When a woman starts to preach about her rigorous beauty regimen ("I never go to bed without carefully removing my makeup") or how she plans to use all the applications of your new tech toy ("I always read the entire instruction manual first"), try following up with "Really?" in your most amazed, shocked voice. Let the word hang in the air for a moment. It's funny how women will laugh and begin to confess how many times they have strayed and what they *really* do.

**Girlfriends are great lie detectors.**

Want to see a Half Truth exposed in front of your eyes? In work we did for a healthcare marketer on chronic heartburn, women claimed that they avoided spicy foods. But when they arrived at the research venue, we put them to the test with a covert experiment. We offered a choice of bland turkey sandwich or lasagna with garlic bread. Guess which entrée was decimated? (Proof that they were telling a Half Truth of Good Intentions!)

Try inviting women into sessions with their girlfriends. The pairs of women can be terrific lie detectors for each other, even as they hide their own truths.

And if you find that you're still uncertain if she's confessing her Whole Truth, try some ethnographic techniques. When we've gone to a woman's home to film our ethnographic DocuDiary of her life, there's no hiding the truth in her closets. Or even easier, ask your

## Truth in Translation

"**I took a vacation from working out when my whole family got sick.** (Whether she was exercising before or not, this is a reasonable excuse that engenders empathy.) **I went through an eight-week period without exercising** (relatable) **and it took me another four weeks just to get remotivated. Supposedly I'm on a diet but I just had two bites of brownie.** (It was probably three or four, but who's counting?) **I know better—less in, more out.** (This rote response is on a repeating loop.) **But all of a sudden for the first time in two years, I've gained five pounds.** (Five is too small and forgivable to even mention, so she's probably gained more.) **But I'm getting back on track."** (And when might that be?)

consumers to take their own digital photos or simple videos for an inside peek at their Good Intentions.

**IKEA** commissioned us to research the state of women's bedrooms. After hearing women describe their bedrooms as well-organized sanctuaries of calm, we asked women to send us pictures. When we reviewed the photos, we were surprised to see the messy Whole Truth of piles of clothes and stacks of paper waiting to be put away . . . someday. These unkept Good Intentions are why IKEA and other retailers like **THE CONTAINER STORE** clean up and a magazine like *REAL SIMPLE* is a huge success. Each is a temple of good organizing intentions where women can experience pathways to neatness nirvana, even if they're just browsing a color-coded fantasy.

# give her a cover story

Creating a cover story for women wary of being busted for failing at their Good Intentions is a smart strategy. **MCDONALD'S** is a case in point.

Previously, every time their kids begged for McDonald's Happy Meals, moms either succumbed to their own french fry temptation or skipped lunch entirely. (Don't be misled: if calories didn't count, she would be sidled up next to her toddler with her own Value Meal.) McDonald's picked up on her intention to be "good" by launching a line of fresh salads. These salads might as well have had "mom" written all over them. Adding them to the menu was a genius move to make women feel better about their choice at the Golden Arches. Who cares if the salad is covered in full-fat dressing and crispy chicken (notice they don't say "fried")?

The reason salads worked is that they nailed this Whole Truth: "Every time I take my son to McDonald's, I'm embarrassed that I'm eating fast food, too." Mom felt guilty admitting to her kid-enabled bad habit and she needed a justification for going. Now, mom can say to her friends, "The kids and I stopped at McDonald's, but I just had a salad." McDonald's marketed to the Whole Truth that she didn't only need to save calories; she needed to save face.

The cherry on top of this Whole Truth example is that the salad to-go bag isn't the same, incriminating burger sack but rather a veggie-decorated plastic bag that won't out her as a fast-food-eating slug.

Let a woman give you her definition of her Good Intentions. What's she really after? Does she really want to win an Olympic medal or is she just grateful to make a good effort and get the credit for going for the gold?

## help her keep her promises

Women are responsible for more than 80% of their families' healthcare-related decisions. Whether it's for her own health or her kids', husband's, or parents', women are the darlings of the pharmaceutical industry. The healthcare industry, however, is more in tune with the needs of the medical community than the needs of patients. Many major healthcare companies spend little time listening to consumers and, therefore, may not pick up on the difference between what a woman promises and the reality of what she actually does.

A great example of this is the human papilloma virus (HPV) test. Several years ago, a medical diagnostic company developed a test to detect HPV strains that could cause cervical cancer. This test was invented to pair with the PAP, the annual test gynecologists have relied on for decades for cell abnormality detection. This new DNA test was superior in that it could identify strains of HPV that could cause cervical cancer. In our research, women were honest enough to admit that even though they didn't even know why they got PAP tests or what HPV was, they were intrigued.

In-market tracking showed that her Good Intentions were being stalled on the examining table when she faced resistance from the doctors, who were reluctant to do the second test (mostly because it meant more time for counseling, putting longer wait time onto

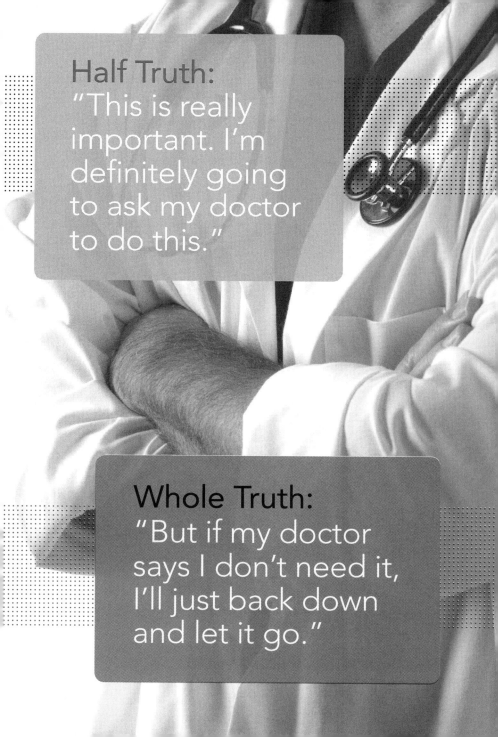

the other patients). So doctors balked and even the most assertive patients backed down rather than argue.

(There's also a bit of Approval Seeking thwarting their Good Intentions, since women hate to raise a conflict with a trusted authority or partner, but more on that in the next chapter.)

So we recommended to our clients that they create a guide for women that would give them the words to say when a doctor said no

In work we did to discover how women researched their healthcare questions, one woman admitted that although she told her doctor that she checked legitimate medical websites, "I really got all my information from an episode of ER."

Think that's funny? In a survey published in the *New York Times*, 35% of women polled said they learned about the HPV Test from an episode of ER, more than twice the number who said they'd heard about it from a doctor. Placing Good Intentions in the right media helps make the most of them!

to their requests for the test—they could keep their Good Intentions and their relationships intact. The company developed an online "script" as an easy way to rehearse the conversation.

The results of this online tool and the concurrent PR were so outstanding that now insurance covers the test, and recent reports claim that the HPV test will soon replace the PAP as the key diagnostic tool for gynecologists. It's not enough to know her Good Intentions; a good marketer helps her keep them.

## call it as she sees it

The supermarket shelves are packed with siren call promises of good and good for you. With so many products overpromising whole grains and trans-fat free, it's not surprising that women are skeptical about whether food marketers are partners or saboteurs.

And yet women look for ways to have their chocolate and eat it too. So food marketers plunge in with pseudo-nutrition, like whole grain Chips Ahoy cookies or Splenda with fiber. Both have quasi health/nutrition claims and neither will ever be blessed as good for you. But at least consumers can attribute some small Good Intention as the rationale for indulging a sweet tooth.

To fill this gap between taste and control, **KRAFT** asserted leadership years ago with a new brand based on portion-control packaging, creating a new calorie denomination with 100-calorie packs of products, such as **OREO** cookies. Kraft didn't try to bait and switch women with an envelope containing a single full-size Oreo, knowing the Whole Truth that women customers still needed a sensation of quantity to get satisfaction. So they redesigned Oreos into tiny creamless cookies, to deliver both the beloved taste and extended snacking satisfaction of more than one.

The act of ripping the envelope is enough to restore a woman's sense of control. One weight-conscious woman told Jen: "If I have a

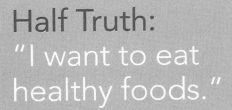

Half Truth:
"I want to eat healthy foods."

Whole Truth:
"Sometimes the less-bad-for-me version of my favorite foods is good enough."

bag of chips, I'll eat the whole bag. If I eat the whole 100-calorie pack, I get the same psychological closure. I'd never eat two in a row."

Kraft discovered Good Intentions gold: new labeling, new packaging, new psychology. The 100-calorie portions, soon copycatted across categories, simplified decision making and helped women keep their Good Intentions without sacrifice or fear of bingeing. It is perfect Whole Truth marketing.

## smoothing the way to her Good Intentions

Women's Good Intentions are often foiled due to the "yucky/boring" factor of doing the right thing. How can you spin some marketing sugar to make the medicine go down?

Let's stay with food for a moment. Women might say they know they need more fiber but they associate it with gritty dull flavor. Products like **FIBER ONE** have penetrated the women's market by pumping the brand's fiber content into pancake mix and Pop-Tart-like treats, a great way to make a tasty treat good inside, too.

In various categories, marketers have found ways to navigate women's Half Truth Good Intentions by making them more fun.

For instance, many moms want to spend more together time with their kids, but are roadblocked by video games. Though a mom might say she wants to play, the Whole Truth is that she often has neither the interest nor the time to learn. Enter **Wii**, with a portfolio of games, sports, and now WiiFit, all geared not only to engage women with their families in fun activities, but also, and even better, to increase the utility of a device that was sitting dormant in homes from 8 a.m. to 3 p.m.

Another Good Intention that women profess but don't act on is learning simple home repair. The growing numbers of single women and the many women whose husbands don't even watch HGTV fantasize that someday they'll install their own bath tile or new lighting. **HOME DEPOT**'s Do It Herself workshops provided the perfect way to put the fun of an all-female DIY training session right in the stores. The classes were a way to help women not just dream, but actually do—and then of course, spend. With the economy encouraging more DIY projects over paying professionals, this strategy is starting to pay off.

## taking the long view of short-attention intentions

One of the critical Good Intentions that too many women profess is the plan to get their finances under control. If there's anything the recession of 2009 taught us all is that money that's taken for granted is soon taken for good.

Women unfortunately will talk a good game about money, but the reality is far different. They'll say, "I really think that this year I will put in the time to educate myself about my money management." Too often, the Whole Truth is, "I haven't even made out my will, let alone have a clue where to start." While men are quick to pull the trigger on these decisions, women tend to be more deliberate and examine options and even delay signing on the bottom line until they are certain they are taking the right step for themselves and their families.

So women will start collecting and coding paperwork or checking out advisors, then stash it all for a rainy day. This stop-and-go procrastination has frustrated even the best financial services marketers who don't have the patience to wait for women. Insurance companies like **STATE FARM** and **FARMER'S INSURANCE** decided that the dollar potential of the female audience was worth taking the long view and have created vibrant websites for women that serve as a resource for whatever stage of financial readiness women are in. In addition, hiring female agents and featuring them in TV commercials have helped demonstrate that State Farm wants women's business, whenever they are ready to follow up on their intentions.

Expecting immediate results ignores Good Intentions.

**AMERICAN EXPRESS** created OPEN as a way to support small businesses but quickly recognized the power of women in this market; so year after year, the company has sponsored events for networking and skill building as a feeding ground for new accounts. They've hooked up with Nell Merlino's "Make Mine a $Million Business," a not-for-profit group that helps female entrepreneurs succeed through financing, education, mentoring, and marketing help. Expecting immediate results, as too many financial companies have done and then failed, ignores the slow path to her Good Intentions.

# build a brand out of failed Good Intentions

Women's beauty drawers are the graveyard of failed Good Intentions, from abandoned skin care regimens to tricky eyebrow kits. The proliferation of two-in-one products, fast-acting creams, and long-lasting formulations all testify to marketer's success at supporting her Good Intentions.

Women know they should wear sunscreen every day, but don't. So cosmetic marketers pour SPF into everything from lip balm to hair conditioners, so women can live with their broken promises, even if the SPF "dose" is barely effective. Women claim that they wash their makeup off every night, except if they're out late, too tired, etc., etc., etc. No wonder mineral makeup brands have gained a reputation for being so good for your skin you can sleep in them and actually improve your looks—it's incredible marketing sleight of hand!

Sometimes women need an easy way to keep their bad beauty behavior undercover until they can make good on their intentions. In research we've done on hair color, women claim to color as often as every four to six weeks to keep up with root regrowth, when in reality, many wait three months or longer. If confronted (a mirror will do!), women will blame their delays on the time required and pretend that a baseball cap can conceal their procrastination.

Like many marketers, **CLAIROL** may have been reluctant to give women a way out of buying a new box of their product. But when it was evident that women were dabbing on their full-size product inappropriately, they came up with a solution: the Nice 'N Easy Root Touch-Up kit, a way to help women pretend they color religiously, even though they don't. The product is a blow-away success because it allows a woman's Good Intentions to stay intact.

## making her Good Intentions work for you

Maneuvering around the landmines of this Half Truth does not mean giving up on aspiration; it does mean that marketers need to navigate the bumpy waters of ego, excuses, and ever-changing promises to discover the Whole Truth underneath.

As you look at your category or business and try to apply these lessons to your consumers, avoid being undermined by a woman's Good Intentions and turn her promises into your profits.

Give her permission to fail,
ways to keep her promises
painlessly, and the chance
to save face.

# how to avoid the Half Truth of Good Intentions

1. Her Good Intentions are not necessarily what you think. Let her express her needs for your product or category in her words, no matter how inflated, then push her to answer the question, "Really?" to be sure she isn't hiding her real desires. Her definition of what being good means in your category is what matters, not yours.

2. Give her permission to fail, ways to keep her promises painlessly, and the chance to save face even if she doesn't comply with all of your "rules." Remember, she's trying to do her best by buying your product and that's what counts. Don't make your subterfuge obvious; she will see that you "get" her just by the shortcuts you offer to her intentions.

3. If you fake your way into her favor and then fail her Good Intentions, prepare to be found out. It's less risky to create something she will count on and tell friends about than to give her a reason to mistrust you the next time around.

# CHAPTER FOUR

# approval seeking

Finally the day has arrived when your ad agency is presenting new creative work for your leading brand. While they're a little past deadline, the team is excited and so are you. (Though you might not admit it, you're wearing your cool jeans and boots that give you that "I'm hip enough to be taken for an outside agency creative" look.)

The copywriter and art director begin their pitch, and though they show lots of ideas, you can't find a single thing you like. But you know that this team has hit home runs before and you don't want to deflate their balloon too quickly.

"So, what do you think?" they ask hopefully (though they're already preening like they're advertising rockstars).

"There's a lot of work here, that's for sure," you say (a timeworn dodge that passes for the positive answer they want to hear).

"We all really loved the last two boards best," they say (trying to build a quorum of creative love).

"Yeah, the celebrity bit is funny if we can afford it," you offer (an easy out until you ask their boss for a total do-over).

"Great meeting! We can't wait to start working out the production details" (an agency tactic to build the pressure to agree).

"Hey, did you catch *Entourage* last night?" (a trick to change the subject to keep the friendly vibe going).

If you see yourself or a colleague in this story, you know what this chapter is about. The Half Truth of Approval Seeking is the collection of covert behaviors, such as faked chumminess or clever diversion, designed to build consensus or get along. Whether we dress to impress, stretch to find common ground, mini- **Seeking** mize differences, or flatter our way to yes, these **Approval is a** everyday approval-seeking behaviors aren't that **natural instinct.** dangerous. But they can be deadly for marketers. When women resort to this Half Truth instead of coming clean with what they really feel and want, they can thwart your marketing success with a smile and you won't even know it.

Seeking Approval is a perfectly natural instinct, a way that human beings pursue affiliation. If you are protesting, "I don't care if I'm liked!" (how often do you tell yourself *this* Half Truth?), then you are probably alone more than you care to confess.

In the situation at the start of this chapter, let's assume that you're tempted to yell, "These ads stink. You're fired!" But rather than descend into a downward spiral of spite, you, a seasoned marketer, instead find a way to preserve the relationship and then work the system before throwing in the towel.

It's important that you understand how significant and motivating Approval Seeking is to women. In general, women are keenly driven to belong and they sense how others see them. They will turn themselves inside out in an effort to find something good, even in your bad idea. Likewise, they are attuned to how you regard *them*. In their interactions with your brand (and if you are a retailer, with your store), their antennae are wired for details and nuance, all the small signals that demonstrate either respect or rejection. Just as they are tough judges of themselves, they can be tough on you; yet in their quest to please, they won't always tell you you've crossed a line until it's too late. In this chapter, we'll identify three minefields where women's Approval Seeking can either derail or deliver results for your brand: market research, brand development, and at the moment of truth—at the register, in the showroom, or on the website where she buys your product or services.

## why women seek approval

Before we begin, let's explore why women seem especially prone to Approval Seeking. Psychologists have studied the effects of "social anxiety," which occurs when people are concerned about how they're evaluated by others. Social psychologists have noted the incredible power of the need to belong and its companion, the fear of social rejection. We often observe how far women will go to earn an A or to avoid an F from others.

Many researchers believe there are two different aspects of this social self-consciousness: private (the running tape in her head that continually asks "How am I feeling?") and public (the self-awareness meter of how she's perceived externally: "What do they think of me?"). The higher her level of public self-consciousness, the more likely it is that a woman will focus on the opinions of everyone else, while carefully trying to avoid criticism.

In our experience, and perhaps in your everyday life, you may have noticed that women seem to strive for social validation more than men. (Otherwise, why would overweight men strut the beach in Speedos while average-size women cover up in sarongs?)

Even when they are complimented, women will fixate on whether the kudos are genuine, and they will hoard a personal slight far longer than it's worth.

Women will share the story of a bad experience with four to seven others, but they've been known to repeat a really hurtful incident for as long as 23 years. Avoiding criticism becomes a full-time job.

## it starts with market research

At the market research stage of a project, women will display their Approval Seeking skills in an effort to avoid sticking out and to improve their odds of securing support. They will try to get along even though they disagree, and likewise, they will all silently agree to hate something even if individually they don't. Now, imagine yourself in the back room as all the women pile on the criticism train and you're trying to keep your agency calm while their work is being gang-ripped through the glass. Your agency colleagues are in their own approval search because everyone likes to feel liked (even if they aren't). Ironically, all this faux agreement has the opposite effect, pitting you against consumers and blocking your ability to listen.

### The Frustration of Too Much "Yes"

In research, it's common to see women robotically nodding at each other, acquiescing to whatever the moderator asks of them or whatever the self-designated "group leader" insists is true. They'll even pleasantly pledge to buy what you're selling. But rather than be delighted, many marketers become skeptical, even ticked off by a group of female consumers who agree with each other.

Many attribute a round of unanimous yeses or nos to mob mentality and are quick to claim that women in research are victims of groupthink and to discard what they've said. This is a big mistake.

If you believe they love your idea in research, you risk launching a loser no one really likes unless you got lucky with a good idea. And if you believe nothing they say just because they all agree to love or to hate your idea, that misconception will also come back to bite you.

The allure of too much agreement in research is that you are lulled into believing women mean what they say without challenging it. Even if a chorus hates your ideas in unison, there's always the reality that a few in the room like the ideas. That's why when we listen to women, we break the approval cycle. In our talk-show research

Your brand can get hurt if you fall for the notion that all the women love your idea *or* if you dismiss their opinions as **groupthink**.

format, Just Ask a Woman LIVE™, we keep our eyes trained on the most timid woman in the group while challenging the big talker who's getting all the head nods, catching her when she contradicts herself so that the quiet woman gets up the nerve to speak out.

What you learn from market research will either anchor your brand to a strong, provocative foundation or send it down the slippery slope to an acceptable but boring nowhere. Don't settle for gratuitous smiles. Never, ever let women off the hook, even if it means confronting their enthusiastic yeses or dour nos with a "Do you really believe that?" It's worth ruffling feathers to achieve what's right for women and your brand.

In our work, we face this Half Truth right up front. We always begin our sessions by saying, "While we're together for the next couple hours, let's agree to disagree. You can all sing 'Kumbaya' in the hall when this is over." We always get a knowing laugh, since women are onto their own game.

## Screening Yourself from the Truth

Approval Seeking comes with the territory of market research. More than that, you might be surprised to know that you unintentionally bring it on yourself. What else would you expect but agreement from a group of eight moms, aged 35 to 40, all with young kids, some college education, household income between $40,000 and $55,000, living in the same neighborhood, and suffering from migraines? Of course, they get along and think alike! You personally cast them that way!

Your accomplice in creating an "all yes" atmosphere is the screener, the questionnaire that recruits the "perfect" set of women and screens out differences of experience, opinion, and personality. Paid recruiters tally up family status, income, education, media habits, product consumption, even answers to attitudinal questions such as, "Are you someone who thinks of herself as creative?"

## SCREENED OUT

Jen was conducting a session on health care in Kansas City and, scarily, a woman in the group had a seizure. Everyone froze. Jen ran out of the room into the hotel to call for help. The EMS folks arrived quickly and attended to the suffering woman. (She was ultimately fine.) During the commotion, the client said, "I can't believe that no one in this group was a nurse or medical worker who could have helped." Jen sighed. "That's because you screened them all out!"

Many women, in turn, give good enough answers, especially if they really need the money paid for making the cut.

How hard is it to be accepted for research? We've seen 17-page questionnaires. If you answered your home phone at night while the kids were trying to get your attention and the dog was out of control and someone asked you 17 pages of questions, what are the chances you'd (A) stay on the phone, (B) answer each question thoughtfully, and (C) tell the Whole Truth to a perfect stranger? The answer is D. You'd hang up.

Still, marketers rely on screeners to be absolutely sure that all the *right* women are in the room (aka all those who share the same problems or carry the same prejudices), so no wonder all the women agree, or disagree together, as much as they do. You cloned them to be identical.

Screeners also eliminate anyone with any knowledge of the subject, especially if they have marketing experience. If anyone has an odd predisposition toward the category, then she's thrown out, too. Though screening is necessary to guard confidentiality and to kabosh women who fundamentally hate your brand, some screeners border on the absurd.

Still, women sometimes slip through by concealing what would keep them out. Even with our scrutiny, we've had outliers, like the woman who wore scrubs to a medical interview, or another who brought her oxygen tank to a session on fitness.

You might think that online surveys would elicit honesty and stifle the reflexive yes factor. But in online screening questionnaires women can guess the "right" answer pretty easily after a couple of questions.

**Get real about the screening process**

In a recent online questionnaire I was using to recruit women to appear onstage with me, the first respondent described herself as witty and outspoken. The second woman had checked the exact same thing. The third, ditto! Could they all truly be witty and outspoken? It was clear that they had just checked off the responses to get chosen for a good gig. With no one to monitor the truth of her clicks, imagine how many Half Truths you might be buying when you use online surveys as a substitute for in-person research!

To get the right women into research in the first place, marketers need to get real about the screening process. Here are some helpful tips to avoid research sabotage: Challenge your team to shorten your screeners so smart people won't hang up on your research invitation. Stop worrying if the women have ever worked in marketing. The ones who have will be quicker to get what you're talking about.

Too many screeners focus nearly every question on insider details rather than on discovering those personal qualities that can prevent the epidemic of too much agreement. Rebalance your screeners to recruit for women who will speak out, be creative problem solvers, and withstand the strong opinions of others. Choose individuality over "Miss Congeniality" so you'll find someone bold enough to disclose personal stuff even if it ticks off other women in the group.

Finally, give yourself a deeper insight into the women in whom you're investing market research dollars and time. We ask women to do homework before the assignment as a way to gauge their creativity and real association with the marketing problem at hand. Time and money well spent on screening upfront will pay handsomely in the truth you need down the line.

# deciphering the meanings of "yes"

The Half Truth of Seeking Approval is fraught with confusion. Think of two women playing a game of indecision with a restaurant lunch menu, until one cops out with, "Okay, I'll just order whatever you're having." By being so noncommittal and agreeable, neither gets what she really wants. Here are some ways women condition their yeses rather than 'fess up.

## She Agrees, Sort Of

In our research for this book, we asked marketers which focus group responses really drive them crazy. These approval zingers zoomed to the top (with some translation from us):

- **"I agree with her."** (Please like me because I just supported you.)
- **"This is just my opinion, but . . ."** (I am not disagreeing, just stating my insignificant, different idea, which you can ignore.)
- **"This isn't my experience, but others may feel . . ."** (Even though I disagree, I am going to make everyone else feel like their ideas are smart.)

"This isn't my experience, but others may feel . . ."

"I agree with her."

"This is just my opinion, but . . ."

We often remind women to answer for themselves, not the mysterious "other" women they defer to. We cut in with, "I'm not asking about other women, I'm asking what do *you* want?" We call them up short and honesty follows.

## She Avoids Saying No

Despite the obvious physical gestures of camaraderie and interest, women's language tells a different story if you listen carefully.

I'm guilty of this myself. When faced with youthful indecision, my mom always coached me: "Just say yes. You can always say no later." This still comes in handy. And it works for a lot of women in market research who know that by seeming to agree, even if they disagree, they can stay in the inner circle that's been created.

Rather than risking criticism for a negative reaction, a woman might employ various strategies to say no without uttering the word. Here's how:

- **She ducks the question:** "I think this product would be great for camping." (I've never gone camping, and I never will.)
- **She likes your product on someone else's behalf:** "I think this would be great for my sister." (My sister's not here, but she'll buy anything.)
- **She puts a price caveat on her yes:** "I'd really like this as long as the price was low." (She would only buy it if the price were so low that you'd never make a dime.)
- **She sits it out:** "I don't know. I'd have to do more research on this to tell you what I think." (I'd rather not trash your idea on the spot, so I'll pass.)

## products based on belonging

Some marketers co-opt the concept of women's desire for affinity and leverage it for product success.

An example of a brand whose success hinges on helping enable women's desire to connect is **WEIGHT WATCHERS**. While the brand understands the Half Truth of acceptance of like-minded peers, they recognize the Whole Truth, that the badge of membership is as important as actually following the regimen. Women claim compliance with the point program (even if they're not), and when they reach their goal weight, they will cling to their record book for years.

The Weight Watchers brand is proof that a support network of women who all share weight challenges yields results. In addition to the meetings, the online community expands access to the club as a place for learning real-world tips, admitting trip-ups, and sharing solutions. The brand also carries a seal of "righteous effectiveness" so that advocates can pass along the endorsement that "only Weight Watchers really works" or is doctor-approved, burnishing their Approval Seeking halo.

## Weight Is Contagious

A study from Harvard medical researchers and the University of California, San Diego showed that gaining or losing weight is "contagious" among overweight friends. The more excuses are shared, the more everyone gains weight. The more support within the circle of friends, the better the loss. Women, as the gender more likely to diet, know how susceptible they are to jumping on the bandwagon of their friend's broken promises.

But the real genius of attaching this clubby feeling to a product is to recognize the bigger Whole Truth that although women crave belonging, they also want to feel unique within the group.

The **MINI COOPER** can trace its success with women to tweaking this clubbiness with a twist of personalization. Driving a MINI Cooper says she belongs to a smart, fun group of energy-conscious, stylish, quirky folks. A woman might join one of their cross-country rallies, but her customization makes the car hers alone and, in essence, allows her personality to shine.

Smart marketers are realizing that women actually like to flaunt their unique differences and even "bad" behavior. **FRITO-LAY'S** Flat Earth, Lay's Chips, and Smartfood teamed up to create "Only in a Woman's World," a site that features four women and their idiosyncrasies, which allows visitors to play games with the virtual women, imagine their snarky comments, even send e-cards reflecting their unique spins on life.

# Just because two women are moms doesn't mean they are blood sisters.

## bringing sisterhood to brand development

Another big Approval Seeking manhole or opportunity in product development is the trap of sisterhood, where marketers, having observed how connected women are when together, try to tap into the value of that "sisterhood" for their brands. But they may be over-reaching when they assume that just because women are alike, they want to be clones.

While marketers see the power of women online, especially on social-networking and shopping sites, all's not sweetness and light in cyberland. Women are tough judges of just who gets to be in their approved circle. Look at how a wedding website like **THEKNOT.COM** works for women. You might think that all brides have a bond and that all advice is created equal. Not so. When Jen was getting married, she'd check out pictures of the happy couples before she took their decorating ideas. If the brides looked tacky or their taste was questionable, Jen wasn't so eager to sign up for their florists.

Here's how misinterpreting this feel-good Approval Seeking Half Truth steered some brands wrong—and some right. Women can get ticked off when you assume affinity they don't really feel. For instance, hotels set up all-women floors, largely in the name of security. But women business travelers, especially those traveling with male colleagues, don't want to come off as separate or wimpy and certainly don't want to be embarrassed at the front desk with a key that says, "Women floor only."

Interestingly, some women's travel websites have stumbled by going too pink, suggesting book clubs and cute woman-y tips that leave professional women annoyed. Women aren't looking to join the sisterhood of the traveling laptops, they just want to get where they're going.

In 1995, **WYNDHAM HOTELS** was the first hotel chain to launch a women's initiative, "Women on Their Way," and recently updated the program to make it even more right for women today. While they offer an online community and blogs for bonding and commiserating over the trials of travel, most of the program serves women's self-interests, like special deals, destination information, and shortcuts to make travel more bearable.

Another approach to this is the way that **KIMPTON HOTELS** create a women-friendly oasis. In addition to offering female-centric amenities like static guard and eye-makeup remover pads, Kimpton allows guests to leave a small bag of their toiletries at their frequently visited properties. (And since women carry five times the products men do, that's a big benefit!) And for all the women who'd like to relax together at the end of a busy travel day but dread the typical hotel bar scene, Kimpton offers Wine, Women, and Fun, an end of day wine hour for women only.

# Approval Seeking at the register

It's one thing for a market researcher who's got two hours to interview a woman to figure out her motivations or for a brand manager to synthesize the insights from thousands of women for months at a time. But at the point of sale, the typical associate or agent or website gets just seconds to assess her yes, so no wonder there are so many snafus. Getting your messaging right at the point of sale calls on your ability to be fast on your feet.

Retailers in technology, financial services, automotive, and even health care wrestle with what women really want and can discover too late that a woman's tacit approval disguises a customer on the verge of meltdown. Salespeople don't understand that a nodding woman isn't the same as a nodding man. A man will generally nod when he means he agrees. A woman will nod to acknowledge that she hears what you're saying, but by no means does it guarantee assent. Only direct follow up such as "Now that you've heard what we're offering, are you interested?" will get you closer to that truth.

When women feel rejected or disrespected, they can use their Approval Seeking skills to get their way. In work we did for a major insurance company, a particularly sweet, unassuming woman described how she'd been ignored by her agent after he'd smooth-talked his way into a contract. She tolerated his unresponsive service for months on end, until she finally called and asked for him under the guise of a friendly follow-up call, only to tell him that she was firing him for incompetence and wanted him to know it.

In research about car buying, one young mom calmly stated her tactics for dealing with the frustrating runaround in the showroom: "When I shop, I usually bring my children along. And I keep an eye on them. But when the salesman starts the 'I've got to talk to my manager' runaround, I don't control my children anymore."

## She Sees Through "Fake Sincerity"

Some companies go overboard to satisfy this Half Truth of feeling respected and liked. And faux friendliness falls as flat as the über-cozy waiter oozing, "My name is Jason and I can't wait to serve your table tonight." Uh-huh.

Thinking that prescribed small talk will pass muster with women is a big mistake. Veterans at making nice, women are expert at sensing insincerity. The authentic support women want is exemplified by the customer service reps at **LANDS' END**, who will actually try on a

## SCRIPTED **EMPATHY**

Jen shares this recent experience with the **T-MOBILE** customer service representative after she had a **BLACKBERRY** meltdown: I predicted a long, frustrating call after navigating out of the voice-automated system, but I was quickly greeted by the world's happiest young woman. "It's a great day at T-Mobile in BlackBerry Support, how can I help you?" After I gave my name, rank, and serial number, I told her my problem, which sent her empathy into overdrive. She chirped, "That must be just awful to be inconvenienced like that. I am so sorry that this happened to you, and we will find a way to fix it right now." She was reading from the world's most patronizing and annoying script. I was tempted to ask about the weather to see if she could answer a question without the script. She put me on hold for a millisecond and came back with, "I am *so* sorry that I put you on hold. I know that your time is important and waiting can be frustrating." It took her longer to apologize than I had been on hold!

pair of shoes while you're on the phone to tell you if they run large. Even better, a representative from Lands' End called Jen just to let her know that she was granted free shipping for a month as a reward for being a good customer. That's a way to get her approval for good.

Later, we will focus on how this Half Truth and others run rampant at retail, but it's important to acknowledge that women expect that a brand will get it right end to end. And to a marketer, that means that a powerful research insight that infuses a product with differentiation and value must connect with women in an ad or on a shelf or online. All that came before is moot if she doesn't see her Whole Truth when it's time to buy.

# how to avoid the Half Truth of Approval Seeking

1. Stop fighting groupthink. Affinity among women helps them confess what they don't want to tell you. Just be sure to dig deep enough to understand what's really behind her yes or no.

2. Before you let the Approval Seeking truth seep into your product idea, don't force her into "clubs" she doesn't want to join, or at least find ways to acknowledge her uniqueness in the group.

3. At the moment of sale, watch out for the temptation to read her yes as agreement or to overdo the nicey-nice talk. She can spot fake approval, because she's so good at giving it.

# CHAPTER FIVE

# martyrdom

"I just wish I didn't have to repeat myself a million times a day. If I could only record myself and just play the tape over and over . . . Like, 'If you eat that piece of cheese, the wrapper doesn't just stay on the counter, you throw it away.' And why am I the only one who can see that the pile of laundry at the foot of the stairs needs to be taken up? And what about the toilet paper? Sometimes I'm sitting there thinking, *Why can't anyone else put toilet paper on the roll?* Someday I'm gonna make the whole family come and sit down and we're gonna have a lesson."

# welcome to her worst day ever (so far)

Ask a woman about her busy life and you'll be smacked in the face with the realities of her never-ending to-do list, the marker of Martyrdom. The Half Truth of Martyrdom is women's irresistible need to express and describe the minute details of her daily stresses so that others understand just how overworked and sometimes overwhelmed she feels.

## she has a right to complain

Women *are* the gatekeepers, family doctors, caretakers, shoppers, and wallet watchers of America, even as more men, especially Gen Y dads, start to pitch in. With increasing numbers of single moms, divorcees, and widows, there are more women left holding the bag.

Just as the legendary martyrs endured bizarre, medieval torture as sacrifice for the greater good, women grin and bear it while compensating for everyone else's deficiencies, from the smallest irritation, such as the empty toilet paper holder, to the bigger issues of their family's welfare. But even the most capable women can't conceal the frustration that bubbles beneath the surface, ready to erupt. Yet, underneath the resentment, women are proud and even possessive of their role as chief operating officer of the household. Here's an example of a woman's pride and unwillingness to delegate: "We have our own business and I run it. I wake up between 4:30 and 5:00 a.m. to get everything done. We have four children, three schools. It works better if I'm the one multitasking because I have more patience. But I'm mentally tired."

A woman's motive for voicing Martyrdom to marketers isn't to get rid of responsibilities. She just wants to be heard. In a survey on Parenting.com, 60% of moms feel they don't tell their friends what they're going through in their lives, so they crave someone—anyone—who will listen.

When women wax on about their sacrifices, marketers react in one of two ways: They shut down because they really don't want to deal ("Not my department!"), or they go overboard with sympathy and stumble headfirst into her rage.

An example of this is the public flogging of **MOTRIN**, the analgesic marketed by the **MCNEIL CONSUMER HEALTHCARE** division of **JOHNSON & JOHNSON**.

Motrin had developed a strong profile among moms by positioning itself as "Mom's Motrin," solving the aches and pains that come from the physical strains of raising children. Their brand personality was well matched to women's truth: in control and impatient with pain that interfered with busy motherhood. But a single commercial where they tried to apply that brand empathy to new moms got slammed in the blogosphere and bashed in mainstream media. Motrin seemingly interpreted the Half Truth of Martyrdom too literally with a well-intentioned ad that focused on baby slings, the fabric baby carriers so popular today.

**She says it because it's true, but she repeats it to make a point.**

In the spot, Motrin linked the sling to back pain, a legitimate way for the brand to strike a chord with new moms. But in an effort to be on mom's sides, the cheeky copy and snarky tone struck out, making the product's user seem self-centered by complaining about backaches from slings.

Though meant to be humorous, the commercial enraged mom bloggers who lashed out and put their own video testimonials on YouTube. The division's vice president posted an apology and, within days, withdrew the spot. In the pre-Internet age, that anger might have amounted to a few nasty letters to the J&J Consumer Info Center; instead the ad incited a public hanging.

If only Motrin had tapped into the Whole Truth that yes, mom's back hurts from carrying a baby, but that pain is a small price for the nurturing value of slings. How could this have been avoided? The ad had all the markings of being written by a junior copywriter pregnant for the first time. A big brand like Motrin should have enlisted a squadron of moms to either contribute to this creative effort or at least vet the copy for a more inclusive tone.

Lessons learned? Women expect both consistency and authenticity from brands they love. Stay true to who you are, even as you court women. The brand was built on a supportive voice, not a sarcastic one. Tread carefully when your brand attempts empathy with Martyrdom. And don't take her complaints at face value. When probed, she'll admit that she actually feels stronger for enduring life's hardships; not to mention, she knows she brings much of her "misery" on herself.

## the Whole Truths behind Martyrdom

Ironically, the Whole Truth is that even though a woman might present herself as an overwrought victim, much of her stress is admittedly self-inflicted and she knows it. She's the one who volunteered to organize the carpool. She's the one who filled her calendar with promises.

Women willingly take on most of their to-dos, and given the choice, wouldn't revise the commitments they've made.

Another Whole Truth is that deep down, women believe that without their leadership, nothing would ever get done . . . certainly not well. We've heard women tell stories of their everyday efforts to orchestrate order with families who seem oblivious. One mom told Tracy a story about her family's chronic lateness: "Sometimes I scream, 'Doesn't anyone around here wear a watch? How come I'm the only one who is always watching the clock?'" Tracy asked, "What would happen if you didn't?" The mom looked at her incredulously and then said, with a semi-straight face, "No one would get anywhere on time."

Most marketers wouldn't have poked at what the woman said as Tracy did. But making her recognize that she inflated some of her overwork helped clarify what her Whole Truth really is, which is that she's convinced she does it better than anyone else.

Still, whether it's the pride of female machismo (she can do it all), or her conviction of superiority (no one else can do what she does), some women are unwilling to step away from their self-imposed servitude.

How can a marketer sing her praises to their brand's benefit? **TYSON CHICKEN** tried with a campaign called "Thank You," which wobbled on the tightrope between saluting and insulting overworked moms.

In the TV spots, Tyson featured a mom cooking up an easy meal of chicken pieces, while her kids and husband performed a deadpan, mock tribute. As Dad silently held up his boom box blasting faux Olympic music, the son solemnly thanked Mom. In his next breath, the son suggested that since she'd mastered the quick meal, she'd have more time to help him with his homework. In essence, he was saying, "Thanks, Mom, now do more for me." We haven't seen sales figures on whether this tactic worked, but we'd be shocked if most moms didn't want to club the creative director with a skillet.

Contending with Martyrdom is the trickiest Half Truth. Just talking about Martyrdom and women in the same breath begs for a fight. Indeed, to women, the "martyr" label is an insult. Still, women are quick to jump on the Martyrdom bandwagon, given the chance.

# the phenomenon of "out-martyring"

The Half Truth of Martyrdom is so pervasive because it's contagious. Just picture several women standing in line at the supermarket checkout and one woman sighs, "I'm tired." Cue the inevitable chorus

# Since she feels that she's the unsung heroine, the marketer's job is to jump on that Whole Truth bandwagon and either reward her for all she's doing, take something annoying off her plate, or make it easier/faster/more fun to do those things she won't let go of.

of "Me, too!" Misery may love company, but sometimes women compete to be the *most* miserable.

If marketers start to ask women about their lives in qualitative research, they're treated to the "out-Martyrdom" phenomenon. As soon as one woman tells her story, she's reflexively out-martyred by others. Marketers who hear multiple women describe hardships and stress, can be misled. What they might not realize is that women pile on for reasons of their own—to wear and share the badge, to be part of the group, to validate their own lives.

**Tune into her martyrdom, don't wallow in it.**

We saw a great example of this martyr fever at a big retailer event we hosted a few years ago where I moderated an onstage consumer discussion on stress.

One woman on the panel talked about her lack of a boyfriend. Another mom of one ticked through her typical day, starting with a 6:45 a.m. wakeup. Another mentioned a stressful job.

The audience was getting a little restless so I invited questions. Instead, I got speeches. One woman declared, "Let me tell you about *my* typical day. I get up at 5 a.m., I have four kids, two jobs, and more headaches than I can count." Then another: "I want to say to that woman with no boyfriend, I'm sorry, but I'm your age and I have this life-threatening disease" . . . and on and on. What started as feedback escalated to competition.

The women onstage felt one-upped, and the women in the audience dug deeper into their own miseries. When women do this during research, a marketer may assume a higher level of unhappiness than is really true . . . and overreact.

# la, la, la, i can't hear you

Another challenge of the Half Truth of Martyrdom is that marketers have a hard time listening to women talk about their stressed lives.

Marketers recoil when women bemoan how busy they are. To many, women's Martyrdom conjures the annoying and unappealing image of a whiner. (And that's not the picture of the customer they want to have.) So often, when we show videos of women mired in Martyrdom, marketers get pulled into their quicksand of complaints. Additionally, this Half Truth of Martyrdom puts marketers, especially male ones on the defensive. We can tell this is happening when male clients start citing all the examples of how in their well-balanced families, men do all the heavy lifting.

**Stress is not a contest.**

As a marketer, beware of competing with women's stress, especially if she's your customer. As we love to say, "Stress is not a contest." Even if it were, you've got to let your customer win.

## help solve her stress

Women can be incredibly empathetic, but they love to play the pity card, so successful marketers need to base ideas on solving stress rather than compete with it or amplify it. The first step is getting the facts, not just the feelings.

To help linen manufacturer **WELSPUN** come up with new concepts for sheets and bedding, we conducted a sleep survey to understand women's needs and opportunities. We knew that women everywhere feel a desperate need for more sleep, but we wanted to discover the biggest culprit keeping them up at night.

The survey revealed that stress was the leading villain at 54%, followed by women blaming their nighttime scrolling to-do lists. This information opened up naming opportunities and even new ways for fabrics to help fight incessant tossing for more stress-free sleep.

Another marketer, **SEALY POSTUREPEDIC**, was smart enough to see the opportunity in the stress–sleep war. Rather than harping on the elusive eight hours of sleep that are so far out of reach, Sealy promises "Get A Better Six," playing to the Whole Truth of a woman's

dream of even six uninterrupted hours. What woman wouldn't kill for six hours of zzzs? The lesson? Listen to the Whole Truth behind her Half Truth of Martyrdom to learn how you can redefine your product in her terms and you may find you can reposition your current offering into a Whole Truth winner.

A business that's plagued with consumers' stress management is the airline industry, and some brands have navigated this better than others. While both men and women business travelers will trumpet the very true Martyrdom refrain, "I'm so exhausted by business travel," women, especially those with kids waiting at home, take the indignities of travel personally. **CONTINENTAL AIRLINES** was the first to roll out the red carpet at check-in (in their case, it was blue) so that all Elite members, even the straggling latecomers, could bypass the long line of nonmembers. The blue carpet practically shouted, "We know you travel constantly, so here's one annoyance you can take off your plate." They also seem to be the most aggressive about filling any empty business class seat with worthy upgrade candidates, again a life raft for a woman on the edge.

## the Whole Truth evolution

The more we've studied this Half Truth, the more we've seen it evolve. Over the last couple of years, we have started to notice another trend. Even the busiest women are finding all kinds of ways to play hooky by either accepting less ambitious goals for themselves or secretly doing fun stuff, like spending hours online under the guise of work.

In research we did for megasite **ABOUT.COM**, women, claiming they are doing research for their families, admitted that they quickly drift into shopping, downloading from iTunes, playing games, posting product reviews, and just zoning out on favorite blogs and sites.

If women are so pressed for time, you'd think surfing the Internet would be squeezed into the scarce wee hours. But though midnight

pops for women's online usage, the Whole Truth is she's online all day—at her computer in the office, her BlackBerry in the checkout line, checking her cell when she awakes. Interestingly, moms of young kids, likely the most time-squeezed women, are online the most.

Brands that create escapes for women find that they are only too willing to spend their time and money, when the reason is right. Look at the hours spent posting e-pinions and downloading music. How many women get intoxicated with the craft details on etsy or the product descriptions on eBay? **TRIPADVISOR** is a delicious way to fantasize about potential vacations, and photo websites such as **KODAKGALLERY** have women cataloguing memories like professionals. All these activities take time women are willing to give, no matter how crammed their schedules are. Don't assume that "I'm too busy" means she is. She's only too busy for what's boring or unrewarding.

## Internet Usage

Is the Internet an escape from busyness or a cause?
- More than half of all moms are online one to five hours a day.
- More than 36 million moms read or write blogs.

## Whole Truths, segmented by stage

Marketers also need to know that all stress is not created equal. And Martyrdom offers all kinds of segmentation opportunities. A young woman may tell you that her schedule of school, work, and social

# The Half Truth of Martyrdom can either scare you into just leaving women alone or encourage you to create products and services that ease their stress or help them escape. The choice is yours.

life is just too overwhelming. An Alpha Mom (a media darling who's supposedly maniacally monitoring her family's every move) will tell you that her biggest stress is keeping her highly organized life under control. A boomer woman will tell you she's just weary of putting up with stupid people. Fine-tune the Martyrdom of a segment and you'll find ways to solve it.

For instance, we see a booming market in what we call Beta Moms, women who are doing the best they can with what they have, constantly reshuffling the to-do lists of their lives in order to survive. Her house might not be perfectly clean, but as one woman told us, "The president isn't coming for dinner, so it's all right."

Bestselling books like *Peeing in Peace* and *I Was a Perfect Mom Until I Had Kids* are clarion calls to the millions of women who have decided that good enough has to be good enough. Yes, Beta Mom may sound a lot less camera ready than Alpha Mom, but she's the mother who's the engine of the economy. So marketers have found ways to play to her special brand of Martyrdom.

**KFC**'s "What's for Dinner" campaign managed to transform a bucket of fried chicken into a healthy, nutritious meal option for Beta Moms, despite its superhigh calorie count. The selling point? At least, it's easy

and counts as a sit-down hot meal that moms can pick up on the way home from work. With the introduction of Kentucky Grilled Chicken, which surely was designed to appeal to mom's guilt, if not her Good Intentions for lighter fare, KGC for dinner is likely to become a staple. (Oprah offering a coupon for a free KGC meal didn't hurt, either!)

Other marketers capitalizing on making life easier for Beta Moms are **OSCAR MAYER LUNCHABLES** premade lunch kits and **SMUCKERS UNCRUSTABLES** frozen PB&J sandwiches (both successes because they make "easy" easier). And since beverage maker **MOTT'S** knows moms add water to cut the sugar content of juices, they created Motts for Tots, which is essentially juice diluted with water that's "vitamin-fortified" to give Mom a cover for buying it instead of just turning on the tap.

# how to avoid the Half Truth of Martyrdom

1. When you invite women to share the difficulties of their stress, try to shut down your personal reactions and focus instead on how you can solve their problems with escape valves and time savers.

2. Humor works, but vet your creative work carefully first with a woman. Don't wallow in a woman's misery, but don't treat it so lightly that she thinks you are making fun of her.

3. Build in a cover story benefit for buying or using your product so that she can keep her martyr badge shiny, even as she buys or enjoys what you're selling.

# ego protection

A few months ago I was shopping for sexy evening shoes, a Rorschach test for any woman's mojo. Ballet flats are practical for everyday, but stilettos keep a woman in the game.

All around me, 20-something shoppers were picking out the most gorgeous and painful-looking styles, while I kept looking for the perfect pair of great but not too high sandals. But suddenly I spotted *them*. I picked up a pair of superhigh, sparkly Stuart Weitzman pumps and asked the balding salesman for them in my size. (I only mention "balding" to give you a heads up where this is headed.)

He brought them out and I slipped them on (or rather tried to stuff my toes inside) and gingerly stepped to the mirror, feeling not quite like a Vegas showgirl but darn close. I asked casually if he had the next bigger size and he said no. But I was smitten, and I couldn't take them off. I said to him, "Maybe I can make these work." And he looked at me, shook his head, and whispered, "When you get to be *our* age, you don't do dumb things the second time around. You need to order a bigger size."

*Our* age? *Second* time around? But I'm only . . . !

Somehow the shoes had lost their shine.

Ego-shattering moments lurk just around the bend for women of every age and at every stage of life, like being asked when you're due when you're not even pregnant, or being called "ma'am" for the first time (yes, we know it's a courtesy but not when you're only 32).

In everyday life, women dodge the slings and arrows hurled their way in the form of left-handed compliments or unintended disrespect. It's bad enough when a teen son rejects his mom's friend request on Facebook; it's unforgiveable when women feel dissed or underestimated by the products they buy and the people they buy from. So it's not surprising that women adopt the coping mechanism of Ego Protection, the fourth Half Truth, to shore up their best beliefs about who they are.

# believing her own Half Truth

This Half Truth of Ego Protection is pervasive and addictive. Some women will repeat their alter-ego stories so often that they begin to believe them. Their Half Truths become kind of überwishful thinking that's deeply internalized and believed.

Why does this matter to marketers? If you're a technology marketer and your prospective customer presents herself in research as a "techie" but hasn't even taken her new digital camera out of the box, and you tailor your new high-tech toy for her maximum utility, prepare for a sales shortfall. If she walks into your auto dealership with her midlife ego starving for a sexy convertible and you steer her toward the sedans, prepare to meet her wrath. (One 60-plus woman told us that she was in the market for a sporty two-seater, one seat for her, and the other for her purse.) Unfortunately for marketers, women become artful dodgers when their ego is threatened, and public exposure in research or at the counter is just that kind of threat.

# meet the real women inside

As a marketer, you need to know that you are marketing to at least two women with every *one* you sell to—the woman you see and the woman you don't.

What we've observed from a decade of interviewing women is that many have adopted what Sigmund Freud first identified as the "ego-ideal" (or in our words, the idealized ego), a perfected version of themselves, their talents, or personalities, even when untrue. Dr. Freud traced the roots of this idealized self to childhood narcissism, where, as young girls, women yearned to be seen as perfect in their parents' eyes. As adults, and perhaps under the glare of a marketer's microscope or the scrutiny of other authority figures, women protect that idealized ego as the expression of their best (happier, smarter, prettier, younger) self. Their endgame might be being loved, admired, or just recognized as special by those they respect or fear.

Women present themselves as whom they choose to be, depending on circumstances, and channel the persona that works for them. Sometimes those personalities have been nurtured for years, other times they are just responses to the issue at hand. At the parent–teacher conference,

the working woman wants to be taken seriously as a dedicated mom, so she dresses casually and stashes her BlackBerry inside her purse. The 50-something mother of the bride tells the bridal shop owner that she's content with whatever simple dress doesn't outshine her daughter's, but inwardly sees herself making her big entrance to the ensuing gasps of "Wow! She *can't* be the mother!" Today's new grandmothers have taken to refusing the "Grandma" moniker, asking for "Glamma" or their first names instead.

These assumed or hidden identities are really a form of Ego Protection, a way for women to shield their fears and promote their inner hopes by crafting a self-image for the outside world. Marketers might be surprised at who's inside.

**As a marketer, you need to know you are marketing to at least two women with every one you sell to—the woman you see and the woman you don't.**

For example, a financial service advisor may assume he's selling securities to a successful careerist, who's prepared to make a deal. But the astute broker might notice that she's dragging her feet on the decision. Why? Inside, that same woman may be an anxious and skeptical worrier who's suffering from bag lady syndrome, fearful that she will lose all her money one day and turn to selling apples on the corner.

The wealth management group of **US TRUST** hit this dual personality nail on the head with a commercial that showed a confident businesswoman and described her this way: "She owns a villa in St. Barths, a condo in Sun Valley . . . yet a part of her still lives in a cul de sac in (smalltown) Ohio." The bank recognized that even a financial highflier can be a conservative investor. Only by reading her right on the outside can you get the chance to mine the deeper, more profound insights within.

It is interesting that the current economic downturn is breeding a new kind of Ego Protection, where even someone who could afford to chill in St. Barth's will proclaim they're staycationing instead, to show prudence and avoid the whiff of wastefulness.

# marketer's ego check

Maybe marketers get fooled by this Half Truth because they're caught up in an Ego Protection game of their own. Examine the profile of your target customer in your brand strategy. We get a kick out of how many ad agencies describe their client's ideal customer as . . . ideal. Let's face it. We're not going to hear this descriptor: She's an overweight, undisciplined woman with a poor self-image and a big dose of resentment toward skinny people. (But wouldn't approaching the project from this angle encourage the most amazing creative work?!)

A more typical strategy is the figment of an agency's aspirations: "Our customer is young, attractive, fashionable, has a good sense of style and humor and a Portuguese Water Spaniel, likes to Tweet while eating Pinkberry, and has an active social life."

With one retail client, we recruited women **She's NOT** based on their own store's credit card reports, so **our customer!** we knew they were the brand's legitimate high spenders. Yet the retailer was so uncomfortable being confronted with the "wrong women" who didn't fit their idealized customer image that we actually posted annual product spend under each woman's photograph in our report to help underline the truth.

Your own Ego Protection can undermine your business success. If you can't love your brand for what it is and who it's for, then it's time to shove your ego and your résumé out the door.

# branding her ego

The most obvious place where ego comes in to play in marketing is in the most aspirational brand names, particularly those designer names that function as badges. In those categories, which are conspicuous when used or worn, your product itself is a surrogate for a woman's ego. It's not new news that a designer label adds ego cachet.

The ego play of designer names or expert celebrities at mass-retail features a parade of Martha Stewart, Emeril Lagasse, and Rachel Ray, who are marketed across media, from product to in-store appearances to ads. Their success plays to the truth that women may pretend not to care about endorsements, but they really do. But how can a marketer know when a woman's telling the truth about whether a designer works for your brand?

One way is to be sure she knows whose name she's dropping. For one project, we were so convinced that women were exaggerating just how much they really knew some designer names that we tucked in a fictitious brand between Donna Karan and Calvin Klein in our list of names to check off as labels they owned. Check, check, check! So much for their label expertise!

Another test is the "coffee test." When you research a series of potential designers or celebrities to endorse a brand, ask women, "Which of these women would you like to meet for a cup of coffee?" It's a great way to weed out the names of celebrities who might be ego inflators but are actually perceived as frenemies.

## is she green or . . . green-ish?

Thanks to the strength of their convictions, women often make marketers think trends are bigger than they are. The green trend, for example, is a case of women being selectively honest. Women will spout their green credentials effortlessly because it presents them as more conscientious consumers. "I only buy organic." "My home is healthier because of green products." Saying you're exclusively green or that you are scrupulously earth conscious is accurate for some, but we have found it's claimed more often than it's true. Women know that green is good and waste is bad, so after adopting a green behavior or two, they will start to talk as if they're

**Is she as squeaky green as she claims to be?**

actually growing their dinner and recycling the plates, even if their only green gesture is a bottle of Method tile spray in the shower.

A way to judge the degree of Ego Protection is to listen to not only what she *says* she cares about but also how *confidently* she asserts what she says to others.

While the green trend is huge and obviously not retreating, we think that marketers who buy all of women's protestations of perfection in this area could lose their shirts. Note how the economy is affecting the more discretionary green buying. Look at the Rodale magazine *Organic Style*. Actually you can't read it now because it failed, yet it was a clearly targeted magazine, well-researched and before it's time, intended to help women make the decisions they claim to be so important. The magazine teetered between her Half Truth, "I want to be as green as I can be," and her Whole Truth, "I'll go green as long as it still tastes good, looks pretty, and doesn't cost more." Green, organic, natural, locally grown, no matter what the language, intent to purchase is often overturned when pricing comes

## PROTESTING TOO MUCH

Jen cracked up at her own comment while interviewing moms about baby apparel and supplies. One mom killed every idea with her principle of buying only natural products. She knocked down concept after concept for not being squeaky green. In exasperation, as the woman nixed a baby bottle carrier made of sturdy and safe BPA-free plastics, Jen said, "Okay, would you like it if I said it was made of hemp?!"

up. Our take on the Whole Truth? She's "green-ish" and can be more practical than purist.

In work we did on towels, women were excited about a bamboo eco-towel that promised to dry faster in the dryer. Women liked it all right, but their reason was more practical (and selfish!): "I want it to dry *me* faster, and I want it to dry fast on the rack, so that it doesn't get rank and I don't have to wash it as often." What was that about the earth-sustaining bamboo?

We don't mean to underestimate the power of the green movement and the growing number of consumers who try to make choices that sustain the planet. Niche, squeaky green brands like **SEVENTH GENERATION** have penetrated the cleaning aisles of the biggest chains. But mass brands like **CLOROX GREENWORKS** cleaned up by offering a dose of feel-good green clean with the silent but mighty hero name of Clorox to assure germ killing. By securing the imprimatur of the Sierra Club and others, the brand has managed to tread the narrow line between green and effective. And we've heard that many women are displaying their Greenworks products on their countertops, a giveaway to their badge value.

Women are still figuring out their green ground rules. Be careful that you don't assume that the green game she talks will end up as cash in the register at the end of the day.

## playing to her undercover ego

Women lying about their age to strangers is a running joke. But why would a woman conceal the truth about her appearance from people she loves? Often, she's guarding her idealized self-image. But if she's not telling her significant other a key truth, how can you expect her to tell it to you? (One in seven women buy a bridal gown one or more sizes smaller than they wear.)

We like to ask questions that unveil the hidden ego. In a beauty session, we asked women to describe themselves three ways: "What age are you? What age do you feel inside? And what age do people take you for?" The first question was answered accurately. The second answer always drew on her humor: "I'm either 30 or I'm 80. Nothing in between!"

But the third question was the most revealing of her Ego Protection because that's where she was able to admit what she was feeling inside, using her perceptions of others' assessments. Women bragged about being carded or being hit on by younger men. This bravado may be a cover for their Whole Truth that compliments may be harder to come by so they concoct their own. A brand that recognizes that women's fragile egos need a mental hug every once in a while wins.

For years, **EILEEN FISHER** apparel has catered to aging egos with her high-fashion sensibility. Midlife women constantly complain there are no clothes that fit their changing bodies and their only choices are baggy or matronly. Most fashion marketers avoid even showing imagery of older women, for fear of bruising their own youth-obsessed egos!

Eileen Fisher hit on the perfect lifestyle and psychic imagery with a campaign featuring beautiful women, many of them graying, fit but not stick-thin, and most of all happy in their gracefully ageless outfits instead of screaming "This comes with elastic waistbands and an AARP card in the pocket!"

In addition to branding products to convey that you understand women's ego frustrations, it's also key to include features that will pay off your promise. **NOT YOUR DAUGHTER'S JEANS** is a great example of this. The brand understands that women are mocked by their teen daughters for wearing high-waisted, boring "mom jeans" yet are freaked at the idea of muffin-top midriffs over low-cut, skin-tight teen jeans. The jeans, with just enough lycra and edgy attitude, do such a good job connecting with women in a fashionable and comfortable way that they command a price that her ego will happily pay.

Age and appearance issues can stretch beyond fashion and cosmetics into unlikely areas such as healthcare. We were retained by a pharmaceutical company to figure out the barriers to women's interest in hormone therapy. The obvious answers were related to widespread negative media reports and highly publicized product trials. Yet even as those results were mitigated or overturned, women still resisted the drugs. By Power Listening, we discovered that Ego Protection turned out to be the unseen culprit when one 50-year-old admitted that she didn't want to investigate her nagging hot flashes because if her younger husband found out she was menopausal, he'd think she was old.

Why does a marketer care if a woman hides the truth from her husband? In the case of the menopausal patient, marketers need to realize that the barrier to usage can be more than a lack of information or a fear of drug side-effects; her ego faced the block of her own mortality or the risk of losing her appeal. Messaging that helps her see herself as young enough (rather than old enough!) for this product would connect.

## protect her ego with stealth products

In the area of product development, it's important to adapt to the workings of her "idealized ego." Note that her idealized ego is not to be confused with her aspirations. Aspirations are what she dreams of being. Her idealized ego is the composite of who she presents herself as in everyday life. And you've got to observe her in everyday life and conversation to find those loopholes. If she never wears her reading glasses, that's a sign that she's in age denial.

Rather than force women to expose their assumed identities, smart marketers find ways to sneak past women's resistance and fulfill their needs with products that include stealth features.

The **JITTERBUG** phone was invented as an antidote to cell phones with tiny keypads and superfeatures that are de rigueur for younger people. The Jitterbug features large keys, simple features, even the ability to use voice commands for frequently used numbers. While the phone is marketed for older folks with visual limitations or technophobia, many younger consumers have taken a shine to a cell that's a no-brainer and requires no reading glasses to read.

Likewise, **AMAZON'S KINDLE** has a benefit that will be instantly understandable to most boomers: all the downloaded books can be read in the font size you prefer. Though most boomer readers aren't ready to be caught reading large-print books on a bus, a flick of a button on the Kindle allows readers to change the font size undetected by others. The ego remains protected!

Apparel sizing is another ego killer that puts a woman's vital statistics right out on the selling floor. Apparel maker **CHICO'S** brilliantly challenged the traditions of women's sizing that forced any larger women into high double digits. Chico's recognized that women, when not at their ideal weights, didn't want to be relegated to the muumuu ghetto. At Chico's, women are a size one, two, or

three, that's it. Their egos are intact, as are those of millions of like-minded Chico's aficionados.

# bracing for her ego revenge

What's fascinating about a woman's Ego Protection is that she may stew silently until she hits a boiling point with marketers and salespeople that blows her cover. Women, who may be mild or diplomatic under most circumstances, will whip out their evil twin when it's time to duel with errant sales and service people.

When we've asked women to describe their identities as shoppers, they are proud to claim their power. As one woman told us, "I'm a 'you've got one chance to screw up' shopper."

Another woman we interviewed demonstrated her revenge technique on a salesman who made her feel he was too busy to take her call. In what was clearly an oft-repeated performance, she mimicked her best imperious voice, as she raved at the hapless receptionist, "You tell your boss, this is an *escalated* phone call, use that *word* and tell him *I want service right now!*" As the other women in the group applauded, I could see her relax into the knowledge that this story only got better with the telling, securing her place as queen of customer service revenge.

> I'm a you've-got-one-chance-to-screw-up shopper!

Marketers of services faced with an irate customer like this can figure out whether her anger is real or manufactured by starting with the magic words, "You're right. Now, how can I make this better for you?" Play to her ego; all she's really wanting is the respect she deserves—and to not be seen as the cowering, customer chump.

In the car business, moms will say that one of the toughest rites of passage is the moment they are faced with the inevitable minivan

## MINIVAN **REVENGE**

Jen adds this dose of Whole Truth revenge to a mini-van purchase: The birth of my twins and an exodus from the city to the 'burbs turned my life upside down. But it was buying a minivan that nearly killed me. I went to the **HONDA** dealer kicking and screaming, but the choice was out of my hands. If we wanted the infant car seats to fit in the car and have room for a spare adult, we had to take the plunge. I was floating in the air looking down on someone else's life. How could I drive it and still hold my head up high? But my husband and I bought a loaded Odyssey and I immediately tried to protect my ego. I even coined a new acronym (MUV, multiuse vehicle) so we wouldn't have to utter the word minivan. It didn't stick. I decided the only way I was going to teach this minivan a lesson was if the first time I drove it, I wore stilettos. After the inaugural ride, I felt much better. And since then, I've even driven it in my pajamas.

decision. As much as women will try to stall or delay, the arrival of multiple little ones and their friends forces the minivan moment.

Rather than try to talk women out of their minivan resentment, **VOLKSWAGEN** turned the tables with a humorous campaign featuring Brooke Shields. In one spot, she deadpans, "There's an epidemic sweeping our nation. Women everywhere are having babies just to get the Volkswagen Routan. Have a baby for love, not for German engineering." In an online long-form ad, she fronts a mockumentary that shows how the baby boom is really an excuse to allow parents to buy the Routan. Brooke literally switches the irritation of minivan revenge to unbridled minivan desire. This creative jujitsu is a genius way to anticipate and understand her Ego Protection and convert it to your brand's advantage.

# detecting her ego trap

One area where women are superguarded about their egos is with luxury or higher-priced purchases. Outing their true identity requires some clever espionage. We once asked women who claimed they were luxury shoppers to bring their favorite shoes to a department store's research session. Funny how the lower priced, scuffed-up "comfort brands" dominated the room! (Maybe the Manolos inspired their visits, but Naturalizers filled their closets.)

Cosmetics usage is another mixed bag. Most women use a mix of expensive and cheaper brands, but will name-drop the fancier products when they are with other women. Worse, they will tell an online survey that they exclusively use brands that they may have only tried once. Ask a woman to empty her purse on the spot. If she says she only wears department store cosmetics, see what falls out onto her lap—Vaseline lip balm or Chanel gloss?

In our conversations with women, they are more open with us than with most other people. Sometimes, they don't have to open their purses, or their jackets! In sessions we did discussing the meaning of femininity, one woman in work boots and jeans literally pulled back her EMS uniform to reveal her "hoochie bra," as she called it, the symbol of who she really was inside.

If you're not quite that personal with your customers, then ask them to bring something to your research session that might reveal a truth that she may be hiding. When doing work for **SPECIAL K**, we asked women to bring clothes that didn't fit any longer but that they were still hoping to wear and couldn't bear to toss. Women brought dresses three sizes too small, jeans lingering from college days, all garments that spoke to their true identities. Both the sizes and the sexier styling of those lost outfits taught us about their aspirations, as well as how far they'd go to fit into them again.

We were most amazed at how convinced each woman was that inside she was still the woman who was sexier or younger than the woman sitting before us. While it's tempting to respond to this situation with "we love you the way you are" advertising, the Whole Truth is that women see themselves as their better selves. That's why Special K, an extraordinarily successful brand, continues to hold out the hope of the tight jeans or the slinky red dress, even if they are a few pounds beyond that. Market to the truth in *her* mirror, that's what she's buying.

# how to avoid the Half Truth of Ego Protection

1. Remember each woman harbors some degree of Ego Protection and may be describing her ideal self to you rather than her real self. Try on-the-spot surprise questions to keep her "perfect script" at bay.

2. Taking her ideal ego seriously does not mean being serious. Humor is one of the best ways to be frontal about what she's hiding inside.

3. Zigging when competitors zag can help you own a woman's unspoken fantasies better than conforming to category norms.

# secret keeping

**Search**

[                    ]

[ search ]

**RSS Feeds**

» Entries RSS

» Comments RSS

**Subscribe by Email**

[                    ]

(email address)

[ submit ]

Preview | Powered by FeedBlitz

**Recent Posts**

» Clean Water for Loggee

‹ Our Family Vacation                    My Insane Day at the Office »

## Spilling My Guts

Posted by Cecilia on Friday, February 20th

It's after midnight here in Michigan, where I am visiting with friends and family. I am surrounded daily by love and attention and support.

So why am I awake and crying?

Because for many months I've been hiding my health issues. Ok, maybe hiding isn't the best word. But since about ...oh, last year Christmas I've failed to mention to you - the people whom I tell EVERYTHING- that I've been sick. So tonight I'm awake and crying because yet ANOTHER symptom has appeared in this long and exhausting road

---

**F**ormer supermodel Tyra Banks, enraged by media criticism of her extra pounds, walked onto the set of her TV talk show, wearing a red swimsuit and a sign that read "160," her weight, in defiant, giant numbers. Surprise! The entire studio audience did the same.

Teenage girls email naked self-portraits to high school boyfriends and sadly, the entire class gets a peek.

New moms describe every detail of labor on their blogs and post videos of every one of their child's burps and bumps on YouTube for millions to share.

Do women really keep secrets anymore? In this culture of confession, with Oprah as high priestess, why would anyone keep a secret when telling them is so easy? In a real-time, digital, Twitter world, where every private thought can be broadcast in a split second, Are today's women just more calculating about what they reveal and what they conceal? How many women post their most flattering (if out of date) pictures on Facebook? Ever read someone's supposedly accurate profile on Match.com?

The Whole Truth is that women share those secrets, online and off, that portray them the way they like to be perceived and support the personalities they aspire to. Conversely, they safeguard the secrets that damage that image.

Secrets don't have to be damaging. They can be "little white secrets." Ask a beauty marketer how many women play down their sins of self-inflicted sun damage while bragging that they wear SPFs all the time. Ask a pharmaceutical marketer how many female consumers promise compliance, yet double down on dosage based on their own doctoring. Ask a furniture marketer how many women claim to have modern, simple taste, yet actually fill their houses with overstuffed furniture and knickknack collections?

You say you don't keep secrets? Is there a small blip on your resume that seems to have been deleted? Was there an event in your life you've never confessed to your spouse? Ever eat a cookie in the bathroom? Keeping secrets is something we learn to do when we are as young as three or four years old. Holding some things inside is part of human nature.

So if you think women don't keep secrets from you, you're in for an awakening. We've certainly exposed more than our share of them.

## why she hides

While this entire book dissects those Half Truths that women tell you, this chapter will take on those secrets that are conscious. Secret Keeping is the collection of deliberate behaviors motivated by women's deeper reasons to hide: shame, embarrassment, pride, self-delusion, and fear. Her Secret Keeping can be a means of preserving denial, of withholding trust, or of safe-guarding personal relationships from prying eyes. And sometimes, Secret Keeping is just her private way of telling the world, "None of your business!"

When Secret Keeping squelches key information you need to know, it can undermine your plans in a big way. Some marketers have nonetheless figured out how to crack the code, but many others are unknowingly in the dark, wondering why she's not buying or believing what their brands have to say. This chapter should turn on the light.

Why do women keep secrets from others and from the marketers who want their business? Naturally, the reasons vary depending on how big the secret, but here are a few we've noticed. We'll start with the more innocent ones and work up to the serious whoppers.

## secrets she proudly hides or flaunts

Some secrets are meant to be shared, as social currency. Women love the idea of a secret because it bestows credibility and insider power on the teller and then when she spreads the word, she blesses the "tell-ee" as a co-conspirator. The fashion industry understands this idea of a fascinating game of "insider" deception. An example is a brand like **ZARA**, exploding globally thanks to the company's talent for quickly adapting designer trends into more accessibly priced apparel. It's both a best-kept insider's secret and a bragging point for women.

She gets to decide whether to squirrel away the price tag or flash it as social currency among like-minded friends.

In a tight economy, keeping shopping secrets is becoming an Olympic sport for higher income women who feel compelled to hide whatever they spend rather than appear shallow. The frugal rich are finding themselves shipping purchases rather than being seen toting designer bags while others scrimp and bargain shop.

We've come a long way from hair coloring that "only your hairdresser knows for sure" to bragging about how we've whitened our teeth, injected our lines, or pumped up body parts. Know whether your brand is a secret she wants to keep or one she'll proudly broadcast.

# chagrined into silence

Secrets about small transgressions or life's everyday mistakes keep brand marketers from getting at a woman's Whole Truth. Sometimes her smallest "bad" behaviors will loom large in a woman's mind and she'll block your access. Will she tell you how many hours she really spent downloading music instead of organizing her home office? Did she really convince the kids to clean their rooms as promised or did she do it herself because she does it better and faster? Sometimes these small secrets make the difference in a creative strategy.

For example, while women today like to refer to their homes as "comfortable" and aren't that worked up about housekeeping faux pas, they do feel some of the blame when things aren't up to snuff.

Successful brands fix the small mistakes so that there's no emotional blowback on women. Bounty's new campaign "Bring It" recently veered from years of focusing on the annoyance of kids' spills to moms treating acci-

dents as nonevents. Likewise, products that provide instant amnesty, like Procter & Gamble's **TIDE-TO-GO**, **MR. CLEAN MAGIC ERASER**, or **FEBREZE**, get rid of life's small embarrassments so that women don't even have to try to hide the stains or smudges or smells that give away spotty cleaning habits. It's not that women won't divulge these "secret" problems, it's that they will downplay their importance

Half Truth:
"Our home is the one where everyone can come and put their feet up."

Whole Truth:
"I feel the pressure to always be ready, but I make it seem like I don't."

because they're bothered that they reflect on them, even when it's not their fault.

Some products are actually designed to guard her secrets of chagrin, like **SPANX**, the booming "foundation" garment brand. Spanx has built an entire business out of hiding unwanted bumps, lumps, and cellulite. Women know that they can get away with a few extra pounds if they're wearing this highly elastic underwear. The brand was pretty undercover until actress Gwyneth Paltrow appeared on Oprah, just weeks after giving birth, and confessed that she was wearing two pairs of Spanx to fit into her skirt. Instant bragging rights for a secret!

Are there other marketing opportunities in these chagrin-inducing secrets? Case in point: women might not like to confess that they spend many hours online at work, researching travel plans or playing poker. By getting her to come clean about when and where she's online (without marking her as a slacker!), advertisers can discover her attention apertures, no matter what time of day. That's why brands from **POTTERY BARN** to **J.CREW** pop-up online all day long to attract the deskbound shopper. As one working woman said to us, "I'd rather order it online and wait for it than waste my lunch hour in line at the Gap with the locusts at the mall waiting for that same black turtleneck."

One thing to remember about these small chagrin-inducing secrets is that you shouldn't rub them in. While advertisers are long past the annoying "Ring around the collar" harangues of **WISK** laundry detergent, there are still examples of companies who seem to think it's funny to show women having to deal with the grime of life. Give women a break! Make the dirt fun, like the **SWIFFER** campaign that humorously shows a woman's old-fashioned but ineffective mop begging to get her back, like a rejected boyfriend. That's putting chagrin where it belongs . . . behind her.

# silent pride and embarrassment

When a woman harbors a secret that is tied deeply to her feelings of either failure or disappointing others, she's hiding secrets of shame. These are the kind of secrets that keep healthcare marketers up at night. For instance, from an early age, women are expected and wired to be strong guardians of their families and loved ones. But when their own illness compromises their caretaking, women will try to keep symptoms secret to avoid "wasting time" going to the doctor or getting a prescription. The Whole Truth? Women are often too proud to say that they're scared and too embarrassed to admit they need help. How can you sell a cure to someone who's hiding out?

For instance, incontinence sufferers mask a problem that is just too publicly embarrassing to share aloud. Women are willing to laugh about the occasional leak when they sneeze but shy away from acknowledging the hugely restrictive effect of serious incontinence, like having to mentally map where every restroom is or stashing extra underwear in their glove compartments. So they withhold the gory details, not just from marketers, but also from doctors and family members.

Ethnography is a great way to get at what's too embarrassing for group discussion. Tracy filmed a woman with incontinence who shared her system for back-up bed linens and another who confessed the toll the problem was taking on her marriage. That video was helpful to the creative teams developing the messaging, as well as for their audience of doctors, who needed a dose of women's reality to up their own empathy levels and interviewing techniques.

And how can a marketer create advertising to appeal to a woman when she squirms at even the mention of your product? Finding ways through humor or new language or stealth marketing is often an answer.

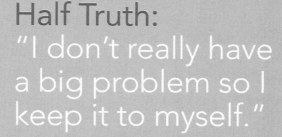

Some brands creatively cope with embarrassing secrets. **ATTENDS** Healthcare products are shipped from **WALGREENS'** online pharmacy in discreet packaging so customers don't have to be red faced with the delivery guy. **WOMEN'S TYLENOL** Menstrual Relief, which we named, purposely packaged itself in purple so that husbands sent out on menstrual reconnaissance missions at night could just grab the "purple one" and not make a mistake.

Secret Keeping is not only a mom or boomer issue. Young women have been known to keep secrets from their doctors on everything from sexual activity to drinking and smoking to avoid reprimands or embarrassment. And doctors play the secret avoiders when they don't want to deal with a long conversation about sex in their 15 minutes of patient time.

While it's an easy laugh to see women trying not to be seen buying a pregnancy kit in a drugstore, more marketers in the feminine categories would be wise to help her keep a little dignity in the aisle, or the "pink ghetto" as Jen calls it. Perhaps the best efforts belong to **TAMPAX**, who've taken a cue from younger women's comfort with "down there" and lightened up the tone of the category with commercials that brought tampons front and center, like using one to stop a leak in a rowboat on a date, so that no one needs to feel weird in the drugstore aisle.

## protecting self-delusion

Women will purposely keep some secrets from you as a way to keep themselves in a blissful state of denial. Smoking cessation is a category where this is chronic.

When Jen was interviewing women who had registered as smokers in advance, she was surprised when several said they didn't smoke. "But you are a smoker, aren't you?" she asked. One woman answered, "No,

I'm not a smoker because I don't buy cigarettes. I just bum them from my girlfriends after work."

Several other women agreed with that same train of thought, hiding their secret for such a long time that they denied the behavior they were actually doing.

Marketers who contend with serious Secret Keeping would be well advised to put themselves personally into the dialogue. To put one group at ease, Jen admitted that she herself had smoked, which not only opened them up but let them know that there was no fooling someone who'd clearly been there.

The women, so committed to concealing their habit, demonstrated the inconvenient and extreme lengths of Secret Keeping. One respondent drove a mile away from her office parking lot to catch a smoke on break. A mom said she only smoked in the backyard so her kids couldn't see. Anyone who's ever loved a smoker knows the smell lingers no matter how much mouthwash or fragrance is involved, and yet mature women had such a deep need to preserve their secret that they believed they weren't getting caught.

By refusing to disclose these delusional secrets, women keep the truth from being real or inviting the displeasure of others, as if denying the secret makes it untrue.

Imagine how much this Secret Keeping limited the potential target audience for smoking-cessation products that would "out" women's habit. That's why **NICODERM** patches come in clear instead of just beige bandage colors, and **COMMIT** gum could pass for a blister pack of Trident to hide the cure that would give away the habit.

How can a marketer sell women a product that solves a problem they won't admit they even have? **GLAXOSMITHKLINE** took an interesting tack when, rather than present the obvious and well-known cancer dangers of smoking, they took a backdoor approach by connecting smoking to aging skin. It's a fact that smokers get a grayish tinge to their skin, lines around their mouths from the puffing action, and premature, deep facial lines. By presenting Commit as a product that could slow, even reverse, the aging signs from smoking, marketers made women take notice.

When a woman is in denial, the burden is on the marketer to search for language, imagery, and benefits that she's willing to talk about. Call it camouflage marketing, but it works.

## the pain of shame

The "worst" kind of secrets women keep are likely those that relate to something as serious as contending with addiction or a past trauma. The toll of guarding this kind of secret weighs heavy on a woman's heart, but the risk of confessing comes at too high a price.

Marketers in the public service space grapple with this all the time. Several years ago, in order to help create sensitive public service messaging for victims of domestic abuse, **LIFETIME TELEVISION** assigned us to figure out the right words to use to connect with abused women.

We proceeded very, very carefully. Though we'd assembled prior abuse victims, at first, none even acknowledged it. We recognized that only by Power Listening, slowly letting women tell their stories, at their pace and timing, could we learn what we needed to know.

A technique I used in that situation was to share my own story, not of abuse but of receiving frightening, anonymous phone calls. That was a way to remove the stigma that it was "their" problem and create a safe haven that encouraged a brave woman to share her story, which inspired others to follow.

The **PARTNERSHIP FOR A DRUG-FREE AMERICA** organization wanted to probe the mindset of moms troubled by their kid's early drug experimentation. At first, women were in a state of "not my kid" denial, despite the fact that prior to the sessions they had all admitted that their kids had problems.

Tracy worried that the one outspoken mom felt suddenly exposed as the lone truth teller in the group. Tracy said, "Everyone in this room is in a similar situation. Don't feel that you're the only one. We can all learn from each other." By normalizing something shameful, Tracy was able to get other women to share the information we needed to help the Partnership.

Women will hide secrets of shame from those who come across as judges rather than as counselors and commiserators. Secret Keeping calls for a big dose of humanity, empathy, and unabashed candor. If you don't feel it, hire it.

## marketers' secrets put her on guard

But how about the secrets you keep from her? You might examine your own conscience as to whether your own behavior is contributing to distrust that makes her reluctant to divulge things to you specifically and marketers in general. Hidden fees for credit cards, magazine subscriptions that trap her with automatic renewal, pricing that disguises hidden costs, punitive return policies, and downsized products all are culprits in their own way. While her Secret Keeping annoys you, consider how many marketers and retailers have kept the truth from her. No wonder she's got a few secrets of her own.

Building a brand that welcomes the truth, stands behind its products, and creates a two-way dialogue at every touch point gives you a better chance of being the one she'll trust with her Whole Truth.

Interestingly, some of the big private-label brands from chains such as supermarket **PUBLIX** and mass-market **TARGET** are gaining share because it's clear that consumers aren't paying for marketing expenses like advertising and fancy packaging. It's not necessary to be "plain" to show you're not a secret-hoarding brand, but being plainspoken is a step in the right direction.

## the benefits of unearthing secrets

This section may have scared you a little into thinking that there are secrets you could never unveil. We thought that too, at first. When we set out to build Just Ask a Woman, we didn't plan to morph from marketers to therapists for thousands of women (and funnily enough, sometimes for our clients, too). But that's exactly what happened. We really didn't realize the power of what happens when our more personal and probing techniques spur women to reveal the deeper secrets they hide. In nearly every one of our hundreds of group sessions, there is always at least one huge a-ha moment among the women. And the reward for telling a secret within a supportive atmosphere is a kind of therapy in itself, thanks to the tips they learn from other women.

In one healthcare research session, a woman suffering from the brain fog of fibromyalgia sat with tears running down her face, clutching a handmade calendar that she carried to keep track of

what day it was. When we asked about it, she whispered that she had two or three duplicates placed around the house in case she lost one. With that startling revelation, four other women raised their hands to confess that they too were often "lost." Suddenly, the symptom of disorientation was verified and clarified in a very human way for the brand.

So often in our work, women will applaud each other for coming out for the first time about a shared but unspoken problem. And our sponsoring brands get the credit for providing the truth-telling environment. So, while we aren't trained psychologists or counselors, somehow we have grown to be brand therapists and that's what's driven our success and our clients'.

# how to avoid the Half Truth of Secret Keeping

1. Her secrets can actually work to your advantage if your brand can tap into the "best-kept secret" brand territory. Ask her if your brand has bragging rights.

2. To get her to open up her deeper secrets to you, prepare to do the same with her. A woman will trust the marketers who are unafraid of showing their own vulnerabilities.

3. If she's got a secret that's standing between your brand and success, you may have to employ stealth techniques, like affinity groups of friends who will force her to tell her truth even if she resists. Remember, the best marketers need this truth to do right by her, not to be busybodies!

# the five
# Half Truths
# at retail

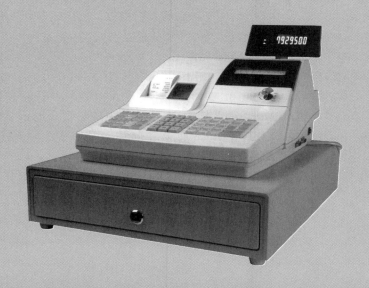

N ow that you've got a grip on the five Half Truths that can give your marketing plans a run for the money, let's look at how all of them come to play at retail. Here's where the GAMES of Good Intentions, Approval Seeking, Martyrdom, Ego Protection, and Secret Keeping can surprise you.

Even the most insightful strategies and the most innovative products can fail at the moment of sale. At every touch point, from presentation and store environment to customer service and loyalty programs to checkout and returns, the realities of retail can either deliver a brand marketer's hopes or dash them.

To women, marketing is retail. They don't know or think about the hard work of brand managers, product developers, and ad agency–types. They don't care about the things you agonize over. They are much more interested in where they buy, how they're treated, and what kind of value they get. And they define the buying experience broadly, including online, on the phone, in the catalog, from the agent, in the showroom, and yes, in the store.

In marketing circles, the buying decision has come to be called "the moment of truth" but is that moment built on women's Half Truths or Whole Truths? This case will truth-detect the two giants of mass retailing—**WAL-MART**, retail's biggest player, and **TARGET**, their closest competitor—to determine which is tapping into a woman's Whole Truth and which is stuck in the Half Truth zone, and how both are dealing with her G-A-M-E-S.

# the truth about Wal-Mart

There is hardly a major product marketer who shouldn't thank his or her lucky stars for Wal-Mart. Wal-Mart is the 8-million-pound gorilla that's both respected and feared for its huge leverage over so many suppliers' fates through its hard-knuckled price negotiations.

Though the brand has been plagued with criticism for its faults (crowded aisles, dowdy clothes, lowbrow image), the fact is that its low prices entice women to shop there more than anywhere else. Since the proof of a woman's retail Whole Truth isn't just what she says but where she actually buys, Wal-Mart is a Whole Truth brand, hands down.

Tight economic times play to Wal-Mart's success. This is true not only because of the company's lowest-price philosophy, but because the chain is now able to reap the fruit of years of renovation and policy change. Newer stores with more organized layouts, better customer service, prolific grocery selection, low-priced prescriptions, and well-stocked electronics at phenomenal prices meet most consumers' demands. And yet, if asked, "Which is the Whole Truth brand, Wal-Mart or Target?" most marketers would probably still answer "Target." Why?

For years, the inner circles of ad agencies and marketing insiders loved to bash Wal-Mart and worship Target. Pick a battle, from employee discrimination to environmental impact of new stores,

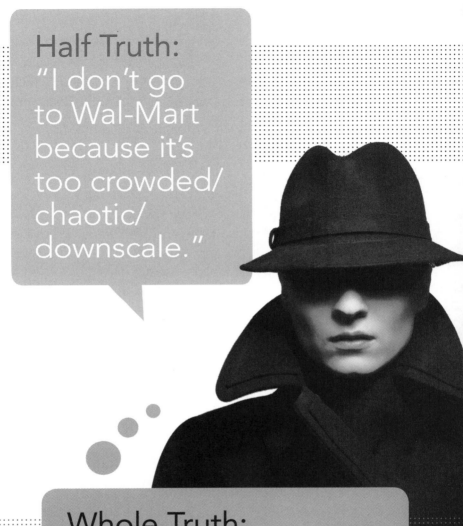

and marketing cognoscenti, Wall Street analysts, and major media piled on Wal-Mart as the enemy. Marketers were guilty of their own Half Truths of Ego Protection of status ("I'd never shop there") and Approval Seeking among peers ("Isn't it awful how little they pay their people?"). Bashing Wal-Mart while fawning over Target's cool factor seemed to be a common way of asserting one's hipness, political correctness, and high-minded superiority.

Women, while putting more of their dollars into Wal-Mart's registers, held their own negative images of the retailer. Although millions turned to Wal-Mart for groceries and household basics for kids,

| | Half Truth | Whole Truth |
|---|---|---|
| Good Intentions | I want to save money so I shop Wal-Mart. | Wal-Mart is okay for food and kid's stuff, but I would rather splurge on myself somewhere else. |
| Martyrdom | Wal-Mart is a "have to do" because I've got so much shopping to do and it's easier to get everything in one place. | But when I get a few precious minutes to spend on me, I deserve to shop somewhere more fun. |
| Ego Protection | I know it's smart to shop at Wal-Mart. | When I go, I always hope I don't run into anyone I know because I don't want them to think I'm that desperate. |
| Secret Keeping | I don't buy Wal-Mart gift cards for kids' parties because the other kids' moms would look down on my cheapness. | I buy lots of cheap presents there, but I don't include a gift receipt when I give them. |

many drew the line on image-related purchases, such as apparel, home items, and anything of badge value.

Changing a brand's image is a challenging task for any marketer. But turning around a big ship like Wal-Mart with more than 4,100 U.S. stores doesn't happen overnight. Wal-Mart knew that longer-term growth required some upgrades in store environment, merchandise, and image, so over the past several years, they tested ways to overcome some of those Half Truth barriers. Some changes are showing the markings of success, like their partnership with *Better Homes and Gardens* to enhance their design credentials and their cut-rate prices on a big selection of brand name consumer electronics. Wal-Mart's substantial commitment to sustainability and green products and their $4 prescriptions in the face of rising healthcare costs are all right on trend.

But Wal-Mart stumbled in women's apparel as they pursued their core shoppers' Half Truth desire for trendier fashions.

In an effort to appeal to women's Half Truth of fashion hopefulness, Wal-Mart inserted an eight-page ad in *Vogue*, a media misfire for their customers who read *Good Housekeeping* and *Woman's Day*, as well as a fashion faux pas since no real fashionista would believe that Wal-Mart's taste was up to runway standards.

But even as the chain fought the stereotypes and perceptions that warped their image, they never wavered from their commitment to value, which turns opinion and spending in their favor during economic stress. With the wind of store improvements at the company's back, in 2007 Wal-Mart anticipated the downturn and launched an ad campaign that saluted smart women who chose to maximize their purchasing dollars to benefit their families' lives: "Save money. Live Better."

The campaign transformed consumers' financial angst into proud accomplishment and presented Wal-Mart not as a concession but as a choice.

What's ironic is that despite the fact that Wal-Mart's 2009 current monthly performance versus year ago is stellar in the current retail wasteland, marketers still lag behind consumers' improved attitudes towards the brand. In a 2009 survey by *The Hub* magazine through reveries.com, when marketers were asked about their opinion of the campaign's emotional appeal, most were unmoved and still saw Wal-Mart as just a low priced, mass behemoth. More telling was their response to a question that asked if they had shopped Wal-Mart more during the recent recession—more than 71% had never or only sporadically done so. But given the contribution of Wal-Mart to their annual sales, it's most surprising that, when asked if they had *ever* shopped alongside a consumer in the store that literally pays their salary, 32% of the readers said they never had. (Wonder how many times had they been in an Apple store or a luxury car showroom?)

One wonders if marketers are as ahead of the curve as they like to think they are, or lagging behind women and their needs for real value and low prices at retail. Our advice for marketers whose personal prejudices keep them in an ivory tower: Wake up. Love it or hate it, Wal-Mart is connecting with women and commanding more of their dollars with every month that passes. Get in a car, grab a cart, and start learning the Whole Truth of why women are shopping there. (You might even pick up a bargain!)

Now it's time for the Whole Truth about a much-loved brand called Target.

## off target

In contrast to Wal-Mart, Target is the image darling, beloved by Wall Street analysts, ad agency creative directors, and the millions of women who brag "I bought it at Tar-zhay." We'd be denying our own Whole Truth if we concealed the fact that all of us at Just Ask a Woman are addicted to Target's allure. Who doesn't love their yoga pants, their cosmetic selection, and their cute home decorative stuff that you don't need but have to have?

Target's retail operation, made glossy by its provocative and iconic advertising, sparkles with the cheap chic that beckons women to their door. Where Wal-Mart might be perceived by women as a shopping chore, Target is seen as a treat, even an indulgence for a busy woman making ends meet.

Target's early designer labels like Isaac Mizrahi and Michael Graves lifted the brand beyond its price appeal and attracted the press pickup reserved for cool retailers way above Target's price range. And the labels at great prices gave the women shoppers bragging rights.

| | Half Truth | Whole Truth |
|---|---|---|
| Ego Protection | I shop Target because it makes me feel upbeat and cool. | I actually buy mostly staples there but I like the idea that they have cool designers, even if I can't pronounce their names. |
| Approval Seeking | When I shop at Target, I feel like I am in a "cool" club. | But I know that the good deals are what give me bragging rights. |
| Secret Keeping | I never buy clothes at Wal-Mart. | But if I did, I would say they were from Target. |

But along the way, Target, revered as being fashion-forward on so many fronts, started to believe their own press. Target's merchandising strategy reflected an assumption that their customer was getting cooler and cooler, so they added even more obscure, young, and

ultra-hip designers, as if the buyers at Target had forgotten who was shopping there (a customer whose demos were nearly identical to Wal-Mart's, by the way).

The shoe department was flooded with names the average woman on a budget had never heard of, such as Miss Trish of Capri or Sigerson Morrison. Their Sonia Kashuk makeup line, a hit as the first mass makeup artist brand, got crowded out by four or five new, unknown "artists," complicating the shopping for a mascara buyer in a hurry. The apparel department parted ways with the likable and accessible Mizrahi and moved to a superyoung group of unknowns—and soon unboughts.

Unfortunately, Target's cool factor, which built the brand's success during the bullish years, backfired when the recession arrived in late 2008.

Even though their pricing is not hugely different than Wal-Mart's, suddenly Target's image made the store feel like a splurge, and worse, a waste of money. And the designers who might have been able to hold their own during flush economic times seemed "too cool for school" when things got tight.

**Was Target cool or "too cool for school"?**

And those brand marketers who told the reveries.com survey that they were smitten by Target's ads and proposition don't drive the quarterly numbers. Women do. Target's slogan, "Expect More, Pay Less," which worked to lift the brand through better times, spoke more to her pre-recession Half Truth than her newly pinched Whole Truth. If anything, "Expect More" was the mantra of behavior that led to keeping up with the Joneses and maxing out credit cards. (Sure, you deserved it. But at some point, the bill collector comes banging at the door!)

The Target team went back to the drawing board to create a new campaign to reposition the brand for women's leaner Whole Truth by trying to focus more on how shoppers get more for less.

The proof of shifting women's behavior was revealed in an April 2009 survey by The Gordman Group, which asked 526 shoppers, 367 of them women, about their reasons for shopping and their store preferences during the recession. Results showed that, while trendier, Target was pulling fewer customers through the doors than Wal-Mart, with 55% of customers planning to spend more of their budget with Wal-Mart and just 25% of those surveyed expecting to do the same at Target. Wal-Mart's gain was Target's loss, thanks to 80% of those surveyed acknowledging that the "current economic conditions" have influenced their choice of store.

Still, women's Half and Whole Truths are confounding. Within that survey, even as they directed their dollars to Wal-Mart, respondents indicated nearly equal numbers for why they choose a store. Thirty-five percent of consumers identified price or sale price as the factor that most influences their purchase behavior, while 39% identified style, quality, and having what they want as the primary drivers. While they may say both price and style are practically equal influences, we'd venture to say that in the end they would choose price over style and quality, based on the fact that their words belie the voice of their wallets.

This case shows that even the savviest marketers can get tangled in women's Half and Whole Truths, because, like retail, women change every day. Beware falling into the trap of your personal preferences or those of elite pundits. If "expert" voices don't include female consumers, the real experts, you can be misled.

## so, what can a marketer learn from this case?

Get out of your office and into the stores where your customers shop if you want to understand what's working at the shelf. Better yet, find a way to get into your customer's closets, pantries, and glove compartments, where her promises of Good Intentions or her cover of Ego Protection cannot hide.

Be watchful that your own prejudices about retailers aren't coloring your marketing focus and innovation plans for the women who shop there. Face it, even if you think you're not paid enough, you're earning more than the average consumer who's struggling to make ends meet—by a lot! Get comfortable with the average female consumer's lifestyle even if it doesn't mimic your own. (The same is advisable if you're marketing to luxury consumers, with whom you may have the opposite challenge.)

Pick up the clues and cues that tell you her Whole Truth. We noted that women who bragged that they loved Target when Isaac Mizrahi was featured referred to him as everything from "Masserati" to "that designer guy," innocently revealing the Whole Truth that even though they tried to name-drop, they really weren't buying his clothes. Listen hard to learn what women aren't telling you.

# CHAPTER EIGHT

# what we're not telling you

With five Half Truths, hundreds of examples, and two big "do and don't" cases, what could we possibly have not told you? Actually, quite a bit, otherwise why would you hire us or call on us for our help?

The Whole Truth is that the more marketers get to know about women, the more questions they have. We know that by revealing all of these truths, we may hear "That's what I always thought" or "Of course that's what women think." Sometimes the most obvious findings are the truest, and they are also right under our nose, so natural and accepted that they escape detection. Our goal is not to complicate but to simplify, not to offer out-of-reach theories, but to make women's truths accessible to businesses large and small.

Yet, you may still have some questions even after getting this far in the book.

# why didn't we report the sales results of all of these cases?

Marketers are justifiably infatuated with numbers (though the Whole Truth is that they know they can make numbers say anything). Sales results don't always tell the whole story, though, since even the best insights can get killed with an inventory shortage on launch or an ambush of competitive ad spending.

On top of that, last week's success is next week's failure in a marketplace that's frankly gone haywire. Writing this book in the midst of one of the most bizarre financial scenes of recent years encouraged us to take a more circumspect look at marketing cases and train our detective's eyes on women's behavior, the greater constant.

# why didn't we spend more time discussing digital marketing, social media, and whatever follows Facebook and Twitter?

The cyber world changes faster than we can write. Any book out now on the subject is already old, so we decided to skip being dated. Instead, on our blog at justaskawoman.com we offer real time analysis of emerging media and new patterns of women's behavior.

Additionally, the five Half Truths are fully operational in new media. Think of the woman who says she Tweets to gain approval of her technologically active colleagues, but is only a dabbler. Or look at the composition of the social media sites that collect like-minded women who self-select, like irreverent Beta Moms or master home chefs or parent extraordinaires, who wouldn't be caught dead on a site that doesn't fluff their ego. Psychologically, women's behaviors in online networking and digital media aren't that different than in the real world; they're just more anonymous and private.

Our advice? Keep your eye on the trends with the biggest growth rate, like women's word of mouth, which now boasts at least two marketing associations, the **SOCIETY OF WORD OF MOUTH** and the **WORD OF MOUTH MARKETING ASSOCIATION**. Figuring out how to co-opt and operationalize this natural behavior of women to a brand's advantage will only grow as a marketing tactic.

Also, note that the women's blogging universe is like an uncaged lioness. Each day, another stay-at-home mom or chatty boomer launches yet another blog, adding a homegrown buzz to the giant sites like **WOWOWOW.COM**, **IVILLAGE.COM**, and others. Issues like buying mom blogger's affections with freebies and blog in-fighting among women will come with the territory. Stay tuned.

# why can't i just do this myself?

You *can* do this yourself, since we gave you lots of suggestions for how to truth detect and how to untangle the Half Truths you may find in your brand's relationship with women. But all the techniques in the world can't replace what we humbly affirm: women don't tell their hidden truths to just anybody, no matter how practiced or slick.

We have earned women's respect after years of refining our approach and by never forgetting who's the real star of the marketing show. It's tempting to think that it's about us. But we know that getting to the Whole Truth comes only because we never forget it's all about her. Demonstrating that in every touchpoint of our work has been our hallmark, and as any marketer will admit, setting aside our own egos and keeping true to our own Good Intentions is often the hardest promise to keep.

# but my business is different . . . what about me?

What about cause marketing, business-to-business marketing, not-for-profit marketing, or marketing to women of different cultures, women from Mars, etc.? Yes, there are dozens of marketing disciplines that merit their own examination. Perhaps we will take these on in a future book. But for now, the lessons here should provide enough analogs for figuring out what's happening in your unique situation. Again, our blog at justaskawoman.com takes on a wide array of issues each week that may be just what's on your radar.

We've found that it's easy to discard theories about women by deciding that unless the information aligns exactly with your specific problem, it's off the table. That's only a way to stay blindly in your world, while women would tell you that they have more in common than they have differences. We have seen marketers in Barcelona laugh at the same Good Intentions realities as brand managers in Chicago. We have noted business-to-business experts who've seen that their female B-to-B customer's Ego Protection is holding up the order or that her need to express her overworked Martyrdom becomes the core of the relationship with a successful salesperson. Look at the forest instead of the trees.

## in summary

There's a saying that you may have heard: "It's just business, it's not personal." While there's wisdom in keeping your emotions in check at the office, this phrase is also a Half Truth as far as marketing and women are concerned. Women take the buying experience personally. They watch ads with their own lives in mind. The products they buy come into their homes and are indeed very personal. The most powerful advice we can offer is to take women personally. See your customer as your sister, your wife, your daughter, your best friend.

Get out of your comfort zone that might worship statistics and data and ignore real life behavior. The art of Power Listening and detecting women's Whole Truths will take as much heart as brainpower. And taking it personally with women is good business.

### Respect What You Don't Know

The biggest enemy to successful marketing with women is complacency, the "we already know that" syndrome. Given that women are such powerful consumers— way beyond their 51%–plus representation in the population—we've been asked why there aren't more serious initiatives devoted to understanding them or why conferences focused on marketing to women are attended largely by women and not men. We believe that there's a high degree of confidence among marketers, warranted or not, that they know women. Maybe they extrapolate their personal experience as enough grounding for marketing decisions. Maybe they think that women have already been "done" with one big study or program, so that they know all they need to know. Or maybe, as stated earlier in the book, marketers are victims of their own ADD, and they have already moved onto some new, bright, shiny object in terms of target, media, or trend.

Since we founded Just Ask a Woman ten years ago, women have only grown in economic clout and emotional complexity. Assuming the marketing-to-women job is done is naïve. Sharpening insights and digging deeper is the only route to staying ahead of her changing game and giving your product or brand a chance at a place on her dance card.

## Let Yourself Be Uncomfortable

Marketers who stay at arm's length in an effort to preserve their dignity or stature with their customers forfeit the chance to understand women intimately. And when you let your brand get close to women, literally reading over her shoulder as she lives, she will tell you what you need to know. Women are tough judges of your interest. They respond only to those marketers whose behavior with them is consistent, authentic, and female-centric. Lip service doesn't cut it, nor do intermittent efforts at "women's programs." The good news about this is that once you have gained a woman's confidence, she will cut you a break when you falter and still spread your good word for you. The bad news is, if you toy with her she will tell more people than you will ever know.

## Truth Detect Your Existing Research

You may be wondering if you've been buying Half Truths or Whole Truths and if you've been Half Listening over the years. In the world of marketing, some internal brand legends spawn other ones, leading to a pile of conjecture that may not be true, and in fact, may be hog-tieing your opportunities. We review existing research all the time to identify lurking Half Truths and raise areas where a new segmentation or insight may underlay work you've already invested in. Be sure that you aren't throwing good money after bad insights.

## Renovate Your Listening Habits

Our discussion of Half Listening often hits homes with "guilty as charged" marketers. It's funny to joke about M&M overdoses and backroom shenanigans, but the truth is this is a non-listening epidemic that needs to stop. If only as a way to maximize the investment you make in research, consider whether your team is really trained in Power Listening or allowed to use focus group travel as boondogles. Sure marketers need to stay in touch with the home office while on the road, but two hours of listening to the women who pay most marketers' salaries isn't that taxing. Treat consumer listening as an art worth refining, rather than a chore to be checked off the list.

## Listen to the Women Inside

We are big believers that every marketer, male or female, is responsible for knowing their customers. But we'd be wrong not to suggest that the women inside a company or on a brand team are amazing secret weapons in the battle for relevance. Too often, women inside aren't asked to add their personal experiences to the brand's intelligence reservoir. Creating an atmosphere where it's not only encouraged but also expected that women will speak up about their own experiences can help you avoid costly marketing mistakes. And to women, who sometimes shy away from adding their personal two cents at the office, get over it.

## Love the One You're With

The first step to getting the Whole Truth is to learn to like your customer. This sounds simple, but so many times we see marketers who wish their "woman" were someone else. The job we are called most often to do is to help marketers understand "who is *she* really." And that may be because, as we said earlier, that the brand is tying its own ego to a customer you want to have rather than the one who loves you. While acquiring new customers or "upgrading" to higher-spending ones is a fair marketing goal, be careful that you aren't doing it at the expense of those you have. Also, you may find that you could get a better share of your existing customer's dollar by understanding her needs more deeply. Today's marketplace, with women already wielding 85% of spending, isn't about getting them to 90% (men have to buy something, after all!). The game is about taking market share and building profits. Expanding the universe of women who are like your existing customer or finding which of your customers are starting to dangle their dollars in front of a competitor is a much easier and less expensive task than courting someone new.

Finally, as we have said since we first opened our doors, start marketing *with* women, and stop marketing *to* them (a phrase so contagious, it's been copycatted). Marketing to women is over. Marketing to women means targeting them, going for their wallets and treating them as a necessary evil on your way to the bank. Marketing with women means trusting them enough to bring them into your processes early and often. Marketing with women means asking before it's a disaster check, being willing to believe that they might have a better idea than you do. And marketing with women means you return to them, again and again, to check in to see how you're doing. You're not done till they say you're done.

Start marketing *with* women,
and stop marketing *to* them.

# ACKNOWLEDGMENTS

We would like to thank the best marketers in the world, our best in class clients for their partnership and encouragement and for entrusting their most important and powerful consumers to us. We are grateful to the many thousands of women who shared their deepest secrets, as well as their Half and Whole Truths, with the humor, candor, and spirit that is uniquely female and extremely generous. And we especially thank our families for their support of our decade of creating a company that makes a difference, with special love to Joe Quinlan, Greg Drechsler, and Dave Chapman who are the answer to all we could ever ask.

We also thank our team members Jean Crawford and Lily Wagner whose attention, ideas, and experience have filled these pages with insight and whose spirit and support fill our company with joy.

And here we thank each other for working so hard together at something we believe in. We set out to be the most compelling interpreters of women's voices in the marketplace today. We never knew we'd have so much fun, just telling the truth.

And, on a personal note, Jen sends love to Charlotte and Max, Tracy to Hannah, and Mary Lou would like to thank Lauren, Manjeet, Ranya, Jennifer, Ira and Gail, Susan, Nancy, Amy, Sandy, and Ginny for their amazing talent and kindness.

# MORE JUST ASK A WOMAN BOOKS
## BY MARY LOU QUINLAN

*Just Ask a Woman: Cracking the Code of What Women Want and How They Buy* (Wiley, 2003)

"Just when you think you know it all, Mary Lou Quinlan helps you with your thinking in a new and wonderful way. If you want to capture a larger piece of your market, read this book."

—**GORDON BETHUNE**, former chairman/CEO, Continental Airlines

"Highly readable, this book speaks cogently to practicing and aspiring marketers about tapping into the minds and pocketbooks of women."

—**STEPHEN A. GREYSER,** professor of marketing and communications emeritus, Harvard Business School

*Time Off for Good Behavior: How Hard-working Women Can Take a Break and Change Their Lives* (Broadway Books, 2005)

"A must-read for every high-achieving woman who's working more and enjoying it less. If you've ever wanted to step out of the rat race and start living your dreams, this book is the perfect guide."

—**CAROLE BLACK**, former president and CEO, Lifetime TV

"This book not only gives hardworking women 'permission' to slow down and ease up, but tells, with real-life examples and simple tools, how women can thrive while smelling the flowers."

—**SHEILA WELLINGTON**, professor of management, NYU/Stern School of Business, and former president, Catalyst